MONEY AND ITS USES
IN THE ANCIENT GREEK WORLD

MONEY AND ITS USES IN THE ANCIENT GREEK WORLD

Edited by

ANDREW MEADOWS
AND
KIRSTY SHIPTON

OXFORD
UNIVERSITY PRESS

OXFORD

UNIVERSITY PRESS

Great Clarendon Street, Oxford OX2 6DP

Oxford University Press is a department of the University of Oxford.
It furthers the University's objective of excellence in research, scholarship,
and education by publishing worldwide in

Oxford New York

Auckland Bangkok Buenos Aires Cape Town Chennai
Dar es Salaam Delhi Hong Kong Istanbul Karachi Kolkata
Kuala Lumpur Madrid Melbourne Mexico City Mumbai Nairobi
São Paulo Shanghai Taipei Tokyo Toronto

Oxford is a registered trade mark of Oxford University Press
in the UK and certain other countries

Published in the United States
by Oxford University Press Inc., New York

British Library Cataloguing in Publication Data

Data available

Library of Congress Cataloging in Publication Data

Money and its uses in the ancient Greek world / Andrew Meadows and Kirsty Shipton [eds].
p. cm.
Includes bibliographical references and index.
Papers presented at two conferences held at Corpus Christi College, Oxford. 1995 and 1997.
1. Money–Greece–History–Congresses. 2. Coinage–Greece–History–Congresses.
3. Numismatics, Greek–History–Congresses. I. Meadows, Andrew. II. Shipton, Kirsty.
HG237 .M66 2001
332.4'938–dc21   00-065241

ISBN 0-19-924012-4 (hbk)
ISBN 0-19-927142-9 (pbk)

1 3 5 7 9 10 8 6 4 2

Typeset by Newgen Imaging Systems (P) Ltd., Chennai, India
Printed in Great Britain by
St. Edmundsbury Press, Bury St. Edmunds, Suffolk

Preface

The papers collected in this book adopt new approaches to an important area of Greek economic history—the use of coined money—and suggest new lines of enquiry. A major purpose of this collection is to make the results of numismatic research more readily accessible to a wider range of students and scholars of ancient history. The book also aims to provide a more wide-ranging account than is currently available of the social and economic contexts within which coined money was actually used in the Greek world. The papers explore money and its uses over a wide geographical area of the Greek-speaking world including Asia Minor, Egypt, and Rhodes. At the same time the Chapters cover a broad chronological range from archaic Greece to Roman Egypt.

Most of the chapters were originally delivered as papers at two conferences held at Corpus Christi College, Oxford, on 16 November 1995 and 1 March 1997. The editors are grateful to the participants at these conferences and to the other scholars who provided further chapters for this collection. We are also grateful to the Society for the Promotion of Hellenic Studies and the Craven Committee for financial assistance and to Corpus Christi College for providing hospitality. The editors would particularly like to thank Robin Osborne, Alan Bowman, and Chris Howgego for their advice and support.

ANDREW MEADOWS
KIRSTY SHIPTON

Contents

The Contributors

R. H. J. ASHTON is co-editor (ancient) of *Numismatic Chronicle*.

JOHN K. DAVIES is Professor of Ancient History and Classical Archaeology and Leverhulme Research Professor at the University of Liverpool.

HENRY S. KIM is the University Lecturer in Greek Numismatics, University of Oxford, and the Assistant Keeper responsible for Greek coins at the Ashmolean Museum.

ANDREW MEADOWS is a Curator of Greek coins at the British Museum.

GRAHAM OLIVER is Senior Research Fellow at the School of Archaeology, Classics and Oriental Studies at the University of Liverpool.

SITTA VON REDEN is a Lecturer in Classics and Ancient History at the University of Bristol.

JANE ROWLANDSON is a Lecturer in Classics and Ancient History at King's College, London.

KIRSTY SHIPTON is a Lecturer in Ancient History at the University of Leicester and Visiting Fellow at the School of Advanced Study, University of London.

JEREMY TREVETT is Assistant Professor of Ancient History at York University, Toronto.

List of Figures

List of Maps

List of Tables

List of Abbreviations

Abbreviations of the names of Greek authors and their works follow or are fuller versions of those used in *LSJ*.

Full details of papyri and related works appear in J. F. Oates *et al.*, *Checklist of Editions of Greek and Latin Papyri, Ostraka and Tablets*, fourth edn. (*BASP* supp. 7, 1992); http://scriptorium.lib.duk.edu/papyrus/texts/clist.html.

Illustrations of coins use the following abbreviations:

AE	bronze
AR	silver
AU	gold

ABSA	*Annual of the British School at Athens*
AD	*Αρχαιολογικον Δελτιον*
AfP	*Archiv für Papyrusforschung*
Agora	*The Athenian Agora: Results of Excavations Conducted by the American School of Classical Studies at Athens* (Princeton, NJ, 1953–)
AIIN	*Annali del Istituto Italiano di Numismatica*
AJA	*American Journal of Archaeology*
AJN	*American Journal of Numismatics*
AKG	*Archiv für Kulturgeschichte*
AM	*Mitteilungen der deutschen archäologischen Instituts. Athenische ableitung*
AMUGS	*Antike Münzen und Geschnittene Steine*
ANRW	H. Temporini and W. Haase (eds.), *Aufstieg und Niedergang der Römischen Welt* (Berlin–New York, 1972–)
ANS	American Numismatic Society
ANSNS	*American Numismatic Society Numismatic Studies*
ANSMN	*American Numismatic Society Museum Notes*
AR	*Archaeological Reports*
AS	*Anatolian Studies*
ATL	B. D. Meritt, H. T. Wade-Gery, M. F. McGregor, *The Athenian Tribute Lists* (4 vols.; Cambridge–Princeton, 1939–53)
BAR	*British Archaeological Reports* (International Series, Oxford)
BASP	*Bulletin of the American Society of Papyrologists*
BCH	*Bulletin de Correspondance Hellénique*
BE	*Bulletin Épigraphique* (in *Revue des Études Grecques*)
BGU	*Aegyptische Urkunden aus den Königlichen* (later *Staatlichen*) *Museen zu Berlin, Griechische Urkunden* (Berlin, 1895–)
BICS	*Bulletin of the Institute of Classical Studies*
BM	British Museum
BMC	*British Museum Catalogue*
CAH	*Cambridge Ancient History*

Cd'E	*Chronique d'Égypte*
CH	*Coin Hoards*
CID	*Corpus des Inscriptions de Delphes* (Paris, 1978–)
CJ	*The Classical Journal*
CNA	Classical Numismatic Auctions
CNG	Classical Numismatic Group
CNR	*Classical Numismatic Review*
CPh	*Classical Philology*
CPR	*Corpus Papyrorum Raineri*
CQ	*Classical Quarterly*
FdeD	*Fouilles de Delphes*
FGrH	F. Jacoby, *Fragmente der Griechischen Historiker* (Berlin, then Leiden, 1923–)
FHG	C. Müller, *Fragmenta Historicorum Graecorum* (Paris, 1841–70)
FPL	Fixed Price List
GR	*Greece and Rome*
GGA	*Göttingische Gelehrte Anzeiger* (Göttingen, 1739–)
GIBM	*The Collection of Ancient Greek Inscriptions in the British Museum* (Oxford, 1874–1916)
GRBS	*Greek, Roman and Byzantine Studies*
Hesp.	*Hesperia*
HN^2	B. V. Head, *Historia Nummorum*, 2nd edn. (Oxford, 1911)
IC	*Inscriptiones Creticae*
ID	*Inscriptions de Délos*
IG	*Inscriptiones Graecae*
IGCH	M. Thompson, O. Mørkholm, and C. M. Kraay (eds.), *Inventory of Greek Coin Hoards* (New York, 1973)
IK	*Inschriften griechischer Städte aus Kleinasien* (Bonn, 1972–)
ISE	L. Moretti, *Iscrizioni storiche ellenistiche*, i (Florence, 1967) and ii (Florence, 1975)
JEA	*Journal of Egyptian Archaeology*
JHS	*Journal of Hellenic Studies*
JIAN	*Journal International d'Archéologie Numismatique*
JNG	*Jahrbuch für Numismatik und Geldgeschichte*
JRA	*Journal of Roman Archaeology*
JRS	*Journal of Roman Studies*
LÄ	*Lexikon der Aegyptologie* (Wiesbaden, 1973–)
LGPN i	P. M. Fraser, E. Matthews, *A Lexicon of Greek Personal Names*, i, The Aegean Islands, Cyprus, Cyrenaica (Oxford, 1987)
LGPN ii	M. J. Osborne and S. G. Byrne, *A Lexicon of Greek Personal Names*, ii, Attica (Oxford, 1994)
LGPN iii	P. M. Fraser and E. Matthews, *A Lexicon of Greek Personal Names*, iii, part A, The Peloponnese, Western Greece, Sicily, and Magna Graecia (Oxford, 1997)
LSJ	H. G. Liddell and R. Scott, *A Greek–English Lexicon*, revised and augmented by H. Stuart Jones (Oxford, 1940)
MAI	*Mémoires de L'Académie des Inscriptions et Belles Lettres*
MBAH	*Münsterische Beiträge zur antiken Handelgeschichte*
MH	*Museum Helveticum*
MIN	*Metallurgy in Numismatics*
ML	R. Meiggs and D. M. Lewis (eds.), *A Selection of Greek Historical Inscriptions to the End of the Fifth Century B.C.* (revised edn. Oxford, 1988)
MMAG	Münzen und Medaillon AG, Basel

Montagu I and II	Sotheby, Wilkinson and Hodge, 23 March 1896 and 15 March 1897 (Hyman Montagu Collection, parts I and II)
NAC	Numismatic Ars Classica
NC	*Numismatic Chronicle*
NFA	Numismatic Fine Arts Inc., Los Angeles
NNÅ	*Nordisk Numismatisk Årsskrift*
NZ	*Numismatische Zeitschrift*
OGIS	W. Dittenberger (ed.), *Orientis Graeci Inscriptiones Selectae* (Leipzig, 1903–5)
Pap.Brux.	*Papyrologica Bruxellensia*
P.Cair.Zen.	C. C. Edgar *et al.* (eds.), *Zenon Papyri, Catalogue général des antiquités égyptiennes du Musée du Caire* (Cairo 1925–40)
P.Coll.Youtie	A. E. Hanson *et al.* (eds.), *Collectanea Papyrologica: Texts Published in Honor of H. C. Youtie* (Bonn, 1976)
P.Coll.Zen.	W. L. Westermann and E. S. Hasenoehrl (eds.), *Columbia Papryi*, iii, *Zenon Papyri*, i (New York, 1934)
P.Eleph.	O. Rubensohn (ed.), *Aegyptische Urkunden aus den königlichen Museen in Berlin: Griechische Urkunden*, Sonderheft. *Elephantine-Papyri* (Berlin, 1907)
P.Fay.	B. P. Grenfell, A. S. Hunt, and D. G. Hogarth (eds.), *Fayum Towns and their Papyri* (London, 1900)
Pap.Flor.	*Papyrologica Florentin* (Florence, 1976–)
P.Giss.	O. Eger, E. Kornemann, and P. M. Meyer (eds.), *Griechische Papyri im Museum des oberhessischen Geschichtsvereins zu Giessen* (Leipzig–Berlin, 1910–12)
P.Hercul.	M. Gigante (ed.), *Catalogo dei Papiri Ercolanesi* (Naples, 1979) and M. Capasso, *Manuale di Papirologia Ercolanese* (Lecce, 1991)
P.Kron.	D. Foraboschi (ed.), *L'Archivio di Kronion* (Milan, 1971)
P.Lond.	*Greek Papyri in the British Museum* (London, 1893–1974)
Pap.Lugd.Bat.	*Papyrologica Lugduno–Batava* (Leiden, 1941–)
P.Mert.	H. I. Bell *et al.* (eds.), *A Descriptive Catalogue of the Greek Papyri in the Collection of Wilfred Merton* (London, 1948–67)
P.Mich.Zen.	C. C. Edgar (ed.), *Michigan Papyri*, i, *Zenon Papyri* (Ann Arbor, Mich., 1931)
P.Mil.Vogl.	A. Vogliano (ed.), *Papiri della R. Università di Milano* (Milan, 1937)
P.Oxy.	B. P. Grenfell and A. S. Hunt *et al.* (eds.), *The Oxyrhynchus Papyri* (London, 1898–)
P.Petrie	J. P. Mahaffy and J. G. Smyly, *The Flinders Petrie Papyri* (Dublin, 1891–1905)
P.Rev.Law.	B. P. Grenfell (ed.), *Revenue Laws of Ptolemy Philadelphus* (Oxford, 1896)
Proc INC	*Proceedings of the International Numismatic Congress*
P.Ryl.	*Catalogue of the Greek and Latin Papyri in the John Rylands Library, Manchester* (Manchester, 1911–52)
P.Soter.	S. Omar (ed.), *Das Archiv des Soterichos* (Cologne/Opladen, 1979)
P.Tebt.	B. P. Grenfell *et al.* (eds.), *The Tebtunis Papyri* (London, 1902–)
PCPS	*Proceedings of the Cambridge Philological Society*
Proc. Cong. Pap.	*Proceedings of the Congress of Papyrology*
PSI	*Papiri greci e latini* (Pubblicazioni della Società Italiana per la ricerca dei papiri greci e latini in Egitto) (Florence 1912–)
QT	*Quaderni Ticinesi di Numismatica et Antichità Classische*
RBN	*Revue Belge de Numismatique*
RE	*Pauly's Real-Encyclopädie der classischen Altertumswissenschaft*
REA	*Revue des Études Anciennes*
RN	*Revue Numismatique*

RPC	A. Burnett, M. Amandry, P. P. Ripollès, *Roman Provincial Coinage* (London and Paris, 1992–)
SAN	*Journal of the Society for Ancient Numismatics*
SB	F. Preisigke *et al.*, *Sammelbuch griechischer Urkunden aus Aegypten* (Strasbourg, 1915–)
SCI	*Scripta Classica Israelica*
SEG	*Supplementum Epigraphicum Graecum*
SGDI	F. Bechtel, H. Collitz, *Sammlung der griechischen Dialekt-Inschriften* (Göttingen, 1884–1915)
SIG³	W. Dittenberger (ed.), *Sylloge Inscriptionum Graecarum*, 3rd edn. (Leipzig, 1915–24)
SIMA	*Studies in Mediterranean Archaeology*
SKAB	Schweizerische Kreditanstalte, Bern
SM	*Schweizer Münzblätter*
SNG	*Sylloge Nummorum Graecorum*
SNR	*Schweizerische Numismatische Rundschau*
Stud.Hell.	*Studia Hellenistica*
TAPA	*Transactions of the American Philological Association*
TINC	*Transactions of the International Numismatic Congress*
TN	J. R. Melville Jones, *Testimonia Numaria: Greek and Latin Texts concerning Ancient Greek Coinage* (London, 1993)
ZPE	*Zeitschrift für Papyrologie und Epigraphik*

INTRODUCTION

The Greek passion for coins, and for beautiful coins at that, is well known and sometimes misunderstood. For a long time this passion was not shared by many of their most advanced neighbours, Phoenicians, Egyptians, Etruscans, Romans, because it was essentially a political phenomenon, 'a piece of local vanity, patriotism or advertisement with no far reaching importance'[1]

Twenty-five years after the first appearance of Finley's seminal work is a good time to reassess the role of coined money in the ancient Greek economy. Given the pre-eminence of Finley and the authority of the work from which the above quotation comes, one must inevitably suppose that this unfortunate pronouncement has been one of the major causes of the lack of dialogue between economic historians and the students of ancient coinage. The conferences that inspired this volume sought to bring numismatists back into the fold of mainstream ancient history, as well as encouraging historians to listen to what numismatists have to say, and the resulting papers have provided stimulating examples of how numismatic research can proceed in new directions, and also how numismatic material can and should be integrated into the writing of social, political, and economic history.

Finley is not, of course, entirely to blame. His insistence on the political nature of coinage did not so much usher in that *Geist* as provide an early shiver of realization that it was upon us. Today the equation of national currency and national essence has become a commonplace. Coinage has become one of the prime identifiers of our imagined communities, and it was this modernistic interpretation that Finley (and

Keynes) sought to retroject upon the ancient world. And so it is that two of the papers in the first part of the volume (Meadows and Oliver) tackle head on the question of the political interpretation of coinage, challenging the assumptions that are all too readily made about coinage and 'patriotism'. A third (Trevett) seeks to add nuance to the debate in ideological terms.

The world of numismatics, it must be said, has not provided the help that it might. Until comparatively recently, the emphasis of much Greek numismatic work has lain upon the die-study of the aesthetically pleasing, rather than the understanding and quantification of the workaday. Herein lie the roots of the modern view of ancient coinage as local vanity or advertisement, rather than an economic or socially embedded phenomenon. The resulting lack of integration of numismatic data into historical debate has been an obvious limiting factor in the writing of Greek social and economic history. The remaining two papers in Part I (Kim and von Reden) seek to begin the process of this integration, one by offering a view of the possibilities, the other by providing a practical demonstration of some in action.

Kim begins the collection with an attempt to reintroduce coinage into the debate about the nature of money and exchange in archaic and early classical Greece. In a valuable *mise en scène* he presents the current state of numismatic thought on the origins and beginning of coinage in the Greek world, as well as suggesting ways in which the physical nature of coinage itself may present some of the answers to the questions of its role in archaic society. His insistence on paying close attention to the artefacts themselves leads him to the important conclusion that the position of early coinage in the economic sphere should not be neglected, and indeed is to be seen as an

[1] Finley (1973) 166: the quotation is from J. M. Keynes, *A Treatise on Money* (London, 1930), i. 12.

important element in the dynamic of the adoption of coinage in archaic Greece. By beginning to quantify the production of the workaday, low-value coinages of the early sixth century BC, Kim offers a window on the level and nature of monetary exchange at this period not available from any other source. His results are all the more interesting when considered in comparison with those produced by Ashton.

The paper from Trevett turns to focus precisely on the Finley question of 'local vanity, patriotism or advertisement'. Taking as his focus a single city, Athens, and examining its coinage output against the background of the political regime that produced it, he examines the numismatic record as evidence for civic self-expression. His conclusion, that coinage as it manifests itself at Athens is a function of the political system that produced it, brings a new sophistication to the interpretation of coin types as political products. On his reading, no less than on those of Oliver and Meadows which follow, coinage thus becomes an index of the political system that issued it. It comes as no surprise that the multiplicity of such systems operative in the ancient Greek world corresponds to a broad range of responses to coinage: from Athenian conservatism to Cyzicene exuberance to Spartan recusance.

The closely connected chapters by Oliver and Meadows take the debate on the political resonance of coinage a stage further and later. Continuing Trevett's concentration on the city of Athens, Oliver moves on into the Hellenistic period. Through a detailed look at the period of Macedonian control of Athens in the third century BC, Oliver takes forward the question of the role of Athenian coinage as a political symbol. The question he sets himself is: Did Macedonian control have a noticeable effect on the ability of the Athenians to issue coin? Crucial to such an inquiry is the comparison of the numismatic material with all other forms of evidence—epigraphic, papyrological, and literary—in an attempt to reconstruct the precise nature of Macedonian control. By setting coinage against the background produced by close consideration of all other source material, Oliver seeks to identify the place of coinage in the spectrum of Greek thought about civic autonomy in the Hellenistic age. His conclusions reinforce those of scholars working on earlier periods of coinage and history, but importantly begin to explain precisely

where coinage was located in the nexus of accommodations between kings and their subject cities.

Meadows carries a similar enquiry beyond Athens to the broader Hellenistic East. Starting again with the question of the nature and extent of the impact of royal control of cities on their coinage in the Hellenistic period, he approaches the problem both comparatively, across cities and kingdoms, and diachronically. Like Oliver he locates coinage in its place among the civic institutions of the Hellenistic *poleis*. But, in the absence of the sort of detailed background available for Athens, he uses the evidence provided by the physical appearance and nature of the coinage itself as a means of gauging its place in royal–civic relations. By thus examining the coinages produced by various cities at various periods he reconstructs a process of shift in the role of coinage in the relations between kings and their subject cities over time. In this development of the attitudes of kings and cities towards coin issue, he thus finds an analogue in coinage for the encroachment of the Roman mode in other political spheres.

Von Reden's chapter on coinage and money in Ptolemaic Egypt serves as the first section of the bridge between the two parts of the collection, as well as offering an analysis of the role of coinage at the other end of the spectrum from Kim's. She begins with an analysis of the symbolic significance of coinage in such élite display activity as the Grand Procession of Ptolemy Philadelphus, suggesting a quasi-programmatic use of high-value coinage on the part of the Ptolemaic kings. Moving on to consider coin use at the other end of Egyptian society, up-country and in everyday transactions, she goes on to outline the use of sophisticated operations for creating and increasing a money supply beyond the limits enforced by inadequate supplies of precious metals.

Ashton provides a second link between the two parts. His Chapter is at once a set piece of numismatic method based on years of research, while at the same time it offers a rare example of how such research can be integrated into the reconstruction of ancient political and economic history. The essential problem that faces any economic historian seeking to use Greek numismatic material is the relative lack (by comparison with the Roman world, for example) of quantified, quantifiable, and thus comparable data. By providing for the first time a full account of the coinage of the important state of Rhodes from its unification in 408 down to the early second century BC, Ashton creates an opportunity to weigh the evidence of coinage against other known economic data for the Rhodian state at various periods. At the same time he provides valuable comparanda for the measuring of the size of other cities' output of coinage. The results of both are startling and likely to require a certain amount of rethinking of the role of coinage in the Hellenistic economy, by comparison with, say, the picture painted by Kim of the archaic world.

The other papers in Part II continue Part I's discussion of the meanings of coined money, but they do so through case-studies based on documentary, rather than numismatic, evidence. They also extend the timescale of Ashton's paper, beginning with the early fifth century (Davies) and continuing down to Roman Egypt (Rowlandson).

Davies addresses the question of how, in the classical period, the spread of monetization discussed by Kim (Part I) affected the economic activities and attitudes of public bodies both at the level of demes or phratries and at the level of individual *poleis*. Focusing on the ideological change in attitude to the use of temple funds which coined money brought about, Davies illustrates how coinage could act both as a symbol and as a hard commodity. Once temple resources could be held in, or converted into, coinage the officials in charge were faced with a possible conflict of priorities between sacred, apparently 'uneconomic', uses of money and rational, 'economic', uses of money so as to build up resources further. Davies argues that the need of some Greek states to meet the enormous costs of trireme fleets may have been an important factor in causing an economically rational use of coined money. Shrines belonging to powers which did not need money for naval warfare were less likely to view their money as a hard commodity, preferring instead to be influenced in their use of their resources by the demands of ritual propriety. For naval powers, at least, the adoption of coinage will have resulted in the linking of cult with public administration and warfare.

The remaining papers in the collection both return to the initial question raised by Kim's study of early Greek coinage: How far did money use penetrate various segments of the population? Focusing like Trevett on classical Athens, Shipton uses the

documentary evidence of the silver-mine leases and the leases of public land to explore the issue of how coined money was conceived by different social groups. The paper thus continues Davies's discussion of how coined money produced changes in the ideological attitude to the use of wealth. The different ways in which the élite used money within the public economy suggest that monetization will have produced different types of relationship between the wealthy élite and the State. More widely, the study suggests a need to reconsider the social complexion of both landed and non-landed sectors of the state economy.

The final contribution in this collection, building on von Reden's paper in Part I, examines a 'limiting case' of monetization in the Greek world: the use of money in the rural areas of Ptolemaic and Roman Egypt. Like many of the earlier chapters by both numismatists and historians Rowlandson's study points up the symbolic significance of coinage. Using evidence from the land-lease documents, Rowlandson demonstrates the ritual element involved in the economic activity of Egyptian peasantry, a feature of money use which Davies drew attention to in his chapter on Greek microstates of the classical period. Rowlandson also emphasizes the complex nature of monetization in a system where accounts can be held in granaries and gold coins set into necklaces. Coined money is thus 'more closely assimilated to other potential bearers of meaning, from piglets to gold bracelets, than it is differentiated from them' (Rowlandson, p. 154). This conclusion is an effective reminder that the use of coined money did not necessarily have a different significance from economic activity which was not based on coinage.

The documentary evidence used by Rowlandson has thus taken us back to the point from which Kim's numismatic study began. Coined money does not work in a vacuum. It arises naturally out of pre-coin money use and, equally naturally, once coinage is introduced it can function in remarkably similar ways to commodities which have an economic value but do not involve coined metals.

The papers described above reveal two important advantages of the interdisciplinary approach adopted in this collection. First, documentary evidence such as that used in the historical case-studies of Part II allows us to address issues which are different from those which numismatic material can illuminate. Thus Kim's numismatic analysis of early coinage enables us to set the major question of how coinage was conceived in the early Greek economy within the wider and important context of pre-coinage money. This in turn casts light on the issue of what we mean by 'monetization'. But for detailed insight into how monetization actually worked on a day-to-day basis we need to turn to documentary evidence. Case-studies such as those produced by Shipton and Rowlandson allow us to construct detailed pictures of how different sectors of Greek society were affected by the adoption of coinage which numismatic work reveals. Secondly, by combining numismatic and documents-based approaches we can at times gain fuller insight into the same issue. This is well exemplified by individual papers like von Reden's, which combines numismatic and documentary material. The two approaches used in this collection thus complement each other. Both numismatic and documentary evidence have to be employed if we are to gain a rounded picture of the uses of money in the ancient Greek world.

REFERENCES

[1] FINLEY, M. I. (1973). *The Ancient Economy*. (London)

PART I

MONETIZATION, MONEY SUPPLY, AND THE POLITICS OF COINAGE

I

ARCHAIC COINAGE AS EVIDENCE FOR THE USE OF MONEY

Henry S. Kim

S THE PAPERS IN THIS VOLUME UNDERSCORE, our understanding and appreciation of money in the ancient Greek world has undergone a remarkable transformation in recent years. The prime force behind this rethink of money has come from a number of studies which have explored the phenomenon of exchange, especially in its non-market-driven forms of social exchange. Scholars such as Seaford, von Reden, and Kurke have all contributed to reframing money by looking at the roles money took in the development of social commensurability, in non-economic exchange, and in how attitudes towards money use were formed.[1] One of the most positive results to come from all of this is that the study of money has been liberated from concentration on its primary role as a key cog in the gears of the market economy. Money no longer needs to be treated as an object, and focus has now shifted towards examining its roles in legal and religious contexts, and how its presence may be a cause or consequence of social change. As a whole our conceptual understanding of money in the Greek world has rapidly evolved, benefiting greatly from a refreshing infusion of new approaches provided by anthropologists and social historians.

Despite all of the attention that has been paid to early money, one important aspect has been left behind: how coinage fits into the overall picture. Previously, coinage has been identified as a watershed in the use of money, introducing a new form of money which could be used as an absolute value for civic and commercial activities. More recently, the cultural impact of 'coinage' has been explored, on the basis that its invention either coincided with or fostered the growth of impersonal transactions. Yet, throughout most of these new studies, coinage has not had a separate identity of its own and has often followed lock step with money. In some, it is even difficult to distinguish between the two, as coinage and money are considered one and the same. Such conflation risks missing not only the subtle conceptual differences between the two, but also the greater practical differences between the two as evidence for the use of money and the development of moneyed economies. As invigorating and exciting as many of these studies may be, they have inadvertently muddied the waters surrounding coinage and money, clouding an already complex issue.

To complicate matters further, the state of scholarship on early silver coinage has changed greatly over the last few decades. Numismatic scholarship has lowered the dates of the beginnings of many of the chronologically important silver coinages from the first half of the sixth century to the second, shifting coinage into very different historical contexts. New low-value denominations have appeared where previously there had been few or

[1] Seaford (1994), esp. 199–206, 220–34; von Reden (1995), esp. 171–221; von Reden (1997) 154–76; Kurke (1995) 36–64.

none, unsettling prior assumptions on how and by whom early silver coinage was used. Many of these changes are relatively new and are not readily accessible to non-specialists, widening the gap between what is generally perceived and what the material evidence now supports. For those currently working on money, these changes must be acknowledged, as they are essential to establishing the context in which coinage fed into the use of money.

What is apparent in light of all the recent activity is that a re-examination of the relationship between coinage and money is long overdue. How can the two be distinguished from one another and what difference does this make in the way we examine how money was used? How has the material record changed and how do these changes affect our understanding of how coinage and money were used? From the historiographical point of view, can the currently popular social and political explanations offered by cultural historians satisfactorily be used as the prime explanations for coinage, or should economic factors be considered again? The purpose of this paper is to provide a first step in this direction by establishing a number of guidelines for discussion and by examining what the material evidence from coins can tell us about how early coins were used. At the heart of the matter is the fundamental question of how early coinage should be handled as a body of evidence. No doubt the discussion that follows will add fuel to the fire, but what it will, one hopes, do as well is redirect the approach to the question. Only then will it be possible to tap the potential information archaic coinage can offer as evidence for the use of money.

Coinage and Money

It is important to begin by drawing a sharp distinction between the terms coinage and money. One of the underlying assumptions of this article is that the two are not synonymous and that it is important to be careful in how the two are used in relation to one another. A number of recent works, unwittingly or not, confuse the two, leading to claims that money was not abundant before coinage or that the creation of money by states was an important step in the development and growth of market economies. If only the relationships between coinage, money, moneyed economies, and market economies were so

simple; however, they are complex, and our understanding of them is not helped by the shifting sands which characterize their relationship depending on where and when they are considered. Within the Greek world these relationships are especially important, as we believe coinage and money may be closely tied to the development of the Greek *polis*. Before launching into any discussion of coinage and money it may be time to get back to basics and relearn what has long been assumed.

Money is commonly defined as a store of wealth, a medium of exchange, a measure of value, and a means for making payments. Such a definition is technically sound, but it does miss out on the less tangible aspects of what makes up money. Perhaps the most important feature of money is that it is culturally biased, acceptable to some but not to others. What makes lumps of silver money in one place and salt money in another is something which cannot easily be explained, and we are well advised to be cautious about our own cultural assumptions when we think about what forms money could potentially take. We have to be aware that a range of items could be used, from grain, to scraps of silver, to coins. While there is no universal or absolute form of money, non-perishable materials have a distinct advantage over perishable, transportable over fixed.

Coinage, on the other hand, is a very specific form of money. It is normally defined as a piece of metal which has been stamped by an issuing authority, to be of definite value or weight. It is unusual among recognized forms of money in that its origins are known and we can actually think of coinage as having a beginning. Its introduction in the form of electrum coins minted in Lydia and along the Ionian coast is variously placed from the middle of the seventh to the beginning of the sixth century BC. However, coinage as a widespread phenomenon develops somewhat later and in a different metal. It becomes prevalent with the introduction and spread of silver coinage through much of the Greek world during the last half if not the last quarter of the sixth century. During this period and down to c.480, nearly 100 mints begin operating, confined to the Greek world and its immediate neighbours.

Appreciating the difference between coinage and money is conceptually difficult for a culture like ours which naturally conflates the two. Yet, the dangers of not adjusting one's sights are readily apparent when one questions the nature of money before or in the absence of coinage. As difficult as it may be, we must keep in mind that a moneyed economy does not require coinage in the first place, as can be documented in 'moneyed economies' which operated in the absence of coinage.[2] Furthermore, the invention of coinage does not need to be considered the starting point of a moneyed economy, as can be documented in numerous 'moneyed economies' which eventually adopted coinage from the Greek world.

Understanding these two points is fundamental to any consideration of coinage and money, as they remind us to consider forms of money beyond coinage. We should be aware of the possibilities of pre-coin money which may have operated prior to the development of coinage as 'general-purpose' or 'limited-purpose' forms of money.[3] Even once coinage appears in the Greek world, we must be aware of various forms of non-coin money which may have been used alongside coins or even in very different contexts. What should be appreciated throughout this discussion is that the invention of coinage is not so important as a single event as it is as part of an overall change in the way that exchange operated. It is the increasing importance of money in social, political, and economic activities which should be examined as the precursor to coinage.

These observations should not be taken in any way as an attempt to de-emphasize the importance of coinage to monetization. They are intended to re-focus and resight the lines which the discussion should follow. When we think of the monetization of the Greek world and the development of moneyed economies, coinage should not be seen as the starting point so much as a milestone along a much longer road in the use of money. It is left to us to discover the tell-tale signs which will help realize the utility of archaic coinage as evidence for the early use of money. It is appropriate to turn first to coinage itself to examine what certain aspects of early coinage can tell us about the use of money and the development of a moneyed economy.

Coinage as Money

Origins and Spread of Greek Coinage

As mentioned above, coinage is an unusual form of money as its origins are known and it can be said to have a definite beginning. In contrast, the origins of many other forms of money are difficult to trace as some may have developed out of a prior use as commodities. As Rowlandson points out in her contribution to the present volume, grain was used as a limited form of currency in Roman Egypt, suitable for grain-tax payments and rent (Ch. 9). Bronze arrowhead 'coins' were used in the Black Sea region during the sixth and fifth centuries, produced in imitation of actual arrowheads which had become recognized as a form of money.[4] Coinage stands apart from such forms as these in that it was a conscious invention. Cities and *ethne* consciously chose to produce coinage, and they did so in a new form regulated in weight and purity.

Where the beginnings are placed and who was responsible for its introduction have been the matter of some debate within the numismatic community, and what will be outlined here has been dealt with in greater detail elsewhere.[5] In recent years, the discussion has evolved to include questions of how closely linked coinage was to the development of the *polis* and whether early coinage can be described as Greek. Pertinent to the present discussion are a few points which are highlighted here as they shed important light on the dynamics of how coinage became part of the Greek world.

What can be said with little likelihood of dissent is that the first coins appear in western Asia Minor produced in the alloy of gold and silver commonly known as electrum. A date for these issues of

---

[2] The ancient New East is a prominent example where a moneyed economy existed in the absence of coinage (see Kuhrt (1995), esp. index entries under 'taxes', 'currency/coins', 'debt'. Moneyed economies could also exist with the shortage of coinage, as von Reden and Rowlandson document in the cases of Ptolemaic and Roman Egypt in the present volume.

[3] The terms '"general-purpose" money' and '"limited-purpose" money' are not without their problems. I am inclined to shy away from Seaford's definition of money as 'a universal equivalent used as a medium of exchange' (Seaford (1994) 222) and accept that there are differing degrees to which various forms of money were recognized and used in exchange (see discussion below on 'Coinage and its Uses' and 'Money Before Coinage').

[4] Wells (1981); Sorda (1980).

[5] Howgego (1995) 1–4. Reasons for the introduction of early electrum coins are treated by Wallace (1987); Price (1983); Weidauer (1975). Models for coinage having a long developmental history, starting with the use of metal bullion, are provided by Furtwängler (1986); Balmuth (1971). Both rely heavily upon Near Eastern examples as antecedents for coinage.

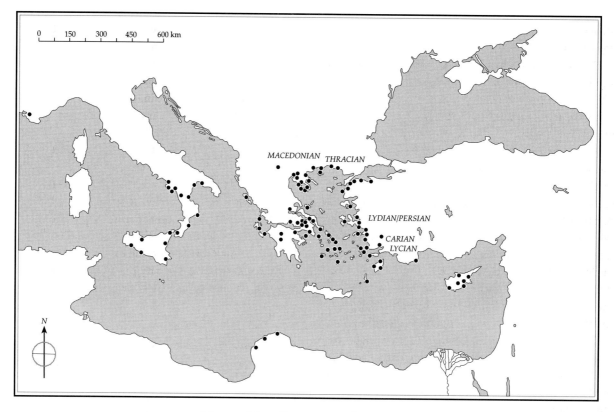

Map 1.1. Map of active mints by *c*.480 BC

sometime before the middle of the sixth century is provided by finds of electrum coins in the foundations of the archaic Artemesium at Ephesus.[6] How much earlier coinage was produced is difficult to determine with any precision, but dates around and prior to 600 have been suggested based on the dating of related materials in the find and the style of the 'pot-hoard' pot.[7] As for who was responsible for these issues, one large producer was the royal Lydian mint, identified by a lion-head obverse type. These coins appear to have been produced in large quantities and have been found as far east as Gordion. However, Lydia was not alone, and the large number of other types of electrum coins suggests the involvement of a number of other issuers, several of which can be identified as Greek cities. Miletus and Teos are commonly associated with series of coins which feature types used in their later silver issues (Miletus—recumbant lion and a 'rosette'-patterned punch; Teos—griffin head).

Phocaea is linked to a type which includes a seal (*phoke*) and letter phi, punning on the civic name.

Based on what we know about who minted coins, the idea of coinage may not have been solely 'Greek' in origin, although even from the very beginning it was used in an area which saw much intermingling between Greeks and non-Greeks. Where coinage develops a Greek flavour is in how the initial idea for coinage spread. Even though the original idea may have 'non-Greek' (Lydian) origins, it is within the Greek world and with silver that coinage becomes a widespread phenomenon. In contrast to the limited sphere in which electrum coins were produced, when coinage appears in silver it spreads through much of the Greek world and to some areas on its periphery. By *c*.480, some 100 mints began producing coins, distributed as far afield as Massalia and Cyrene, through much of western and eastern Greece, and closer to home in the heartland of the Greek mainland.[8] Amid

---

[6] Bammer (1990); Robinson (1951).
[7] Carradice and Price (1988) 24; Kraay (1976) 21; Howgego (1995) 2; Williams (1991–3).

[8] For a listing of mints see Osborne (1996*a*) 253–5. To this should be added the colony of Massalia (see Furtwängler (1978)) as well as the various mints operated by Persian, Carian, and Lycian dynasts.

all of this, we should be aware that the diffusion of coinage could also have a regional flavour, as the coinages of different cities within a region could appear quite similar, employing similar methods of production (fabric), shared weight systems, or shared types.

While the geographic distribution of early silver mints may be impressive, what is even more so is the rate at which the spread occurred. The time frame for the spread of silver coinage has shrunk considerably in the last two decades as a number of previously secure fixed points have fallen, as a result in large part of careful work on key series. Associations of coinage with Solon and Pheidon during the early part of the sixth century are no longer trusted.[9] Even the attribution of the 'Croesids' to Croesus has been called into question in recent years as our understanding of the chronologies of late archaic hoards has become more secure.[10] It is now difficult to attribute any silver issues before c.550, pushing the phenomenon of silver coinage entirely into the second half of the sixth century. Key fixed points begin to emerge mainly in the last two decades of the sixth century, securing the chronology against any further falls.[11]

The importance of this shift in the time frame beyond the middle of the century can be felt in how the dynamics of the spread may be described. Instead of a gradual diffusion spaced over a century or more, coinage appears to have spread rapidly during the last quarter of the sixth century and first quarter of the fifth. This shift downwards changes the context in which coinage spread, placing it significantly later in the development of the Greek polis and importantly closer in time to the formalization of a number of key civic institutions such as legal codes, liturgies,[12] religious ceremonies, and civic offices. Perhaps more important, the compression of the chronology forces us to look more closely at how the development of coinage may be correlated to some common changes which were occurring at the time.[13]

While much more work needs to be done to assess what impact silver coinage had, a few key ideas must

be kept in mind. The spread of coinage should not be taken as a blanket covering of coinage through the Greek world, as not all states produced coinage.[14] The development of the polis may not be the sole factor in the creation of coinage, as Persians, Lycians, Carians, and various Thraco-Macedonian peoples produced coinage as well.[15] Nonetheless, it is in the Greek world that most of the activity occurred and it is in this context that the development of coinage must sensibly be placed. When it comes to evidence for the early use of money, it is coinage which can provide one of the most complete and coherent bodies of evidence available. For, unlike literary sources or special ceramics, the evidence of coinage is not skewed towards one city or region, but reflects a broader phenomenon which cuts across regions.

Coinage and its Uses

While new finds and new work have greatly improved our understanding of the dynamics of the spread of early silver coinage, our understanding of how it functioned as a form of money has remained more or less unchanged. Its immediate impact on money is still considered relatively little. Early coinage is largely seen as being used for only a limited range of activities and by a limited circle of participants, and it is still popular to believe that the moneyed economy only really advanced in the fifth century when state payments in coin finally percolated through to the body of individual citizens who became involved in civic duties. We are left with the distinct impression of early coinage being used in very limited contexts, far from the general-purpose applications of money we normally expect of coinage. One result of this is that it severely limits how coinage can be used as evidence for monetary use.

How coins were used is crucial to our understanding of the development of money. Few would argue with the notion that coinage was used in the archaic period as a form of money. Irrespective of what reasons we may attribute to the minting of the first coins, coins were intended to be used as money in various contexts such as tribute, state payments, or 'overseas trade'. What is less clear, though, is the

---

[9] Waggoner and Kroll (1984).   [10] Carradice (1987).
[11] Fixed points include the following: (1) coins impressed on datable clay tablets (see Root (1988)); (2) coins found in the foundation deposit at Persepolis (see Herzfeld (1938)); (3) the production of coins at Sybaris prior to its destruction in 510.
[12] An argument has recently been made in favour of coinage originating from the liturgical system (see Martin (1996)).
[13] Morris (1994).

[14] Notable among the non-producers before c.480 are Sparta, much of the Peloponnese, and the Greek colonies of the Black Sea.
[15] Williams (1996).

degree to which early coinage could be used for a wide variety of purposes; when the use of coin became normal for a wide proportion of the population; and when the Greek economy became 'moneyed'. Current views on the matter place the development of a 'moneyed' economy well into the fifth century, nearly 100 years after the minting of the first silver coins.[16] While such a long gap may seem something of a curiosity, it is based on a number of key observations about the nature of early Greek coinage which limit what can be said about the immediate impact of coinage on the development of a moneyed economy.

One of the observations which remains popular is that early coins were of considerably high value and that small change was not widespread. This assumption of predominance of high-value coins limits our impression of how coins could be used and it has been suggested that early coinage was used for specialized transactions and by a relatively small pool of users. To some, this means that archaic coinage was not used immediately as a widespread form of money. Rather, it would have been used as a specialist currency, as money in overseas trade, for tribute, or as a means of redistribution. Only after some time, especially once coinage was minted in low denominations, did coinage become useful as money in everyday exchange.

This perception of coinage—what may be described as a 'limited-purpose and limited-user' interpretation—is one of the most commonly expressed, and there is some material support for this view. At the time of the spread of Greek coinage, coins weighing between eight and seventeen grams were struck in substantial quantities, and most of the 100 or so states which minted coins did so with these large-denomination coins. As for how these coins were used, a good number of them ended up in hoards which have survived to the present day. Most of the coin hoards from the archaic period contain only these large-denomination coins. Low-denomination coins are largely absent. Archaic coins also ended up great distances from their issuing cities, and general patterns of movement, such as towards Egypt and western Greece, can be established, suggesting the

use of coins on the winds of trade. As a whole, hoards and individual coin find-spots show coinage used in overseas commerce, booty, and possibly as tribute. They provide little evidence towards coins being used in everyday commerce and within their city of issue.

This picture of early Greek coinage has persisted over the years and was probably best voiced by Kraay some thirty-five years ago.[17] Rutter confirmed most of these points in his examination of coinage at the beginning of the Athenian empire.[18] However, it has become increasingly difficult to support either case. Recent finds of early silver coins have overturned these models for early coinage, demonstrating how new bodies of evidence can still produce fundamental shifts in our perspective on a problem. While this is not the appropriate place to present a detailed account of the new material,[19] what is offered below is a brief overview to show how great a difference new finds can make to our perception of how coins were used.

One of the most important additions to our understanding of archaic coinage comes in the form of the large numbers of fractional silver coins which have appeared over the last few decades. The importance of such small coins should not be underestimated as they represent what might be thought of as the lowest common denominator in coinage. The smallest weigh as little as a tenth of a gram, although most mints which produced fractional silver tended to mint coins between a quarter and a full gram. As money, they differ significantly from their large-denomination counterparts. Unlike larger coins, it is easier to imagine their use in transactions of the everyday sort. Perhaps more striking, when documentary evidence for the use of coins begins to improve towards the middle and end of the fifth century, the fractional silver coins appear very often as money used in everyday transactions in the market place. These are the coins which may plausibly be called small change.

What is perhaps most astonishing about the recent appearance of early fractional silver is the quantities involved and how this new influx affects our understanding of the prevalence of small change. When Kraay sketched the picture of the prevalence of small change in the mid-1960s, he found that many prominent mints, such as the South Italian incuse mints,

---

[16] von Reden (1997) 156–7; Rutter (1981) 5; Kraay (1964) 88–91.

[17] Kraay (1964).   [18] Rutter (1981).
[19] Kim (1994); Bérend (1984).

Athens (early owls), Syracuse, Aenus, Abdera, Thasos, Mende, and Acanthus, either lacked small change or produced it in insufficient quantities.[20] In contrast, it is now apparent that nearly all of the mints which Kraay pointed to show significant levels of production. Some areas, such as Ionia and northern Greece, display a bewildering array of new types, many of which defy traditional attempts at identifying civic authorities.

As surprising as the recent appearance of new types may be, more surprising discoveries await in gauging the extent of fractional silver coinages. One case offers a salutary lesson of the potential output of some fractional series. A series of Ionian coins bearing a profile archaic head and sometimes attributed as the early series of Colophon has until now been relatively uncommon (Pl. 1.1–4). However, a single hoard containing 906 twelfths and twenty-fourths of a Persian *siglos* has broken the silence to reveal a most remarkable scale of production.[21] A die-study of this hoard (*CH* 1, 3) has shown that over 400 obverse and 400 reverse dies were used to produce the coins found in the hoard. While relating die numbers to original production levels remains a problematic issue,[22] the numbers are staggering. Even if these dies only produced as few as a thousand coins in their productive lives, we would have to envisage the production, use, and circulation of hundreds of thousands of coins.

The problem with finding so much coinage produced in one location is in how to envision its use. Substantial production of large-denomination coins can at times be attributed to requirements beyond city walls in terms of payments of tribute, the export of bullion, or military expenditures. However, finds of small coins do not display patterns of dispersal remotely similar to large coins. As a whole, small coins tend not to travel far from their issuing cities.[23] When found in hoards, they tend to be found only with similarly small coins. It is difficult to envisage substantial production of small coins being directed to export or major expenditures. More plausibly, their existence ought to be considered in the context of local needs.

The amount of fractional silver coinage produced during the early stages of Greek coinage should provide substantial evidence to raise doubts about the 'limited-purpose and limited-user' interpretations for early silver coinage. For some mints, we may surmise that the amount of small change produced must have been plentiful enough for use by a significant segment of a population. This revised picture of early silver coinage is very different from what could have been outlined as recently as a decade ago. It represents a fundamental change in our understanding of how early coins could be used.

Money Before Coinage

One aspect of silver coinage which is often overlooked is that when it emerged it did so in a fully developed form. In most coinages we are faced with carefully manufactured pieces of silver, bearing a stamp of authority, conforming to a consistent weight standard, and including a system of denominations which stretch downwards to fractions of under a gram in weight. There is little evidence in the Greek world of a transitional period in which a 'proto-coinage' consisting of unmarked, weight-adjusted pieces of silver circulated.[24] Nor is there any evidence of official stamps, whether civic or private, appearing on silver bullion in the Greek world prior to the appearance of coinage.[25]

The relatively short period of time it took for a fully developed coinage to spread through the Greek world poses a pressing question: Was there money before coinage? The speed of its development and spread makes it hard to imagine that the use of money was unfamiliar when coinage was introduced. If anything, it suggests that the notion of money use and some forms of money preceded coinage, and that when coinage appeared it slotted into a system which was already well established, serving as an improved substitute. If so, what was this pre-coin form of money and what functions did money serve?

The most obvious suspect for a form of money prior to coinage is silver bullion, as the features of early coinage would have improved its usage, providing

---

[20] Kraay (1964) 85–8.   [21] *CH* 1, 3; Kim (1994) 23–6.
[22] deCallataÿ (1995); Buttrey (1993); Buttrey (1994).
[23] Kim (forthcoming).

[24] Furtwängler suggests some evidence of weight-adjusted gold bars (see Furtwängler (1986)). He cites the cases of Knossos, Crete (Boardman (1967)), and Eretria (Themelis (1982); Themelis (1983)). Boardman, while noting the uniformity of some of the gold bars and dumps, argues against considering them currency (Boardman (1967) 62). Themelis comes to the same conclusions (Themelis (1983) 161).
[25] For the appearance of stamps on bullion contemporary to coinage see Arnold-Biucchi, Beer-Tobey, and Waggoner (1988); Babelon (1912) 32–3.

assurance of the weight and purity of the metal. Yet, it has recently been asserted that coinage was introduced at a time when 'silver was scarce' and the 'possession of monetary wealth [was not] excessive'.[26] If both observations are true, this proposition would need to be called into question, as well as the prospect of whether we can identify money use before coinage.

In answer to the latter, there should be little doubt that the concept of money and that some forms of (limited-purpose) money did exist before coinage. Von Reden has illustrated a number of cases in which awards, fines, and payments in the form of metal containers, metal objects, and foodstuffs were used in legal, marital, athletic, and political contexts prior to and concurrent with coinage.[27] Central to her case is her proposition that the importance of rendering value quantifiable grew out of the institutionalization of social, religious, and legal practices, in which valuables (symbolic and intrinsic) were exchanged to meet obligations or as compensation. This notion of money being a social construct is extremely important, and offers us a key model for seeing how money and the idea of assessing value may have developed out of much wider concerns than disembedded economic exchange.[28] When looking at the development of coinage in the archaic Greek *polis* these factors cannot be ignored, as they point to a number of emergent institutions which influenced and also were influenced by its development.

This focus on the 'actions' and contexts rather than the 'objects' makes much sense and provides a valuable new line of investigation into the development of money in the *polis*. However, we have to be cautious in placing too much weight on the priority of these cases over other models for money use and monetization. If monetization involved the spread of money use through a society, its infiltration should have been felt within a relatively wide spectrum of society.[29] Yet, many of the early laws were concerned with procedural matters in which those fined were of a relatively exclusive social class.[30] Likewise, regulations controlling the maximum value of marriage dowries would have been aimed at the few. If the experience of money use emerged as a result of

participation in or obligation to civic institutions, we would have to imagine monetization spreading or 'trickling down' through strata of society. This 'top-down' model for monetization fits extremely well with a model of early coinage which sees its use as restricted to coins of relatively high value. However, as outlined above, the recent evidence of fractional silver coins suggests that when early silver coinage began it had a much broader base of uses and users.

We should also wonder whether the monetary payments prescribed by these various institutions should be viewed as engines for monetization or simply as a reflection of a growing reality of money use and a movement towards a more disembedded system of exchange. Von Reden sees in these institutions a smooth transition from the exchange of valuables to the exchange of coinage, both functionally and symbolically.[31] The implication is that coinage had distinct 'political' values, symbolizing the authority of the *polis* and slotting into the élite culture of the time. It is tempting to read much political symbolism in early coinage; however, we have to tread very carefully, especially in ascribing coinage to a particular social class.[32] There is a natural tendency to do this, especially when attempting to explain coinage specifically in the context of the *polis*. However, in the end we are still left with the question of why coinage spread within the greater Greek world (both *polis* and non-*polis*). What was so special about the emergent institutions of the Greek *poleis* which promoted the adoption of coinage versus other factors which made coinage equally attractive to the non-Greeks who minted coins at the same time?

The models developed in recent years are offered in contrast to popular economic explanations which have been proposed over the years. However, it seems unlikely that economic explanations do not have some bearing on the matter. While much recent attention has been paid to social and political developments which were specific to the archaic Greek *polis*, we should equally wonder whether there were factors external to the developing institutions of the *polis* which made the need to assess value important.

[26] von Reden (1995) 175.   [27] von Reden (1997) 156–68.
[28] von Reden (1997) 160–1.   [29] Kim (1994).
[30] von Reden (1997) 162–3.   [31] von Reden (1997) 168–70.

[32] See Kurke (1995) 42, for coinage posing a threat to traditional aristocrats; von Reden (1997) 168, for coinage distributed by the élites; Martin (1996) 280–3, for coinage facilitating redistributions from the rich to the community.

Casting an eye across the archaeology of the archaic period, which is replete with evidence for inter-regional activities and contacts with the outside world, we should not think of the development of the archaic Greek *polis* as having occurred within a vacuum. Could there have been external factors which contributed to the growth in the use of money? Need we restrict ourselves entirely to the Greek *polis* in seeking models for how money use evolved?

At this point, it is appropriate to return to the question of silver as a commodity whose use as money may have been the antecedent to coinage. The 'silver-poor' picture of the Greek world prior to the introduction of coinage is problematic and requires careful scrutiny. If true, it undermines one of the key elements for building a case for an economic explanation of coinage. Its effect should not be underestimated as it sets coinage into a very different context. If silver coinage had no bullion predecessor, its invention would have introduced a new medium of exchange. Monetization would have largely been a phenomenon of coinage, and coinage would then become an extremely important marker for the use of money.

The new evidence of early silver coinage as presented above should raise some doubts about whether Greece during the archaic period was 'silver-poor'. In contrast, what is proposed here is a model in which the use of silver and money was already quite advanced by the time that coinage was invented. It is an observation which can be supported from two forms of material evidence; first, from finds of uncoined silver, some of which are remarkable because of their inclusion of very low-weight silver fragments; second, from the high level of sophistication apparent in early coin-weighing systems, especially at weights of under a gram. Both point to a strong familiarity with and developed use of silver as a form of money prior to the start of coinage, and both are important elements for promoting an economic explanation (or component) for the development of coinage.

Uncoined Silver

The question of money before coinage inevitably turns to uncoined (or pre-coin) silver. Adherents of a market-driven explanation for coinage suggest that silver was used as money prior to coinage, but what remains unproven is how extensively silver was used

and, more importantly, whether it was actually used as money. Answering these questions is not easy, as evidence for the prevalence, context, and uses for uncoined silver still remains woefully poor. Despite this, building a positive case for the prevalence of silver can be done by piecing together a range of material finds, scientific findings, and literary references.

Assessing the prevalence of silver prior to coinage is not straightforward. The sorts of documentary evidence we would want to have for the use of silver in exchange contexts exists in only a handful of sources. As for material finds, one of the problems immediately faced is that the nature of the survival and dating of silver objects may prejudice us to believe that silver was relatively scarce before the spread of coinage. Hoards of silver scraps are virtually undatable in the absence of coins or other manufactured material, resulting in their loss from the material record. Compounding the problem is the fact that, unlike manufactured objects such as pottery, silver is a reusable and valuable commodity which may not leave tell-tale trails of use and reuse.

Finds of uncoined silver in the Greek world are mainly confined to hoards which include a combination of coined and uncoined silver.[33] Hoards such as Selinus (*CH* 8, 35), Taranto (*IGCH* 1874), Sambiase (*IGCH* 1872), Ras Shamra (*IGCH* 1478), Asyut (*CH* 2, 17), and Asia Minor (*CH* 1, 3) display how coins and uncoined silver were used side by side. *CH* 1, 3 shows the use of silver bullion alongside some of the earliest and smallest silver coins. Even though the hoard contained some 906 coins, the bulk of the hoard, some 316 grams (versus 245), consisted of small pieces of silver, some cut up, others intentionally manufactured as small disks (Pl. 1.5–10). What separates this hoard from many of the other bullion hoards is the prevalence of these low-weight pieces, the majority under three grams in weight. It is tempting to see their inclusion together with small coins as suggestive of coins and bullion functioning side by side as forms of small change.

While the number of finds of pre-coin silver is small, evidence for pre-coin production and use of silver can be found in a number of material and literary sources.[34]

---

[33] One exception is the case of the find at Knossos (Boardman (1967)), where one bar of silver was found alongside several gold bars.

[34] See Kroll (1998) 230.

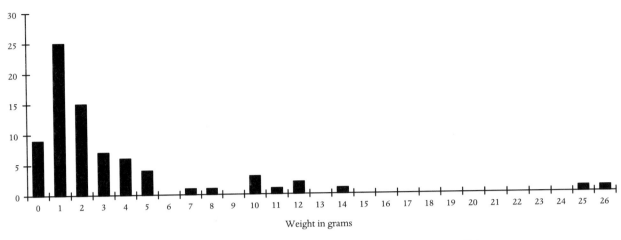

Figure 1.2: Weight histogram of the silver disks and fragments in *CH* i, 3.

Scientific analysis has revealed that the well-known and extremely productive mines at Laureion in Attica may have been producing silver as early as the Bronze Age.[35] Literary evidence for the exploitation of mines provides very promising evidence for silver refinement during the archaic period. The mines at Siphnos apparently produced large quantities of precious metal until they were flooded and presumably abandoned around 525,[36] and the lyric poets of the sixth and fifth centuries make numerous references to metals being weighed, purified, and tested.[37] The long-distance movement of silver should not be forgotten, as lead-isotope analysis of an ingot from the Selinus hoard provides some evidence for the movement of silver from Iberian mines to the Greek world before 500.[38]

Lead-isotope analysis also provides some rather surprising clues on the sources of silvers used in early archaic coinage.[39] Far from showing that mints generally relied on single mines for their silver, analysis has shown that most mints drew their silver from a much wider and less coherent pool, suggesting that circulating silver provided a significant portion of the metal used for coins. The mint at Aegina which had no native source of silver appears to have used silver derived from nearby Attica and Siphnos as well as from a range of others.[40] Even mints which had direct

access to sources of silver show little reliance on their native silvers. The early *Wappenmünzen* coins of Athens include silver from its native mines as well as a host of other mines further afield.[41] The silver in Thasian coins, despite Thasos' control of mines on the island and mainland, appears to come from a number of different sources.[42] Few mints actually display dependence on a single source of silver.[43]

This incoherence in the sourcing of silver is by no means surprising given the growing number of long-distance contacts characteristic of the archaic period. During this time we see a significant movement of commodities between regions, as documented in the export of foodstuffs and manufactured wares.[44] What should be kept in mind is that few of these economic developments were unique to the Greek world. The Greek world was part of a wider Mediterranean economy which saw a growing level of regional interdependence.[45] Silver was a key commodity, used by most of the cultures bordering the Greek world, and it appears that Greeks treated it in much the same way.

While a case can be made for the prevalence of uncoined silver, what should be kept in mind is that

[35] Stos-Gale and Macdonald (1991).
[36] Herodotus, 3. 57.   [37] Kurke (1995) 39 ff.
[38] Beer-Tobey, Gale, Kim, Stos-Gale (1998). Steisichorus fr. 7 (184) refers to Spanish silver.
[39] Gale, Gentner, Wagner (1980) 3–49.
[40] Gale, Gentner, Wagner (1980) 33–43.

[41] Gale, Gentner, Wagner (1980) 30, 49.
[42] Gale, Gentner, Wagner (1980) 44–5.
[43] The one strong case is of the coins of the Orescii, a Macedonian 'tribe', which appears to have drawn its silver from Thasos (Gale, Gentner, Wagner (1980) 44).
[44] Osborne (1996*b*) 39–40.
[45] Sherratt and Sherratt (1993) 371–4. For 'interdependence' see Osborne (1996*b*) 31.

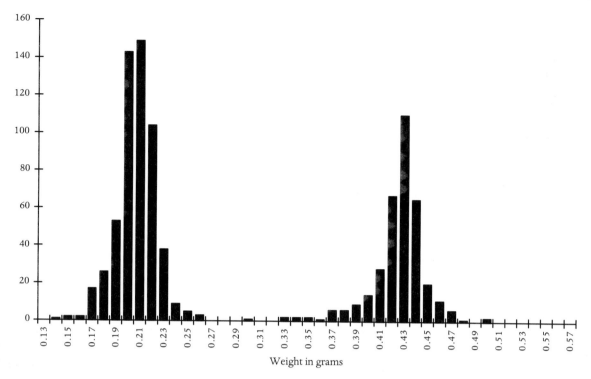

Figure 1.3: Weight histogram of the coins contained in *CH* 1, 3.

much of this evidence does not prove that silver was used as money. It could be argued that silver was used simply as a commodity in overseas trade. For silver to be used as money, we must turn to literary and epigraphic evidence to pin down its use in legal, religious, and political contexts. While material evidence for the use of silver before coinage is far from ideal—a number of datable finds of silver scraps would be helpful—the scattering of literary sources gives a stronger impression that silver was not scarce before coinage and that it was probably used as money in exchange.

Evidence for the use of silver bullion comes from a number of literary and epigraphic sources. The most pertinent are those which concern the Solonian laws of the early sixth century. As Kroll has recently outlined, twelve of the laws attributed to Solon involve payments in silver bullion at a time when silver coinage had yet to be invented.[46] Fines of low (two-drachma) and high (100-drachma) values are imposed on transgressors, to be paid to the public treasury.[47]

The administrative office of the naucrary dealt in silver.[48] Payments to victors in games were also reckoned in drachmas.[49] Perhaps most important, private debt (i.e. the interest accrued) appears to have been handled by the weighing out of silver.[50] Epigraphic evidence elsewhere points to similar practices. Fines levied in Eretria during the last quarter of the sixth century were probably paid in uncoined silver.[51] From the lyric poets, there are a number of metaphors of metals being used in exchange.[52]

Weighing Systems

One aspect of the use of silver bullion as money which has not received much attention is the weighing systems which were employed. Part of the reason for this may have to do with how chaotic the

[46] Kroll (1998).
[47] Plutarch, *Solon* 21. 1 (fr. 32, 33), 23. 1 (fr. 26, 30), and 24. 1 (fr. 65).

[48] Aristotle, *Ath. Pol.* 8. 3 (fr. 79).
[49] Plutarch, *Solon* 23. 3 (fr. 143).   [50] Lysias, 10. 18 (fr. 68).
[51] Cairns (1994).
[52] Kurke (1995) 39 ff. Also, Heracleitos' statement (fr. 90) that 'all things are an equal exchange for fire and fire for all things, as goods are for gold and gold for all goods' indicates some notion of the use of metals as money. (See Seaford (1994) 221–5, for the development of money as a universal equivalent as a medium of exchange.)

multitude of weighing systems employed though the Greek world appears. In his survey of archaic Greece, Osborne lists no fewer than fourteen weight standards which were employed at the outset of silver coinage.[53] To this number should be added several more and the figure further multiplied to take into account differing systems of denomination.[54]

As complicated as weighing systems may be, they do provide important information from which a number of inferences can be made. One important inference which Osborne has recently made is that by being minted according to the local systems of weighing, coins were not produced in order to facilitate transactions across state boundaries. The weights of coins from one city were often at variance with coins of another, and yet there is no evidence that this precluded their mixing together. The reason for this is that coins were not tokens of nominal value, but were intrinsically valuable. Provided that good scales were available, coins of differing standards could be used with ease, as the mixed hoards of the archaic period demonstrate.[55]

This inference is quite important as it reinforces the economic or market-based value of coins and the importance of weighing silver, even after coinage had been invented. But what about before coinage? Have we any evidence for the practice of silver being carefully weighed to determine its value for both large and small transactions?

In answer to this, we need only go as far as the Solonian and Eretrian laws mentioned above. But further support for a growing familiarity with the practice of weighing out silver may actually come from the weighing systems themselves. There are two features of weighing systems which are of some interest: the high level of precision evident in weights of early coins, and the formalization of various weighing standards prior to the invention of coinage.

It is often overlooked that the very first coins were produced to remarkably precise weights. Electrum coins minted in western Asia Minor display a remarkable sensitivity and precision in their weights, even at extremely low levels. The smallest fraction, the 1/96 of a stater, was minted at 0.14 g., and few specimens deviate from this weight by more than a few hundredths of a gram. Fractional silver coins display a similar level of precision and sensitivity. The weights of the 906 coins from *CH* 1, 3 are distributed so precisely that few deviate from the median by more than 0.02 g.

What should be concluded from the existence of such precise weighing systems? The first point is that it seems unlikely that such accurate and sensitive weighing systems developed overnight. Such precision and sensitivity suggest that when coinage began, highly developed methods of weighing were already in place in certain regions of the Greek world. The second point to be made is that, while the technology for precision weighing need not be complicated, the desire to weigh objects accurately to less than a tenth of a gram must come from the need for precision in handling precious material in minute quantities on a regular basis. Grain, timber, and stone are certainly not the products involved. More precious materials such as metals and plant or animal derivatives come to mind as the objects of meticulous handling. Certainly weighing systems had achieved high levels of sensitivity prior to the introduction of coinage, paving the way for minting coins to a remarkable consistency.

Equally remarkable are the number of reforms which are alleged to have occurred to weighing systems prior to the invention of coinage.[56] Both Pheidon of Argos and Solon are credited with inventing coinage and reforming the weighing systems of their respective cities. While it is unlikely that either historical figure contributed to the establishment of coinage in their respective cities,[57] their reputations as founders or reformers of weighing standards cannot be dismissed as easily. The conflation of weighing systems and coinage seems natural enough, when viewed through the eyes of the various commentators a few centuries after the fact. This should not cloud the basic conclusion that the reforms were considered important actions in their own right and that the need to have a reliable system of weights was of great importance. We might wonder whether the standardization of weights served as an important first step before the creation of coinage.[58]

---

[53] Osborne (1996a) 253–5.
[54] See Grayson (1974). For a survey of recent work on weighing systems see Parise (1997) 5–9.
[55] Osborne (1996a) 251–5.

[56] Grayson (1974) 338–49.
[57] Waggoner and Kroll (1984) 326–33, 335–9.
[58] *Contra* Grayson (1980) 338–49, who believes the development of coinage helped pave the way for the standardization of weights.

Taken together, the evidence for silver production and use and the evidence for the formalization of weights should suggest that silver was probably used as a form of money prior to the invention of coinage. This is an important recognition for building an economic explanation for the invention of coinage. Coinage should be seen not so much as a radically new invention, but as a formalization of the use of silver bullion. We might imagine that coinage does not so much stand at the headwaters of the use of silver, as it is a tributary feeding on to a much wider flow of silver which in turn fed into the wider Mediterranean economy.

The Moneyed Economy

The picture of early Greek coinage and pre-coin money outlined above differs significantly from what could have been outlined as recently as a decade or two ago. During this time the material record of early silver coinage has improved greatly, forcing us to reconsider what functions early coinage could serve. At the same time, the intellectual climate surrounding money has changed, allowing new approaches to age-old problems. This paper has set out to join up these two new developments to provide a framework for continued work on how coinage developed and influenced the archaic Greek world.

At the heart of the discussion is the question of how coinage can be used as evidence for the development of the moneyed economy. As the recent generation of works has pointed out, the 'monetization' of the Greek world played a crucial part in the development in the social, political, economic, and cultural history of the Greek *polis*. It occurred alongside a crucial change in the way in which exchange could be carried out, and is a reflection of changes in the nature of social exchange and personal relationships. It re-aligned power relationships within society, and is imbued with strong moral overtones for the closed *polis* community. Within this context, it is easy to appreciate the important role coinage has to play as a form of evidence.

One of the key points which this discussion has attempted to develop is the notion that coinage should be viewed as one marker along a longer road in the use of money. This point is by no means original, as many

recent works have seen the origins of socially constructed money in traditional practices. What this paper argues is that it is possible to identify certain features of early coinage—small change, precise weights—which may have had antecedents in pre-coin money use. Silver, it has been argued, was probably the main antecedent. One result of this observation is that, far from being a radically new invention, coinage should be viewed as a simple convenience.

A second point which needs further emphasis is that when we think of a moneyed economy, we should not limit ourselves simply to seeking just one form of 'general-purpose' money or just one inspiration for monetization. A moneyed economy presupposes a widespread familiarity with the notion of money use, whether in the daily economic activities of the household or in the activities which brought the individual citizen in contact with civic obligations and duties. There should be little doubt that the development of the *polis* had a role to play in the spread of money use. The workings of a radical democracy such as was seen in Athens needed coins to function, as Jeremy Trevett explores in the present volume (Ch. 2). The systems of taxes, liturgies, and political pay, the increased expenditures made for public projects, and the centralization of legal bodies all contributed to accelerating the amount of money going around the *polis* and in obliging wider segments of the population to partake in moneyed exchange.

The emphasis of recent works towards the *polis* has been a great development, as it has helped to show how culturally specific was the Greek notion of money. It has also helped emphasize how unique coinage was to the Greek world. Where criticism may be levelled is in that it risks being short-sighted and fails to consider the factors external to the *polis* which may have promoted the growth of money use. Economic explanations have often been dismissed and practices external to the Greek world ignored.

While there were a number of key developments in the Greek world which were unique, the general economic climate, of which the Greek world was an integral part, was one which was shared by many others. Not all of the changes which led to the invention of coinage can be attributed to social or political developments. What has been traced above suggests that there may have been economic conditions which promoted the development and spread of coinage. The uses of pre-coin silver in the Greek world may be roughly analogous to the use of uncoined silver in much of the rest of the Mediterranean. It may be tied into the rise in commoditization and the growing importance of regional interdependence in supplying basic and luxury goods. While we should exercise some caution in trying to relate the relatively poorly documented experience of the Greek world to the silver-rich practices of the Near East, we cannot deny how interlinked the Mediterranean had become.

Far from undermining the uniqueness of the Greek contribution, this acknowledgement should heighten our awareness of the importance of the social and political strands which contributed to the formation of Greek *poleis*. It should be conceded that economic explanations cannot explain fully why coinage was invented and why so many cities adopted it. Other societies bordering the Greek world did not develop coinage at this time and failed to do so for a century or more, yet probably experienced a similar level of trade in precious metals and possessed sophisticated weighing systems. Just because economic conditions were similar does not mean that the same route must have been taken.

In one sense, what is needed among historians is to accept the Aristotelian duality of the nature of coinage, being both a symbol and a hard commodity. Studies of money in the archaic Greek world need to balance models which emphasize the unique developments of *polis*-based society against economic models of the wider Mediterranean world. Money and coinage can be both symbolic concepts of a society, and objects which held value when removed from it. Can we accept that the notion of money use developed out of social experiences *and* that it was made possible by using a commodity which was already being used as money? We probably should.

This contribution is only one step on the longer road which lies ahead in developing our understanding of how money developed and was used in the Greek world. The key first steps have been provided by investigations which have examined the importance of non-economic exchange in the development and use of general-purpose monies. Still, the economic climate should not be forgotten, and placing coinage in this context remains an important avenue of research.

REFERENCES

ARNOLD-BIUCCHI, C., L. BEER-TOBEY, and N. M. WAGGONER (1988). 'A Greek Archaic Silver Hoard from Selinus', *ANSMN* 33: 1–35.

BABELON, E. (1912). 'Trouvaille de Tarente', *RN*[4] 16: 1–40.

BALMUTH, M. A. (1971). 'Remarks on the Appearance of the Earliest Coins', in D. G. Mitten, J. G. Pedley, and J. A. Scott (eds.), *Studies Presented to George M. A. Hanfmann* (Mainz), 1–7.

BAMMER, A. (1990). 'A Peripteros of the Geometric Period in the Artemesion of Ephesus', *AS* 40: 137–60.

BEER-TOBEY, L., N. H. GALE, H. S. KIM, Z. A. STOS-GALE (1998). 'Lead Isotope Analysis of Four Late Archaic Silver Ingots from the Selinus Hoard', *MIN* 4: 385–92.

BÉREND, D. (1984). 'Reflexions sur les fractions grecques', in A. Houghton, S. Hurter, *et al.* (eds.), *Festschrift für Leo Mildenberg* (Wettern), 7–30.

BOARDMAN, J. (1967). 'The Khaniale Tekke tombs, II', *BSA* 62: 57–75.

BUTTREY, T. V. (1993). 'Calculating Ancient Coin Productions: Facts and Fantasies', *NC* 153: 335–51.

——(1994). 'Calculating Coin Production II: Why it Cannot be Done', *NC* 154: 341–52.

CAIRNS, F. (1994). '*Chremata dokima*: IG XII, 9, 1273.1274 and the Early Coinage of Eretria', *ZPE* 54: 145–55.

CARRADICE, I. (1987). 'Coinage of the Persian Empire', in I. Carradice (ed.), *Coinage and Administration in the Athenian and Persian Empires* (Oxford), 73–107.

——and M. PRICE (1988). *Coinage in the Greek World* (London).

DE CALLATAŸ, F. (1995). 'Calculating Ancient Coin Production: Seeking a Balance', *NC* 155: 289–311.

FURTWÄNGLER, A. (1978). *Monnaies grecques en Gaul: Le trésor d'Auriol et le monnayage de Massalia 525/520–460 ac. J.-C.* (Fribourg).

——(1986). 'Neue beobachtungen zur frühesten Münzprägung', *SNR* 65: 153–65.

GALE, N. H., W. GENTNER, and G. A. WAGNER (1980). 'Mineralogical Silver Sources of Archaic Greek Coinage', in D. M. Metcalf and W. A. Oddy (eds.), *MIN* 1: 3–49.

GRAYSON, C. (1974). 'Greek Weighing' (Univ. of Oxford D.Phil. Thesis).

HERZFELD, E. (1938). 'Notes on the Achaemenid Coinage and some Sassanian Mint Names', *TINC 1936*: 413–26.

HOWGEGO, C. J. (1995). *Ancient History from Coins* (London).

KIM, H. S. (1994). 'Greek Fractional Silver Coinage: A Reassessment of the Inception, Development, Prevalence, and Functions of Small Change during the Late Archaic and Early Classical Periods' (Univ. of Oxford M.Phil. Thesis).

——(forthcoming). 'Small Change and the Moneyed Economy', in L. Foxhall, P. Cartledge, and E. E. Cohen (eds.), *Kerdos: Money, Labour and Land in Ancient Greece* (London).

KRAAY, C. M. (1964). 'Hoards, Small Change and the Origin of Coinage', *JHS* 84: 76–91.

——(1976). *Archaic and Classical Greek Coins* (Berkeley Calif.).

KROLL, J. H. (1998). 'Silver in Solon's Laws', in R. Ashton and S. Hurter (eds.), *Studies in Greek Numismatics in Memory of Martin Jessop Price* (London), 225–32.

KUHRT, A. (1995). *The Ancient Near East* (London).

KURKE, L. (1995). 'Herodotus and the Language of Metals', *Helios*, 22/1: 36–64.

MARTIN, T. (1996). 'Why Did the Greek Polis Originally Need Coins?', *Historia*, 45/3: 257–83.

MORRIS, I. (1994). 'The Athenian Economy Twenty Years after *The Ancient Economy*', *CP* 89: 351–66.

OSBORNE, R. (1996a). *Greece in the Making: 1200–479 BC* (London).

——(1996b). 'Pots, Trade and the Archaic Greek Economy', *Antiquity*, 70: 31–44.

PARISE, N. (1997). 'Metallic Currency and Weight Units in the Mediterranean Before Coinage', in C. Morrison and B. Kluge, *A Survey of Numismatic Research 1990–1995* (Berlin), 5–9.

PRICE, M. J. (1983). 'Thoughts on the Beginning of Coinage', in C. N. L. Brooke, B. H. I. H. Stewart, J. G. Pollard, and T. R. Volk (eds.), *Studies in Numismatic Method Presented to Philip Grierson* (Cambridge), 1–10.

ROBINSON, E. S. G. (1951). 'The Coins from the Ephesian Artemision Reconsidered', *JHS* 76: 156–67.

ROOT, M. C. (1988). 'Evidence from Persepolis for the Dating of Persian and Archaic Greek Coinage', *NC* 148: 1–12.

RUTTER, N. K. (1981). 'Early Greek Coinage and the Influence of the Athenian State', in B. Cunliffe (ed.), *Coinage and Society in Britain and Gaul: Some Current Problems* (London), 1–9.

SEAFORD, R. A. S. (1994). *Reciprocity and Ritual* (Oxford).

SHERRATT, S., and A. SHERRATT (1993). 'The Growth of the Mediterranean Economy in the Early First Millenium BC', *World Archaeology*, 24/3: 361–78.

SORDA, S. [1979] (1980). 'A proposito di un rinvenimento di punte di freccia', *AIIN* 26: 185–206.

STOS-GALE, Z. A., and C. F. MACDONALD (1991). 'Sources of Metal and Trade in the Bronze Age Aegean', in N. H. Gale (ed.), *Bronze Age Trade in the Mediterranean*, *SIMA* 90 (Jonsered) 248–80.

THEMELIS, P. G. [1980] (1982). 'Anaskaphi Eretrias', *Praktika*, 135: 78–102.

——(1983). 'An Eighth Century Goldsmith's Workshop at Eretria', in R. Hägg, *The Greek Renaissance of the Eighth Century B.C.* (Stockholm), 157–65.

VON REDEN, S. (1995). *Exchange in Ancient Greece* (London).

——(1997). 'Money, Law and Exchange: Coinage in the Greek Polis', *JHS* 117: 154–76.

WAGGONER, N. M., and J. H. KROLL (1984). 'Dating the Earliest Coins of Athens, Corinth and Aegina', *AJA* 88: 325–39.

WALLACE, R. W. (1987). 'The Origin of Electrum Coinage', *AJA* 91: 385–97.

WEIDAUER, L. (1995). *Probleme der frühen Elektronprägung* (Fribourg).

WELLS, H. B. (1981). 'A Further Study of the Arrowhead-money', *SAN* 12/3: 53–4.

WILLIAMS, D. J. R. (1991–3). 'The "Pot-hoard" Pot from the Archaic Artemesion at Ephesus', *BICS* 38: 98–104.

WILLIAMS, J. H. C. (1996). Review of C. J. Howgego, *Ancient History from Coins*, in *NC* 156: 333–5.

2
COINAGE AND DEMOCRACY AT ATHENS

Jeremy Trevett

Introduction

THE AIM OF THIS PAPER IS TO EXPLORE THE relationship between coinage and democracy in late archaic and classical Athens. The subject is a large one, and the treatment of it will inevitably be somewhat impressionistic. My argument is that Athenian coinage cannot be considered apart from the political circumstances that produced it—coinage is after all nothing if not a political phenomenon[1]—and that certain features of Athens' coins can best be understood in the light of Athens' democratic ideologies and practices.[2]

Democracy and Coinage

No direct connection can be shown to have existed between democracy and coinage in ancient Greece. No ancient text asserts it, and many *poleis* that issued coins were not democracies at the time they did so.[3] It is, however, possible to argue for an indirect connection, on the basis of several passages of Aristotle's *Politics* in which democracy is associated with public pay. For example, he writes that in democracies: 'Payment for services, in the assembly, in the law courts, and in the magistracies, is regular for all (or at

any rate in the magistracies, law courts, council, and the sovereign meetings of the assembly, or in the magistracies where it is obligatory to have meals together).'[4] Unfortunately we cannot confirm his statement from other sources, since for the classical period there is next to no evidence for political pay outside Athens. Indeed, the only certain instance is fourth-century Rhodes.[5] Yet Aristotle's text clearly suggests that he had a number of different *poleis* in mind. And since he collected copious material on the constitutional histories of Greek states, it would be an error of method to suppose that he is either mistaken or generalizing from the case of Athens.[6] It must, of course, be granted that at Athens democracy was established half a century before the introduction of public pay,[7] and that Greece in general was much more highly monetized in the later fourth century, when Aristotle was writing, than it had been in the fifth. Consequently his statement linking democracy with public pay will doubtless have been truer of his own day than of earlier periods. But it should not for that reason be rejected.

Since it is unlikely that many democracies made regular official payments to their citizens in either foreign coin or non-monetary form, we may conclude that, if Aristotle is correct, most democracies, in

---

[1] Cf. the dictum of Finley (1985) 166 that: 'The Greek passion for coins . . . was essentially a political phenomenon.' and above, 1–2.

[2] My approach in some respects resembles that of Leslie Kurke in her recent book *Coins, Bodies, Games, and Gold*. Specifically, I endorse her insistence that Greek coins must be regarded as 'both material and symbol, both matter and trope' (Kurke (1999) 300).

[3] Oligarchic Corinth issued coins throughout this period: see Kraay (1976) 78–88.

[4] 1317^{b}35–8. Cf. also 1294^{a}37–41; 1297^{a}35–8; 1304^{b}26–7.

[5] Ar. *Pol.* 1304^{b}26–7. On state pay in general see de Ste Croix (1975); on the coinage of Rhodes see Ashton (this volume).

[6] de Ste Croix (1981) 289–90, 602–3.

[7] I am here accepting the conventional view that democracy was introduced by Kleisthenes: for discussion of this question see the various contributions in Part I of Morris and Raaflaub (1998): 'The Beginnings of Athenian Democracy'.

so far as they paid their citizens, will also have issued coins. Indeed, an important reason why archaic *poleis* started to issue coins was precisely to make state payments.[8] Furthermore, if such a connection did exist, we might hope to find some correlation between *poleis* that issued coins and those that were democracies. Unfortunately, however, the present state of our knowledge makes it virtually impossible to determine whether this was the case. Not only is little known about democracies outside Athens,[9] but we also lack securely dated numismatic material for the majority of Greek *poleis*. The danger of circular argument in assigning coins to periods of democracy is evident, and it seems safest to leave this line of investigation to one side.

Coinage and Democracy at Athens

State Pay

That coined money played an integral role in the operation of the democracy of classical Athens can hardly be disputed. Pericles called Athens 'a salary-drawing city',[10] and the author of the pseudo-Xenophontic *Athenian Constitution* refers to the common people holding magistracies 'for the sake of the pay they receive'.[11] Jury pay[12] and magisterial salaries[13] were introduced in the middle of the fifth century, assembly pay in the early fourth.[14] Payment for military service was also instituted in the fifth century.[15] The development of state pay and of democracy are linked phenomena. In this respect, indeed, one might argue that the democracy was more radical in the fourth century than it had been in the fifth.[16] The numismatic evidence is wholly consistent with this picture. There was a sharp increase in the middle of the fifth century in the quantity of coins of all denominations that were issued.[17] Some of this increase was prompted by the needs of public pay.

Smaller coins would have been needed to pay daily wages; payments for such regular duties as magistracies and military service might have been made in larger coins every prytany, or month, or at the end of the campaign.

Conversely, the abolition of state pay was one of the first acts of the oligarchs in 411. Peisandros referred to it in his speech to the assembly at Kolonos, where he stated that no one was to draw public pay.[18] According to pseudo-Aristotle it was decided that all magistrates except the Archons and Prytaneis were to be unsalaried for the duration of the war.[19] Moreover, the oligarchs' policy that revenue was to be spent only on the waging of war implied the ending of jury pay. Finally, political power was to be restricted, again for the duration of the war, to those Athenians 'most able to serve with their bodies and with their possessions', in other words to those who were rich enough to be able to take part in public life without monetary compensation. State pay was presumably also abolished by the Thirty in 404, in so far as it was still being paid, though no source refers to it.[20]

What the effect on Athens' coinage would have been if an oligarchy had established itself in power can only be guessed. David Whitehead has argued that the Thirty sought in various ways to reform Athens along broadly Spartan lines, at the instigation of the strongly pro-Spartan Kritias.[21] One prominent feature of Spartan society was the failure to issue coins, indeed the virtual absence of coined money (see p. 33 below). Cessation of coinage is not mentioned in connection with the Thirty, and would have been hard to implement in such a highly monetized economy, but public pay would presumably have been substantially curtailed. Also relevant is the failed proposal of Phormisios in 403 to restrict Athenian citizenship to those who owned land—a proposal that was advanced with Spartan support.[22] Its effect would have been to disfranchise not only the landless poor, but also any Athenians whose wealth was held exclusively in the form of money. At the least, the numismatic history of Athens would have been quite different if Kritias and his supporters had remained in power.

---

⁸ See Martin (1996), esp. pp. 275–9.
⁹ For what little is known see O'Neil (1995); E. W. Robinson (1997).
¹⁰ Plut. *Per.* 12.   ¹¹ [Xen.] *AP* 1. 3.
¹² *AP* 27. 3 with Rhodes (1981) 338; Loomis (1998) 9–10.
¹³ Loomis (1998) 10–12, and, more generally, Ch. 1, on pay to public office holders.
¹⁴ [Ar.] *AP* 41. 3.   ¹⁵ Pritchett (1971) 3–29; Loomis (1998) Ch. 2.
¹⁶ On the differences between fifth- and fourth-century democracy see Rhodes (1980).
¹⁷ Starr (1970) 64–75. I am not of course suggesting that public pay was the sole reason for the increase in minting.

¹⁸ Thuc. 8. 67. 3.   ¹⁹ [Ar.] *AP* 29. 5.
²⁰ Xen. *Hell.* 2. 3. 12.   ²¹ Whitehead (1982/3).
²² Dion. Hal. *Lys.* 34.

We might also note the effect of Spartan policies on coinage in the cities of the Peloponnese during this period. Kraay concluded that: 'The zenith of Spartan power [in the early fourth century] seems generally to have restricted coinage.' Democratic Mantinea had issued coins; when the city was destroyed by Sparta and its population forcibly resettled in villages it ceased to do so.[23]

The link between democracy and coined money at Athens is apparent also in the fact that some democratic institutions were referred to informally by the coin or sum that participants in them received. In Aristophanes' *Knights* jury service is called by metonymy 'the triobol', when the Paphlagonian addresses the elderly jurors as 'clansmen of the triobol'.[24] A public payment of uncertain purpose, perhaps a daily dole to needy Athenians, is referred to even in official documents simply as 'the two-obol payments'.[25]

This metonymy is graphically represented on the fourth-century bronze plaques used to allocate jurors to courts.[26] These are stamped with a seal which is either an exact copy or, in some cases, a slight variation of the obverse type of the Athenian silver triobol (the type is an owl facing, with olive sprigs on either side). According to John Kroll, these 'could have been struck with dies engraved and originally used for the minting of coins'.[27] Similarly the double-bodied owls used as secondary seals on these plaques are modelled on the reverse types of fourth-century silver diobols,[28] and the 'owl-in-square' seals reproduce the type of the owl familiar from tetradrachms and their fractions.[29]

There was indeed a close connection between the performance of jury service and the receipt of jury pay. The juror in Aristotle's day received 'a bronze token with the three-obol design; when he gives this up he is paid three obols' (tr. Rhodes).[30] The exact form of these tokens is disputed. A recent study argues that they

were marked with either a gamma or three parallel strokes, although no such tokens have been found.[31] Lead tokens with the triobol type (owl) on the obverse and the letters alpha to kappa on the reverse are argued to have served a different purpose, but could perhaps have been either precursors or successors of the bronze tokens referred to by pseudo-Aristotle.[32] Other official tokens also had types familiar from coins, and may have been used in connection with state payments. Specifically, there exist bronze monetiform tokens with the helmeted head of Athena on the obverse, which were once wrongly regarded as small-denomination coins.[33]

In these and other ways coined money was both necessary for and closely implicated in the operation of the Athenian democracy.[34] Without it, it is hardly an exaggeration to say that democracy could not have existed.

Democratic Types?

Let us now consider the coins themselves, and ask what, if any, connection there is between their types and democracy.

The earliest Athenian coins are the so-called *Wappenmünzen*, didrachms which carry a variety of different types on the obverse and an incuse square on the reverse. Their introduction is generally dated to the reign of Peisistratos.[35] The *Wappenmünzen* take their name (lit. 'heraldic coins' in German) from their obverse types, which were once believed to depict the badges of aristocratic families.[36] Although this theory is now discredited, it remains plausible to interpret the changes from one coin type to another as evidence for changes in the personnel responsible for minting. Kroll notes that elsewhere in Greece changing types were 'the personally chosen devices of mint magistrates', and suggests that the same may have been true of archaic Athens. Indeed, it is possible that some, at any rate, of the coin types are canting allusions to the name of the individual in charge of the mint, and that others derive from

[23] Kraay (1976) 100–2.   [24] φράτερες τριωβόλου (I. 255).

[25] [Ar.] *AP* 28. 3; Loomis (1998) 222–3.

[26] See, in general, Kroll (1972).

[27] Kroll (1972) 41–4. In fact Kroll found no instance of the same die being used for both coins and plaques (41, n. 31).

[28] Kroll (1972) 45–6.   [29] Kroll (1972) 46–7.

[30] [Ar.] *AP* 68. 2. On the precise meaning of the text see next note.

[31] So Boegehold (1995) 67–76. According to the papyrus text the tokens bore a gamma (μετὰ τον γ), but Rhodes (1981) 731 argues that their 'value' was probably indicated by three strokes, since the alphabetic system of numerals was not used before the Hellenistic period.

[32] Rhodes (1981) 712.

[33] Svoronos (1923) pl. 100–2; see Rhodes (1981) 712; Boegehold (1995).

[34] I have said nothing, for example, about liturgies, on which see Martin (1996), who argues that one of the reasons coinage was taken up by the Greeks was to facilitate their performance.

[35] Kroll and Waggoner (1984) 76–91. For the suggestion that the Athenians used weighed silver before the introduction of coinage, and that it is to this that the literary sources refer, see Kroll (1998).

[36] Seltman (1924) 23–38.

shield emblems, as indeed Seltman believed.[37] The *Wappenmünzen* lack any specifically Athenian symbol or legend, and their changing types reflect choices made by individuals, presumably aristocrats, rather than by the community as a whole. To that extent, they reflect an archaic society of powerful noble families and a relatively weak sense of community. This remains true even if, as now seems certain, they were first issued under the tyranny, rather than before its establishment. They are, one might say, a quintessentially pre-democratic coinage.

Towards the end of the sixth century the *Wappenmünzen* were replaced by tetradrachms with the head of Athena on the obverse, an owl and abbreviated Athenian ethnic on the reverse, together with their associated fractions. These coins are commonly referred to as 'Owls'. The date of this change is much disputed, although there is general agreement about the range within which it must fall.[38] In his fundamental study of the archaic Owls, Kraay assigned the change to the last quarter of the sixth century, and almost all scholars accept his view.[39] There is, however, little agreement as to when within this period it occurred. During the tyranny? After the expulsion of Hippias? Or after Kleisthenes' constitutional reforms? In order to determine the political significance of the new coin types, it is clearly desirable to have a more precise date than Kraay was able to provide.

Kraay in fact argued that the Owls were probably introduced by the tyrant Hippias (i.e. before 510), for two reasons. First, he believed that the introduction of new coin types is better placed in a period of political stability; in other words, neither after the expulsion of Hippias nor in the early years of the democracy. Second, the large quantity of early Owls suggests, other things being equal, that they were issued over a longer rather than a shorter period. In other words, the date of their introduction should be pushed back, at any rate earlier than 510. This view is endorsed by Kroll, who sees the Owls as the final stage in a deliberate process of reform, which was 'the achievement of a single, stable, and economically minded government'.[40]

A different view was taken by Martin Price and Nancy Waggoner, who argued from the evidence of coin hoards that the Owls were introduced no earlier than 510. In their view 'a date of 510, or indeed of 506, for the introduction of the owls becomes not only a possibility, but an attractive probability, explaining why the types remained unchanged for 300 years, as a symbol of the democracy itself and freedom from tyranny'.[41] More recent discussions have added little of significance.[42]

It is always tempting to associate changes in coin type with constitutional change. So, for example, John Barron, writing on the fifth-century coinage of Samos, interpreted a series of tetradrachms with the letters [alpha] to xi on the reverse as annual issues of an oligarchy that held power from 454/3 to 440/39.[43] The date of the establishment of the oligarchy was calculated *ex hypothesi*, since no other evidence indicates that an oligarchy was founded in that year, and the thesis is controversial.[44] That a change of constitution *sometimes* led to a change in the coinage is undeniable, but not all changes of coin type need be explained in this way. Too often political events have been used as 'fixed points' by which to date changes in the coins.[45]

There are several objections that might be raised against the thesis of Price and Waggoner as it stands. First, two different events, the expulsion of Hippias and the constitutional reforms of Kleisthenes, are proposed as explanations for the change in type. Second, it is assumed rather than demonstrated that the new types symbolized either democracy or freedom from tyranny. In fact, such civic emblems are commonly found on the coins of democratic and oligarchic *poleis* alike.[46] Third, no reason is given why Hippias could not have issued these coins.[47] The replacement of changing types, which, as we saw (pp. 25–6), may have been chosen by and associated

---

[37] Kroll (1981) 1–10.
[38] Shapiro (1993) 223: 'perhaps the greatest crux in Greek numismatics'.
[39] Kraay (1956). *Contra* Vickers (1985).   [40] Kroll (1981) 24–5.
[41] Price and Waggoner (1975) 64–5.
[42] See also Rutter (1981) 2–3; Kroll and Waggoner (1984); Ober (1998) 80; Raaflaub (1998) 93.
[43] Barron (1966) 90–1. No examples of coins with alpha have yet been found, so far as I know.
[44] The date of the end of the oligarchy is known, since Samos tried to secede from the Athenian empire in that year. For criticism see Kraay (1976) app. 3.
[45] For example, the belief that on epigraphic grounds the Athenian Coinage Decree can be dated *c*.445 (which is now hotly debated) has been fundamental to several important studies of fifth-century mints. On this see most recently Figueira (1998).
[46] Kraay (1976) 2–5.
[47] Seltman (1924) 76 discusses a unique obol with the legend *HIΠ*, which was probably issued by Hippias after his expulsion from Athens.

with individual aristocrats, by a single explicitly Athenian type is consistent with what is known of the Pisistratids' cultural and political policies.[48] Price and Waggoner may in fact have been correct, but they provided no compelling argument in favour of a Kleisthenic date, and the question remains open.

The debate has thus far been conducted primarily in numismatic terms. It might be helpful to alter our focus by considering, first, how if at all the expulsion of Hippias and the reforms of Kleisthenes were represented in other artistic media at the time, and, second, how far the public art of early fifth-century Athens can usefully be characterized as 'democratic'. Such questions have been addressed by contributors to two recent volumes, the consensus of which is that neither event received much public commemoration at the time.[49] Thus David Castriota, writing about the relationship between democracy and art in the late sixth and early fifth centuries, concludes that: 'Athenian art approached the celebration of democracy in oblique, allusive terms for at least a century or more after the reforms of Kleisthenes.'[50] Thus, *contra* Price and Waggoner, we might not expect to find coins being used to announce or celebrate the institution of democracy.

In a similar vein Alan Shapiro has recently discussed the depiction of the owl on Athenian coins, in the context of representations of Athena's owl on Athenian vases. He argues that the owl evolved during the second half of the sixth century from an attribute of Athena to a symbol of Athens, and concludes that 'the iconographical development strongly suggests that the use of the owl as a symbol of Athena, hence of her city, is probably unthinkable before the late sixth century'.[51] He is, however, unable to offer any greater chronological precision. He then discusses Athenian coins, in the light of the vase evidence, and suggests that the Owls may have been introduced by Hippias with the owl facing to the left, and that the new democracy altered the design by making the owl face to the right. Once again, the precise relationship between iconographic and political developments remains elusive.

There is a danger of regarding the exact date of the introduction of the Owls as of decisive importance, and of losing sight of the larger picture. In a sense the question is irrelevant, since, even if the Owls were introduced by Hippias, they were sufficiently acceptable to the new democracy that their design remained substantially unaltered throughout the classical period.[52] Indeed, the tyrants and the new democracy had a common interest in creating a civic focus as a means of diminishing the powers of over-mighty aristocrats—potential rivals to the former and oppressors of the latter. As has recently been argued by Ian Morris, the roots of democracy, at Athens and elsewhere, lie in the early archaic period, in popular resentment to aristocratic rule, and in the egalitarianism inherent in the institution of the *polis*.[53] Taking the long view, tyranny at Athens can be seen as a stage, perhaps indeed a necessary one, on the road from aristocracy to democracy. In fitting the coins into the political history of Athens, what matters is not so much whether the Owls were introduced by Hippias or by Kleisthenes, but the fact that the *Wappenmünzen* were replaced by explicitly civic coin types. The introduction of democracy was a process more than an event, and the institution of the Owls was part of that process. What makes the coins democratic is the emphasis on Athens' patron goddess and animal, and (in the legend) on the Athenians themselves, and the permanent exclusion from the coins of anything else.

Although there is nothing overtly democratic about the Owls, as we have seen, some Athenian coin types of the early fifth century have been regarded as political, and should briefly be considered here.[54] The first is a hemidrachm with on its reverse the head of a Negro, who has been identified as Delphos the son of Melantho. On this basis the coin is commonly taken to allude to the role played by Delphi in the expulsion of Hippias from Athens. The identification of Delphos has, however, been challenged by L. Lacroix,

---

[48] See Shapiro (1989) (although he does not discuss coins).

[49] Morris and Raaflaub (1998); Boedeker and Raaflaub (1998). The absence of coinage from both volumes is a disappointing omission.

[50] Castriota (1998) 201.   [51] Shapiro (1993), quotation from 218.

[52] Similarly Kraay (1976) 79 observes that at Corinth 'the coinage itself carries no discernible allusion to the tyrants, nor is there any change in its types which could be the consequence of their fall'.

[53] Morris (1996) emphasizes the principle of equality—the 'middling tradition'—as an important feature of the archaic period. Cf. Wallace (1998), who attributes Athenian democracy in essence to Solon, and stresses the popular (because anti-aristocratic) character of tyranny; *contra*, on this last point, Cawkwell (1995).

[54] Kroll (1981) 25–9; Spier (1990) 120–1.

who prefers to see a reference to the signally pious Ethiopians.[55] The second coin is a quarter-drachm with a Janiform female head on the obverse, which has been interpreted as depicting Athena looking both backward and forward (sc. in time), in other words marking the end of one era and the beginning of another. The third is a drachm with as its reverse type an owl with its right wing raised. This gesture has been viewed as an auspicious omen, and the coin as referring to the liberation of Athens from tyranny, on the ground that this was a notably auspicious event. A little later, allusions to victory over Persia have been detected in two changes made to the design of the tetradrachms after 480: the addition of a wreath of olive leaves to the crown of Athena's helmet on the obverse, and the insertion of a crescent moon beside the owl on the reverse.[56]

It is not clear that either the early variants or the changes made to the tetradrachm after 480 have any commemorative significance. All of the claims made about them are speculative and tendentious, and motivated largely, it would appear, by a desire to detect in the coins even the smallest reference to Athenian political history.

Thereafter the types of Athenian tetradrachms remain essentially the same, despite certain stylistic developments.[57] In the fourth century the coins retain only the semblance of archaism. Athena's head is modernized—most notably her eye is shown in profile rather than in full—but the design remains essentially unchanged.

If there is nothing specifically democratic about Athenian coin types, it may be suggested that two features of the coins, while by no means unique to Athens, exemplify Athenian democratic principles. The first is the absence from the coins of magistrates' signatures or symbols. These occur elsewhere during the classical period, especially in the fourth century. Kraay documented a sharp increase in the naming of magistrates on coins from western Asia Minor in the fourth century.[58] The second is the absence of engravers' signatures, although less weight should be given to this, since signatures are uncommon outside Sicily and southern Italy. These two features are connected, in that the Athenians avoided anything that might detract from the coin types as civic emblems. Athena, owl, and legend together formed a democratic emblem, the *dêmosios charaktêr* referred to in the fourth-century Coinage Law.[59] The linking of coins with individual magistrates or artists would have been regarded as undemocratic.

In this respect it is instructive to compare the Owls both with *Wappenmünzen* and with Hellenistic 'New Style' tetradrachms. *Wappenmünzen* are anepigraphic, but the varying types have been plausibly associated with the individuals who were responsible for producing them (see above pp. 25–6). Much later, under the markedly less democratic conditions of the second century BC, Athenian 'New Style' tetradrachms carry several different magistrates' names and monograms.[60] By contrast, the coinage issued by the democracy eschews any mention of or reference to individuals, be they magistrate or engraver. In other words, at those periods in Athenian history when democracy was strong, the coins are uniform; when an élite predominated, they are more individuated.[61]

The Conservatism of Athenian Coin Types

I suggested above that democratic coin types were consistent with democratic values in their uniformity and avoidance of reference to named individuals. But some explanation is still required for the retention of an archaic, or archaistic, appearance into the fourth century and beyond, a phenomenon which is hard to parallel in other major coinages. Why did Athenian coins change so little?

In an influential passage Kraay argued that the Athenians left their coin types unchanged for reasons of commercial advantage: 'the need to preserve the acceptability of Athenian coinage in foreign markets imposed upon it a uniformity of appearance rarely encountered elsewhere'.[62] Although it is true that many Owls were exported, this explanation seems to me inadequate, for the following reasons. First, the Athenians issued coins for their own use in the first

[55] Lacroix (1974) 37–51.   [56] See Spier (1990) 120–1 with refs.
[57] These have been catalogued only for the period 480 to 449: see Starr (1970).
[58] Kraay (1976) 253–4.

[59] L. 4 with Stroud's (1974) comment (strictly the *character* is the punch die, which produces the reverse).
[60] I owe this point to E. S. G. Robinson (1960) 2.
[61] Cf. Kurke (1999) 305: 'In the symbolism of the democratic city, all coins, like all citizens, were made of the same stuff, and all were pure and precious matter.' I would add that they were also all alike, small cogs in a great machine.
[62] Kraay (1976) 2.

instance; there is no reason to think that they were interested in their acceptability in foreign markets, except to the extent that state payments could be made abroad.[63] Second, it is questionable whether a change of type, still less stylistic alterations to that type, would have detracted significantly from the coins' acceptability, assuming that they were of good silver, as Athenian coins always were. Third, the Athenian type was not in itself a guarantee of quality, since it is clear from surviving examples, as well as from the fourth-century Coinage Law, that both foreign copies and counterfeits were in circulation in large numbers.[64] Finally, Cyzicene electrum staters were routinely accepted as an international coinage, even though their main type changed frequently, with only the small tunny fish remaining constant. Thus commercial advantage seems to be at best a partial explanation for the conservatism of Athens' coin types.[65]

That Athena and the owl were retained as the two types can readily be attributed to patriotic sentiment: one face depicted the patron goddess of the city, the other the animal that was associated with her. Moreover, coin and type were fused in the popular mind, so that tetradrachms were commonly referred to as 'Owls' and possibly also, with reference to Athena, 'Maidens'.[66] But it remains to be explained why the coins show so little stylistic development, and why archaic types were reproduced by engravers who no longer had an archaic sensibility. Particularly noticeable is the fact that in the legend epsilon rather than eta was retained, even though eta was routinely used in public documents from the end of the fifth century onwards.[67] Other states retained long-standing types, but Athens is exceptional in the degree of its conservatism. This point can be illustrated from the coinage of two other leading states. One is Corinth, where the types (Pegasus/Aphrodite head) remained the same, but the treatment of those types shows stylistic development and innovation. The other is Syracuse, cited by Kraay: 'The minimal change in the types, fabric and style of Athenian coinage over a period of three centuries should be compared with the variation permitted within the established types of the tetradrachms at Syracuse during the fifth century alone.'[68]

In place of Kraay's economic explanation for the conservatism of Athenian coin types, I suggest that the reason was primarily political, and is connected in two different ways with the fact that Athens was a democracy. First, with two brief interruptions, in 411–410 and 404–403, Athens remained a democracy throughout the classical period. In so far as changes of coin type are associated with changes of constitution (see p. 26 above), Athens' conservatism is an index of her constitutional stability. Second, to qualify this, the only certain break in the minting of silver coins was soon followed by the overthrow of democracy and the establishment of an oligarchy. Athens stopped minting silver coins at some time before the production of Aristophanes' Frogs of 405, and resumed some time before his Ecclesiazusae of 392 or 391.[69] The length of the break is unknown, although the return of Konon in 393 with Persian money has been thought a plausible occasion for the resumption of minting.[70] When Athens did so, it was with the oligarchic terror fresh in everyone's mind. Under those circumstances, their decision to reproduce the coin types of the fifth century was all but inevitable—it proclaimed continuity between the restored democracy and its fifth-century predecessor.[71] We might compare the clause in the decree of Teisamenos, recorded by Andokides, that the restored democracy should use the laws and weights and measures of Solon.[72] The continued use of coin types that had been current at the time of the Persian Wars and of the heyday of the Athenian empire also projected to the wider Greek world an image of self-confidence and continuity. Normal service had been resumed.

Conversely, I suggest that the continued use during the fourth century of coin types that had been current in the late sixth and fifth centuries in fact betrays

[63] Thus E. S. G. Robinson (1960) 2.

[64] On foreign copies see Kraay (1976) 73–4, Stroud (1974) 168–71; on counterfeit coins see Stroud (1974) 171–8.

[65] On Cyzicene staters see Kraay (1976) 260–7.

[66] Owls: TN 55–8; Maidens: Pollux 9. 75 (TN 656).

[67] AΘH is found on bronze coins generally taken to be an emergency issue of the general Timotheus: see Robinson and Price (1967).

[68] Kraay (1976) 55.   [69] Frogs 718–36; Eccl. 815–22.
[70] Xen. Hell. 4. 8. 9–10.
[71] Cf. Kurke (1999) 327: the silver coinage was restored 'with an almost audible sigh of relief'.
[72] Andoc. 1. 83: πολιτεύεσθαι κατὰ τὰ πάτρια, νόμοις δὲ χρῆσθαι τοῖς Σόλωνος καὶ μέτροις καὶ σταθμοῖς. It is unclear whether the Thirty had in fact changed Athens' weights and measures. Ostwald (1986) 515 suggests that: 'Probably the Solonian weights and measures were included in this fundamental statement in order to reassure all Athenians that no economic changes were envisaged.'

Athens' *lack* of self-confidence. The archaic coin types served as a sentimental link to the fifth century. By retaining them, the Athenians sought to convince themselves that in this respect at least things had not changed for the worse. This accords with the nostalgia for the fifth century that is pervasive in so much fourth-century Athenian literature. We see it already, I believe, in the parabasis of Aristophanes' *Frogs*, where the silver coinage is called *archaios*, which should be rendered 'ancient' rather than simply 'old' (in the sense of prior to the current gold and bronze coins).[73]

I have assumed so far that the conservatism of Athenian coin types was a matter of deliberate policy; that, as it were, the Athenians from time to time pondered their coinage, and on each occasion decided that it was good, and that no changes needed to be made. So far as we know this never happened, although it was open to them to vote to alter their coinage at any time.[74] I want to suggest next that democratic Athens lacked any ready mechanism for changing its coinage, and that the conservatism of its coin types was in part a matter of what might be termed democratic inertia.

Very little is known about the administration of the mint, or about coinage policy in general. The mint is referred to in a number of texts and has been identified with a large building in the south-east corner of the Agora.[75] It is unclear whether this had always been the site of the mint, since the building belongs to the latter part of the fifth century, and the bronze flans found there must belong to the fourth century at the earliest. The mint was run by officials named *Epistatai* (*tou argyrokopeiou*). These are referred to in the Coinage Decree, of the second half of the fifth century, wherein they are instructed to erect a copy of the decree in front of the mint.[76] They also appear as dedicators in one fourth-century inscription,[77] and should possibly be restored in two other inscriptions.[78] They were ten in number, one from each tribe,[79] and were presumably chosen by lot, although there is no evidence on this point.

Major decisions relating to the coinage were taken by the Assembly, or in the fourth century by the *Nomothetai*. Aristophanes refers to a vote (sc. of the Assembly) to introduce bronze coinage in the late fifth century.[80] Presumably the Coinage Decree was a decree of the people, although its prescript does not survive. The Coinage Law of 375/4 was passed by the *Nomothetai*.[81]

Nothing is known of the duties of the *Epistatai*, and what follows is necessarily speculative. It is likely that their responsibilities were exclusively administrative—that they were required only to operate the mint efficiently and securely.[82] Under their control were various staff. Andokides alleged that the father of Hyperbolos was a public slave who worked in the mint,[83] and a curse tablet refers to a bellows-blower from the mint named Lysanias.[84] There must also have been die-cutters and others. David Lewis argued that these were all public slaves, referring to an apparently decisive unpublished law of 354/3 found in the Agora.[85] The Coinage Law of 375/4 states that payments to the tester of coins, who is a public slave, are to come from the same fund as payments to the mint-workers, although this strictly proves nothing about the latter's status.[86]

Presumably neither the *Epistatai* nor the die-cutters had the authority to alter the design of the coins in any significant way. The latter will certainly have had no right to innovate on their own initiative, although stylistic developments inevitably occurred over time. Indeed, the mechanical look of many coins suggests that the cutters largely copied existing coins. Athens seems not to have employed skilled engravers, such as the expert craftsmen at Syracuse who signed their handiwork (see p. 28 above).[87] Nor are the *Epistatai* likely to have altered the coinage. Given the Athenians' well-attested distrust of magistrates, especially of those in positions of financial

---

[73] See *LSJ* s.v. ἀρχαῖος.

[74] Strictly speaking, in the fourth century any alteration to the coinage probably required the passing of a new law by the process of *nomothesia*. (See below n. 81).

[75] For testimonia see Wycherley (1957) 160–1; on the building see Thompson and Wycherley (1972) 78–9.

[76] ML 45 (*IG* i³ 1453) para. 10.   [77] *SEG* 21. 667. 64.

[78] *Hesp.* 32 (1963) 31–2; *IG* i³ 90 (TN 79).

[79] The inscription in fact lists eleven men, in reverse tribal order, tribe IV being represented twice. Presumably a member of the board had died in office and been replaced.

[80] *Eccl.* 815–16.   [81] *Hesp.* 43 (1974) 157–88 (TN 91), l. 1.

[82] What, if any, responsibility the Boule may have had over them is unclear: see Rhodes (1972) 88–113 on its financial responsibilities.

[83] Schol. Arist. *Wasps* 1007 = Andoc. fr. III. 2 Maidment.

[84] See E. S. G. Robinson (1960) 6.

[85] Lewis (1997) 71. The inscription is I 7495.

[86] *Hesp.* 43 (1974) 157–88 (TN 91), ll. 53–5.

[87] On the artistic and technical quality of the coins see further pp. 31–2 below.

responsibility, it is hard to see what benefit the *Epistatai* would have derived, and easy to see the risk they would have run, if they had done so without the authorization of the people.

Turning to the Assembly, it is harder to imagine how a proposal to alter the design of the coinage might have been made than to imagine how it would have been opposed, as an act of treason, impiety, or the like. Indeed, Demosthenes refers to tampering with the coinage as an offence punishable by death: 'for those who tamper with the currency, death is the penalty among you'.[88] This law is not otherwise attested, but there is no reason to doubt its existence. Precisely what was forbidden is unclear. Counterfeit coins are specified in the Coinage Law of 375/4 as being either 'bronze beneath or lead beneath or base', and one might suppose that tampering with the coinage meant making counterfeit coins.[89] Perhaps, however, the law did not define the offence, and it was left to the jury to decide whether the coinage had been tampered with. We might compare the law of *hybris*, which notoriously left the offence undefined.[90] If this was the case, any perceived malpractice on the part of the mint officials might have been prosecuted under this law, with death as the penalty.

We know in fact of one earlier occasion on which a change to the coinage was proposed. Probably in the middle of the fifth century, a certain Dionysios proposed that Athens adopt bronze coinage, and as a result acquired the nickname 'the Brazen'. The proposal must have failed, since no bronze coins were issued in that period. Presumably he advocated the introduction of bronze fractions to replace the impractically small silver fractional coins then being issued.[91] He did not suffer for the proposal, so far as we know, but a sensible monetary reform was turned down.

Alteration to the coinage seems often to have been associated either with political crisis or with tyranny (see p. 26). The decision in the last years of the Peloponnesian War to replace Athens' silver coinage with gold coins for foreign payments, and plated bronze coins for domestic use, was precipitated by the total depletion of her stock of silver, and only briefly preceded defeat by Sparta and the overthrow of democracy.[92] The new bronze coinage is associated with political decline in the parabasis of the *Frogs*: 'Wicked little bronzes, struck yesterday and the day before with the worst possible striking' are likened to the political leaders who are now prominent: 'for-eigners, redheads, villains from evil stock, recent arrivals whom the city in the past would not have used even in the most random way as scapegoats'.[93] The ancient silver coinage is associated with the good old days. Silver is not explicitly linked with democracy, but the new bronze coins are clearly associated with sickness in the body politic. This argument dovetails nicely with that recently advanced by Kurke, that in Greece silver was symbolically associated with democracy, or at any rate with the 'middling' ethos of the *polis*, as compared with the élitist connotations of gold.[94] Kurke also argues that silver was associated with the cardinal Athenian quality of autochthony, since the silver from which the coins were made came, as the Athenians believed themselves to have come, from the soil of Attica.

The association between tyranny and alteration to the coinage has recently been discussed by Deborah Tarn Steiner,[95] and I shall limit myself to giving a few examples. Hippias of Athens was reputed to have re-called the existing coins, restruck them, and given them back to their owners.[96] Presumably he was thought to have reduced the weight standard, given back the same sums as had been surrendered, and kept the remaining silver for himself. Dionysios of Syracuse is said to have done precisely that, and Polykrates of Samos to have minted plated coins in order to deceive the besieging Spartans.[97] In short, little good could be expected to come from altering the coinage.

The Quality of Athenian Coins

The chorus of Aristophanes' *Frogs* claims (ll. 722–3) that Athens' silver coinage, which at the time of the play was no longer being issued, was 'the fairest, it seems, of all, and the only ones struck well'. This line

[88] τοῖς τὸ νόμισμα διαφθείροισι θάνατος παρ' ὑμῖν ἐστιν ἡ ζημία (20. 167). Cf. Dem. 24. 212–14 and Kurke (1999) 317–18.
[89] ὑπόχαλκον ἢ ὑπομόλυβδον ἢ κίβδηλον. For the meaning of κίβδηλον see Buttrey (1979) 35.
[90] The law is cited at Dem. 21. 47.
[91] E. S. G. Robinson (1960) 6; *RE* s.v. Dionysios 97; cf. Kurke (1999) 308, who attributes to Dionysios the proposal to issue plated bronze at the end of the fifth century. This is chronologically awkward.

[92] On the gold coins see Thompson (1970); on the bronze, Kroll (1976).
[93] *Frogs* 725–6, 730–3.   [94] Kurke (1999) 302–6.
[95] Steiner (1994) 159–65.   [96] [Ar.] *Econ.* 1347a (*TN* 54).
[97] [Ar.] *Econ.* 1349b (*TN* 538); Hdt. 3. 56 (*TN* 535): in reality this may have been an emergency measure.

proves that beauty is in the eye of the beholder, since Athenian coins of the late fifth and fourth centuries are of low artistic and technical quality, albeit still of very pure silver. A more realistic assessment is attributed to the Hellenistic philosopher Zeno, who 'used to say that the well-polished speeches of those who avoided solecisms were like the silver of Alexander, pleasing to the eye and neatly formed like the coinage itself, but no better for that; while he compared those of the opposite kind to Attic tetradrachms, struck in a random manner with the occasional mistake, but often outweighing the more artistic orations'.[98] This verdict is repeated in the modern numismatic literature.[99] Specifically, the dies are crudely engraved, and the flans often so thick that their diameter is smaller than the die size, resulting in incomplete reproduction of the image. Technically, Athenian coins fall far short of those from many other states. What was the reason for this? It might be suggested that at certain periods the volume of coin production led to corners being cut. Certainly in the middle and later years of the fifth century coins were struck in very large numbers. But the quality of Athenian coins is no better in those periods when the volume of production is agreed to have been low, such as the early fourth century. Nor is volume of production in itself a satisfactory explanation for the coins' poor quality, since the Athenians could easily have assigned more resources to the mint had they so wished.

Once again a narrowly economic argument could be advanced. Moses Finley argued that the Greeks' taste for attractive coins was a function of local patriotism and vanity: 'Hence the insistence, with the important exception of Athens, on artistic coins, economically a nonsense (no money-changer gives a better rate for a four-drachma Syracusan coin because it was signed by Euainetos).'[100] Finley leaves the exceptional nature of Athens' coinage unexplained: were the Athenians simply more hard-headed than others in minimizing the expense of minting? There is no reason to think so, and, if it were the case, we would still have to ask why Athens was so

exceptionally deficient in local pride as to produce unattractive coins.[101]

I want to suggest instead that the poor quality of Athenian coins was largely a result of the lack of any body responsible for producing aesthetically pleasing coins. The *Epistatai*, like all other magistrates, had to pass an end-of-year scrutiny and have their accounts approved. In other words, they had to avoid doing anything demonstrably wrong, and be able to account for every scrap of silver that passed through the mint. There was no incentive for them to produce beautiful coins, and indeed, unless they were given the funds to hire more skilled die-cutters, no means for them to do so. We might profitably compare those states which included the name of the mint magistrate on the type. There, unattractive coins might reflect badly on the man whose name appeared on them. Athens' lacklustre coinage is not untypical of a *polis* where, if it was important that a public service be done conspicuously well, it was generally made into a liturgy. Unelected boards of magistrates had no expertise in the areas for which they were responsible, and often did no more than they needed. This mentality is nicely illustrated by the records of the Superintendents of the Dockyards, who year by year sedulously recorded the debts incurred by trierarchs, but generally made little effort to collect them.[102] When coinage was everyone's business, it became no one's business.

Thus I would attribute both the conservatism of Athenian coin types and the poor quality of the coins themselves not so much to a calculation of commercial advantage, as, positively, to an association of the silver Owls with democracy, specifically that of the golden years of the earlier fifth century, and, negatively, to democratic inertia.

Conclusion: Hostility to Coinage and Hostility to Democracy

We noted earlier (p. 23) that many coin-issuing states were oligarchies, and that there is only a weak

[98] Diog. Laert. 7. 1. 18 (TN 104): τοῖς Ἀττικοῖς τετραδράχμοις εἰκῆ μὲν κεκομμένοις καὶ σολοίκως.
[99] Thus (e.g.) Head (1911) 374: 'The tetradrachms of the fourth century are roughly engraved and carelessly struck. They are, in fact, only imitations of the older coins.'
[100] Finley (1985) 166–7.
[101] A similar point is advanced by Martin (1996) 262 against the view that Greek states issued coins as an expression of civic pride: Are we to assume that the fifty per cent of states that issued no coins were deficient in that quality?
[102] See E. S. G. Robinson (1960) 2.

connection between democracy and coinage, through the institution of public pay. Nevertheless, any discussion of the significance of coinage at Athens requires at least a glance at its ideological antipode, Sparta.[103]

In the archaic and classical periods Sparta issued no coins. Spartan society was organized in such a way that money was largely unnecessary, iron spits being used as a deliberately cumbersome form of token money. Member states of the Peloponnesian League contributed mostly men rather than money. There is also a persistent tradition that Sparta largely eschewed coined money until her defeat of Athens in 404, and that its introduction thereafter was the root of her decline. Although this tradition is overstated in many of our sources, it goes back to the fourth century.[104] At the same time, whether or not the Spartan constitution can properly be called oligarchic, Sparta was closely associated with oligarchy from the time of the Peloponnesian War onwards. Athenian oligarchs looked to Sparta as their spiritual home. The Spartans tended to support rural oligarchies and to oppose urban democracies, whilst Athens did the opposite.[105] Thus Sparta was associated with both oligarchy and the absence of coinage. We have already seen that at Mantinea the Spartans overthrew the democracy and put an end to its coinage, whilst at Athens the Spartan-backed and laconizing regime of the Thirty scrapped public pay, and sought to establish a polity in which power was monopolized by a landed élite.[106]

This fits with the hostility to money found in the writings of anti-democratic political theorists, Plato above all. In the *Republic* he asserts that while the ideal city may have coinage, the Guardians must not use it.[107] And in the *Laws* he draws a distinction between foreign and local money: necessary state expenditure can be met with what he calls Greek money; but for domestic exchange, which he admits is unavoidable, a token local currency must be used. No individual is allowed to own either gold or silver, and any foreign money that is brought into the city must be surrendered to the authorities.[108]

The anti-democratic ideal was of a world without coinage. Conversely, the democratic *polis*, and Athens in particular, was a world of coins.[109]

REFERENCES

BARRON, J. (1966). *The Silver Coins of Samos* (London: The Athlone Press).

BOEDEKER, D., and K. A. RAAFLAUB (eds.) (1998). *Democracy, Empire, and the Arts in Fifth-Century Athens* (Cambridge, Mass., and London: Harvard University Press).

BOEGEHOLD, A. L. (1995). *The Lawcourts at Athens: Sites, Buildings, Equipment, Procedure, and Testimonia* (The Athenian Agora, xxviii) (Princeton, NJ: American School of Classical Studies at Athens).

BUTTREY, T. V. (1979). 'The Athenian Currency Law of 375/4 B.C.', in O. Mørkholm and N. M. Waggoner (eds.), *Greek Numismatics and Archaeology: Essays in Honor of Margaret Thompson* (Wetteren: Éditions NR), 33–45.

CASTRIOTA, D. (1998). 'Democracy and Art in Late-Sixth- and Fifth-Century-B.C. Athens', in Morris and Raaflaub (1998), 197–216.

CAWKWELL, G. L. (1995). 'Early Greek Tyranny and the People', *CQ* 45: 73–86.

FIGUEIRA, T. (1998). *The Power of Money: Coinage and Politics in the Athenian Empire* (Philadelphia, Pa.: University of Pennsylvania Press).

FINLEY, M. I. (1985). *The Ancient Economy*, 2nd edn. (London: Hogarth Press).

HEAD, B. V. (1911). *Historia Numorum: A Manual of Greek Numismatics*, 2nd edn. (Oxford: Clarendon Press).

HODKINSON, S. (1994). '"Blind Ploutos"? Contemporary Images of the Role of Wealth in Classical Sparta', in A. Powell and S. Hodkinson (eds.), *The Shadow of Sparta* (London and New York: Routledge for The Classical Press of Wales).

KRAAY, C. M. (1956). 'The Archaic Owls of Athens: Classification and Chronology', *NC*[6] 16: 43–68.

——(1976). *Archaic and Classical Greek Coins* (Berkeley and Los Angeles, Calif.: University of California Press).

KROLL, J. H. (1972). *Athenian Bronze Allotment Tokens* (Cambridge, Mass.: Harvard University Press).

——(1976). 'Aristophanes' πονηρὰ χαλκία: A Reply' *GRBS* 17: 329–41.

——(1981). 'From Wappenmünzen to Gorgoneia to Owls', *ANSMN* 26: 1–32.

——(1998). 'Silver in Solon's Laws', in R. Ashton and S. Hurter (eds.), *Studies in Greek Numismatics in Memory of Martin Jessop Price* (London: Spink), 225–32.

---

[103] Sources: TN 381–8, 569–71, 925–6. [104] Hodkinson (1994).
[105] See Th. 3. 82. 1; Xen. *Hell.* 5. 2. 1–7.
[106] See pp. 24–5 above.
[107] *Rep.* 2. 371b (TN 2); 3. 416e–417a (TN 3).
[108] *Laws* 5. 741e–742b (TN 4). See Morrow (1960) 139–40.

[109] An earlier version of this chapter was given at a conference at the University of Exeter. I should like to thank the organizers and participants for their comments on it.

KROLL, J. H., and N. M. WAGGONER (1984). 'Dating the Earliest Coins of Athens, Corinth and Aegina', *AJA* 88: 76–91.

KURKE, L. (1999). *Coins, Bodies, Games, and Gold: The Politics of Meaning in Archaic Greece* (Princeton, NJ: Princeton University Press).

LACROIX, L. (1974). *Études d'archéologie numismatique* (Paris: Boccard).

LEWIS, D. M. (1997). 'Public Property in the City', in *Selected Papers in Greek and Near Eastern History* (Cambridge: Cambridge University Press), 60–76.

LOOMIS, W. T. (1998). *Wages, Welfare Costs and Inflation in Classical Athens* (Ann Arbor, Mich.: University of Michigan Press).

MARTIN, T. R. (1996). 'Why Did the Greek *polis* Originally Need Coins?' *Historia* 45: 257–83.

MELVILLE JONES, J. R. (1993). *Testimonia Numaria: Greek and Latin Texts Concerning Ancient Greek Coinage* (London: Spink).

MORRIS, I. (1996). 'The Strong Principle of Equality and the Archaic Origins of Greek Democracy', in J. Ober and C. Hedrick (eds.), *Demokratia: A Conversation on Democracies, Ancient and Modern* (Princeton, NJ: Princeton University Press), 19–48.

—— and K. A. RAAFLAUB (eds.) (1998). *Democracy 2500? Questions and Challenges* (Dubuque, Ia.: Kendall/Hunt Publishing Co.).

MORROW, G. R. (1960). *Plato's Cretan City: A Historical Interpretation of the Laws* (Princeton, NJ: Princeton University Press).

OBER, J. (1998). 'Revolution Matters: Democracy as Demotic Action (A Response to Kurt A. Raaflaub)', in Morris and Raaflaub (1998), 67–85.

O'NEIL, J. L. (1995). *The Origins and Development of Ancient Greek Democracy* (Lanham, Md.: Rowman and Littlefield).

OSTWALD, M. (1986). *From Popular Sovereignty to the Sovereignty of Law: Law, Society, and Politics in Fifth-Century Athens* (Berkeley and Los Angeles, Calif., and London: University of California Press).

PRICE, M., and N. WAGGONER (1975). *Archaic Greek Coinage: The 'Asyut' Hoard* (London: V. C. Vecchi).

PRITCHETT, W. K. (1971). *The Greek State at War*, i. (Berkeley and Los Angeles, Calif.: University of California Press).

RAAFLAUB, K. A. (1998). 'The Thetes and Democracy (A Response to Josiah Ober)', in Morris and Raaflaub (1998), 87–103.

RHODES, P. J. (1972). *The Athenian Boule* (Oxford: Oxford University Press).

—— (1980). 'Athenian Democracy after 403 B.C.', *CJ* 75: 305–23.

—— (1981). *A Commentary on the Aristotelian Athenaion Politeia* (Oxford: Oxford University Press).

ROBINSON, E. S. G. (1960). 'Some Problems in the Later Fifth Century Coinage of Athens', *ANSMN* 9: 1–15.

—— and M. J. PRICE (1967). 'An Emergency Coinage of Timotheus', *NC*[7]7: 1–6.

ROBINSON, E. W. (1997). *The First Democracies: Early Popular Government Outside Athens* (*Historia*, Einzelschriften 107) (Stuttgart: Franz Steiner Verlag).

RUTTER, K. (1981). 'Early Greek Coinage and the Influence of the Athenian State', in B. Cunliffe (ed.), *Coinage and Society in Britain and Gaul: Some Current Problems* (London: Council for British Archeology), 1–9.

STE CROIX, G. E. M. DE (1975). 'Political Pay Outside Athens', *CQ* 25: 48–52.

—— (1981). *The Class Struggle in the Ancient Greek World* (London: Duckworth).

SELTMAN, C. T. (1924). *Athens: Its History and Coinage Before the Persian Invasion* (Cambridge: Cambridge University Press).

SHAPIRO, H. A. (1989). *Art and Cult under the Tyrants in Athens* (Mainz am Rhein: Phillip von Zabern).

—— (1993). 'From Athena's Owl to the Owl of Athens', in R. M. Rosen and J. Farrell (eds.), *Nomodeiktes: Greek Studies in Honor of Martin Ostwald* (Ann Arbor, Mich.: University of Michigan Press), 213–24.

SPIER, J. (1990). 'Emblems in Archaic Greece', *BICS* 37: 107–29.

STARR, C. G. (1970). *Athenian Coinage 480–449 B.C.* (Oxford: Oxford University Press).

STEINER, D. (1994). *The Tyrant's Writ: Myths and Images of Writing in Ancient Greece* (Princeton, NJ: Princeton University Press).

STROUD, R. S. (1974). 'An Athenian Law on Silver Coinage', *Hesperia*, 43: 157–88.

SVORONOS, J. (1923). *Les Monnaies d'Athènes* (Munich: F. Bruckmann).

THOMPSON, H. A., and R. E. WYCHERLEY (1972). *The Agora of Athens: The History, Shape and Uses of an Ancient City Center* (*The Athenian Agora*, xiv) (Princeton, NJ: American School of Classical Studies at Athens).

THOMPSON, W. E. (1970). 'The Golden Nikai and the Coinage of Athens', *NC*[7]10: 1–6.

VICKERS, M. (1985). 'Early Greek Coinage: A 'Reassessment', *NC* 145: 108–28.

WALLACE, R. W. (1998). 'Solonian Democracy', in Morris and Raaflaub (1998), 11–29.

WHITEHEAD, D. (1982/3). 'Sparta and the Thirty Tyrants', *Ancient Society* 13/14: 105–30.

WYCHERLEY, R. E. (1957). *Literary and Epigraphical Testimonia* (*The Athenian Agora*, iii) (Princeton, NJ: American School of Classical Studies at Athens).

3
THE POLITICS OF COINAGE: ATHENS AND ANTIGONUS GONATAS

Graham Oliver

Introduction

THE *POLIS* WAS NOT A MONOLITHIC structure but a fluid and dynamic organism which was always the sum of its constituent parts, namely its citizens. The life and freedom of the *politai* of the *poleis* in the Hellenistic period are generally cast in a negative light; some have even suggested that the *polis* had disappeared by this time.[1] For many modern commentators the ideas of freedom and autonomy had become so devalued during the Hellenistic age that promises of *eleutheria* and *autonomia* had become mere slogans.[2] Historians of the Hellenistic period need to revise their perceptions of these terms. What was really understood in ancient sources by *eleutheria* and *autonomia*? This chapter highlights the need for clarification about what ancient *poleis* understood by terms like freedom and autonomy. How did the decision-making processes and the control of the *politai* over their internal affairs and relations with the outside world develop? What did it mean to be free in the Greek *polis* during the Hellenistic period? These are big questions. Although they cannot be answered in depth here, it will be important to keep them in mind.

If we can approach an answer to such questions, we will need to consider the relationship between Hellenistic monarchs and the Greek *polis*. Such an investigation might be considered futile by some: Cawkwell has argued that Greek liberty had already been removed when Philip II defeated Athens, Thebes, and their allies at Chaeronea in 338 BC: 'It is of no importance that the heart of Athens, her democratic system, continued fitfully to beat when her power to defend herself was largely paralysed'.[3] Cawkwell's main target was Gomme, who had suggested that Greek independence terminated at the end of the Chremonidean war (268–263/2).[4] The war was fought by Athens, Sparta, their Greek allies, and Ptolemy II against Antigonus Gonatas; its aftermath provides the focus for this chapter, which questions the assumption that Athens lost her freedom after 263/2.

Particular attention will be given to the role that coinage played in Athens. Did Athens or any Greek city lose the right to produce coinage if they were consumed by an external power? This question has been aired in Thomas Martin's book *Sovereignty and Coinage in Classical Greece*.[5] In the last few years, however, the utility of the term 'sovereignty' has been questioned: John Davies has argued that it has been applied with insufficient clarity to archaic and classical Greece. Ideas which we might identify under the term 'sovereignty' were frequently being expressed through the terms freedom (*eleutheria*) and autonomy

I would like to thank the late D. M. Lewis and Dr. C. Howgego, who read material on which much of this chapter was based, in 1992 and 1993. I have benefited from questions posed in the conference in 1997 at which a version of this paper was presented, and discussions with Dr. Katerina Panagopoulou. The editors and the anonymous readers for OUP made many useful criticisms of this chapter; I have tried to incorporate their improvements, but any errors remain my own responsibility. The map was drawn by Alison Wilkins, and Andy Meadows helped to supply the photographs of coins from the British Museum collection. Dreyer (1999) appeared too late to be incorporated into this chapter.

[1] Runciman (1990).   [2] Seager and Tuplin (1980); Seager (1981).

[3] Cawkwell (1996) 98.   [4] Gomme (1937) 223.
[5] Martin (1985).

(*autonomia*), terms which are often seen as a pair.[6] While this chapter cannot incorporate a full discussion of semantics, it will assume that what Martin understood by sovereignty can be expressed within the terms 'freedom' and 'autonomy' in the late classical and Hellenistic periods: 'what Greeks therefore seem to have done, in an attempt to verbalise what we call genuine sovereignty, was to put the two words [*eleutheria* and *autonomia*] together'.[7]

It is familiar to us that in the Hellenistic period the greatest potential threat to the freedom of a Greek *polis* came from one or a combination of Hellenistic monarchies. In this respect freedom is being used in a much more limited way than is applied in Cawkwell's discussion of the Greeks after Chaeronea. Monarchy had considerable impact on Athens. It is generally believed that Antigonus Gonatas, victor in the Chremonidean war, removed Athenian freedom, at least for a limited period: 'Defeated in the [Chremonidean] war against Macedonia, Athens lost its independence, falling under the rule of Antigonus Gonatas.'[8] It was thought for some time that coinage was among those 'rights' that Gonatas terminated.[9] Habicht questioned that assumption, and further doubt has been cast by the current debate about the relationship between coinage and sovereignty—or autonomy.[10] This chapter re-examines the evidence and analyses the relationship between Athens and the Hellenistic monarch, Antigonus Gonatas, King of the Macedonians. The role of coinage in this relationship will be re-assessed and with it our preconceptions about what we understand by freedom when studying the Greek *polis* in the Hellenistic age.

Athenian Freedom in the Early Hellenistic Period

In terms of international politics in the eastern Mediterranean, Athens fell further than many other Greek *poleis* in the 200 years from the fifth to the third centuries. Periclean Athens commanded a considerable position in the Aegean and in her relations with other Greek cities, at the head of a maritime empire, but that position was redefined at the end of the Peloponnesian war (431–403) and readjusted throughout the fourth century. The process of change at Athens was gradual; in the first few decades of the third century the city faced problems similar to those of the second half of the fourth century. For Philip, read Alexander, then Kassander, Demetrius Poliorcetes, and Antigonus Gonatas. The regular threats to Athenian security and self-government demanded the formation of diplomatic and political alliances with other powers. Political associations came thick and fast in the years following the death of Alexander. His reign engulfed a vast world which was subsequently dominated by his successors. The globalization of Greek monarchy was the central characteristic of the so-called Hellenistic age. In the east this period was clearly defined by the impact of Macedonian monarchs. The cities of old Greece, like Athens, had been responding gradually to the rise of autocratic power throughout much of the earlier fourth century. Perhaps in particular for mainland and maritime Greece, 'Hellenistic' marked less of a break, more of a continuity.

For Athens, the support of one Hellenistic power or another became crucial to the city's ambitions. The glorious revival of democracy in 307 BC was only possible with the outside support of Antigonus the One-Eyed and Demetrius Poliorcetes; then, just over ten years later, the city was incapable of withstanding siege from Demetrius Poliorcetes and both harbour and city centre saw the return of foreign garrisons; in 288/7 the city had the opportunity to expel Demetrius' garrison from the Mouseion only with the aid of outsiders—Ptolemy I, Pyrrhus, and Lysimachus. The success of the 280s was limited, and it is unlikely that Athens was able to recover Piraeus and perhaps Sunium for some time, if at all. Twenty years later, in the 260s, Antigonus Gonatas had become the *bête noire*. The efforts made against him by the Greek states, led by Sparta and Athens, and supported by Ptolemy II, were to prove unsuccessful: the Chremonidean war saw the defeat of Sparta and Athens at the hands of Gonatas.[11]

As in the second half of the fourth century when Greek *poleis* confronted Philip II, so in the Hellenistic period, the resources of the monarchs far surpassed even those of allied Greek states. Invariably the support of other powers was now required. For Athens,

---

[6] Davies (1994). [7] Davies (1994) 61. [8] Habicht (1997) 150.
[9] Habicht (1982) 34–42; Kroll and Nicolet-Pierre (1990).
[10] Habicht (1997) 155 and n. 19.

[11] See Habicht (1997) chs. 3–4.

defeat in the Chremonidean war highlighted the fragility of such support. The victory of Antigonus Gonatas opened an important chapter but continued a familiar story in the history of the city and its relations with the King of the Macedonians. The nature of that relationship lies at the heart of this chapter.

At the close of the Chremonidean war, Pausanias the travel writer describes how Athens was forced to surrender to the Macedonian king after withstanding a lengthy siege:

Antigonus [Gonatas] made peace with the Athenians who had held out for a very long time. It was a condition that he put a garrison on the Mouseion [hill]. In time Antigonus himself voluntarily removed the garrison.[12]

The precise terms of the settlement are unclear. The other sources we have are fragmentary and of uncertain reliability, but on them whole edifices of historical interpretation have been built. It is worth revisiting them here. In some ways there is a relative richness in 'sources' which relate to the end of the Chremonidean war and in particular Antigonus' involvement with Athens. It is often difficult to identify who the contemporary authors might have been. The third book of Phylarchus' detailed but colourful account of the period from Pyrrhus to Cleomenes (272 to 220/19) is readily identified as the origin of the story of Patroclus, the Ptolemaic general, sending fish and figs to Antigonus Gonatas.[13] Phylarchus has also been suggested as the source of Pausanias' account of the end of the war, particularly given its strong Spartan flavour.[14]

Another source, a fragment of Apollodorus, tells us the date of Gonatas' victory over Athens; that he moved a garrison on to the Mouseion hill; that he removed the offices and, possibly, that he put the affairs of the city into the hands of one person:

Apollodorus puts the submission of the city in the archonship of Antipatros, the year before that of Arrhenides. [At that time] a garrison was brought into the Mouseion by Antigonus [and the] offices [removed] and everything was being [dealt with on the] decision (?) of one man.[15]

Apollodorus had been writing around the middle of the second century BC. It is thought that the bulk of his major historical chronicle, Chronika, had been completed or was virtually complete at the time of his flight from Ptolemy VIII's Alexandria. Considerable accuracy was achieved by his use of archontic dating, and the Chronika ultimately replaced that produced by Eratosthenes at the end of the third century. The specific use of the two archons in fragment 44 is testimony to the chronological accuracy. But can Apollodorus' sources be identified? It is likely that Apollodorus had access to vast amounts of material in Alexandria; it is also possible that he returned to his native Athens.[16] But little is known of specific sources, apart from those which supplied material about philosophers.[17] Philochorus may have been able to include the Chremonidean war in his historical works before his execution by Antigonus;[18] Hieronymus may have drawn parallels between the Lamian and Chremonidean war.[19] There is little to say that either had any impact on Apollodorus. Both, however, would have something to say about Antigonus Gonatas.

The latest, and possibly most important, source is Eusebius from around the early fourth century AD. It tells us that 'Antigonus gave back freedom to the Athenians' in the year 256 BC.[20] In the case of Eusebius we have even less idea about his sources. The summary nature of this stark notice has carried considerable weight; it is the only extant source which mentions specifically the return of freedom to Athens, a term which is not used by Apollodorus. An intricate source tradition makes up this chronicle. Eusebius' original text is lost, but we do have an Armenian version, a Latin adaptation by Eusebius Hieronymus (St. Jerome), and, principal among other Greek versions, Syncellus. The tight chronologies presented in the Armenian and Latin of Jerome concur that Antigonus returned freedom to the Athenians in the first year of the 131st Olympiad, 256 BC. Whilst this date has been assumed to be secure, one should note that Jerome and the Armenian version do not always agree on the chronology of events. The crucial date given for the death of Zeno occurs in the Armenian version in 272 (128th

---

[12] Paus. 3. 6. 6.

[13] Phylarchus of Naucratis, FGrH 81 f. 1 = Ath. Deipnosophistae 8, 334 A–B; Phylarchus probably devoted two years of history to each book; see Lissone (1969) 187.

[14] See Musti (1997) 180.

[15] Translation of the Greek text revised by Dorandi (1990b) 130, no. 39 = Phld. De Stoicis, 4. 6–12 (PHerc. 155e339) = Apollod. FGrH 244 fr.44.

[16] Pfeiffer (1968) 253.

[17] Jacoby (1902) 51–7; see 375f. fr. 85 for the relevant text.

[18] Ferguson (1911) 188 on Philochorus' death; on the content of his work, see Jacoby (1949) 115 f. and Rhodes (1990) 79.

[19] Hornblower (1980) 171 and 175.

[20] Eus., Chronica, ed. A. Schöne (Berlin, 1866), ii. 120.

Olympiad) but in Jerome in 264 (first year of the 129th Olympiad). But neither of these dates agrees with the date of Zeno's death offered by Philodemos; this offers a date thirty-nine years and three months after the archonship of Klearchos (301/300) which might be either 263/2 or 262/1. How reliable is Eusebius? The discrepancy in the years offered for the death of Zeno is worrying, but at least one version of Eusebius offers a date close to the text preserved in Philodemos. Notwithstanding the chronological doubts, the content of Eusebius' notice continues to direct our interpretation of Athenian history in the 250s.

Athens and the 'Freedom' to Mint Coins

What was the nature of the 'freedom' that Antigonus restored to Athens in 256 BC? Whatever it was, it certainly would not have satisfied Cawkwell's view of Greek liberty. The nature of the settlement and the subsequent history of Athens following the defeat against Antigonus raises the issue of Athenian independence: How did Gonatas affect her freedom, her autonomy, her democracy? It is within this context that we need to re-examine the role of coinage at Athens: the pivotal fragment of Apollodorus makes no mention of coinage, nor does any other written source. But the accumulated evidence of Pausanias, Apollodorus, and Eusebius led to the well-established belief that Antigonus interfered in the administration of the Athenian *polis* and that he altered many aspects of civic life. Did that extend to coinage? The possible interference in coin production at Athens requires a reassessment of Martin's arguments: Does issuing coinage indicate autonomy, or freedom? Is 'sovereignty' necessary to issue coinage?

For some time, numismatists assumed that the right to mint coins was among the changes introduced by Antigonus. Until the early 1990s it was generally held that Athens produced no silver tetradrachms between 262 and 229 BC, a position which Habicht had already questioned earlier.[21] But Kroll and Nicolet-Pierre's new study identified groups of Athenian silver tetradrachms which seemed to belong to a period from the late 260s or 250s down to the late 230s. These groups, termed heterogeneous, differed from the

Athenian pi-style coinage of the late fourth and first few decades of the third century and those issues which can be placed at the end of the third century (compare Pl. 3.1.3 (heterogeneous), 3.1.1 (pi-style), and 3.1.4 (early second century BC)). After 229 Athens introduced a new series of owl coins following the expulsion of the Macedonian garrisons.[22] Kroll and Nicolet-Pierre argued that Athens would not have produced coinage herself in this period because Antigonus Gonatas had removed the right to produce coinage. The 'heterogeneous' groups must therefore have been good imitations of Athenian silver coinage.[23]

This argument overlooked Martin's thesis on sovereignty and coinage, but was considerably revised by Kroll in his recent magisterial publication of the coinage from the Athenian Agora. Kroll updated his analysis of the heterogeneous groups in light of Martin's work.[24] In the belief that no assumptions should be made about the relationship between the loss of freedom and the removal of the right to issue coinage, Kroll now holds that Athens may well have been producing silver tetradrachms after the Chremonidean war: 'there is still a very good possibility that many of the heterogeneous tetradrachms may be bona fide Athenian emissions'.[25] The whole discussion raises a number of problems: Is Kroll's application of Martin's thesis valid at Athens in the middle of the third century BC? How was Athens affected by Gonatas at the end of the Chremonidean war? Is there any reason to suppose that Athens did not have the capacity to issue its own coinage in this period?

The question surrounding Martin's thesis is crucial particularly now that challenges are being made against it.[26] It is worthwhile outlining the sovereignty/autonomy and coinage debate. In 1985 Thomas Martin argued that no Greek *polis* was ever prevented from issuing coinage as a result of interference by an external power. A close study of Thessalian coinage minted during the rule of Philip II suggested that no interruption in local-coinage production can be identified during Philip's period of rule over Thessaly.[27] In short, Martin argues that one needs to prove a link

---

[21] Habicht (1982) 38–9.

[22] Kroll and Nicolet-Pierre (1990) 13.
[23] See below, pp. 46–8 for further discussion.
[24] Kroll (1993) 11 f.   [25] Kroll (1993) 12.
[26] See below, ch. 4 and Howgego (1995).
[27] Martin (1985), ch. 8. On the chronology of Philip II's coinage in Thessaly see now Le Rider (1996).

between sovereignty and coinage rather than assuming it was a given factor. Martin was concerned with classical Greece but he envisaged that the Hellenistic period should be treated with similar scepticism:

If we are to believe that an abstract notion of the sovereignty of the state became a central component of decisions on who in the Greek world should mint coins and who should not, I submit that there is no compelling evidence for such a development any earlier than the last decade of the fourth century, when a variety of self-appointed kings began to compete for status, recognition, and territory.[28]

Martin suggested there might be a stronger possibility that coinage and sovereignty were linked from the end of the fourth century onwards but such a connection should be seen neither as a necessary given nor an absolute truth.

Coin production and civic administration in the Greek *polis* should be distanced from the impact of Hellenistic kings. Of fundamental importance is the nature of the relationship between the *polis* and the Hellenistic king and the ways in which that relationship was negotiated, if at all. Concepts of freedom and autonomy must be applied carefully. Nor can the role of terms like sovereignty be taken for granted: 'In our current state of knowledge, it always seems better to start historical investigation of the relations between the Hellenistic kings and the Greek city-states from the premise that these relations were a matter of practical arrangements worked out in a context unaffected by consideration of the *theoretical components* [my emphasis] of royal and civic sovereignty'.[29] If we are to investigate fully concerns about the role of coinage in the Hellenistic period, we will ultimately have to return to fundamentals and reconsider what it is we understand, and crucially what the Greeks understood, when talking about freedom and autonomy.

Some have criticized Martin's thesis for removing coinage too readily from the concepts of sovereignty or autonomy. Howgego has argued that coinage must be seen as one of a number of negotiable entities which might have been subject to debate when a city was accommodated into an empire: 'It is wrong ... to exclude imposition from consideration, and to deny that there is a connection between coinage and autonomy ... The degree of autonomy enjoyed by the subject cities (or peoples) within empires was the result of a series of negotiations and accommodations'.[30] While Martin has broken what had been an assumed link between coinage and autonomy, Howgego asks that such a link must still be considered. One cannot assume either way that coinage was or was not linked to political changes in the relations of a *polis* to an outside power. If we bear Howgego's caution in mind, the application of Martin's thesis by Kroll to mid-third-century Athens may not be as simple as it appears.

In the Hellenistic period, and surely throughout antiquity, more thought must be given to the ways in which the internal organization of a community—particularly a Greek *polis*—was affected by its relationship with a Hellenistic king or other empire. Recovering the motivation for issuing coinage is, of course, difficult. Figueira has argued recently that the allies in the Athenian Empire were motivated more by economic and fiscal factors than any other reason in their decisions to stop minting coins.[31] But the picture may be more complex still. Meadows (Ch. 4) takes Howgego's objection to Martin's thesis some stages further and suggest not only that sovereignty and coinage were certainly connected but that there is evidence for interference in coin production in Asia Minor by imperial Rome in the first century AD.[32]

Political and economic motives can both underlie the production of coinage: they are not mutually exclusive. Coins issued by a *polis* were still *nomismata* and as such were a symbolic extension of a city's laws and therefore identifiable with the *polis* (see Trevett's argument in Ch. 2). The question remains: Can an autonomous city issue coins but not be free? Indeed, did it mean much to be autonomous without freedom? As Davies has suggested, autonomy alone may not have been much to have preserved when faced with the loss of other freedoms.[33]

Autonomy in Athens under Antigonus Gonatas

Before looking in more detail at the numismatic evidence, it will be worth considering the historical

[28] Martin (1985) 263.   [29] Martin (1985) 246.

[30] Howgego (1995) 40.   [31] Figueira (1998) 481.
[32] See below, ch. 4.
[33] Davies (1994) 62. Figueira (1998, 247–52) argues that Aegina was autonomous but a member of the Athenian Empire when she resumed the minting of coins.

and economic background in Attica to provide a wider context in which we can understand the role of coinage at Athens in the middle of the third century BC. Rather than focusing on the relationship between coinage and autonomy, let us assess the existence or degree of freedom and autonomy at Athens at this time.

Apollodorus tells us that at the end of the 260s Antigonus removed the offices from Athens; the fragmentary text may suggest that he put the control of the city in the hands of one man. Such manipulations of civic administration and autonomy would have impaired any rightful claim for Athens to have been free. Eusebius says that Antigonus Gonatas returned freedom to Athens in 256. Can we assume that this entailed returning the offices to the Athenians and not leaving the affairs of the state in the hands of one man? To answer these questions, we need to reassess the political organization at Athens after the Chremonidean war. Both of the sources, Apollodorus and Eusebius, require considerable scrutiny: Is there any other evidence to suggest that Athenian autonomy was affected at the end of the Chremonidean war? Should autonomy even be equated with the loss of the right to appoint officials?[34] Can any change in the appointment and role of officials be identified under Antigonus? Is there anything which suggests that Antigonus did interfere in the running of the Athenian *polis*?

Different aspects of Athenian political organization have been used to calibrate levels of self-government: the titles used to describe officials or an official, the election of various city offices, and the references to Antigonus on inscriptions in Athens and Attica all indicate the relationship with the king. In addition, the presence of Antigonus' own soldiers and officers sheds further light on the situation. These factors do not present a conclusive picture of the relationship between Athens and Gonatas, but a complex one. The clarity of that picture is more blurred when we consider the wider political context of Athens' position in central Greece and the Aegean during the mid-third century BC.

It used to be thought that the public decrees of Athens erected between the years 262 and 229 showed that the city in this period was under the control of a foreign power, that the city did not have complete control of its own affairs, even that its government was no longer democratic. Among the reasons for this opinion was the belief that in this period, 'a single officer for the distribution' was responsible for the erection of public inscriptions authorized by the Council (Boule) or Assembly. In contrast, in previous periods of government considered as democratic, identified in the period before 262, all inscribed civic decrees in Athens were erected by a group of officials, 'the plural board'. On this basis, the evidence seemed to support the belief that Antigonus Gonatas had interfered with the workings of the Athenian government, because inscriptions funded by the single officer dated to the period between 262 and 229 and those by the plural board to before 262.[35] However, the discovery of a new inscribed text from central Athens, undoubtedly belonging to the period between 262 and 229, forced a rethink.[36] The new text identified the plural board as the authority setting up inscriptions. Although this remains the only securely dated instance of the plural board's existence after the Chremonidean war, it cannot be easily explained away as an error by a stonecutter. The single officer and the plural board cannot be used simply to distinguish periods of free and unfree government in Athens before and after the defeat at the end of the Chremonidean war respectively.[37]

Other apparent distinctions in the operation of the Athenian government before and after the Chremonidean war have also been identified. The election of generals is one example. It was once thought that the hoplite general at Athens had been removed by Antigonus Gonatas, but it is now known that he continued to be elected by the Athenians throughout the third century.[38] The other generals who served in Attica were the generals 'appointed for the countryside': one operating with the specific remit at Eleusis, covering also Panakton and Phyle, the other general for the countryside operating from Rhamnous and covering the coastal area probably down to Sunium. Although the honorific decrees of

---

[34] This is implied as a criterion by Meadows: see Ch. 4.

[35] See, e.g., Henry (1988).   [36] Dontas (1983).
[37] Rhodes (1993) and Rhodes with Lewis (1997) 51.
[38] Habicht (1997) 155, correcting Habicht (1982) 47. See also Oliver (1996) 129, n. 26.

these generals emphasize their connection with Gonatas, there is no evidence to suggest that their election was dependent on the king. In all cases, the language of these decrees emphasizes that the appointment of the generals to the countryside after the Chremonidean war relied upon public support.

One instance suggests that Antigonus directly appointed a general, Apollodorus of Otryne.[39] But this is the solitary example. It is significant that a general's specific role was voted for by the Athenian people.[40] The year of the appointment is uncertain since the crucial archon name is no longer legible. The possible archon names suggest that the general would have served some time in the 250s.[41] Apollodorus' appointment does not correlate with the other evidence for the appointment of the generals; his honours are proposed by the *isoteleis* at Rhamnous, non-Athenians given special privileges. The inconsistency in the evidence makes any interpretation difficult.

The strongest indication of interference in the appointment of officials comes from a literary source and remains the hardest to explain away. A story from Hegesander of Delphi, preserved by Athenaeus, describes the excessive behaviour of Demetrius of Phalerum, the grandson of the governor of Athens (317 and 307 BC).[42] Demetrius kept a mistress, Aristagora of Corinth, and boasted that he lived a sumptuous life but within his means; he drank Chian wine and never wronged anyone. Demetrius proceeded to name some members of the Council of the Areopagus who did not live in such a worthy manner. The story goes that, on hearing this, Antigonus appointed Demetrius *thesmothetes*. The appointment of an Athenian official by Antigonus is the only attested instance of direct interference in Athenian government. One wonders whether Demetrius' appointment as *thesmothetes* is a doublet; his grandfather had served in this office during the period of Kassander's rule. Justifiable uneasiness about the validity of the sources does not, however, remove the evidence.

Habicht has suggested recently that Demetrius' appointment as *thesmothetes* should be identified with

the empowering of Athenian government in the hands of one man: 'Demetrius was the royal governor between 262 and 255 ... Demetrius adopted the less offensive name of *thesmothetes*, which recalled its original, all-but-forgotten sense of "giver of ordinances" '.[43] In other words, the Hegesander passage in Athenaeus, in Habicht's view, supports the fragmentary passage of Apollodorus quoted by Philodemus which speaks of Antigonus' settlement in Athens after the Chremonidean war.

Epigraphical research has expanded our knowledge of Demetrius of Phalerum, grandson of the more famous Demetrius. Tracy has redated a well-known honorific inscription from Eleusis on the basis of the identity of the letter-cutter.[44] The inscription is set up by Athenian soldiers at Eleusis, Panakton, and Phyle who have crowned Demetrius. He has served as general and as hipparch. As Habicht argues, it is difficult to imagine Gonatas appointing Demetrius as *thesmothetes* at any time other than in the years immediately after the Chremonidean war. To identify Demetrius with the single ruler, the royal governor of Athens at this time, is, I think, doubtful. The Apollodorus fragment is incomplete and cannot be decisive in the reading it offers. Any irony in appointing the grandson of Demetrius of Phalerum to this post might not have been lost on Antigonus. Kassander, who had made Demetrius of Phalerum, *epistates* in 317, had also been the enemy of Gonatas' grandfather, Antigonus the One Eyed.[45] Neither Demetrius' appointment nor subsequent Antigonid appointments in Athens offer conclusive evidence for the presence of a 'royal governor' in Athens.

It may be preferable to return to Ferguson's original reconstruction of events at this time and see Demetrius' appointment as part of a wider process: 'Antigonus ... discharged the magistrates elected before the capture of the city, and put in their places others whom he could trust. One of the new *thesmothetae* was Demetrius'.[46] Ferguson goes on to say that the new government was made up of the oligarchic faction. The suggestion is characteristic of Ferguson's polarization of Athenian politics into

[39] *SEG* 3. 122 = Pouilloux 1954, no. 7 = *ISE* 22.
[40] Oliver (1996) 139 and Table 9.
[41] Archonship of Apollodorus' office: Habicht (1982) 48 argues for Euboulos; Henry (1992) opposes this. It is possible that Antimachos was the archon (Oliver (1996) 139, n. 53).
[42] Ath. *Deipnosophistae* 4. 167 E–F = Hegesand., *FHG* IV, 415, no. 8.

[43] Habicht (1997) 153 f.
[44] *IG* II² 2971, Tracy (1994), and Tracy (1995) 43–4, 171–4.
[45] I thank Dr J. D. Morgan for this observation.
[46] Ferguson (1911) 183.

democratic (anti-Macedonian) and oligarchic (pro-Macedonian) groups. The political climate in Athens after the Chremonidean war is difficult to clarify. Another of Gonatas' actions following the war was the commemoration of Zeno of Citium, the philosopher. Zeno had died shortly after the defeat of Athens, in the archonship of Arrhenides.[47] Dorandi has argued that the fragment of Philodemus gives an *inclusive* dating for Zenon's death thirty-nine years and three months after the archonship of Klearchos (301/300), the year in which he founded the Stoic school.[48] He suggests that Zeno's death belongs in the archonship of Arrhenides: 262/1. This dating remains insecure, but has been accepted by Habicht, for example.[49] Shortly afterwards, the Athenians passed a decree awarding Zeno a gold crown, a public burial in the Kerameikos, and two stelae in honour of him, one in the Lyceum, the other in the Academy.[50] Antigonus Gonatas is believed to have asked the proposer of the decree, Thraso, that Zeno should be given a burial in the Kerameikos.[51] This 'intervention' offers more evidence for the preservation and continuity of political mechanisms in Athens than it does for the weakening of local government. The machinery of Athenian government continued despite the reservations which had to be retained for the new external force.

Did the appointment of Demetrius mark a break from normal political organization? Habicht does not suppose that Demetrius' office can be identified with the normal body of six *thesmothetai* who would have held office each year.[52] These would normally have been drawn from the archons; archons were chosen by lot from a previously identified group. In what capacity Antigonus 'appointed' Demetrius is uncertain. It is possible that the technical procedure of appointment was unaffected despite the King's apparent interference. Other political and legal bodies continued: there is no suggestion that *nomothetai*, for

example, did not operate in the mid-third century.[53]

It is clearly problematic trying to establish the degree, if any, to which Antigonus interfered in Athenian administration. Some of the uncertainty can be explained by the lack of clarity surrounding our own expectations of what we think determines the level of freedom or independence. It is here that Ferguson's idiosyncratic view of Athenian politics must come into play. For Ferguson, Antigonus brought cultural decline: 'The creative impulse . . . seems to have spent its entire force upon the generation which witnessed the fall of Athens in 261 [*sic*]'; a view shared by Habicht: 'Athens' defeat in the war coincided with the end of a cultural era'.[54] But Ferguson's view of Athenian history is one in which self-interested groups in Athens waxed and waned; the post-Chremonidean war period is dominated by 'the oligarchic faction'.[55]

At one period or another, political actions in Athens are often sponsored by external powers. So Antigonus encouraged Thraso, an ambassador from Athens, to propose public burial for Zeno. The version of the inscription we have in Diogenes Laertius does little to suggest foul play in proceedings. Contrast the honours for the poet Philippides in the archonship of Euthios, 283/2.[56] How should we interpret the evidence here that King Lysimachus 'has often been witness for Philippides on behalf of all these things to those Athenians on embassy to him'?[57] What does this tell us about the level of involvement Lysimachus had with Athens in the 280s? Such involvement arouses no suspicion because Athens was 'free' in this period, having successfully removed Demetrius Poliorcetes and his garrison from the city of Athens. Antigonus' proposals are tantamount to the sort of requests made on occasion by Hellenistic monarchs. For example, controversy surrounded some decisions, such as Stratokles' manipulation of the Athenian year to initiate Demetrius Poliorcetes into the Eleusinian Mysteries in the late 300s.

There is some degree of relativity and ultimately subjectivity in what we might regard as undue interference. We know, for example, that the Athenians included mention of King Antigonus and his family within the prayers at the opening of

---

[47] T. Dorandi (1990a) 36, argues that Arrhenides' archonship belongs to 262/61 and not 261/60 (cf. Osborne (1989) 209–42). Dorandi bases the redating on PHerc. 339, col. V 9–14, for which see also ZPE 84 (1990) 122 f.
[48] Contrast Ferguson (1911) 185, n. 5 for exclusive dating of the fragment.
[49] Habicht (1997) 153.   [50] Diog. Laert. 7. 10–12.
[51] Diog. Laert. 7. 15.   [52] Habicht (1997) 153.
[53] See further on *nomothetai* Rhodes (1990) 20, n. 67. An unpublished inscription from Brauron, dated around the middle of the third century, proves that the *Nomothetai* were indeed in office and functioning at this time (SEG 35. 83).

[54] Ferguson (1911) 185; Habicht (1997) 142.
[55] Ferguson (1911) 183.   [56] IG ii² 657.
[57] IG ii² 657, ll. 36–8.

Assembly meetings: 'that it is the Council's opinion that the Council and the Demos welcome the good that exists through the sacrifices to the health and security of the Council and the Demos of the Athenians and their children and their women and on behalf of King Antigonus and Phila his Queen and their descendants'.[58] The way in which such expressions were regarded was only considered worthy of destruction in 200 BC when Athens declared war on Philip V.[59] Until then, there is no reason to suppose that such items caused any affront, not even to the liberated city of Athens after 229 BC.

In all there is little direct evidence to support the view that Antigonus Gonatas removed the offices at Athens. Any interference is difficult to assess from the end of the Chremonidean war. In Rhodes' recent assessment of the workings of the government in this period, he concludes that 'Athens in this period does not seem to me to be noticeably oligarchic'.[60] There is ample testimony of the degree to which Gonatas was identified with Athenian interests. The orthodoxy is to regard Gonatas' involvement in Athenian politics and organization as non-productive, but the relationship between the Athenian generals honoured for their actions while serving in Attica and Antigonus need not be seen in a completely negative light. Macedonian troops were stationed alongside Athenians at Rhamnous and their presence gave some security to the countryside and those working it during a period of uncertainty.

It could be argued that Antigonus' involvement in Athens brought some benefit to Athens as a whole. A general responsible for the command of the Piraeus was appointed by the king, but this position was outside the realm of existing or previous civic offices in Athens. Herakleitos of Athmonon, an Athenian, maintained control not only of Piraeus but also of Salamis.[61] The commander of the garrison had authority in an extensive and strategically sensitive area stretching from Piraeus across to Salamis. As far as we know, the appointment to this command continued from the end of the Chremonidean war right down to 229 and the return of the Piraeus to

Athens. His appointment was not an Athenian office but the hallmark of the Macedonian presence in Attica since the end of the Chremonidean war. The continued presence of this position after 256 did not prevent Eusebius from identifying this year as that of the return of freedom to Athens.

If anything could be readily identified with the loss of freedom at Athens, it has been the presence of a garrison on the Mouseion hill, imposed at the end of the Chremonidean war. Its existence was almost certainly short-lived.[62] Most have dated its removal to the mid-250s, on the evidence of Eusebius' date for the restoration of freedom to Athens. If there is any one action which symbolized the loss of freedom it was the presence of a foreign garrison in the city itself. The removal of the garrison from the Mouseion in 288/7 had introduced a period of renewed democratic values and a sense of liberation. If there is any sense at all in Athens having lost her freedom in the period of the Chremonidean war, the Mouseion garrison might be held responsible.

Ultimately, problems about whether Athens lost or regained freedom, and autonomy, exist largely because of the quotation from Eusebius. The historical reliability of Eusebius has been questioned already. Some criteria must be established if we are to apply 'freedom' (and 'autonomy') to describe any one particular situation. Modern criteria imposed by historians all too readily identify the period in Athens between 262 and 229 as a period without independence, a time when no foreign policy could be pursued. But such criteria may not always be appropriate or illuminating, and I suggest that we need to rethink precisely what is understood by loss of freedom at Athens under Antigonus Gonatas. It is not clear that the normal processes of government were radically altered.

Economic Resources in Athens

There is no argument based on historical evidence that proves coin production was interrupted by Antigonus Gonatas. Even the presence of a garrison was not crucial; Thomas Martin has asserted that 'autonomous coinage could continue without

---

[58] Dontas (1983) 52, ll. 19–25. For inscriptions offering such sacrifices to Antigonus and his family see Habicht (1982) 148, n. 137.
[59] Habicht (1997) 197, n. 10.
[60] Rhodes with Lewis (1997) 52.
[61] IG II[2] 1225 and Taylor (1997) 250 ff.

[62] Pausanias 3. 6. 6, quoted above (p. 37).

hindrance even in cities which were occupied by a garrison': coin production at Corinth extended beyond the end of the fourth century when Demetrius Poliorcetes had placed a garrison in the city.[63] The evidence of Athens may be more convincing still than that of Corinth. A Macedonian garrison had been present in the Piraeus in the 280s, and possibly later, and yet Athens was minting in this period the silver tetradrachms of the quadridigité style (e.g. Pl. 3.1.2). That a garrison was present in the Piraeus from 262 to 229 need not have prevented Athens from minting coins.

Were there any limitations on the capacity at Athens to mint and issue coins, especially silver coins? The isotopic analysis of third-century Athenian silver tetradrachms by Kroll and Nicolet-Pierre suggests the silver coinage from the first half of the third century in Athens revealed much greater impurities in the silver content than was normal for silver 'Owls'.[64] The quality of the silver in the Athenian coinage had been consistently high in the classical period; the reduction of silver quality was thought by Kroll and Nicolet-Pierre to reflect the use of gifts of silver to produce coinage in the 280s and beyond. 'Imported' silver would have been required, they argue, because of the demise of the silver-mining region of Laurium in the south-east of Attica. The evidence of isotopic analysis is notoriously controversial and the results delivered by Kroll and Nicolet-Pierre are not sufficient to prove that the Laurium mines or Laurium silver were not being used in some part.[65]

Is there any evidence to indicate that this region had been abandoned in the third century? It is very difficult to be certain that the Laurium hills continued to be mined for silver at the time. It is generally thought that the disruptions, especially during the first thirty to forty years of the third century, would have been sufficient to reduce any mining activity to almost nothing. The production of the pi-style coinage at Athens seems to have broken off some time around the 290s. In terms of direct evidence, the latest of the extant *poletai* inscriptions which deal with

the mines belongs to the end of the fourth century.[66] But the inscription concerned is dated on the basis of letter forms. There is little other epigraphical evidence which helps: the *poletai* themselves continue well beyond the end of the fourth century.

Archaeological material is not conclusive, but indicates signs of activity related to the working of ores in the Laurium region during the third century. The only relatively accessible excavated mining installation, in the Agrileza valley, suggests that there was little datable activity beyond the end of the fourth century.[67] Similarly, the Belgian excavations at Thorikos have produced very little which might be connected with the mining industry or processing of extracted ores in the third century. But elsewhere there is some important and significant evidence. The majority of identifiable sites active in the Hellenistic period are on the coast.[68] The evidence for activity would seem to indicate that some ore processing, even the reworking of slag heaps, was taking place in the third century.

On the northern side of Panormos Bay at Pontazeza a series of furnaces has been known for some time, reported by Young back in 1941.[69] More specific details were provided by Conophagos, reporting the excavation of the site by Marinatos.[70] The excavations found material at the furnace site from the third century. Further north at Gaidouromandra Bay the expansion of the Olympic yacht complex required the excavation of the area. The discovery of establishments with buildings finished in hydraulic (waterproof) cement and cisterns all pointed to this site being used for the processing of minerals. Such activities required ample water supplies—the cisterns—but no washing tables were found, which would have confirmed the function of the area. Activity could be traced from the fourth through to the second century. In 1941 Young noted at the south-west end of the bay some traces of ancient furnaces. The evidence seems to point to Gaidouromandra Bay having been connected in some way with ore processing, and there is nothing to say that the site fell into disuse in the third century BC.[71]

---

[63] Martin (1985) 183.
[64] Kroll and Nicolet-Pierre (1990) 10 and 32–4.
[65] Gale, Gentner, Wagner (1980) 48: Chemical analysis can indicate purity; as regards their archaic silver coins, 'Athenian coins are seen not to be noticeably purer than those from other mints'; on Laurium silver see pp. 29–33.
[66] *Agora*, xix, P. 50–1.

[67] *Archaeological Reports* 1984/5, 106–23.
[68] Ellis Jones (1982).
[69] See Figure 3.1 for location of sites discussed here; Young (1941).
[70] Conophagos (1960, 1974); *Archaiologikon Deltion* 27 (1972) Chron. B1, 147–8.
[71] *Archaeological Reports* 1976/7, 12; *Archaeological Annals of Athens* 9 (1976) 24–44.

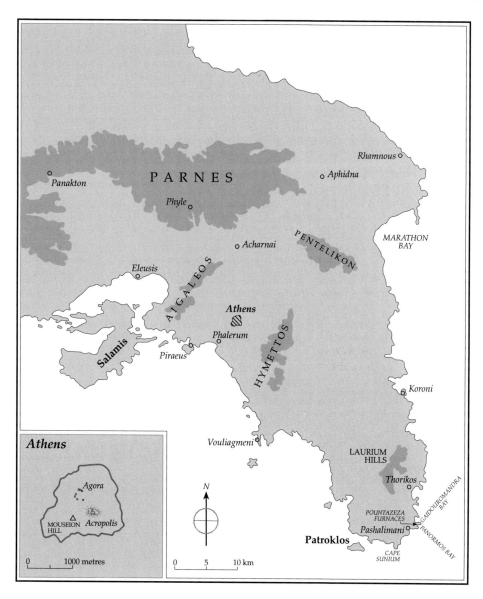

Map 3.1: Attica

Further north, beyond the area of Thorikos excavated by the Belgians, on the northern stretch of the Francolimani Bay, Greek archaeologists carried out the excavation of a site close to the National Electricity Board power station. There five furnaces were found, cut into the bedrock, with a date in either the third or second century BC.[72]

In addition to these isolated discoveries, a major discovery was made south of Panormos Bay, at Pashalimani. Here the Greek Archaeological Service excavated in the late 1970s a large Agora-like area surrounded by buildings.[73] Extensive finds reveal that the site had been occupied and in use without interruption from the fourth until the first century BC. The excavators thought that the site was a major economic trading centre; they identified a thin destruction layer, possibly belonging to a time between the mid-fourth century BC and the early third century.

[72] Conophagos (1974) 343–7; *Archaiologikon Deltion* 27 (1972), Chron. B1, 150–1.

[73] Salliora-Oikonomakou (1979).

Some major developments took place at the site some time in the middle of the third century BC and the bulk of the numismatic and pottery evidence dates to the second half of the third and second centuries BC. The question remains as to what the function of the area was. Various identities have been offered but there is evidence that some activities involved ore processing. Outside the north-west corner of the Agora buildings are traces of a small washery installation which would have been used to process metalliferous rocks. Litharge, a by-product of the cupellation process used to extract silver from argentiferous lead ores has also been found. There is no certainty that Pashalimani was a centre for ore processing, but signs of such activity in a busy centre suggest that activities associated with the production of silver took place here. The number of sites from the Hellenistic period nearby reinforce the relative importance of the area.[74]

Further evidence of Hellenistic activity can be found in the heart of the mining district of the classical period at Laurium. The important set of mining installations excavated in the Botsare valley by Kakavoyiannis in the 1980s has revealed some traces from the Hellenistic era.[75] At mining installation 1, the rebaling tank contained pottery of a Hellenistic date, the type and styles of which have not yet been specified.[76] At nearby mining installation 2, signs of uninterrupted and continued use from the classical period through the Hellenistic into Roman times have been found.[77] If we review the archaeological evidence, there is a significant number of sites in the region which display functions relating to ore processing. Such functions would be what one might expect to find if looking for evidence of the extraction of silver. That this was the actual use of such sites must remain uncertain until further detailed results are published from Attica.

The archaeological evidence does suggest that silver mining could have continued into the Hellenistic period. The evidence from Pashalimani and the rather uneasy silences from elsewhere might be taken as an indication that the first half of the third century had

seen considerable disruptions. The archaeological evidence does not prove that Athens was completely dependent on external sources of metal for the production of silver coinage after the Chremonidean war.

In the earlier part of the third century, activities in south-east Attica will have been disrupted by military actions. The deposit of the large hoard at Thorikos is thought to have been made in the early 280s. Similar disruptions in Attica would have occurred during the 260s, the Chremonidean war. The presence of Ptolemaic camps on Patroklos and at Koroni offers little help in gauging the extent of the impact of warfare in south-east Attica but suggests that the mining district would have been a precarious place for financial speculation.[78] The unfortunate lack of evidence from Sunium adds to these uncertainties, although one can be confident that new epigraphical finds still await discovery from this site.[79]

Athenian Coinage

We have looked extensively at the historical background against which we must view the coin production in the mid-third century at Athens. We have also considered the archaeological evidence for silver production. But what then of the coin evidence itself? There is little evidence to suggest that during the middle of the third century and from the end of the Chremonidean war in particular Athens did not have the expertise to produce new coins. There is *no* evidence to suggest that Athens would not have been able to mint coins in the second half of the third century, and it is possible that some Attic silver might have been available for such purposes. Athens was issuing coins during the Chremonidean war. This is the context in which the silver pentobols were issued. The Attic pentobols (Pl. 3.1.5) were minted to provide a denomination equivalent to the Ptolemaic weight drachm of $c.3.55$ g.[80] The production date is based on

---

[74] The association between this site and the controversial Salaminioi decree from the middle of the third century remains unclear: see Lambert (1997) 96 f. n. 24.

[75] *Archaiologikon Deltion* 39 (1984) Chron. B, 53–4.

[76] Ibid. p. 53, pl. 13B and 14.   [77] Ibid. p. 54.

[78] McCredie (1966).

[79] See Goette (1995) for the recent discovery of an inscription at Sunium.

[80] Kroll (1993) 11; pl. 3, 28A–B. Kroll and Nicolet-Pierre (1990, 30) crucially raised Svoronos' proposed date of the Athenian pentobols, an example of which was found in *IGCH* 193, from $c.255$–229 to the 260s (cf. Hackens (1969) 706 and n. 4). The date of the hoard *IGCH* 193 might be raised to $c.240$ by the presence of fourteen well-preserved Rhodian didrachms which belong to Ashton's third series and were struck in the first half of the third century BC (Ashton (1988) 83–4 and 86). Hackens (1969) 706 and n. 4.

the understanding that the coins were produced to pay the Ptolemaic contingents who were present in various fortified positions in Attica. This still seems a sound argument despite Touratsoglou's suggestion that the Ptolemaic presence would hardly have affected the movement of Ptolemaic *silver* in mainland Greece because the soldiers were paid in *copper* coins.[81] The Athenian tetrobols (Pl. 3.1.6), thought to have been produced to pay mercenaries, were issued on two occasions during the third century but no definite date can be established.[82] Athens also produced a new bronze issue after the Chremonidean war in the shape of the Eleusinian chalkous (one-eighth obol) and its double (one-quarter obol, e.g. Pl. 3.1.7).[83] But the main and most controversial evidence for the production of silver coins at Athens after the Chremonidean war is Kroll's 'heterogeneous silver'. The study by Kroll and Nicolet-Pierre of the so-called 'heterogeneous' coins, on which Kroll bases the subsequent discussion of Athenian coinage from the Agora, relies on the dating of twenty-four hoards. The deposition dates and observations on the wear of the Athenian silver tetradrachms within those relevant hoards containing regal issues provide the chronology for the heterogeneous coins. Athenian silver coinage at the end of the fourth century was typified by the 'bracket' or 'pi-style' tetradrachm (Pl. 3.1.1). These coins displayed a characteristic feature on the obverse at the base of Athena's helmet, a 'T between reversed brackets' or what Bingen later called the 'pi-style', in the most authoritative study of this type.[84] Bingen published a hoard of 282 coins from Thorikos in which he identified five different phases before the introduction of what he called the 'quadridigité' type (e.g. Pl. 3.1.2). Bingen dated the 'pi-style' to c.340–294 and the quadridigité to some time after this, following a break.[85] Kroll and Nicolet-Pierre identified the 'heterogeneous types' as a sub-group of this quadridigité type (e.g. Pl. 3.1.3).[86]

Three phases were indicated within the hoards studied: those buried before 270 BC, before c.240 BC,

and before 215 BC. The deposition date of each hoard and observations on the relative wear of the relevant coins allow a loose chronology of the heterogeneous types to be established. Since their study, there has been little to suggest that Kroll and Nicolet-Pierre's estimate of deposition date for these hoards is wildly inaccurate.[87] In twenty-three of the twenty-four hoards silver coins of both pi- and quadridigité style were found from all three periods.[88] The heterogeneous groups were found in only the second and third phases; groups C, D, and F were found in phase-two hoards; because group B resembles C, groups B, C, and D were in circulation before the Chremonidean war. Coins of groups A, E, and F were in circulation only after the Chremonidean war (see Appendix 1).

Kroll and Nicolet-Pierre's chronology of the heterogeneous coins resembling the Athenian quadridigité types did not necessarily explain who produced them. The authors suggested in 1990 that the coins were more likely to be imitations of Athenian issues. The most striking difference between these and earlier Athenian coinage was the general lack of unity. There was little resemblance between the six groups of heterogeneous types, and sometimes within a group; there is considerable die linkage between a small number of dies: the authors complain of the difficulty in distinguishing different engravers. Although groups A, D, E, and F followed normal Athenian practice in die alignment, the obverses display eight different styles of helmet ornamentation. Kroll and Nicolet-Pierre suggest that these issues blended in with official Athenian types and were thereby preserved in their respective hoards.

Group-B types had a feature not normally seen on the Athenian tetradrachm, 'a volute at the hinge of the visor on Athena's helmet'; and group C had the same feature but used a different die alignment and cylindrical punch dies as opposed to the square punch die normal in the fourth and third centuries BC. Groups B and C had features similar to those preceding the New Style issues of Athens. However,

---

[81] Touratsoglou (1995) 85.   [82] Kroll (1993) 11; pl. 3, 29A–C.
[83] Kroll (1993) 35 f.
[84] Thompson (1957) 6; Bingen (1973) 9 and n. 1.
[85] Bingen (1973) 9 links the deposit to the abandonment of the site. The accuracy of the date may be affected by other evidence for the occupation of the site, such as Tower compound 1 in insula 3 at Thorikos, where the conflicting chronological evidence of the excavated lamps may be important (see Spitaels (1978) 39–110, esp. 103 and 108).
[86] See also Martin (1981) 60, n. 14.

[87] Touratsoglou (1995) suggests more precise dates for some of the hoards: Pherai 1938: 250 BC or later (Table III); Eretria 1937: 235 BC (Table VI); Karditsa 1929: 227–225 BC (Table III); Hija e Korbit 1983: 227–225 BC (Table III); Carystus 1945: 227–225 BC (Table III); Sparta 1908: 222 BC (Table III). For the explanation for the dates in the 220s, see Touratsoglou (1995) 77 and 79.
[88] The exception was *IGCH* 91, Siphnos 1930.

because the Phayttos (buried *c*.260) and Krčedin (buried 270–260) hoards are much earlier than these later examples, Kroll and Nicolet-Pierre thought that Groups B and C were imitations and could not be related to Athenian coins at the end of the third century.[89]

There remains little doubt that some of the heterogeneous types are imitations: 'The eclectic, frequently derivative or uncouth, and highly diverse die cutting leaves little doubt that at least some of the heterogeneous material consists of unofficial imitations'.[90] But there is now far less certainty that all the examples are imitations. Kroll and Nicolet-Pierre originally identified the sole heterogeneous silver tetradrachm from the Agora in Athens (*Agora*, xxvi. no. 30) with one of their larger groups, Group F.[91] However, Kroll now relates features of this coin with an example from Group C of the heterogeneous types: C5.[92] The Agora example displays on the reverse the diagonally aligned ethnic and an owl's head similar to that of C5. This comparison raises further doubts as to the deposition dates of the hoards from Krčedin and Phayttos, dated 270–260 and *c*.260 BC respectively: both contain Athenian tetradrachms from Kroll and Nicolet-Pierre's heterogeneous group C.[93] If these hoards were deposited later, as Kroll suspects, then this may be further proof that the coins from Group C are genuinely Athenian, were a forerunner to the Athenian New Style coinage, and were being minted in the period after the Chremonidean war and before 229 BC.[94]

Kroll and Nicolet-Pierre concluded in 1990 that heterogeneous types 'were not "false" in the absolute sense' because they were accepted within the hoards. Their production was explained by the Athenian political history. 'The suspension of minting at Athens, in or before 262/1, must have stimulated their manufacture, and the prolonged inactivity of the official mint probably encouraged toleration of their circulation'.[95] The conclusions made in this seminal study of the heterogeneous coins were far from secure. The authors admitted then that 'a prima facie

case can be made for considering them a prolongation, intermittent to be sure, but nevertheless official of the QD [quadridigité] coinage, a prolongation, or rather a revival, that would have followed upon the *eleutheria* Antigonus Gonatas conceded to Athens in 255'.[96] What becomes clear is the degree to which any interpretation still relies heavily on the political context of the period.[97]

But the broader numismatic evidence must be considered. Only one example of Athenian heterogeneous types identified by Kroll and Nicolet-Pierre has been discovered in the Agora. The majority of those hoards containing the heterogeneous types are from central and northern Greece. Both pi- and quadridigité-style Athenian silver coins also continue to appear in relatively more hoards throughout the three phases. The proportion of heterogeneous-style coins in those hoards which contain Athenian issues fluctuates over this period (see Appendix 2). Perhaps it is not surprising that relatively more Athenian coins appear in those hoards discovered closer to Athens.[98] It is worth noting that where the heterogeneous types do appear, they invariably outnumber the other Athenian types. The relative numbers of heterogeneous and non-heterogeneous Athenian coins in these hoards tend to suggest that the acceptability of the heterogeneous types might have been underestimated. Of the heterogeneous types, some forms may have been imitations. But there can be little doubt now that this type of silver tetradrachm was in some form an Athenian-produced civic coinage.

Conclusion

The focus of this Chapter has been on the silver coins of Athens. The argument that Athens was minting some form of silver tetradrachm in the period after the Chremonidean war, between the late 260s and 229, has been reasserted. The numismatic evidence does not support a view that Athenian coin production ended in this period. There is then little consequent support on this basis for the suggestion that

[89] Kroll and Nicolet-Pierre (1990) 20 f.   [90] Kroll (1993) 11.
[91] Kroll and Nicolet-Pierre (1990) 17; pl. 6, F23.
[92] Kroll (1993) 12 n. 47; Kroll and Nicolet-Pierre (1990) 15; pl. 4, C5 (from the Sophikon hoard, *IGCH* 179).
[93] Kroll and Nicolet-Pierre (1990) 15; pl. 4, C1 (Krčedin) and C2 (Phayttos).
[94] Kroll (1993) 12 with n. 47.   [95] Kroll and Nicolet-Pierre (1990) 21.

[96] Kroll and Nicolet-Pierre (1990) 20.
[97] See Picard (1996) 254 on the relationship between money and politics at Athens.
[98] Lönnqvist (1997) 134: 'In most of the hoards found in Greece, and in particular in Attica, the Athenian tetradrachms appear in substantial quantities and clearly outnumber the other coinages'.

Antigonus did stop Athens producing coinage after the Chremonidean war. The onus of proof is on those who wish to argue that Antigonus did interrupt this activity.

The context for this analysis of the numismatic evidence has been a close and detailed study of the evidence for Athenian political organization in the years shortly after the Chremonidean war. Although here the evidence is not as decisive as one might have liked, it is reasonable to conclude that Antigonus did very little to affect or disrupt the ways in which the Athenians organized their political structures. The most decisive step that Antigonus took was the imposition of the garrison on the Mouseion hill in the city itself. If any step could be said to have impinged upon the freedom of the Athenians, it will have been the decision to resort to installing a military presence overlooking the functional and symbolic heart of Athenian government in the middle of the city. There can be little doubt that if Eusebius had been referring to any specific action in 256, it will have been to the removal of this garrison from Athens. Any other assumptions built up around Eusebius' statement must be considered very carefully. It is no longer tenable to assume that the right to produce coinage was in any way associated with Antigonus' behaviour towards Athens in the late 260s or 250s.

If we step further back still, and embrace the debate provoked by Thomas Martin, it is difficult to accept that the loss of 'freedom' should in any way have required infringement of a city's right to produce coins. At least, this is the lesson we can take from Athens in the mid-third century. While others have disputed Martin's position, it is clear now that each case needs to be considered in its own right. There can be no clear-cut rule that associates freedom or independence or autonomy with the ability to produce coins. In fact, a more general problem is becoming apparent from this close study of the arguments surrounding Athens' right to produce coins in the third century: understanding of what it was to be free.

For so many historians of Athens, and indeed the Greek city, there have been a number of assumptions made about at what point one can declare independence lost. Gomme's autopsy on the Greek *polis* suggested that independence ceased at the close of the Chremonidean war. His argument was based on

Athens, which of course entailed a consideration of the points this chapter has dealt with:

It is not simply that Macedonian troops now occupied the city itself and Peiraeus, and many places in Attika... and controlled the assembly and the magistrates, but it appears that the assembly met but rarely, and *above all* [my italics] Athens ceased to issue her own coins—her autonomy was gone, as well as her trade, and she never recovered it.[99]

The points mentioned by Gomme have been dealt with. Coin production did not stop. The activity of the Assembly can only be measured by the extant epigraphical output of the city. But epigraphic habit in itself is not a secure indication of independence. We are dealing here with ideas of what autonomy is understood to entail.

Another gloomy commentator on the evolution of the *polis* is Runciman, who argues that the Greek *polis* was unable to change and adapt in a developing environment. It is interesting to note that here too we find signs that attributes of the *polis* are given specific prominence. For instance, Runciman describes cults, coins, and calendars as 'distinctive symbols of independence'.[100] Coins again are assumed to offer a simple symptom of status. It is significant that Runciman, like Gomme, includes coinage as crucial to his diagnosis on the independent or autonomous *polis*.

If it has not already become apparent, it should be obvious by now that as historians of antiquity we frequently make assumptions about what we understand autonomy or independence meant. Cawkwell declared that Greek liberty ended at the battle of Chaeronea: 'independence was gone'.[101] This view too is highly idiosyncratic. It is based on a diagnosis of symptoms that may well have been alien to the patient. Cawkwell's judgement is based on power: the possession of absolute power in Greece passed to Philip in 338, and on this basis alone freedom should be declared dead. This position makes little allowance for the procession of history which followed Chaeronea and the continued evolution of the Greek *polis* after Alexander.

Eusebius or his source made some sort of assumption about what freedom Antigonus had given back

[99] Gomme (1937) 223.   [100] Runciman (1990) 353.
[101] Cawkwell (1996) 100.

to Athens in 256, and in this chapter the removal of the garrison on Mouseion hill has been suggested as the possible criterion. Other possible factors have been argued to be less significant, or dismissed altogether. The relationship between Athens and the Hellenistic monarch Gonatas was a complex one. The *polis* enjoyed freedoms in the 260s which it did not between the end of the Chremonidean war and 256. Between 256 and 229 the city had less freedom than it did after 229.

At the same time, Athens existed in an ever-changing political world. It is wrong to assume that freedom and autonomy in this period were mere slogans. The terms referred to important and emotive issues on which competing external forces could always call. Different media could be employed to communicate ideas and deliver favours. After the Chremonidean war, Gonatas was the most potent force in Athens. He chose to exert that power. Although coinage has its uses, for Antigonus it was not as important as the exertion of military muscle. Athenian freedom was impaired by Gonatas but only briefly. The liberty of the *polis* developed as the relationship with the monarch evolved. While freedom and autonomy were absolutely important to the Hellenistic *polis* they still defy absolute definition.

Appendix 1

Table 3.1: Summary of the hoards containing heterogeneous groups of Athenian silver tetradrachms studied by Kroll and Nicolet-Pierre (1990)

Hoard	Number of hoards studied which contained Athenian silver tetradrachms of the heterogeneous groups	Burial date
PHASE 1 HOARDS:	None out of 7 hoards	
PHASE 2 HOARDS:	4 out of 11, containing Groups C, D, F	
Krčedin 1953	Group C × 1	270–260
Phayttos 1938/*IGCH* 159	Group C × 1; Gp. D × 1	*c*.260
Olympia 1922/*IGCH* 176	Group F × 1	245
Kozani 1955/*IGCH* 457	Group D × 2	245
PHASE 3 HOARDS:	4 out of 6, containing Groups A, B, C, E, F	
Hija e Korbit, 1982/*CH* 8.299	Groups A × 2, B × 2, E × 1, F × 3	230
Sparta 1908/*IGCH* 181	Groups A × 2, B × 1, C × 1, F × 2	230–220
Sophikon 1893/*IGCH* 179	Groups A × 3, B × 1, C × 2, F × 11	230–220
Corinth 1938/*IGCH* 187	Groups A × 3, B × 1, C × 1, D × 2, E × 3, F × 8	220–215

Appendix 2

Table 3.2: Percentages of Athenian coins in hoards studied by Kroll and Nicolet-Pierre (1990)

Hoard	Total coins	Percentage of all coins which are Athenian issues	Percentage of all Athenian coins which are of heterogeneous type
PHASE 2, BEFORE 240 BC			
Pontiolevadi Kilkis 1961/*IGCH* 445	114	4	0
Krčedin 1953	73	14	10
Pherai 1938/*IGCH* 168	549	13+	0
Phayttos 1956/*IGCH* 159	65	12	25
Eretria 1981, 1B/*CH* 8. 282	115	4	0
Jabukovac 1924/*IGCH* 447 458	219	1	0

Table 3.2: *(Cont'd)*

Hoard	Total coins	Percentage of all coins which are Athenian issues	Percentage of all Athenian coins which are of heterogeneous type
Eretria 1937/*IGCH* 175	566	5	0
Olympia 1922/*IGCH* 176	72	4	33
Kozani 1955/*IGCH* 457	29	28+	25
Karditsa 1929/*IGCH* 162	36	19	0
Thessaly 1975/*CH 3.* 43	26	8	0
PHASE 3, BEFORE *c.*215 BC			
Thebes 1935/*IGCH* 193	21	33	0
Hija e Korbit 1982/see now *CH 8.* 299[102]	585	6	27
Carystus 1945/*IGCH* 117	367	2	0
Sparta 1908/*IGCH* 181	96	42	17
Sophikon 1893/*IGCH* 179	838	4	< 48
Corinth 1938/*IGCH* 187	417	35	19

REFERENCES

ALESHIRE, S. (1989). *The Athenian Asklepeion* (Gieben).

ASHTON, R. H. J. (1988). 'Rhodian Coinage and the Colossus', *RN*[6], 30: 75–90.

BELLINGER, A. R. (1963). *Essays on the Coinage of Alexander the Great*, Numismatic Studies, xi (New York).

BINGEN, J. (1973). *Thorikos vi./1969* (Brussels).

BOEHRINGER, C. (1972). *Zur Chronologie Mittelhellenistischen Münzserien* (Berlin).

BRAUN, K. (1970). 'Der Diplyon-Brunnen B₁: Die Funde', *AM* 85: 129–269.

BRISCOE, J. (1978). 'Antigonus and the Greek States, 276–196 B.C.', in P. D. Garnsey and C. R. Whittaker (eds.), *Imperialism in the Ancient World* (Cambridge), 145–57.

CAWKWELL, G. (1996). 'The End of Greek Liberty', in R. W. Wallace and E. M. Harris (eds.), *Transitions to Empire: Essays in Graeco-Roman History, 360–146 B.C., in Honor of E. Badian* (Norman, Okla., and London), 98–121.

CONOPHAGOS, C. E. (1960). 'Une Méthode ignoré de cupellation du plomb argentifère utilisé par les anciens grecs', *Annales Géologiques des Pays Helléniques*, 11: 137–49.

—— ([1974] 1975). 'Kaminoi tēxeōs kai technikē tēs tēxeōs tōn argurouchōn metauevmatōn moluvdou tēs lavreōtikēs upo tōn archaiōn Hellēnōn' ('Smelting Furnaces and the Technology of Smelting Argentiferous Lead Ores in Ancient Greece'), *Annales géologiques des pays helléniques*, 26: 338–66.

—— (1980). *Le Laurium antique, et la technique grecque de la production de l'argent* (Athens).

DAVIES, J. K. (1994). 'On the Non-usability of the Concept of "Sovereignty" in an Ancient Greek Context', in

L. A. Foresti, A. Barzano, C. Bearzot, L. Prandi, G. Zecchini (eds.), *Federazioni e federalismo nell Europa antica*, Bergamo, 21–5 settembre 1992, i (Milan), 51–65.

DONTAS, G. (1983). 'The True Aglaurion', *Hesperia*, 52: 48–63.

DORANDI, T. (1990a). 'Arrenide', *ZPE* 81: 36.

—— (1990b). 'Gli arconti nei papiri ercolanesi', *ZPE* 84: 121–38.

DREYER, B. (1999). *Untersuchungen zur Geschichte des spätklassischen Athen (322–ca. 230. v. Chr.)*, Historia Einzelschriften, cxxxvii (Stuttgart).

ELLIS JONES, J. (1982). 'The Laurion Silver Mines: A Review of Recent Researches and Results', *Greece and Rome*, 29: 169–83.

FERGUSON, W. S. (1911). *Hellenistic Athens* (London).

FIGUEIRA, T. (1998). *The Power of Money: Coinage and Politics in the Athenian Empire* (Philadelphia Pa.).

GALE, N. H., W. GENTNER, and G. A. WAGNER (1980). 'Mineralogical and Geographical Silver Sources of Archaic Greek Coinage', in D. M. Metcalf and W. A. Oddy (eds.), *Metallurgy in Numismatics*, 1: 3–49.

GAUTHIER, Ph. (1985). *Les Cités grecques et leurs bienfaiteurs, IV*ᵉ *et I*ᵉʳ *siècle avant J.C.*, *BCH*, suppl. 12.

GOETTE, H. R. (1995). 'Sounion II: Ein neues *decretum militum qui Sunii in statione erant*', *AM* 110: 175–81.

GOMME, A. W. (1937). *Essays in Greek History and Literature* (Oxford).

GRACE, V. (1974). 'Revisions in Early Hellenistic Chronology', *AM* 89: 193–200.

HABICHT, C. (1982). *Studien zur Geschichte Athens in hellenistischer Zeit*, Hypomnemata, Heft 73 (Göttingen).

—— (1997). *Athens from Alexander to Antony* (Harvard, Mass. and London).

---

[102] *CH* 8.299 reports 618 silver coins, 80 Athenian tetradrachms.

HACKENS, T. (1969). 'La Circulation monétaire dans la Béotie hellénistique', *BCH* 93: 701–29.

HENRY, A. S. (1988). 'The One and the Many: Athenian Financial Officials in the Hellenistic Period', *ZPE* 72: 129–36.

——(1992). 'Lysandros of Anaphlystos and the Decree for Phaidros of Sphettos', *Chiron* 22: 25–33.

HORNBLOWER, J. (1980). *Hieronymus of Cardia* (Oxford).

HOWGEGO, C. (1995). *Ancient History from Coins* (London).

JACOBY, F. (1902). *Apollodors Chronik* (Berlin).

——(1949). *Atthis* (Oxford).

KLEINER, F. (1975). 'The Earliest Athenian New Style Bronze Coins, Some Evidence from the Athenian Agora', *Hesperia*, 44: 302–30.

——(1976). 'The Agora Excavations and the Athenian Bronze Coinage, 200–86 B.C.', *Hesperia*, 75: 1–40.

KNOEPFLER, D. (1987). 'Tétradrachmes attiques et argent ⟨alexandrin⟩ chez Diogéne Laërce: première partie', *MH* 44: 233–53.

——(1989). 'Tétradrachmes attiques et argent ⟨alexandrin⟩ chez Diogéne Laërce: deuxième partie', *MH* 46: 193–230.

KROLL, J. H. (1993). *The Athenian Agora xxvi. The Greek Coins* (Princeton, NJ: American School of Classical Studies at Athens).

—— and H. NICOLET-PIERRE (1990). 'Athenian Tetradrachm Coinage of the Third Century B.C.', *AJN* 2: 1–35.

LAMBERT, S. D. (1997). 'The Attic Genos Salaminioi and the Island of Salamis', *ZPE* 119: 85–106.

LE RIDER, G. (1996). *Monnayage et finances de Philippe II. Un état de la question*, Meletemata 23 (Athens).

LEWIS, D. M. (1962). 'The Chronology of the Athenian New Style Silver', *NC*[7] 2: 275–80.

LISSONE, F. L. V. M. (1969). *De Fragmenten van de Geschiedschrijver Phylarchus* (Nijmegen).

LÖNNQVIST, K. (1997). 'Studies on the Hellenistic Coinage of Athens: The Impact of Macedonia on the Athenian Money Market in the 3rd Century B.C.', in J. Frösén (ed.), *Early Hellenistic Athens: Symptoms of a Change* (Helsinki), 119–45.

McCREDIE, T. R. (1966). *Fortified Military Camps in Attica, Hesperia*, suppl. 11 (American School of Classical Studies at Athens).

MARTIN, T. (1981). 'A Third Century B.C. Hoard from Thessaly at the A.N.S.', *ANSMN* 26: 51–77.

——(1985). *Sovereignty and Coinage in Classical Greece* (Princeton, NJ).

MATHIESEN, R. W. (1981). 'Antigonus Gonatas and the Silver Coinages of Macedonia circa 280–270 B.C.', *ANSMN* 26: 79–123.

MELVILLE JONES, J. R. (1972). 'Epigraphical Notes on Hellenistic Coinage', *NC*[7] 12: 39–42.

MERKER, I. (1960). 'The Silver Coinage of Antigonus Gonatas and Antigonus Doson', *ANSMN* 9: 39–52.

MØRKHOLM, O. (1981). *Early Hellenistic Coinage* (Cambridge).

MUSTI, D. (1997). *Pausania. Guida della Grecia, iii. La Laconia*, 3rd edn., tr. D. Musti, comm. D. Musti and M. Torelli (Lorenza Valla).

OLIVER, G. (1996). 'The Athenian State Under Threat: Politics and Food Supply, 307 to 229 B.C.' (Univ. of Oxford D.Phil thesis).

OSBORNE, M. J. (1989). 'The Chronology of Athens in the mid third century B.C.', *ZPE* 78: 209–42.

PFEIFFER, R. (1968). *History of Classical Scholarship: From the Beginnings to the End of the Hellenistic Age* (Oxford).

PICARD, O. (1969). 'Le Trésor de Kaki Thalassa', *BCH* 93: 823–9.

——(1996). 'Monnaie et démocratie à Athènes', in M. Sakellariou (ed.), *Colloque International Démocratie Athénienne et Culture* (Athens), 243–55.

RHODES, P. J. (1990). 'Atthidographers', in H. Verdin, G. Schepens, E. de Keser (eds.), *Purposes of History: Studies in Greek Historiography from the 4th to the 2nd Centuries B.C.*, Proceedings of the International Colloquium Leuven, 24–6 May 1988 (Louvain), 73–81.

——(1993). 'One Treasurer Oligarchic, Many Treasurers Democratic?', in H. Jocelyn (ed.), *Tria Lustra: Essays and Notes Presented to John Pinsent*, Liverpool Classical Papers, iii (Liverpool), 1–3.

—— with D. M. LEWIS (1997). *The Decrees of the Greek States* (Oxford).

RUNCIMAN, W. G. (1990). 'Doomed to Extinction: The *Polis* as an Evolutionary Dead End', in O. Murray and S. Price (eds.), *The Greek City* (Oxford), 347–67.

SALLIORA-OIKONOMAKOU, M. (1979). 'Archaia agora sto Limani Pasa Lavriou', *Archaiologikon Deltion*, 34A: 161–73.

SEAGER, R. J. (1981). 'The Freedom of the Greeks of Asia: From Alexander to Antiochus', *CQ* 31: 106–12.

—— and C. J. TUPLIN (1980). 'The Freedom of the Greeks of Asia', *JHS* 100: 141–54.

SPITAELS, P. (1978). 'Insula 3. Tower Compound 1', *Thorikos, vii. 1970–71* (Gent), 39–110.

TAYLOR, M. C. (1997). *Salamis and the Salaminioi* (Amsterdam).

THOMPSON, M. (1957). 'A Hoard of Athenian Fractions', *ANSMN* 7: 1–6.

TOURATSOGLOU, G. (1995). *Disjecta Membra: Two New Hellenistic Hoards from Greece* (Athens).

TRACY, S. V. (1994). 'Hands in Greek Epigraphy—Demetrios of Phaleron', in J. M. Fossey (ed.), *Boeotia Antiqua IV: Proceedings of the 7th International Congress on Boiotian Antiquities* (Amsterdam), 151–61.

——(1995). *Athenian Democracy in Transition: Attic Letter Cutters of 340 to 290 B.C.* (Berkeley, Calif.).

YOUNG, J. H. (1941). 'Studies in South Attica: The Salaminians at Panormos', *Hesperia*, 10: 163–91.

4
MONEY, FREEDOM, AND EMPIRE IN THE HELLENISTIC WORLD

Andrew Meadows

Indeed, after law itself, there is nothing of greater consequence than the title, value, and measure of coins … and in every well-ordered state, it is the sovereign prince alone who has this power. This, we read, is the way it was at Rome[1]

IN HIS IMPORTANT BOOK OF 1985, THOMAS Martin tackled head-on the relationship between king and subjects, coinage and sovereignty, in the classical Greek world. Taking as his focus the coinage of Thessaly before, during, and after the Macedonian conquest in the fourth century BC, he found no evidence for the subjection of the region to the Macedonian kings having had any effect on the ability of the Thessalians to produce coin. In a summary review of the other coinages of Greece at the same time he perceived a similar pattern. His conclusion was unequivocal: 'It is my contention that the numismatic, historical, documentary, and literary evidence uniformly fails to support the idea that there was operative in the classical Greek world a strongly felt connection between an abstract notion of sovereignty and the right of coinage which implied the necessity to enforce a uniform monetary circulation.'[2]

Such a conclusion, if correct, is of fundamental importance for two reasons: first, for our appreciation of the abstract concept or concepts of sovereignty[3] and the place of coin issue in the rhetoric of imperialism in the Greek world; and, second, for the practical numismatic purpose of dating many coinages of ancient Greek states. Among numismatists, as well as historians working in all periods of Greek history, it has been common to invoke what Martin has dubbed the *lex Seyrig*, a 'law' which dictates that no state issued coin in its own name if it was ruled by another. This law is (rather like that in Hellenistic epigraphy which requires any king not given his title to be dead) extremely attractive for dating purposes. But if Martin is correct and the *lex Seyrig* is invalidated, then the conventional dating of many coinages must be called into question. In 1986 Philip Kinns seized upon this last point in his review of B. Deppert-Lippitz's corpus of the coinage of Miletus:

D-L is at pains to glean what she can from the historical sources, but two lines of interpretation which are repeatedly invoked depend on assumptions of questionable validity. The first is that issues of local coinage will normally have been made when the city was 'free', rather than controlled by some external power. The second is that issues of coinage will belong to periods of prosperity rather than periods of economic difficulties. Neither proposition has much to recommend it. Despite varying degrees of foreign domination there is no reason to believe that the civic institutions of Miletus were ever suspended, and since the issue of coinage was largely a local civic matter,

---

[1] Jean Bodin, *Six Livres de la République* (Paris, 1583), bk. i, ch. 10, p. 242. The translation is taken from J. H. Franklin (ed.), *Jean Bodin. On Sovereignty*. Cambridge Texts in the History of Political Thought (Cambridge, 1992).

[2] Martin (1985) 219, restated in Martin (1996).

[3] For a recent disentanglement and critique of the use of the term 'sovereignty' by modern scholars apropos of ancient states, see Davies (1994). That at issue here is Davies's Type A: 'The supreme individual authority possessed by a state to enact and enforce its law with respect to all persons, property, and events within its borders'.

striking of silver and bronze might surely have been carried out at almost any time when local need arose.[4]

Kinns thus arrives at essentially the same point as Martin but, importantly, by a different route. Whereas Martin was able adequately to demonstrate the existence of the phenomenon of the continuation of local coinage in a period of foreign rule by analysis of the coinage, Kinns explains the survival of coinage under foreign domination through the institutions that produced it within the city.[5] This is an important point, particularly when we come to consider the inverse of the type of situation identified by Martin; that is, where a local coinage did disappear upon the introduction of foreign rule. Let us take, for example, the case of Lycia when it came under the rule of the Hecatomnid dynasty in the fourth century BC. Previously, from very early times in the development of coinage, Lycia had seen a continuous stream of silver coinages produced by the local dynasts whose rule characterized the history of the area down to the mid fourth century BC. At this point the land of Lycia was taken over *in toto* by the Hecatomnid dynasty of Caria.[6] The Lycian coinage stopped completely. These are the plain facts, but how do we interpret them? It is tempting, of course, to view this disappearance of a long tradition of coinage in Lycia as the result of the suppression of coinage as a political gesture of dominance on the part of the incoming Hecatomnid satraps. Yet, if we follow the lead offered to us by Kinns and look to the institutions within the state responsible for the production of coinage, we will note that the last coinages of fourth-century Lycia were produced by dynasts, and that these dynasts were undoubtedly unseated by the Hecatomnids. Thus the disappearance of coinage at this period becomes not a political act in itself, but merely the corollary of a political act. Coinage disappeared not because it was a symbol of political freedom or sovereignty, but for the simple, practical reason that the men who had previously produced it had now ceased to exist or were no longer in power.

The problem is, Which of these two interpretative positions to adopt in any given case? Martin may

seem to have proved his point for fourth-century Thessaly and Greece, but can it be applied equally later and elsewhere? In his recent introduction to the use of numismatic evidence for historical purposes Chris Howgego has rightly pointed out that matters are not as straightforward in the Greek world at other periods.[7] The most compelling counter example is that of the Greek cities under Roman domination.

In an article published in 1960 Louis Robert collected together the evidence for a particularly interesting group of Roman provincial coins that carried as part of their legend the name of an individual in the genitive and the participle *aitesamenou* ('requesting').[8] The explanation for this legend, Robert argued, was that the individual named had sought permission from the Roman emperor for the issues so inscribed. In the case of one city, Hadrianopolis, he managed to find epigraphic confirmation that an individual so named on the coinage had indeed gone on an embassy to the emperor. The earliest known example is from Ancyra in the reign of Nero (*RPC* 3111) (Pl. 4.1.1). More recently doubt has been cast on Robert's interpretation of these legends, and caution is perhaps required,[9] but another group of coins from Patras and Corinth in Greece proper leave little room for doubt. In the reign of Domitian the former marked its coins INDULGENTIAE AVG MONETA INPETRATA ('coinage obtained through the indulgence of the emperor'), perhaps referring to a restored right to issue coin after its withdrawal by Vespasian. Corinth's coin (Pl. 4.1.2) carried the more abbreviated legend PERM IMP ('by permission of the emperor'), in this respect recalling the legends found earlier on the issues of western provincial mints such as Ebora, Emerita, Italica, Romula, Traducta, Patricia, and Paterna, or an issue of Berytus in Phoenicia from AD 12–14, inscribed with the permission of the provincial governor: PERMISSV SILANI ('by permission of Silanus').[10] There can, it seems, be little doubt that by the end of the first century AD there existed an established link in the Greek world between suzerainty and the right to issue coin.

So, on the one hand we have a classical Greek world where, on Martin's view, emperors and kings

---

[4] Kinns (1986) (quotation from 247–8)—review of Deppert-Lippitz (1984).

[5] On this point cf. Oliver (above, ch. 3).

[6] The precise date of acquisition is uncertain, but it had probably occurred by the reign of Mausolus. See Jacob (1993).

[7] Howgego (1995) 39–61.   [8] Robert (1960).

[9] See *RPC* i. 2–3 and Weiss (1992).

[10] On both types see Levy (1987). For the full range of formulations in the west see *RPC* i. 2–3.

allowed subject states to issue their own coin unfettered; on the other, a Roman empire where Greek states on occasion made explicit reference to the permission they had sought of the emperor or his representative; but in any case where more often than not they placed the emperor's image on their issues. What had happened in the interim; when had this change of attitude occurred? Howgego ((1995) 40–1) has suggested that the effect of an imperial power on the ability of states to issue coin can already be felt in the Hellenistic period. What follows is an attempt to show that he is correct, but at the same time to refine our understanding of the chronology and dynamic of this shift in the significance and use of coinage.

Let us begin not with the question of what impact royal acquisition had on the coinage of a particular area, which we have seen in the case of fourth-century Lycia to be fraught with methodological problems, but rather the reverse. What happened to the pattern of autonomous coinage in an area when royal control was removed? In his criticism of Martin's thesis, Howgego has suggested that there are two areas in which we can clearly see the impact of the withdrawal of royal authority on local coinage: the removal of Ptolemaic control from southern Asia Minor at the end of the third century, and the removal of Seleucid control of Eastern Cilicia, Syria, Phoenicia, and Palestine at the end of the second and beginning of the first century. However, neither example seems to be clear cut.

The question of autonomous city-eras is central to both cases. In Pamphylia the detachment of the province from the Ptolemaic empire seems to have been marked by the beginning of new city-eras at the cities of Perge, Sillyon, Phaselis, Aspendus, Termessus, and Magydus. It should be noted at the outset, though, that not all of these eras started in the same year.[11] All six cities began fairly quickly, in the last quarter of the third century BC, to issue posthumous Alexander coinage marked with the date in their respective eras (see, for example, Pl. 4.1.3–4, issues of Phaselis and Aspendus dated to year 11 (IA) of their respective city-eras). At first glance this looks like a clear case of a burst of coinage as the result of a grant of autonomy, but matters are not quite that

simple. C. Heipp-Tamer's recent corpus of the coinage of one of these cities, Phaselis, makes it quite clear that the city had minted for an extended period in the third century (Pl. 4.1.5), which means certainly under any period of Ptolemaic domination.[12] We are faced with two choices: if we accept the proposition that the Ptolemies did not allow their subject cities to issue coin, then we must accept that Phaselis was not Ptolemaic prior to the creation of her era and the minting of the dated Alexanders, and that consequently these coins can offer no evidence for a burst of coinage upon the grant of autonomy after all. On the other hand, if we accept that the era is an era of freedom, then we must also accept that Phaselis was able to mint coin before she achieved this freedom from the Ptolemies. On this reconstruction too, the Alexanders and their eras can tell us nothing about the ability or lack of it of the Pamphylian cities to mint under the Ptolemies. In fact, when we turn to two of the other cities, Perge and Aspendos, we note that they too had third-century civic coinages prior to the beginning of their eras (Pl. 4.1.6 Perge, and 4.1.7 Aspendos). Since the study of these coinages by Henri Seyrig in 1963, the standard dates assigned to them are c.255–241 BC.[13] There is no hoard evidence to support such a precise dating as this. Rather, Seyrig assumed (according to the *lex Seyrig*) that they belonged not to a period of Ptolemaic control, when local issues would naturally have been suppressed, but must instead have been issued in a period of autonomy that occurred between the Ptolemaic loss of Pamphylia in the course of the second Syrian War, c.255 BC, and its reacquisition during the third Syrian War, c.241 BC. If, with Martin, we reject the *lex Seyrig* with its a priori assumption of the impossibility of civic issues under a monarchy, then we no longer have a firm date for these coins,[14] nor necessarily any evidence for a burst

---

[11] For discussion of the numismatic evidence for the dates of the eras, and bibliography, see Price (1991) 347–8.

[12] Heipp-Tamer (1993). Series 8, dated by her to c.mid third century to c.221 BC, used thirty-five obverse dies (the same number of dies for the dated Alexander series spanned a continuous period of twenty-three years). There are no hoards containing these coins which confirm their date, and Heipp-Tamer relies in part for her dates on the *lex Seyrig* (pp. 60–5). However, their weight standard (Persian) and the appearance of jugate 'Ptolemaic' busts as symbols on one issue strongly suggest a date no later than the third century BC. For the use of the Persic standard elsewhere in the third century, at Selge and Aspendos in Pamphylia, see Mørkholm (1991) 159–60.

[13] Seyrig (1963) 43–6.

[14] The fabric of some of these issues of Perge does bare a resemblance to the third-century issues of Aspendos, Selge, and Phaselis, however, perhaps suggesting rough contemporaneity. (See Seyrig (1963) 43–4 and Heipp-Tamer (1993) 64.)

of coinage after the withdrawal of Ptolemaic control in the 220s.

The question of eras and prior mint histories aside, the nature of these coinages—posthumous issues with the types and in the name of Alexander the Great—must suggest a fundamentally economic reason behind their production. Their appearance is governed not by the desire to give expression to civic autonomy, but by the need to create a currency that will be acceptable on a broad basis. Indeed it is remarkable how many cases there are of the removal of royal or other forms of control leading to the establishment of what we might term 'fashion' coinages. Thanks to the work of Martin Price the phenomenon of the late posthumous Alexander is now clearly traceable: 'With their civic symbols they clearly represent an autonomous form of coinage, and the preference for Alexander types rather than purely autonomous designs may have resulted from the need to produce issues that were recognised to be good money and of neutral political implication.'[15] The list of cities minting Alexanders around the late third and early second century is given by Price ((1991) 76–9) as Samothrace, Ambracia, Carystus, Corinth, Sicyon, Argos, Hermione, Pellene, Megalopolis, Messene, Cabyle, Dionysopolis, Istrus, Mesembria, Odessus, Tomi, Sinope, Heraclea, Alexandria Troas, Pergamum, Assos, Kyme, Myrina, Temnos, Methymna, Mytilene, Clazomenae, Colophon, Erythrae, Magnesia, Miletus, Phocaea, Priene, Smyrna, Teos, Chios, Samos, Alabanda, Antioch on the Maeander, Cnidus, Euromos, Halicarnassus, Mylasa, Cos, Nisyros, Rhodes, Sardis, Phaselis, Aspendus, Perge, Side, Sagalassus, Sillyum, Termessus, Laodicea in Syria, Aradus, Carne, Gabala, and Marathus.

Alexanders were not, however, the only template available. For example, various mints in Greece and Asia Minor began in the first half of the second century to mint coins of Attic weight with the reverse type encircled by a wreath. Such *stephanephoroi* were produced at Athens, Chalcis, Eretria, Syros, Cyzicus, Abydus, Tenedos, Mytilene, Myrina, Aegae, Kyme, Smyrna, Lebedus, Colophon, Magnesia, Heraclea Latmos, and Myndos (Pl. 4.2.8 Athens, 4.2.9 Chalcis, 4.2.10 Cyzicus, and 4.2.11 Heraclea). Mørkholm, seeking to understand these coinages, has rightly

rejected earlier explanations in terms either of Roman intervention or *Münzunion*.[16] His own explanation, that the wreath originates in Epirot and Macedonian royal coinage of the late third century, whence it was transferred to Athens and the rest of the mints in the early second century, must be closer to the truth. In function, the similarity, or fashionability, of the wreaths on these coins must surely be identical to the function of the uniformity of Alexander issues: the creation of a recognizable, widely acceptable currency by individual states.

We should note, though, that 'widely acceptable' need not mean politically neutral. Another example from Lycia illustrates the point well. Here we find the following sequence of events in the second century. The Rhodians received Lycia as a province from the Romans in 188/7 BC. Rhodian control was, we know from literary sources, deeply unpopular.[17] Upon the end of Rhodian control in 167/6 BC the Lycians began to mint their own coinage. Again, a simple sequence of events. But how to interpret it? On the one hand we may opt for a political explanation for the beginning of this coinage: the removal of Rhodian control made it possible for the Lycians to issue coinage. On the other hand we might opt for the economic explanation: removal of Rhodian control had slowed the flow of Rhodian coinage into the region. To make up the shortfall, the Lycians were forced to begin the issue of their own coinage. Once more a glance at the coinage the Lycians chose to produce makes it clear that, while we might instinctively opt for the former explanation, the latter interpretation is certainly true. The Lycians chose a 'fashion' coinage after the model of their erstwhile masters: deity on the obverse, plinthophoric design on the reverse, as well as minting on the Rhodian standard (Pl. 4.2.12, plinthophoric drachm of the Lycian League, 4.2.13 plinthophoric drachm of Rhodes).[18]

Even coinage of the Hellenistic monarchs could serve as the model for autonomous coinages. In 1976

---

[15] Price (1991) 79.

[16] Mørkholm (1980) 145–58. For explanations in terms of Roman intervention or *Münzunion* see, respectively, Giovannini (1978) and Boehringer (1972) 31–9.
[17] Polyb. 22. 5. 1–10; 25. 4. 1–10 with Walbank (1979) *ad* 24. 15. 13. Cf. Livy 41. 6. 8–12; 41. 25. 8. See in general, Fraser and Bean (1954) 114–17.
[18] On the two coinages see Troxell (1982) and Jenkins (1989). For the commencement of the Lycian League silver coinage after 167 BC see Ashton (1987). The coinage continued to be produced well into the first century BC.

Mørkholm demonstrated that the city of Aradus in Phoenicia interspersed its autonomous issues of Alexanders with a series of imitations of Ptolemaic tetradrachms, minted on the Ptolemaic standard.[19] All dated by the city's era of autonomy, there can be little doubt that the types were chosen on the same basis as Alexander types: acceptability (Pl. 4.3.14, a Ptolemaic coin of the second century BC and 4.3.15 an issue of Aradus, dated to year 90 (170/69 BC)). These pseudo-Ptolemies seem to have circulated in the second century in Phoenicia and Palestine, despite the fact that these regions were now under Seleucid control. Moreover it is clear that the Seleucid kings from Antiochus V (164–161 BC) onwards were complicit in the maintenance not just of the Ptolemaic weight standard in this portion of their realm, but also of recognizably Ptolemaic coin design on Seleucid royal coinage produced for use in this area.[20] The Ptolemaic eagle appeared on Ptolemaic-weight issues of Antiochus V at Ptolemais. From here their production spread under Alexander I Balas to Tyre, Sidon, Berytus (Pl. 4.3.16), Byblos, Ascalon and Tripolis. Such issues continued sporadically until the reign of Antiochus IX (Pl. 4.3.17, mint of Ake Ptolemais).

Turning to the Seleucid empire, we find that its coinage might be copied too. The remarkable case of Ascalon in Palestine comes in the wake of the removal of Seleucid control in 104/3 BC. Down to this final year of Seleucid suzerainty the mint of Ascalon produced silver royal issues in the name of Antiochus VIII. The obverse depicted the head of Antiochus, the reverse a left-facing eagle with a dove in front with the legend ΑΝΤΙΟΧΟΥ ΒΑΣΙΛΕΩΣ ('of King Antiochus') (Pl. 4.3.18). When the city began to issue autonomous coin, dated by its era of freedom (the earliest known is from year 6), it retained the types unchanged: head of Antiochus and eagle with dove. The legend now read ΑΣΚΑΛΩΝΙΤΩΝ ΙΕΡΑΣ ΑΣΥ ΑΥΤΟ ('of the city of Ascalon, using its own laws, holy and inviolable'—Pl. 4.3.19) or just ΑΣΚΑΛΩΝΙΤΩΝ ΙΕΡΑΣ ΑΥΤΟ. Nowhere can be seen more clearly the dynamic behind the sudden appearance of autonomous issues in the wake of imperial control. The entire phenomenon of these 'fashion' coinages, with their emphasis on acceptability, points us

towards the conclusion that these cities were minting now because they needed too, not simply because they were able to. By 85/4 BC Ascalon was placing the portraits of Ptolemaic rulers on her autonomous coinage, a move again inspired, no doubt, by prevailing circulation patterns.[21]

Like that at Ascalon, some of the coinages of this region certainly proclaimed the newly found 'freedom' of their cities. But we must beware of inferring from this that the autonomy and the coinage are causally linked: it does not automatically follow. At Seleuceia Pieria, for example, freedom from Seleucid control was attained in 109/8 BC, and her autonomous tetradrachms with legend ΣΕΛΕΥΚΕΩΝ ΤΗΣ ΙΕΡΑΣ ΚΑΙ ΑΥΤΟΝΟΜΟΥ ('of the city of Seleuceia, holy and using its own laws') and date according to the city's new era of freedom (Pl. 4.3.20) began to be issued in year 4 (105/4). Yet, as Mørkholm has pointed out, the beginning of this coinage coincides not with the beginning of Seleuceia's autonomy, but with the beginning of a seven-year cessation of production at the previously prolific mint of Aradus. The coins of Seleuceia were in fact minted (quite extraordinarily) on the local Aradian weight standard of about 15.3 grams. As Mørkholm notes, the lapse in production at Aradus 'may have induced the Pierians to start their own production in order to fill the void'.[22] Interestingly at Tripolis too the first issues of autonomous coinage with their autonomous legend (ΤΡΙΠΟΛΙΤ-ΩΝ ΤΗΣ ΙΕΡΑΣ ΚΑΙ ΑΥΤΟΝΟΜΟΥ ('of the city of Tripolis, holy and using its own laws')) belong to this period, the third year of the city's era (which began between 105 and 95 BC), and were also minted on the Aradian standard (Pl. 4.3.21).[23]

Yet, having divorced the freedom-proclaiming coinages from their circumstances of issue in one sense, we must not lose sight of the fact of the existence of these coins. Their legends are new in the history of Greek coinage, and if their appearance is not to be explained simply as a reaction to new-found political

[21] The early autonomous issues of Ascalon with Seleucid portraits were first pointed out by Spaer (1984). For the earlier Seleucid issues of the mint and later autonomous issues with Ptolemaic portraits see Baldwin Brett (1950) and (1937).

[22] Mørkholm (1983) (quotation from 99). Likewise Laodiceia, having been granted freedom by Tigranes in 81 BC, appears not to have commenced the issue of autonomous coinage until the fourth year of her freedom (ibid. 100).

[23] On the autonomous tetradrachms of Tripolis and their dates see de Callataÿ (1993) 111–26.

[19] Mørkholm (1975–6).
[20] On this phenomenon see, most recently, Le Rider (1995) 391–404.

freedom, then we must seek an alternative explanation for this innovation. To this point we shall return, but first there is a note of caution to be sounded.

In none of the cases outlined above, it might be argued, is the possibility ruled out that both systems of interpretation—economic and political—might be correct: while these coinages were arguably economic responses to the disappearance of royal coinages, might it not also be the case that they had previously been prohibited from production by the royal rulers? Properly to disprove the political approach's validity in favour of the economic, one would like to find a case of a city that, though undoubtedly subject to a Hellenistic monarchy, continued to mint its autonomous coinage under that monarch, and upon the termination of that monarchy began to imitate the coinage of that monarchy with a 'fashion' coinage, in order to make up a shortfall in a widely acceptable type. This seems a very tall order; but, as it happens, we have just such a case at the mint of Ephesus.

The story of the mint of Ephesus in the second century falls into two halves. Following the reform of the Attalid king Eumenes II (197–158 BC), it became a royal mint for the new cistophoric tetradrachms. At the end of the Attalid dynasty in 134/3 BC it, like other cistophoric mints such as Pergamum, Nysa, Sardis, Tralles, Apameia, Laodikeia, and Synnada, continued to mint these cistophori. At Ephesus we note the important change that the city began to date its cistophori by a new era, starting in its first year (Pl. 4.4.22). As K. Rigsby has shown, this era was not, as had previously been thought, the era of the province of Asia, but rather was the city's era of freedom, beginning in the year 134/3.[24] It is clear then that these new cistophoric issues, in contrast to the royal issues before 134/3, are to be regarded as autonomous civic issues. Thus we apparently have another clear case of a city making up supplies of acceptable royal coinage with civic copies. At the same time, as Kinns has now proved beyond any doubt, the Ephesians were issuing a coinage with their traditional civic types of bee and stag on the Attic standard alongside certainly their royal and possibly even their civic cistophori (Pl. 4.4.23).[25]

Here then is a clear case of a city subject to a monarch issuing apparently civic coin. Ephesian magistrates continued production of coinage unabated: in this respect civic institutions were left intact at Ephesus by the Attalid kings. Such a case is encouraging, in as much as it offers grounds for accepting in one case the economic explanation for the existence of a post-imperial-control coinage. But one swallow does not make a summer. One might argue, for example, that a major city like Ephesus achieved some sort of special status. Considerably more evidence is needed before we can claim this state of affairs to have been true for every city under every king.

Although we have cast doubt on the notion that civic coinage following periods of royal control testifies to the prior existence of royal control, in fact we do not have to look far to find instances of very clear royal interference in coinage produced in the name of cities. One of the most striking cases is presented by the various cities of Pontus, Paphlagonia, and Thrace in the reign of Mithridates VI (c.120–63 BC). Under this monarch a number of these cities issued bronze coins with similar designs but with their individual ethnics.[26] Thus, for example, coins with an obverse design of a right-facing head of Zeus and reverse of a left-facing eagle on a thunderbolt are found minted in the names of Amaseia (Pl. 4.4.24), Amisos, Gazioura, Kabera, Pimolisa (Pl. 4.4.25), Taulara, Sinope, Amastris, Laodikeia, Pharnakeia, and Abonouteichos. Coins with the obverse type of right-facing head of Athena and reverse type of Perseus standing holding the head of Medusa are found in the names of Amisos, Kabera, Komana (Pl. 4.4.26), Amastris, Sinope (Pl. 4.4.27), Chabakta, and Laodikeia. At the Bosporan cities of Panticapaeum, Gorgippia, and Phanagoria this policy of uniformity extended even to 'autonomous' issues in silver as well as bronze (Pl. 4.4.28 and 4.4.29, silver didrachms of Panticapaeum and Phanagoria).[27]

There are salutary warnings here against equating coinage with freedom, given the status of Ephesus within the Attalid kingdom'.

[24] Rigsby (1979).
[25] Kinns (1999) and (1987) 107: 'Head's theory that this was latterly an export currency struck alongside the cistophori appears to be correct.

[26] The basic account remains that of Imhoof-Blumer (1912). For adjustments to dating see Amandry, le Guen-Pollet, Özcan, and Rémy (1991) 63–76.
[27] See Anohin (1986), nos. 198 and 202 (silver and bronze of Panticapaeum), 204 and 208 (silver and bronze of Phanagoria), and 209 and 211 (silver and bronze of Gorgippia); for discussion of the common types of these issues see de Callataÿ (1997) 249–50.

MONEY, FREEDOM, AND EMPIRE IN THE HELLENISTIC WORLD 59

Yet these are not simply examples of cities getting on with their own coinage under an indifferent ruler. The appearance of these uniform types over a broad area, as well as shared monograms and even obverse dies across different mints, strongly suggests a 'top-down' rationale, and the appearance of the Mithridatic 'dynastic type' of Perseus makes it clear where the impetus came from.[28] These issues do seem to provide evidence for the enforcement in the early first century BC of 'a uniform monetary circulation' such as Martin was unable to identify in the classical period. But, as we have noted, these are not royal issues, they were produced in the names of the individual cities alone. Moreover, in the cases of all but three of the cities in Pontus and Paphlagonia, these were the first coins they had ever issued. We cannot talk simply of imposition of royal will or curtailment of sovereignty. Something more subtle is going on. At one level Mithridates clearly did regard uniformity of coin type within his kingdom as desirable, or even necessary. At another, he some-how encouraged cities under his control to issue coin for the first time, and to place their names on it. It mattered to Mithridates that the copper coin of his realm be uniform, but not that it be produced in his name. Martin's thesis is not necessarily compromised, but these are far from straightforward civic issues.

It is worth dwelling here on the question of coin design: Mithridates must have imposed this, and there is clear evidence from precisely this period that cities did value the ability to choose and use their own designs. A famous decree from Sestos of the late second century BC honours a citizen called Menas for his role in the production of the city's coinage.[29] The decree explains:

when the people decided to use its own bronze coinage, so that the city's coin type should be used as a current type and the people should receive the profit resulting from this source of revenue, and appointed men who would safe-guard this position of trust piously and justly, Menas was appointed and, together with his colleague in office, showed suitable care, as a result of which the people, thanks to the justice and assiduity of these men, can use its own coinage.[30]

In his analysis of this text Martin seeks to draw attention away from the question of coin type, insisting instead that 'this inscription plainly shows the overriding importance to the demos in this par-ticular case of making a profit from the introduction of bronze coinage'.[31] In this interpretation he dis-misses not only the first stated reason for the pro-duction of Sestian coinage 'so that the city's coin type should be used as the current type',[32] but also one of the concerns of the demos as to how the task should be carried out: by 'men who would safeguard this position of trust piously'. As Robert has suggested, 'their piety must have manifested itself ... in the care they took over the choice and details of the divine images (Demeter), and of the religious emblems. The term should be noted—and emphasized—for this characteristic which is applied to the state money'.[33] Indeed we might go further and question whether the Sestians' pride in this matter was not a reaction to the way in which civic coin types were beginning to slip out of the sphere of civic control elsewhere in northern Asia Minor. It is also worth emphasizing that we are not talking about showy precious metal coinages at Sestos: the issues in question are bronze and otherwise generally unremarkable (Pl. 4.5.30).[34]

If national types were so important a factor in the decision to issue coin, and the choice of them an important function of the men charged with their production, then the imposition of a coin type from above was in fact a curtailment of the normal pre-rogatives of a sovereign state. We might compare in this respect the earlier example of the so-called municipal bronze coinages of the Seleucid king Antiochus IV (175–164 BC).[35] This group of coinages is distinctive for the appearance on the obverse of a portrait either diademed or diademed and radiate of Antiochus, but the appearance of the minting city's name on the reverse. Issues are known from Antioch,

[28] See de Callataÿ (1997) 248–9.
[29] *GIBM* 1000; *OGIS* 339.
[30] ῾τοῦ τε δήμου προελομέ|νου νομίσματι χαλκίνωι χρῆσθαι ἰδίωι, χάριν τοῦ νομειτεύεσθαι μὲν τὸν τῆς πό|λεως χαρακτῆρα, τὸ δὲ λυσιτελὲς τὸ περιγεινόμενον ἐκ τῆς τοιαύτης προσόδου | λαμβάνειν τὸν δῆμον, καὶ

προχειρισαμένου τοὺς τὴν πίστιν εὐσεβῶς τε καὶ | δικαίως τηρήσοντας, Μηνᾶς αἱρεθεὶς μετὰ τοῦ συναποδειχθέντος τὴν κα|θήκουσαν εἰσηνέγκατο ἐπιμέλειαν, ἐξ ὧν ὁ δῆμος διὰ τὴν τῶν ἀνδρῶν δι|καιοσύνην τε καὶ φιλοτιμίαν χρῆται τῶι ἰδίωι νομίσματι᾿ (ll. 43–9).

[31] Martin (1985) 239.
[32] The translation is that of Austin (1981) no. 215. For the meaning, see Melville Jones (1972) 40 and Robert (1973) 49: 'afin qu'ait cours la marque-type de la cité'.
[33] Robert (1973) 51.
[34] For the identification of these issues see von Fritze (1907).
[35] On this coinage see, in general, Mørkholm (1965) and (1984).

Apameia, Laodiceia and Seleuceia in Syria, Byblus, Laodiceia (Berytus), Sidon, Tyre in Phoenicia, Antiocheia in Ptolemais (Ake) and Tripolis in Palestine, Antiocheia ad Kallirhoen (Edessa), Hierapolis Bambyce, and Antiocheia in Mygdonia (Nisibis) on the route eastwards, and Aegeae, Alexandria ad Issum, Seleuceia ad Pyramum (Mopsus), Hierapolis Castabala, and Antiocheia ad Sarum (Adana) in Cilicia.

Mørkholm, collecting the evidence for these issues, noted that those that were dated all began in the same year 144 SE = 169/8 BC. This fact, combined with the common occurrence of Zeus on the reverses at some mints (a god in whom Antiochus took particular interest and who appeared on the royal issues) strongly suggests that in these municipal issues, as in those of Mithridates' kingdom, we are looking at a top-down phenomenon—originating with the king, not the cities. The situation is not absolutely parallel with that of the cities under Mithridates, however. Some of the Seleucid cities had as their reverse types images which look to have been royally instigated such as the seated or standing Zeus, as, for example, at Antiocheia in Ptolemais (Ake) (Pl. 4.5.31), or the eagle of Zeus at Hierapolis Castabala (Pl. 4.5.32). Others took types that had previously appeared on their autonomous issues—so, for example, Sidon with its galley (Pl. 4.5.33)—while others chose designs of apparently local significance: Europa on her bull at Sidon (Pl. 4.5.34), Poseidon at Berytus (Pl. 4.5.35), the prow of a ship at Tyre (Pl. 4.5.36), Nike at Alexandria ad Issum (Pl. 4.5.37), or a dove at Ascalon (Pl. 4.5.38). Legends too were apparently subject to some flexibility. At Byblos, Berytus, Sidon, and Tyre, parts of the legend were inscribed in Phoenician. At Tyre this inscription read 'of Tyre the Metropolis of the Sidonians' (Pl. 4.5.33); this, as Mørkholm puts it, was 'quite outshone by the pompous inscription on some Sidonian coins "of the Sidonians the Metropolis of Cambe, Hippo, Citium and Tyre"' (Pl. 4.5.36).[36] This aspect of the reverse type was presumably governed by the rivalry between the two Phoenician cities, not by any royal edict.

All in all, this coinage gives the impression of being far less uniform than the Mithridatic bronze. Indeed, on the basis of the rare phenomenon of denomination marks on some of these coins, we can

see, as Mørkholm pointed out, that different cities probably minted on different weight standards.[37] It is thus clear that we are dealing not with a standard royal bronze coinage nominally issued with cities' names, but with something more locally driven, at least at the level of execution.

How then do we fit this phenomenon into the overall question of sovereignty and coinage? Pursuing the line of political interpretation and the *lex Seyrig*, these municipal bronzes might be seen as some form of concession on the part of Antiochus to the cities that minted them: a limited grant of the right to issue bronze coin, with limited freedom to choose a reverse type. Implicit in this explanation is, of course, the assumption that kings did not allow cities in their domains to issue bronze coin. This is an extremely difficult assumption to test, since Hellenistic bronze coinage is exceptionally hard to date. Dates indeed are often assigned to bronze coinage on the basis of the *lex Seyrig*, a law which we have seen to be of questionable validity in the case of silver coinage (but in any case producing a complete circularity of argument for our purposes), or on necessarily subjective stylistic considerations.[38] Much work is still needed on the bronze coinage of the Hellenistic period before answers can be found to general questions. If we require a bronze parallel for the case of Ephesus already discussed, one lies ready at Lebedos in Ionia, which seems quite clearly to have minted bronze for a brief period in the mid third century as a Ptolemaic dependency refounded as Ptolemais.[39] Caunus too may well have minted 'autonomous' bronze during its period of Ptolemaic control.[40]

To return to the municipal issues of Antiochus IV: one fact that is quite certain is that none of the mints in question had minted bronze before the arrival of

---

[36] Mørkholm (1965) 65–6.

[37] Mørkholm (1965) 66. Cf. Le Rider (1994), who, while seeking to view the weight standards of Antiochus' empire as more centrally controlled, admits a troubling disparity between certain contemporary issues (pp. 24 and 26).

[38] For another salutary warning from Kinns (1986), see his redating of Deppert-Lippitz's Miletus period VII bronzes from 39–17 BC (on stylistic grounds) to the third century BC, some 200 years earlier (on the basis of hoard evidence and prosopography).

[39] The coinage was first firmly attributed by Dieudonné (1902), following a suggestion by Waddington. Cf. Kinns (1980) 249–52 accepting Dieudonné's dating of the coins to post 246 BC. For a summary of the evidence regarding the refoundation and the coinage see, now, Cohen (1995) 188–91.

[40] For the evidence see Ashton (1999).

the Seleucids; several in fact had never minted at all. These coinages were a new departure for all concerned. Another point that should be stressed is that none of these were old Greek cities. Some were old Phoenician cities, such as Tyre or Sidon, where the pre-Hellenistic coinage had been issued by the local king. The remainder were Seleucid colonies or refoundations: cities which owed their existence to the Seleucid king. Antiochus' motives in stimulating the production of these municipal issues remain a mystery. Mørkholm suggested he was concerned 'to infuse new vigour into city life' by making 'the cities active partners in the work for the inner regeneration of his kingdom'. He cites an interesting passage of Polybius which is drawn from a source hostile to Antiochus, noting that: 'Antiochus seems to have shocked his contemporaries by assuming various magistracies in his capital Antioch. Even greater was the scandal when he went on to take his duties as a magistrate of the city seriously.'[41] The essential point of Polybius' story is, of course, that the king crossed a boundary that divided city from king. Magistracies were the institutions that cities retained intact under kings: a framework that the king and his satraps were required to preserve.

What makes this passage of Polybius doubly interesting is the associations this behaviour invites for Polybius or his source. The passage deserves quoting:

Antiochus would frequently put off his royal robes, and, assuming a white toga, go round the market place like a candidate, and, taking some by the hand and embracing others, would beg them to vote for him, sometimes for the position of *agoranomos*, sometimes for that of *demarch*. Upon being elected he would sit on the ivory chair, as the Roman custom is, listening to lawsuits tried there, and pronouncing judgement with great pains and display of interest. In consequence, all respectable men were entirely puzzled by him, some looking upon him as a simple man, and others as a madman.[42]

He wears a toga, he has a curule chair, he behaves in an explicitly Roman fashion. In one sense, of course, this comes as no surprise, since Antiochus was famous for his importation of things Roman to the Seleucid kingdom—from triumphs, to gladiatorial shows, to military organization.[43] What is remarkable about this particular passage is that it is the interference in the internal affairs of the city by one who should remain aloof that is here being linked with Roman behaviour. Moreover in the first half of the second century BC such interference is seen as distinctively Roman, not Greek, behaviour.

We return to where we began: the best evidence for the interference of rulers in the coinage sphere of civic affairs of the city comes, as we have seen, from the first century AD, and the period of Roman rule. But when the imperial role in the issue of local coinages achieved its final expression in the 'permission' legends, it was not a sweeping new imposition, but rather the culmination of a process that had begun two and a half centuries before. Conceptually, the municipal bronze issues of Antiochus IV were the precursors of the Roman provincial coinage, with their incongruous mixture of royal portrait and civic design. That it was under Antiochus IV, the infamously Romanizing Hellenistic king, that this concept originated is not, I would submit, coincidental. That all the coinages that boasted in their legends of the issuing cities' autonomy belong to the period after the creation of the first Roman province in the east is also no great surprise.[44] Like the citizens of Sestos, the magistrates of these cities were now using their coin designs and legends in a new way, as an expression of their civic identity at a period when this identity was under threat. The clearest testimony that expectations with regard to coinage had changed in the Seleucid realm and among its neighbours comes in the famous words placed in the mouth of Antiochus VII in the first book of Maccabees: 'and I permitted you your own striking, coinage for your

[41] Mørkholm (1965) 67.

[42] Polyb. 26. 1. 5–7: 'πολλάκις δὲ καὶ τὴν βασιλικὴν ἀποθέμενος ἐσθῆτα τήβενναν ἀναλαβὼν περιῄει κατὰ τὴν ἀγορὰν ἀρχαιρεσιάζων καὶ τοὺς μὲν δεξιούμενος, τοὺς δὲ καὶ περιπτύσσων παρεκάλει φέρειν αὐτῷ τὴν ψῆφον, ποτὲ μὲν ὡς ἀγορανόμος γένηται, ποτὲ δὲ καὶ ὡς δήμαρχος. τυχὼν δὲ τῆς ἀρχῆς καὶ καθίσας ἐπὶ τὸν ἐλεφάντινον δίφρον κατὰ τὸ παρὰ Ῥωμαίοις ἔθος διήκουε τῶν κατὰ τὴν ἀγορὰν γινομένων συναλλαγμάτων καὶ διέκρινε μετὰ πολλῆς σπουδῆς καὶ προθυμίας. ἐξ ὧν εἰς ἀπορίαν ἦγε τῶν ἀνθρώπων τοὺς ἐπιεικεῖς· οἱ μὲν γὰρ ἀφελῆ τινα αὐτὸν εἶναι ὑπελάμβανον, οἱ δὲ μαινόμενον'.

[43] For Antiochus' 'triumph' at Daphne in 166 BC see Polyb. 30. 25–6 with Walbank (1979) ad loc. Cf. Livy 41. 10. 9: 'gladiatorum munus, Romanae consuetudinis, primo maiore cum terrore hominum, insuetorum ad tale spectaculum, quam uoluptate dedit' ('he gave a gladiatorial show in the Roman manner, which proved to be more frightening than enjoyable to a people unaccustomed to such a display'). For the introduction of Roman military methods see Sekunda (1994).

[44] The precise effect of the coming of Rome on Greek coin types and legends is one I hope to take up in a forthcoming book.

own country'.[45] That the coinage referred to cannot be identified is only in part a problem: the crucial fact is that a near contemporary source could imagine the concept of a *grant* of coinage in the second half of the second century BC.

The picture that emerges from the Hellenistic evidence is, at one level, tantalizing. But a pattern, I think, begins to appear. Alexander's successors inherited an approach to coinage which he had himself partly inherited from Persia. Royal mints were set to work producing as much coinage as was necessary to conquer and maintain a kingdom. But wherever Greek cities existed with their own institutions—councils, assemblies, magistrates, and coinage—they were left to their own devices. So it was that the grand old cities such as Miletus and Ephesus continued to issue coin as they saw fit. The period of the second and first centuries BC saw an important change as Rome became increasingly involved in the Greek east. This came first in the mere fact of the rolling back of the great Hellenistic empires. The removal of direct control over an area, as provided for by the Peace of Apamea in 188, for example, led to a reduction of flow in royal coinage into that area. Cities affected by this shortage were, of course, perfectly free to issue coins of their own design, but in many cases chose not to, preferring instead to issue Alexanders or other fashion coinages. But at the same time the arrival of Rome brought more pernicious consequences, in the form of intrusion into civic affairs. With the famous rebuff of Q. Caecilius Metellus by the Achaean strategos Aristaenus in 185 BC (Polyb. 22. 10) we are perhaps at the beginning of this process, and before long two related phenomena start to appear: on the one hand, states who retain their civic coinages making clear their claims to autonomy on those coinages; on the other, states that do not beginning to produce 'municipal' coinages, acknowledging in one way or another the ruler of the kingdom in which they lie. By the middle of the first century AD, with Greek states placing the emperor's portraits on their civic issues, just as the cities of Antiochus IV had had on theirs, and some of them explicitly seeking the emperor's approval for their issues, we are at the end. We have arrived in a world where the great and the good of the cities of the Greek east sought the emperor's permission or indulgence for everything from the erection of a public building to the issue of bronze coins.

As John Davies has reminded us in his demonstration of the inapplicability of the term 'sovereignty' to the ancient Greek world, 'applying alien concepts and interpretations unconsciously and unquestioningly' leads to a dead end.[46] This conclusion is no less true for coinage, one of the elements that modern scholars have attempted to employ as an index of sovereignty in the ancient Greek world. In the negotiations that took place between ruler and subject in the Hellenistic world, the role of coinage does not always conform to our own expectations. Moreover, in any attempt to assign coinage a political significance within the framework of an empire we must be aware that this significance changed over time. Once these two simple, but long-overlooked, facts have been absorbed we may begin to see where our own, and Jean Bodin's, preconceptions were formed: not in Greece, but at Rome.

REFERENCES

AMANDRY, M., B. LE GUEN-POLLET, B. ÖZCAN, and B. RÉMY (1991). 'Le trésor de Binbasioğlu (Tokat, Turquie)—monnaies de bronze des villes du Pont frapées sous Mithridate VI Eupator', in B. Rémy (ed.), *Pontica, i. Recherches sur l'histoire du pont dans l'antiquité* (Saint-Étienne/Istanbul/Savoie), 63–76.

ANOHIN, V. A. (1986). *Coinage of the Bosporus* (Moscow).

ASHTON, R. H. J. (1987). 'Pseudo-Rhodian Drachms and the Beginning of the Lycian League Coinage', *NC* 147: 8–25.

—— (1999). 'The Hellenistic Hemidrachms of Caunus', *RBN* 145 (Hackens Memorial Volume): 141–54.

AUSTIN, M. M. (1981). *The Hellenistic World from Alexander to the Roman Conquest* (Cambridge).

BALDWIN BRETT, A. (1937). 'A New Cleopatra Tetradrachm of Ascalon', *AJA* 41: 452–63.

—— (1950). 'The Mint of Ascalon under the Seleucids', *ANSMN* 4: 43–54.

BOEHRINGER, C. (1972). *Zur Chronologie mittelhellenistischer Münzserien* (Berlin).

COHEN, G. M. (1995). *The Hellenistic Settlements in Europe, the Islands, and Asia Minor* (Berkeley and Los Angeles, Calif., and London).

---

[45] 'καὶ ἐπέτρεψά σοι ποιῆσαι κόμμα ἴδιον, νόμισμα τῇ χώρᾳ σου' (*I Maccabees* 15. 6, Antiochus to Simon Maccabeus).

[46] Davies (1994) 56.

DAVIES, J. K. (1994). 'On the Non-usability of the Concept of "Sovereignty" in an Ancient Greek Context', in L. Aigner Foresti et al. (eds.), Federazioni e federalismo nell'Europa antica I: alle radici della casa comune Europea (Milan), 51–65.

DE CALLATAŸ, F. (1993). 'Les Tétradrachmes hellénistiques de Tripolis', QT 22: 111–26.

—— (1997). L'Histoire des guerres mithridatiques vue par les monnaies (Louvain).

DEPPERT-LIPPITZ, B. (1984). Die Münzprägung Milets vom vierten bis ersten Jahrhundert v. Chr. Typos V (Aarau/Frankfurt am Main/Salzburg).

DIEUDONNÉ, A. (1902). 'Ptolemais–Lebedus', JIAN 5: 45–60.

FINLEY, M. I. (1975). The Ancient Economy (London).

FRASER, P. M. and G. E. BEAN (1954). The Rhodian Peraea and Islands (Oxford).

FRITZE, H. VON (1907). 'Sestos, die Menas-Inschrift und das Münzwesen der Stadt', Nomisma 1: 1–13.

GIOVANNINI, A. (1978). Rome et la circulation monétaire en Grèce au 2e. siècle av. J.C. (Basel).

HEIPP-TAMER, C. (1993). Die Münzprägung der Lykischen Stadt Phaselis in Griechischer Zeit (Saarbrücken).

HOWGEGO, C. J. (1995). Ancient History from Coins (London).

IMHOOF-BLUMER, F. (1912). 'Die Kupferprägung des mithridatischen Reiches und andere Münzen des Pontos und Paphlagoniens', NZ, NS, 5: 169–92.

JACOB, B. (1993). 'Die Stellung Lykiens innerhalb der Achämenidisch–Persischen Reichsverwaltung', in Akten des II. Internationalen Lykien Symposiums (Vienna), 63–9.

JENKINS, G. K. (1989). 'Rhodian Plinthophoroi: A Sketch', in G. le Rider et al. (eds.), Kraay–Mørkholm Essays: Numismatic Studies in Memory of C. M. Kraay and O. Mørkholm (Louvain), 101–19.

KINNS, P. (1980). 'Studies in the Coinage of Ionia: Erythrae, Teos, Lebedus and Colophon' (Univ. of Cambridge Ph.D. thesis).

—— (1986). 'The coinage of Miletus', NC 146: 233–60.

—— (1987). 'Asia Minor', in A. M. Burnett and M. H. Crawford (eds.), The Coinage of the Roman World in the Late Republic, BAR Int. Ser. 326 (Oxford), 105–19.

—— (1999). 'The Attic Weight Drachms of Ephesus: A Preliminary Study in the Light of Recent Hoards', NC 159: 47–97.

KLEINER, F. S. and S. P. NOE (1977). The Early Cistophoric Coinage (New York).

LE RIDER, G. (1994). 'Antiochos IV (175–164) et le monnayage de bronze Séleucide', BCH 118: 17–34.

—— (1995). 'La politique monétaire des Séleucides en Coele Syrie et en Phénicie aprés 200', BCH 119: 391–404.

LEVY, B. E. (1987). 'Indulgentiae Augusti Moneta Inpetrata', in H. Huvelin et al. (eds.), Mélanges de numismatique offerts à Pierre Bastien (Wetteren), 39–49.

MARTIN, T. R. (1985). Sovereignty and Coinage in Classical Greece (Princeton, NJ).

—— (1996). 'Why Did the Greek Polis Originally Need Coins?', Historia, 45: 261–83.

MELVILLE JONES, J. R. (1972). 'Epigraphical Notes on Hellenistic Bronze Coinage', NC[7] 12: 39–43.

MØRKHOLM, O. (1965). 'The Municipal Coinages with Portrait of Antiochus IV of Syria', in Congresso Internazionale di Numismatica, Roma 11–16 Settembre, ii., Atti (Rome), 63–7.

—— (1969). 'Some Seleucid Coins from the Mint of Sardis', NNÅ, 5–20.

—— (1975–6). 'The Ptolemaic "Coins of an Uncertain Era"', NNÅ, 23–58.

—— (1979). Review of Simonetta (1977), NC[7] 19: 242–6.

—— (1980). 'Chronology and Meaning of the Wreathed Coinages of the Early Second Century B.C.', QT 9: 145–58.

—— (1981). 'Sculpture and Coins: The Portrait of Alexander Balas of Syria', QT 10: 235–45.

—— (1983). 'The Autonomous Tetradrachms of Laodicea ad Mare', ANSMN 28: 89–107.

—— (1984). 'The Monetary System in the Seleucid Empire after 187 B.C.', in W. Heckel and R. D. Sullivan (eds.), Ancient Coins of the Graeco-Roman World: The Nickle Numismatic Papers (Waterloo, Ont.), 93–113.

—— (1991). Early Hellenistic Coinage from the Accession of Alexander to the Peace of Apamea (Cambridge).

PRICE, M. J. (1991). The Coinage in the Name of Alexander the Great and Philip Arrhidaeus: A British Museum Catalogue (Zurich/London).

RIGSBY, K. J. (1979). 'The Era of the Province of Asia', Phoenix 33: 39–47.

ROBERT, L. (1960). 'ΑΙΤΗΣΑΜΕΝΟΣ sur les monnaies', Hellenica, 11–12: 53–62.

—— (1973). 'Les Monétaires et un décret Hellénistique de Sestos', RN[6] 15: 43–53.

SEKUNDA, N. (1994). Seleucid and Ptolemaic Reformed Armies 168–145 B.C., i. The Seleucid Army (Stockport).

SEYRIG, H. (1963). 'Monnaies hellénistiques', RN[6] 5: 7–64.

SIMONETTA, B. (1977). The Coins of the Cappadocian Kings (Fribourg).

SPAER, A. (1984). 'Ascalon: From Royal Mint to Autonomy', in A. Houghton et al. (eds.), Studies in Honour of Leo Mildenberg (Wetteren), 229–39.

TROXELL, H. A. (1982). The Coinage of the Lycian League (New York).

WALBANK, F. W. (1979). A Historical Commentary on Polybius III (Oxford).

WEISS, P. (1992). 'Zu Münzprägung mit den Formeln ΑΙΤΗΣΑΜΕΝΟΥ und ΕΙΣΑΝΓΕΙΛΑΝΤΟΣ' in Studien zum antiken Kleinasien, ii (Bonn), 167–80.

WESTERMARK, U. (1960). Das Bildnis des Philetairos von Pergamon. Corpus der Münzprägung (Stockholm).

5

THE POLITICS OF MONETIZATION IN THIRD-CENTURY BC EGYPT

Sitta von Reden

THE INTRODUCTION OF A REGULAR COINAGE in Egypt after the Greco-Macedonian conquest in 332 BC has been considered mainly in the context of Ptolemaic imperial policy. More precisely, it has been a matter of debate only in respect of Ptolemaic policy in relation to their provinces outside Egypt. While the older research emphasized an unequivocal enforcement of the regal coinage upon all Ptolemaic subjects inside and outside Egypt, recent scholars have argued for a more differentiated picture.[1] Bagnall saw a pattern according to which an inner circle of Ptolemaic possessions (Cyrene, Cyprus, and Coile Syria) adopted royal mints, while a less homogeneous group of farther provinces were more flexible in their choice of mints and weight standards (Asia Minor, Greece, and the Aegean). Moreover, within the Ptolemaic monetary zone foreign coinages were prohibited by royal decree.[2] Outside the monetary zone circulation of foreign coins did not cease, and minting of Ptolemaic coinage, though not altogether absent, was based on preference and economic requirement, and was not exclusive.[3]

The conditions of the introduction of coinage into Egypt itself, by contrast, have never been discussed in any detail. Yet, especially against the background of a new consensus about the nature of Ptolemaic kingship emerging, the introduction and acceptance of coinage can no longer be regarded as a simple act of enforcement. While the focus has shifted away from Ptolemaic rule as above all a tributary system based on, and motivated by, military force, scholars have looked more carefully at legitimizing strategies of the kings, such as public ritual and royal self-representation.[4] Questions, moreover, about the addressees of such strategies have taken centre stage.[5] Changing perspectives on these issues cannot leave questions about the introduction of coinage unaffected.

Coinage and monetization are closely linked to state building, state power, and the representation of it to the citizens or subjects.[6] Although, according to common-sense assumptions, monetization rests on

---

[1] The older view is exemplified by Rostoftzeff (1953) 401. Préaux (1936) 267 ff. leaves the question open, but, in stating (p. 269) that the 'main Ptolemaic mints' were in Cyrene, Alexandria, and Cyprus, she seems to suggest that different Ptolemaic possessions were not treated differently.

[2] However, Ptolemaic coins from different mints within the zone travelled freely across their internal boundaries; Bagnall (1976) 176–212.

[3] For new hoard evidence since Bagnall (1976) see Le Rider (1991), Lorber (1995/6), Cadell and Le Rider (1997), and Meadows (unpublished).

This evidence, which perhaps suggests that Ptolemaic coinage circulated more widely within Ptolemaic provinces beyond the 'core areas', does not render Bagnall's general hypothesis invalid. It might suggest, however, that minting and circulation of Ptolemaic coins was not just a matter of imperial policy, but also of economic requirement. For the latter see Le Rider (1991) in the case of Ephesus, Howgego (1995) in respect of circulation, Meadows, above ch. 4, in respect of minting.

[4] The literature on Hellenistic kingship in general and Ptolemaic monarchy in particular is immense. See overviews by Walbank (1984) and Gehrke (1995) 165–8.

[5] Again the bibliography is extensive; for the most comprehensive account see Koenen (1993), with ample literature.

[6] Classically formulated by, for example, Weber (1978) i. 196–7, ii. 963–4; Simmel (1990) 185–7, 395–7; Polanyi (1957) 201–5, 214–15.

a simple act of state initiative and the convenience of money in exchange, thoroughgoing monetization of economic activity issues only from an aggressive insistence of the State.[7] This might be realized by an insistence on payments of monetary taxes. The issuing authority, however, must also propagate and implement its own commitment to money in order to promote its acceptance.[8] In the State's control over the fiscal organs and its symbolic identification with a standardized medium of exchange lies a significant potential to integrate a country. Monetization can then be seen as a strategy of political integration and state formation.[9]

In this Chapter I wish to argue that the dynamics of monetization in the first generations of Ptolemaic Egypt rested not only on the enforcement of monetization through taxation, and a prior Greek familiarity with coinage, but also on the importance of coinage in the Ptolemaic imagery of power coupled with the kings' commitment to monetary exchange.[10] The State's commitment to monetary exchange is all the more significant as precious metal resources were scarce, and conditions for non-monetary exchange favourable. Egypt after all had been capable of sustaining a complex, though in many ways decentralized, economy before the arrival of the Greeks, and the Persians, who adopted a notably different strategy of exploitation, had not introduced coinage in the thoroughgoing manner of the Ptolemies.[11] In the first part I shall look at the place of coinage in the imagery of power of Ptolemy II Philadelphus, whose reign is probably to be associated with a rapid

increase of monetary circulation.[12] In the second part I shall discuss some of the papyrological material of the same period which suggests a high degree of monetization of the public economy despite a notable scarcity of coinage in circulation.[13] This seems to me to show a demonstrable commitment of the Ptolemies to a monetary economy under not altogether favourable conditions. In a final section I shall attempt to contrast aspects of the Ptolemaic monetary economy with classical Athens, which might throw into sharper relief the particular social and political dynamics of monetization in Ptolemaic Egypt.

Coinage and the Imagery of Power

In 279/8 BC Ptolemy II Philadelphus inaugurated a dynastic festival in honour of his parents Ptolemy I Soter and Berenike.[14] The festival was held in Alexandria every four years but this first one was so magnificent that still, generations later, Kallixenos of Rhodes described the details of the occasion.[15] Kallixenos' account of the procession is preserved in the *Deipnosophistai* of Athenaios as an illustration

---

have discussed the Pharaonic economy in relation to the Ptolemaic one in von Reden (1996), with further bibliography. For issues of the Persian kings in Egypt, see, most recently, Price (1993).

[12] Lorber (1995/6) argues that the variations of the average weights of coin issues in the Meydancıkkale hoard (deposited, according to its editor, in c.240–235 BC on a Ptolemaic site in Anatolia) are indicators of relative time in, or intensity of, circulation. The *sigma* series which Lorber dates (in slight variation to the original editor) to c.277–268, and of which there are by far the most specimens in the hoard, have also the lowest average weight. For the original publication of the hoard see Davesne (1994). The introduction of a new bronze coinage, the extension of production of silver to mints in Phoenicia, as well as the reform of the gold coinage, also fall in the reign of Ptolemy II.

[13] I can offer at this stage only a sketch of what will be the argument of a more systematic study that I am preparing on the monetization of third-century BC Egypt.

[14] I am following here the date suggested by Rice (1983) 182 (on the basis of the Athenian decree in honour of Kallias of Sphettos; *Hesp.* suppl. 17 (1978) 33 ff.). The date has most recently been confirmed by Thompson (forthcoming, with full bibliography on the *pompe*). Otto (1905) 153 suggested 275/4 (in preparation for the First Syrian War), while Dunand (1981) 13, Gehrke (1982) 260, and Heinen, in *CAH*[2] vii.1 (1984, 417), propose 271/0 (celebrating the end of the Syrian War).

[15] Based, as he claims, on the *graphai* ('festival accounts') of the Penteterides; see Ath. 5. 197d and Thompson (forthcoming) n. 7. Rice (1983, 172) suggests that these were the *basilikai anagraphai* drawn up by Philadelphus at the end of his reign (App. *Proem.* 10). The use of any other literary sources or visual documents is likely (given the Alexandrian collection), but purely speculative. For the date of Kallixenos' writing see Thompson (forthcoming) n. 8 ('some 100 years after the event'), and Rice (1983) 164–71 (third century BC, but no eyewitness).

---

[7] Woodruff (unpublished), Elwert (1987), and Coronil (1997). For a criticism of the spontaneous acceptance of monetary exchange see Anderlini and Sabourian (1992).

[8] Woodruff (unpublished).

[9] The interdependence of monetization and political integration is well recognized in history and anthropology. The modern debate on monetary union is also instructive in this context; see, for example, Holtfrerich (1989), Hammond (1957), and Woodruff (unpublished).

[10] The argument is notably different from the (by now rather obsolete) controversy on the political vs. economic significance of coinage. While Finley (1985) 166–8 argued that coinage was above all a political emblem, a symbol of civic pride and autonomy, Martin (1985) argued that the question of whether states adopted, or ceased having, a coinage was a question of economic requirement (cf. 225–6 on the closed currency system of Ptolemaic Egypt). I am arguing here for a consideration of the political strategies necessary to enforce coinage, and the political effects it had, regardless of whether monetization was of political or economic importance to the Ptolemies.

[11] For the complexities of the Pharaonic economy see, above all, Kemp (1989) 232 ff., but also Janssen (1975) 102 ff., (1981); Maucourant (1990). I

of the outstanding wealth of Ptolemy II. Modern scholars have discussed the religious and political significance of the procession; but the particular meaning attached to coinage in this procession has not been much commented on.[16] The procession began with the rise of the Morning Star, an allegorization of both Amun Re and Helios. It was followed by a Dionysiac procession, the main part of the show, and culminated in the display of objects for dedication, a military parade, a crowning ceremony, and dedications to the royal dynasty. In the ritual demonstration of objects for dedication, Kallixenos writes:

there were also many thrones constructed of ivory and gold; on one of these lay a gold diadem, on another a gilded horn, on still another a gold crown, and on another a horn of solid gold. Upon the throne of Ptolemy Soter lay a crown made of [kateskeuasmenos ek] ten thousand chrusoi [gold coins] (Athen. V. 202ab)

What is given here as an example of outstanding truphê (luxury) is in anthropological terms a typical case of conspicuous consumption: the ritual destruction of wealth and of the paraphernalia of power. The throne of Ptolemy I adorned with the crown made of coinage attached to the ritual a particular political message. Ptolemy Soter had from 321 BC onwards gradually transformed his position of Greek governor to that of King of Egypt. Within the same process Egypt was established as an independent kingdom. The coinage of Ptolemy Soter is source for and symbolic of this policy.[17] In 321/0 he changed the obverse of the so-called Alexander coinage (which so far had been minted in all parts of the Hellenistic world and in many places continued to be struck until well into the second century) from the Herakles type to that of the deified Alexander with elephant's scalp, ram's horn, and royal diadem. This change was arguably connected with Ptolemy's appropriation of Alexander's corpse and its burial in Memphis. As possessor of the human relics of Alexander, Ptolemy could now establish a state cult

of the dead conqueror which enhanced his prestige among the Greeks within and outside Egypt.[18] It was also connected with the confirmation of Ptolemy as governor of Egypt and the victory over his rivals in the same year.

The next significant change was implemented in 315/14 BC when not only was the seated Zeus replaced by a standing Athena but also the personal badge of Ptolemy, an eagle standing on a thunderbolt, was added to the image of the reverse. An early issue of the new series also for the first time bore the name of Ptolemy (Ptolemaiou). Then, in c.310 BC, the weight of the silver tetradrachm was reduced from the Attic standard of about 17.25 g. to about 15.7 g., an apparently idiosyncratic standard, which can be interpreted as neither Phoenician nor Rhodian. After 305/4, when Ptolemy had assumed the title of King of Egypt, the silver tetradrachm of the reduced standard was accompanied by a new gold coinage, also deviating from the Attic standard by about 17 per cent. The obverse of this coinage shows the portrait of Ptolemy wearing the royal diadem and carrying the aegis. The reverse still represents Alexander standing in a quadriga of elephants and holding the thunderbolt, probably emphasizing Ptolemy's dynastic connection with the divinized conqueror. Also on the reverse, the coinage for the first time showed the inscription Ptolemaiou Basileos ([coinage] 'of Ptolemy the King'). The final changes in the coinage of Ptolemy I were introduced just after 300 BC. The same types were now used for all denominations in gold and silver, showing a head of Ptolemy I on the obverse and the eagle standing on the thunderbolt as well as the inscription Ptolemaiou Basileos on the reverse. The silver tetradrachm was reduced to, first, 14.9 g. and, finally, 14.25 g., where it stayed with remarkable stability for the next 200 years.

It is usually argued that the Ptolemies propagated their rule with coinage,[19] but the ritual display of the most splendid coins in a dynastic festival also associated kingship, power, and the prosperity of the new kingdom with coined money. This was the ideology also subtly expressed in Theocritus' Encomium to Ptolemy Philadelphus, which is worth considering for a

---

[16] Rice (1983) 117–18, translating chrusoi as 'gold pieces', underrates, in one case, their significance, and, in another, relates them to the costs of the procession (p. 132). Thompson (forthcoming) gives greater prominence to the passages, but takes them as references to the financing of the procession.

[17] Although certain elements of the chronology of Ptolemaic coinage are debatable, the outlines are generally agreed upon. I am following here the account of Mørkholm (1991) 63–7.

[18] Mørkholm (1991) 63.

[19] For an interesting analysis of Hellenistic royal iconography on coinage and its political and cultic significance see, now, Fleischer (1996).

moment:

In wealth he could outweigh all the kings, so great are the riches that come daily from everywhere to his opulent home; men till the soil in peace. No enemy by land has crossed the teeming Nile to raise the battle cry in villages that do not belong to him, nor has he leaped in arms on to the shore from a swift ship with hostile intent to seize the herds of Egypt. So great is the man who reigns over the broad plains, fair-haired Ptolemy, skilled spearman, who as a good king cares deeply for the preservation of his fatherly inheritance, and adds to it himself. And yet in his wealthy house the gold does not lie useless in piles like the wealth of the ever-toiling ants. Much of it is received by the glorious homes of the gods, where he always offers first fruits together with other offerings, and many are the gifts he has made to mighty kings, many to cities, and many to his trusted friends. Nor has any man come to the sacred competitions of Dionysus, skilled in raising a harmonious song, to whom he has not granted a gift worthy of his art. And so the spokesmen of the Muses celebrate Ptolemy in return for his benefactions. For a man blessed with wealth what more beautiful goal could there be than to win a good reputation among men (Theocr. *Idyll* 17, ll. 36 ff.)

Although money is not mentioned in the poem at all, it lurks everywhere beneath the surface of the traditional language of praise. Read against the background of Philadelphus' Egypt, this passage becomes a parody of the agrarian language traditionally employed in the pastoral genre.[20] 'The riches that come daily from everywhere' to Egypt came—in striking contrast to imperial Athens, where this phrase was coined[21]—in the form of foreign specie. Egypt was an exporting country, above all of grain and papyrus, and what it deliberately imported was foreign coinage, silver and gold.[22] The gold, moreover, that was 'received by the glorious homes of the gods' does not refer unequivocally to dedications to Greek temples, but more straightforwardly to the monetary payments to Egyptian temples and the priesthood on which the internal peace of Egypt rested.[23] And the 'gifts to trusted friends' does not conjure up unspecified munificence, but the reciprocity of the relationships. Hellenistic monarchies could not have functioned without their friends and allied cities; they provided the rulers with officers,

governors, administrators, and ambassadors. The loyalty of these friends was maintained by the benefactions of the king, which most commonly were paid in money.[24] The strength of the encomium lies in that it evokes what it barely conceals: that the power of the king which granted peace and continuity, and which was based on friendship and generosity, was dependent on money.

The link between Ptolemaic imperial power and money occurs forcefully in Kallixenos' account of the procession as well. In the procession of Dionysos a long train of animals was shown, symbolizing Dionysos' (and by inference Alexander's) Indian exploits. Spices were carried in this procession, evoking their association with the East. Ethiopian tribute-bearers, moreover, came along, 'some of whom brought six hundred tusks, others two thousand ebony logs, others sixty craters of gold and silver coins and gold dust' (v. 201a). The imagery was broad and allusive; as Rice comments, the Ptolemies derived glory from the comparison with Dionysos and Alexander, and shared the glory of the Eastern triumphs themselves as their heirs. In this part of the procession, their personal connection with the East is seen in the plethora of spices, luxury goods, and exotic animals, all of which had been obtained through extensive trading connections developed and maintained under royal control. And, although many of the items in the procession came from Ethiopia, the precise geographical origin of the goods was less important than the fact that the Ptolemies could claim credit for their appearance in Alexandria.[25]

The connection of money with internal peace, friendship, and generosity is expressed at the end of the procession. Kallixenos describes the crowning of the athletes, and the dedication of statues to Soter, Berenike, and Philadelphus: 'and the total expense in coin [*nomisma*] amounted to 2,239 talents and 50 minae; and the sum was paid in to the *oikonomoi* before the exhibition was over through the great zeal of those who gave the crowns' (Ath. v. 203b).[26] The demonstrative payment by the benefactors to the *oikonomoi*, and the recording of this detail in the royal archives (from which the figure might have come),

[20] See, in general, Griffiths (1979) 71–82, and, for parody, Goldhill (1991) 246 ff. with further literature.

[21] Thuc. 2. 38. 2; Ps.-Xen. *Ath.Pol.* 2. 9. 7–8; cf. von Reden (1995) 130 ff.

[22] P. Cair. Zen. 59021, the only other resource that was imported was timber; see Préaux (1936) 353 ff; Fraser (1972) i. 136 ff, 148 ff.

[23] Cf. *OGIS* 56, SB 8299, P. Rev. Law col. 24 (on the *apomoira*).

[24] Cf. Gauthier (1985); Herman (1980/1).   [25] Rice (1983) 85–6.

[26] The amount can hardly be related to the cost of the entire *pompe*, but refers, if to be taken seriously at all, to the costs of the crowning ceremony alone; thus Rice (1983) 132, and Thompson (forthcoming).

emphasized again the power of money and the patronage it could buy.[27] Rice rightly suggests that this gesture by those wishing to be seen publicly supporting the royal festival was analogous to the practice of foreign states sending crowns to a host state on the occasion of an important festival.[28] Yet she does not comment on the striking difference, that the benefactors are shown in this passage to have paid money rather than donating a crown. Money was a conspicuous part in the ritualized reciprocities of the dynastic festival.[29]

It is commonly agreed that the Grand Procession targeted the Greek inhabitants of Egypt and visitors from the Greek world. This is certainly suggested by the fact that the procession took place in Alexandria. The Dionysiac procession, moreover, contains a host of allusions to the Ptolemaic claim to Panhellenic hegemony which concerned above all a Greek audience.[30] Theocritus' encomium, too, was addressed to an exclusive audience of Greeks. Nonetheless, it would be misleading to assume that the propaganda of the *pompê* bypassed the indigenous population altogether. As Walbank notes, even if Egyptian mythological themes were given no emphasis in the event, the procession contained images to which Egyptians could easily attach their own cultural interpretations.[31] The procession was led through the stadium of Alexandria and then proceeded through the city, where it could be viewed by everybody.[32] Especially in the passage quoted above (202b) polyvalent imagery abounds. Thrones, to begin with, are not a traditional Greek symbol of kingship. They made to the Greek audience allusions to the deification of Alexander and the dynastic

principle. But the throne was also the most important pharaonic image of divine kingship. The formula 'I give you the throne' expressed the father–son relationship between god and king. In the iconography of Egyptian temples every king was a son of Amun, a young Horus, or in Greek terminology a son of Zeus, a Dionysus.[33] Thrones gave the Dionysiac procession significance for both the Greek and an Egyptian audience. The cornucopias (horns), moreover, were also ambivalent. They were Egyptian symbols of fertility connected with Isis and the Nile, and had connections with Dionysos. If the gilded horn on the first throne was a *dikeras*, as one codex has it, it would be the symbol of Isis, and possibly of the deified queen Berenike in her image.[34] If it was a *keras* it could be identified with the single horn with which Alexander appears on the tetradrachms of Soter and which represented him within the Egyptian imagery as son of Amun Re.[35] The reference to *stephanai*, finally, can also be interpreted in different ways. *Stephanê* was the Greek word for both the Greek diadem and the oriental crown.[36] If it referred to the diadem it could, like the *dikeras*, symbolize the deified Berenike or Isis. If it was a crown (which, arguably, is likely if it was adorned with such a large number of gold coins) it might refer to the Egyptian double crown with which the Ptolemies depicted themselves on Greek-sponsored Egyptian temples at least from the time of Euergetes onwards.[37] Throne and horns, and possibly the combination of Greek and Egyptian crowns, conveyed a complex ideology of power to which both Greeks and Egyptians could relate. It might not be irrelevant in this context that on coins

---

[27] It is interesting that the payments were made, according to Kallixenos, to the *oikonomoi*, who are generally considered to have been the treasurers of the nomes (administrative subdivisions of Egypt). Although it is impossible to reconstruct the reasons for this, it integrated local concerns into the festivities of Alexandria. Rice (1983) 133 suggests that 'people throughout the *chora* may have made contributions to their local *oikonomos*', while Thompson remarks that 'what the passage seems to say is that to some extent it was the visitors who paid for the show'. She also suggests that the payments for the crowns did not just come from Egypt, but from overseas visitors as well (n. 63).

[28] Rice (1983) 131; cf. SIG[3] 390. 42 ff. for an example of this practice.

[29] On the emphasis on reciprocity in the Grand Procession see esp. Thompson (forthcoming).

[30] Rice (1983) 45 ff.   [31] Walbank (1996) 123; Koenen (1993) *passim*.

[32] Walbank (1996) 122 f.; Rice (1983) 31 *contra* Dunand (1981); see also Athen. 5. 197e. Dunand's interpretation rests on a mistranslation of 5. 197d (ἤγετο γὰρ διὰ τοῦ κατὰ τὴν πόλιν σταδίου), which means the procession was 'led through' the stadium, rather than that it was 'held' there.

[33] Koenen (1993) 45 ff.

[34] It might not be irrelevant that the name Isis signified 'throne', that is, the throne of Horus the king. The glyph for the name is a high throne with female ending; see Thompson (forthcoming) n. 55 with LÄ iii, s.v. 'Isis', cols. 186–203, at 186. There are also coins extant depicting the royal couple as Isis and Sarapis; cf. *Cleopatra's Egypt* (ed. the Brooklyn Museum), cat. no 102.

[35] See for example, Howgego (1995) cat. no 76 (Ptolemy I tetradrachm, 310–305 BC: Head of Alexander/Athena).

[36] *Stephanos* refers in third-century papyri also to monetary crown taxes (eg. P. Teb. 746.24; PSI 4.383.5; P. Cair. Zen. 36.27). It is, however, unlikely that this is meant here, as Dunand (1981) 36 suggests; cf. LSJ s.v. 'stephanos'.

[37] E.g. on the Horus temple of Edfu, begun under Ptolemy III Euergetes, 237 BC. Much of the interpretation depends on the question of whether Ptolemaic kings had themselves crowned before Epiphanes for whom coronation is unambiguously attested. The issue is controversial and evidence inconclusive; cf. Koenen (1993) n. 109 and (1977), arguing for coronations since Alexander; see also, however, Gruen (1985) and Burstein (1991).

themselves ideas were expressed that were under-standable for both parts of the population.[38]

Money and Coinage in the Egyptian *Chora*

In significant contrast to the immense quantity of money displayed at the occasion of the festivals, Egypt suffered from a severe lack of precious metal coinage. There were no silver resources in Egypt itself, and the gold coinage which was minted in pieces of 60 and, subsequently, 100 and 50 silver drachmae value was impractical for taxation and everyday exchange. Already under Soter a bronze coinage was minted which was developed in new denominations in large quantities from the reign of Philadelphus onwards.[39] The bronze coins had a fiduciary value only; that is, 1 bronze drachma was equal to 1 drachma of silver. Many payments, espe-cially those to the State, however, remained payable in silver, which meant that if paid in bronze an agio (*allagê, epallagê*) of c.10 per cent was added (i.e. twenty-five and a half bronze obols to the silver stater of twenty-four obols).[40] Bronze had a far more lim-ited commodity value outside Egypt than silver or gold, and it is not surprising that it is rarely found in hoards outside Egypt and its dominions.[41] As a result, the bulk of money that was accumulated in Egypt tied its owners to the Ptolemaic monarchy.

Lack of money in hand is a recurrent theme in the papyri of the third century. The evidence is fre-quently indirect and has not normally been noted by scholars. Much of our knowledge about the first half of the third century BC in Egypt depends on the Zenon archive, a body of 1,700 documents spann-ing the period c.270–240 BC. Zenon is usually regarded

as a well-off Greek immigrant from Kaunos who, in addition to being the manager of a large gift estate, seems to have engaged in some business of his own.[42] In contrast to earlier assumptions, it is now generally agreed that his business was above all of an agrarian nature: exploitation of cleruchic tenures through hired labour and sub-leases, and the possession of some quantities of goats, sheep, and swine which brought in rent in cash and kind.[43] The management of land and animals was clearly profit and cash orientated, and there is no reason to doubt that Zenon was among the group whom Jean Bingen has called 'entrepreneurs'; that is, Greeks who were successfully engaged in the monetary economy of Ptolemaic Egypt.[44]

His finances were nevertheless precarious: in the years 248/7 he appears to have run into serious financial difficulties, with letters of complaint about outstanding debts, wages, and tax payments abounding.[45] But, even under normal circumstances, and in affairs concerning the gift estate he managed, payments were frequently not made on a cash basis.[46] There are many indications that the amount of cash changing hands was reduced to a minimum. While the degree to which coinage appears in the extant accounts as a standard of value and unit of account gives the impression of a vigorous cash flow, it is questionable whether coinage was in all cases used as a means of exchange. At the end of a letter addressed to Zenon, for example, Iason, an employee on the gift estate writes:

Timokles, one of the veterans, has reported to me that the rest of the veterans in Dinneos Koite owe you for what you have expended on the canal 56 dr. 1 obol. His condi-tion is that if we come to account with them and reach agreement, his own share of the 56 dr. 1 ob., that is, 6 dr. 4 ob., shall be deducted. They have now accounted, and have sent an agreement to pay the amount towards the money taxes of the 36th year. If, on the other hand, we make the payment [of the money taxes], we shall deduct the money from the rent due for the 39th year. (P. Lond. 2008 col. 2, 37–51; 1 May 247)

[38] Cf. the horn of Amun Re on Ptolemy I's Alexander coins, or the sceptre formed with lotus leaves on the gold octadrachms of Arsinoe II (struck after her death); Koenen (1993) 27 f. with Kyrieleis (1975) pl. 70. 1 and 2, and 88. 1–3.

[39] Hazzard (1995) 62 (minting of bronze in large quantities under Philadelphus), Weiser (1995), 20 ff. seems to suggest that the bronze currency was introduced with the establishment of the (reduced) Ptolemaic silver standard.

[40] Maresch (1996) 3 f.; cf. P. Lond. 1934.

[41] Third-century evidence: *IGCH* 183 (1/7), 184 (10/14), 190 (many, all from Peloponnese 246–222 BC; 2029 (6/78), 2242 (2/322, both from Italy/Sicily). H. Mattingly draws my attention to Egyptian bronze frequently recorded as stray finds in mainland Greece and the Aegean Islands.

[42] On Zenon's two types of business see, esp., Orrieux (1985); his attempt to separate Zenon's private correspondence from that which concerned the *doreia* remains, however, inconclusive.

[43] Orrieux (1985); Clarysse and Vandorpe (1995).

[44] Bingen (1978); Orrieux (1985) 271: 'entrepreneur sans entreprise'.

[45] Orrieux (1985) 269 ff.

[46] For a comparable financial estate management see Rathbone (1991).

Zenon owed to Timokles an unspecified sum, which Timokles wished to set off against the sum owed by him and the other veterans as a result of canal work financed by Zenon. There were, furthermore, certain debts which the veterans had to settle with each other, and possibly individually with Zenon. About these we learn only that the veterans have to account first among themselves before being able to present the agreement to Zenon. Finally, Zenon, as tenant of some land of the veterans, owed the tax of that land for the year 36 to the State, which the veterans suggest they will pay for Zenon with the money owing to him. Alternatively, he could deduct the sum from the rent due later in the same year. The settlement of the debts between the veterans and Zenon happened in any case without money changing hands.

More complicated is the situation presented in a long papyrus dated to the year 243 BC in which Zenon gives a statement about the sums still owing from Philon the baker in Apollonius' Alexandrian household. In September 259 BC Zenon had lent to Philon 900 drachmae at 2×2 drachmae/mina per month (i.e. 24 per cent per annum) interest. Fifteen years later he went to court to claim back the sums still owing. The papyrus, which comprises 180 lines, was the account drawn up for the court case. An excerpt of this account reads as follows:

According to the contract the loan taken up in Gorpiaios of the 27th year in silver 900 dr. Of this the interest according to the contract is 2 dr. on the mina, from Gorpiaios of the 27th year to Artemisios of the 28th year with the intercalary month Peritios makes 10 months, 18 dr. each month makes 180 dr.

For the interest we have the salary booked in the account of Apollonios of the 28th year in the month Artemisios, for the month Xandikos, and for the month Artemisios in silver 100 dr. which makes in bronze 108 dr. 2 ob.

.   .   .   .

Against the loan we credit him the 3rd part of the female slave A[. . .] who came to us in the 31st year, 66 dr. 4 ob., and of her daughter who came to us in the 3rd year, what is his, 200 dr. in silver.

.   .   .   .

[he owes furthermore] what he received in the 33rd year from Python's bank, and which he still has to pay, 20 dr. in silver, and the interest in bronze, 20 dr.

.   .   .   .

He has also received money from hand to hand as advance payment. In year 28 from Peisikles in silver 32 dr., in bronze 38 dr.; from Mikon in bronze 4 dr. 2 1/12 ob.; from Dromon in silver 4 dr.; from Zenon in silver 60 dr. [. . .] (P. Cair. Zen. 59355 = SB 6771)

It is worth noting that the statement does not list only the obligations between Zenon and Philon, but also payments which Philon had received from third parties. For example, Zenon deducts wage payments from Apollonius to Philon from the sum that Philon owed to him; further loans made by other people 'from hand to hand' to Philon are added to the claims Zenon advanced against Philon. The conclusion must be that behind this account of outstanding debts there were other accounts in which Zenon had listed those payments with which he had settled debts Philon had with other people. These other accounts must have referred not only to other individuals but also to the accounts of Apollonius' gift estate and of the banker Python. Although there is no conclusive evidence that in Ptolemaic Egypt giro transfers between accounts at different banks were possible, the complex web of debt and debt settlement via sums credited to third parties had similar effects: to make payments without the involvement of specie.

Even in the public economy cash was not always readily available. Nevertheless, documents relating to public payments show a strong commitment to wage payments in monetary terms. In a letter dating to 7 August 255 BC and concerned with the building of a canal under the supervision of Kleon we read:

Alexandros to Kleon greeting. In the conduit which we dug last year from Tebetnou and Samaria to Kerkeesis a silting up has taken place. You will therefore do well to deduct from the *laoi* a sum of 200 dr. from their salt tax, out of which they measure out 4 dr. per *aiolia*, in order that the work may be finished, and the land not become saturated (P. Petrie 2. iv (ii)).

Behind this rather difficult formulation lies a typical labour contract for public work. P. Petrie iii, 43 verso col. iii gives the pattern. This is a contract in which Asklepiades, son of Protion, agrees to remove 12,400 *aiolia* of soil at 4 drachmae per 75 *aiolia* with 100 labourers within 40 days, making 661 drachmae 2 obols. The money should be given to him when he has sealed the contract and furnished the sureties.

Column i of the *verso* of the same papyrus indicates that contractors like Asklepiades were paid locally by the royal bank out of the accounts of tax payments or other revenues. The *oikonomos* is advised to pay the contractors in two instalments out of the *helaike*—the revenue from the sale of oil produced under the state monopoly. The document also contains a penalty clause stipulating that the *oikonomos* had to pay by himself one and a half times the amount of the payment to be made to the contractors in case he failed to collect the *helaike*. Both the payment in instalments and the penalty clause show that income and expenditure were closely connected. In case of default the *oikonomos* does not have to compensate for the loss of the tax income and 50 per cent in addition, but has to pay in full the expenditure which was to be financed by it (plus 50 per cent). It seems that local treasuries, managed by royal banks in the district, were organized above all with a view towards collecting revenue for necessary expenses.

In the letter preserved as P. Petrie 2. IV (II) Alexandros suggests that he shall pay for the labour contracted for public works with money which was not yet in hand. Instead it should be taken from the salt tax to be expected. This meant either that the taxpayers were to be employed against remittance of the tax payment, or that the tax farmer farming the salt tax was to make an advance payment. If the tax farmer and the contractor happened to be the same person (which is not unlikely), the whole project could have been undertaken without any cash being involved.

The practice of transferring money, or making payments with money not yet in hand, is illustrated further by another document, dating to 29 October 255 BC, this time again from the Zenon archive:

Philotas to Zenon greeting. Know that I have arrived from Memphis, where in the first place I have given rations to the soldiers, and in the next place have delivered to the *phorologos* [tax gatherer] all the money that was in hand, borrowing an additional sum from the bank in Memphis. But since my arrival nothing has yet been paid in. It is advisable therefore that you write Thrason about this matter, telling him to instruct his agents to transfer the tax collected [*logeumata*] to the bank so that payment can be made immediately (P. Mich. Zen. 32)

It is not known which position Philotas held, but he must have been acting in some kind of official capacity, given that he was expected to pass on tax revenues to the *phorologos*. Also, the rations to the soldiers are likely to have been paid by a public official. The *logeumata*, mentioned in the last sentence of the document, refer to the tax payments which the agents of Apollonius were obliged to collect from the taxpayers on the *doreia*. Thrason may have been late in paying in the tax to the royal bank, or the *phorologos* early in collecting it. In any case Philotas handed over tax money which had actually not yet been accounted for at the bank. Only by helping out with his own money and a loan from the bank was the flow of money from taxpayer to revenue collector not interrupted.

Payment for public work with money not in hand is, finally, the theme of a third papyrus, recently re-edited by W. Clarysse.[47] The text, belonging to the Zenon archive, has no date but the editor suggests the period of 258–256, when Zenon was personal secretary of the *dioiketes* and therefore involved in public finance. It refers to some embankment work on or round an island which was to be financed with funds managed by Apollonius in his capacity of financial minister:

To Apollonios, the *dioiketes*, Kalligenes greeting. The island can be embanked after the harvest [——] in 60 days, if old wheat is given for 10 talents [——] to the workmen, [divided] according to nomarchy [and numbering] 15,000, at 4 dr. each, and 5,000 mattocks and XX stone [——], so that [?] the rest of the expense to be made for the embankment will be 6 talents (SB V 8243).

Kalligenes plans a project of a scale for which the money necessary to pay the wages was not in hand. Whether the labourers should be paid in kind at the rate of grain worth 4 drachmae, or whether they should be paid from the proceeds of the grain sold, is difficult to tell. But the formulation of the text, as well as the fact that such work was routinely paid in monetary terms, make it more likely that the grain was to be sold to finance the wage payments. Take, for example, P. Col. Zen. 70, where Sosos reports to Zenon that Dionysios the farmer had sold the grain which he had 'measured out' (i.e. allocated) for the hay cutting and had applied its proceeds against the outstanding payment (*opheilêma*). If this case is a parallel, the stores of grain mentioned in SB V 8243

[47] Clarysse (1988).

were not used for payment in kind, but for selling to pay the wages. Not only does the document suggest once more that local authorities frequently had problems of liquidity, but also that grain could be used as a store of wealth to be cashed when needed. It can be said that it took over the one function of money, to be a store of wealth, which is the most detrimental to circulation. In this way, even non-monetary stores of wealth promoted the money economy.

The material discussed so far suggests not only that there was a certain scarcity of cash, but also that the economy of public payments was highly monetized. Labourers employed in gangs to execute construction work, embankment work, or low-skill agricultural labour were paid in cash. Stores of wheat or olyra (an inferior type of grain cultivated in Egypt) had to be sold before they could be used for wage payments. Even the *sitarchia* to soldiers was not a pure payment in kind, but involved money in quantities to render banks devoid of money.[48] It should be noted, furthermore, that the *apomoira* (tax on orchards and vineyards) and the *elaike* (tax on oils) were exacted during the third century from the peasants in kind, but ended in the treasuries of state and temples as a cash revenue after the proceeds had been sold in the market.[49] Also, all the personnel involved in the so-called oil monopoly—cultivators, oil producers, and retail traders—were paid for their work in cash, and the *oikonomoi* were advised to reimburse the price of the containers in which the *apomoira* was delivered.[50]

It is true that the labourers on Apollonius' estate received a corn allowance (*sitometria*) alongside their monetary salaries, and it might be argued that grain was used as a medium of exchange especially among the Egyptian peasantry.[51] But the *sitometriai* on Apollonius' estate were of such limited amount that they must have been intended for consumption rather than for use in further payments. It is also true that rents and taxes on land were paid in kind and, given the agrarian nature of the Egyptian economy, that they formed a

significant amount of the State's annual tax income. But, with a few exceptions, all Greek and non-Greek inhabitants of Egypt had to pay a monetary salt tax, which amounted to one and a half drachmae for men and one drachma for women until 254 BC, and one drachma for men and three obols for women thereafter.[52] Although the tax was small, it drew all inhabitants of Egypt into the monetary economy. It has also been shown that the majority of extant loan transactions before the Roman period involve grain rather than money.[53] But in all third-century examples where the purpose of a loan is stated in the contract, or can be inferred, these loans were loans of seed corn.[54] It seems that grain was used as a means of payment only in taxation and in a subsistence economy where it was used for consumption and sowing. As a medium of exchange it was of limited use.[55]

The relative scarcity of precious-metal coinage on the one hand, and the attempt of the State to promote monetization ideologically and practically prompted a variety of strategies to create money beyond the available supply of precious metals. One was the introduction of a bronze coinage as a medium of payment, another the use of grain as a store of wealth. Beyond these strategies a large number of credit operations were deployed whose major function seems to have been to compensate for the scarcity of coinage and to increase its speed of circulation.

Hellenistic Egypt and the Classical *Polis*

This argument is at variance with Bogaert's assumption that the classical Greek *polis*, and Athens in particular, provided the model for credit operations in Ptolemaic Egypt.[56] Bogaert argues, for example, that not only was the institution of banking based on the Athenian tradition, but the accounting

---

[48] See, for example, P. Lond. 1938.
[49] P. Rev. Laws cols. 34 and 40; cf. Bingen (1978a).
[50] P. Rev. Laws col. 45 (payments for cultivators, etc.), col. 32 (reimbursement of expenditure for containers).
[51] On the *sitometria* in the Zenon Archive see Franko (1988). On the use of grain as money see Preisigke (1910), whose work, although no longer authoritative, has not yet been replaced.

[52] On the salt tax see, most recently, Thompson (1997).
[53] Foraboschi and Gara (1981, 1982).
[54] See the evidence listed in Rupprecht (1968) 75 f. The situation was quite different in the second century, but this seems to be not so much a reflection of the low degree of monetization, but of the rapid devaluation of the bronze standard in relation to silver; see Reekmans (1949) for evidence, Maresch (1996) for the relation between bronze and silver in the second century BC.
[55] See, for example, the case of PSI IV 356 (253/2 BC).
[56] Bogaert (1981, 1987); both repr. in Bogaert (1994).

terminology that occurs in the papyrological material had been developed in the Attic orators. While the latter may well be the case, this does not therefore mean that Ptolemaic banking was based on Athenian traditions.

Friedrich Pringsheim has much to do with the failure to distinguish sufficiently between the Athenian and the Ptolemaic monetary economy. In his comprehensive and learned work he collected texts across time and space and joined them together into one 'Greek Law of Sale'. In the wake of Moses Finley's damaging review his work has found little favour among historians of the classical Greek *polis*,[57] but among papyrologists it has led to some misapprehensions about the nature of the classical 'model' for Ptolemaic Egypt.

The nature and function of credit lies at the centre of the problem. Pringsheim argued, probably rightly, that Greek sale was above all cash sale. There was in principle no sale on credit and no purchase without delivery. Yet he also argued that there developed a variety of legal fictions to subvert this principle in practice. The most important of these were the institution of *arrha*, that is, advance purchase of goods to be delivered later, and the drawing up of loan contracts between buyers and sellers in place of credit sale.[58] Pringsheim's study is still fundamental for a number of legal problems in the papyri, but it has been criticized for its lack of a socio-economic framework. Finley argued that as far as the classical *polis* is concerned, Pringsheim had ignored the question of the relative frequency and socio-economic significance of credit institutions.[59] Millett observes that in Pringsheim's chapter of almost a hundred pages on *arrha* only one example was drawn from Athens, and that other formal examples of credit sales in Athens were few and far between.[60]

The situation in Ptolemaic Egypt, by contrast, was quite different. A large variety of credit sales are attested and seem indeed to have been common

practice. Among papyrologists, economic questions do not tend to be discussed on an equally generalizing level as among historians of classical Greece, but, since earlier conceptions of a planned or *dirigiste* economy have become obsolete, the view prevails that the introduction of coinage by the Greeks created its own dynamics.[61] Yet, was Athens the model for the monetary economy in Ptolemaic Egypt?

Surely, from an institutional perspective there were close parallels: banks existed here and there, bank *diagraphai*, *arrha*, credit sale, etc. were known both in Athens and in Ptolemaic Egypt. But the political and economic background was entirely different. While Athens had a rich supply of precious metal but low surplus production, Egypt had a high agrarian productivity but deficient precious-metal resources. The aggregate motivation for using money and credit was therefore different. It may be true that in Athens written orders of payment, credit sale, and professional banking were part of urban market exchange and long-distance trade. In Egypt, by contrast, sophisticated credit operations such as labour contracts based on credit, credit sale, and 'sale on delivery', as well as an extensive use of book money were in practice both in cities and the countryside, and there is no evidence that they were stimulated by commerce.[62] As I have tried to show in this paper, their most important effect was to increase circulation and to maintain the money supply.

The ideological message of the monetary splendour displayed in Alexandria at the occasion of the festival in honour of Soter and Berenike was therefore not entirely unrelated to the reality of monetary circulation in the *chora*. Far from parading the gap between rich and poor, Greeks and Egyptians, and their respective economic traditions, it displayed the terms of economic and political integration and the capacity of the State to provide and maintain. In a tense coincidence of presence and absence, money was a crucial social bond between central and local authorities, Greeks and Egyptians, lenders and borrowers, as well as taxpayers and those who provided the cash with which taxes could be paid.[63]

---

[57] Finley (1951); Millett (1991) 173 ff.
[58] Pringsheim (1950) 244–7, 333–429.   [59] Cf. Millett (1991) 175.
[60] Cohen (1992), by contrast, has created his own frame for Pringsheim's legal analysis by arguing that in Athens consumer credits and bank *diagraphai* (purchase by written bank transfer) were routinely made and were much to the advantage of commerce and economic growth. Without the creation of bank money and a wide variety of credit facilities the Athenian economy could not have operated on the commercial scale it did (see *passim* and 14 f.).

[61] Cf. Bingen (1978b) 212.
[62] An overview of the range of credit arrangements in Greco–Roman Egypt is given in Rupprecht (1994), with further bibliography.
[63] Versions of this paper were given in Freiburg in 1996, in Oxford in 1997, and in Cambridge in 1998. I wish to thank the audiences for helpful

REFERENCES

ALFÖLDI, M. (1978). *Antike Numismatik*, 2 vols. (Mainz).

ANDERLINI, L. and H. SABOURIAN (1992). 'Some notes on the Economics of Barter, Money and Credit', in C. Humphrey and S. Hugh-Jones (eds.), *Barter, Exchange and Value: An Anthropological Approach* (Cambridge), 83–90.

BAGNALL, R. S. (1976). *The Administration of the Ptolemaic Possessions Outside Egypt* (Leiden).

BINGEN, J. (1978a). *Le Papyrus Revenue Laws—Tradition grecque et adaption hellénistique*, Abhandlungen der Rheinisch–Westfälischen Akademie der Wissenschaften (Cologne).

——(1978b). 'Economie grecque et société égyptienne en IIIe siècle', in H. G. T. Maehler and V. M. Strocka (eds.), *Das Ptolemäische Ägypten* (Berlin), 212–19.

BOGAERT, R. (1981). 'Le Statut des banques en Égypte Ptolémaiques', *l'Antiquité Classique*, 50: 86–99.

——(1987). 'Recherches sur la banque en Égypte gréco-romaine', in T. Hackens and P. Marchetti (eds.), *Histoire économique de l'antiquité* (Louvaine-la-Neuve), 49–77.

——(1994). *Trapezitika Aegyptiaca: Receuil de recherche sur la banque en Égypte Gréco–Romaine* (Florence).

BURSTEIN, S. M. (1991). 'Pharaoh Alexander: A Scholarly Myth', *Ancient Society* 22: 139–45.

CADELL, H. and G. LE RIDER (1997). *Prix du blé et numéraire dans l'Égypt Lagide de 305 à 173* (Brussels).

CLARYSSE, W. (1988). 'A New Fragment for a Zenon Papyrus from Athens', in *Proc. XVIII Cong. Pap.* ii: 77–82.

—— and K. VANDORPE (1995). *Zénon, un homme d'affairs grèc à l'ombre des pyramides* (Louvain).

COHEN, E. (1992). *Athenian Economy and Society* (Princeton, NJ).

CORONIL, F. (1997). *The Magical State: Nature, Money and Modernity in Venezuela* (Chicago, Ill.).

DAVESNE, A. (1994). 'The Medancikkale Hoard', in M. Amandry and G. Le Rider (eds.), *Trésors et circulation monétaire en Anatolie antique* (Paris), 37–43.

DUNAND, F. (1981). 'Fête et propagande à Alexandrie sous les Lagides', in F. Dunand (ed.), *La Fête: pratique et discours d'Alexandrie hellénistique* (Besançon), 13–40.

ELWERT, G. (1987). 'Ausdehnung der Käuflichkeit und Einbettung der Wirtschaft. Markt und Moralökonomie', in K. Heinemann (ed.), *Soziologie wirtschaftlichen Handelns* (Opladen), 300–21.

FINLEY, M. I. (1951). 'Some Problems of Greek Law: A Consideration of Pringsheim on Sale', *Seminar* 9: 72–91.

FLEISCHER, R. (1996). 'Hellenistic Royal Iconography on Coins', in P. Bilde *et al.* (eds.) *Aspects of Hellenistic Kingship*, Studies in Hellenistic Civilisation vii (Aarhus).

FORABOSCHI, D. and A. GARA (1981). 'Sulla differenza tra tassi di interesse in natura e in moneta nell' Egitto Greco-Romano', *Proc. XVI Cong. Pap.*, i. 335–43.

——(1982). 'L'economia dei crediti in natura (Egitto), *Athenaeum*, 70: 69–83.

——(1985). *Studies in Land and Credit in Ancient Athens* (New Brunswick, NJ, 1952; new edn. with additional material by P. Millet, New Brunswick, 1985).

FRANKO, G. F. (1988). 'Sitometria in the Zenon Archive', *BASP* 23: 13–98.

FRASER, P. M. (1972). *Ptolemaic Alexandria*, 3 vols. (Oxford).

GAUTHIER, P. (1985). *Les cités greques et leurs bienfaiteurs IVe-Ie siècle avan J.-C. BCH* Suppl. 12. (Paris).

GEHRKE, H.-J. (1982). 'Der siegreiche König. Überlegungen zur Hellenistischen Monarchie', *AKG* 64: 247–77.

——(1995). *Geschichte des Hellenismus* (Munich).

GOLDHILL, S. (1991). *The Poet's Voice* (Cambridge).

GRIFFITHS, F. F. (1979). *Theocritus at Court* (Leiden), 71–81.

GRUEN, E. S. (1985). 'The Coronation of the Diadochoi', in J. W. Eadie and J. Ober (eds.), *The Craft of the Ancient Historian: Essays in Honour of Chester G. Starr* (Princeton, NJ), 253–71.

HAMMOND, B. (1957). *Banks and Politics in America from the Revolution to the Civil War* (Princeton, NJ).

HAZZARD, R. A. (1995). *Ptolemaic Coins: An Introduction for Collectors* (Toronto).

HERMAN, G. (1980/1). 'The "Friends" of the Early Hellenistic Rulers: Servants or Officials?' *Talanta*, 12/13: 103–49.

HOLTFRERICH, L. (1989). 'The Monetary Unification Process in Nineteenth-Century Germany: Relevance and Lessons for Europe Today', in M. de Cecco and A. Giovanni, *A European Central Bank? Perspectives on Monetary Unification After 10 Years of EMS* (Cambridge) 216–40.

HOWGEGO, C. (1995). *Ancient History from Coins* (London).

JANSSEN, J. J. (1975). *Commodity Prices from the Ramessid Period* (Leiden).

——(1981). 'Die Struktur der pharaonischen Wirtschaft', *Göttinger Miszellen*, 48: 59–77.

KEMP, B. (1989). *Ancient Egypt: Anatomy of a Civilisation* (London).

KOENEN, L. (1977). *Eine agonistische Inschrift aus Ägypten und frühptolemäische Königsfeste*, Beiträge zur klassischen Philologie, lvi. (Meisenheim).

——(1993). 'The Ptolemaic King as Religious Figure', in A. Bulloch *et al.* (eds.), *Images and Ideologies* (Berkeley, Calif.), 25–116.

KYRIELEIS, H. (1975). *Bildnisse der Ptolemäer* (Berlin).

LE RIDER, G. (1991). 'Éphèse et Arados au IIe siècle avant notre ère', *QT* 20: 193–212.

discussion; in particular, Alan Bowman, Hans-Joachim Gehrke, and Harold Mattingly. Special thanks to Andy Meadows, Dorothy Thompson, and David Woodruff for letting me have unpublished work.

LORBER, C. C. (1995/6). Review of R. A. Hazzard (1995) and W. Weiser (1995), *AJN* 7/8: 256–76.

MARESCH, K. (1996). *Bronze und Silber. Papyrologische Beiträge zur Geschichte der Währung im ptolemäischen und römischen Ägypten bis zum 2. Jh n. Chr.* Papyrologica Coloniensia, xxv. (Opladen).

MARTIN, T. R. (1985). *Sovereignty and Coinage in Classical Greece* (Princeton, NJ).

MAUCOURANT, J. (1990). 'Pratiques monétaire et individu en Égypte ancienne', *Cahier monnaie et financement* 2: 41–79.

MEADOWS, A. (unpublished). 'Coinage in the Ptolemaic Empire'.

MILLETT, P. (1991). 'Sale, Credit and Exchange in Athenian Economy and Society', in P. Cartledge, P. Millett and S. Todd (eds.), *Nomos* (Cambridge), 167–94.

MØRKHOLM, O. (1991). *Early Hellenistic Coinage: From the Accession of Alexander to the Peace of Apamea (336–188 BC)* (Cambridge).

ORRIEUX, C. (1981). 'Comptes privés de Zénon à Philadelphe', *CdE* 56: 213–39.

——(1985). *Zénon de Caunos, parépidêmos, et le destin grec* (Paris).

OTTO, W. (1905). *Priester und Tempel im hellenistischen Ägypten*, 2 vols. (Berlin).

POLANYI, K. (1957). *The Great Transformation: The Political and Economic Origins of our Time* (Boston, MA).

PRÉAUX, C. (1936). *L'Économie royale des Lagides* (Brussels).

PREISIGKE, F. (1910). *Girowesen im griechischen Ägypten enthaltend Korngiro, Geldgiro, Girobanknotariat mit Einschluß des Archivwesens. Ein Beitrag zur Geschichte des Verwaltungswesens im Altertum* (Strasburg).

PRICE, M. J. (1993). 'More from Memphis and the Syria 1989 hoard', in M. J. Price, A. M. Burnett, and R. F. Bland (eds.), *Essays in Honour of Robert Carson and Kenneth Jenkins* (London), 31–5.

PRINGSHEIM, F. (1950). *The Greek Law of Sale* (Berlin).

RATHBONE, D. (1991). *Economic Rationalism and Rural Society in Third-Century AD Egypt: The Heroninus Archive and the Appianus Estate* (Cambridge).

REEKMANS, T. (1949). 'Economic and Social Repercussions of the Ptolemaic Copper Inflation', *CdE* 24: 324–42.

RICE, E. E. (1983). *The Grand Procession of Ptolemy Philadelphus* (Oxford).

ROSTOVTZEFF, M. (1953). *The Social and Economic History of the Hellenistic World*. 3 vols. (Oxford).

RUPPRECHT, H. A. (1968). *Untersuchungen zum Darlehen im Recht der gräko-ägyptischen Papyri der Ptolemäerzeit* (Munich).

——(1994). *Kleine Einführung in die Papyruskunde* (Darmstadt).

SAMUEL, A. E. (1984). 'The Money Economy and the Ptolemaic Peasantry', *BASP* 21: 187–206.

SIMMEL, G. (1990). *The Philosophy of Money*, tr. from German orig. (London).

THOMPSON, D. J. (1997). 'The Infrastructure of Splendour: Census and Taxes in Ptolemaic Egypt', in P. A Cartledge, P. D. A. Garnsey, and E. Gruen (eds.), *Hellenistic Constructs* (Berkeley, Calif.), 242–57.

——(forthcoming). 'Philadelphus' Procession: Dynastic Power in a Mediterranean Context', *Stud. Hell.*

VON REDEN, S. (1995). *Exchange in Ancient Greece* (London).

——(1997). 'Money and Coinage in Ptolemaic Egypt: Some Preliminary Remarks', *Proc. XXI Cong. Pap.* ii. *AfP*, Beiheft 3: 1003–8.

WALBANK, F. W. (1984). 'Monarchy and Monarchic Ideas', *CAH*[2] vii.1. (Cambridge), ch. 3.

——(1996). 'Two Hellenistic Processions: A Matter of Self-Definition', *SCI* 15: 119–30.

WEBER, M. (1978). *Economy and Society: An Outline of Interpretive Sociology*, trans. from German orig. (Berkeley, Calif.).

WEISER, W. (1995). *Katalog Ptolemäischer Bronzemünzen der Sammlung des Instituts für Altertumskunde der Universität zu Köln*, Papyrologica Coloniensia xxiii, Abhandlungen der Nordrhein–Westfälischen Akademie der Wissenschaften (Opladen).

WOODRUFF, D. (unpublished). 'Barter of the Bankrupt: The Politics of Demonetization in Russia's Federal State'.

PART II

MONEY AND SOCIETY— CASE STUDIES ON THE USES OF MONEY

6

THE COINAGE OF RHODES
408–*c*.190 BC

R. H. J. Ashton[1]

W HEN IALYSOS, KAMIROS, AND LINDOS synoecized in 408/7, the new coinage of the unified state bore little resemblance to the disparate coinages which the three old cities had produced in silver and electrum from the late sixth century until, probably, the third quarter of the fifth.[2] The rose, the punning reverse design, had already appeared on fractions from Kamiros (*BMC* 14) and Ialysos (*BMC* 9), but not as a dominant type.[3] The heads of Helios and of the nymph Rhodos, the obverse types of almost all the late classical and Hellenistic coinage of Rhodes, do not occur on the coinages of the three old cities, and illustrate the adoption of Helios as the patron deity of the newly unified state.[4] Moreover, whereas Ialysos had used an apparently individual weight standard, Kamiros the Aeginetan, and Lindos the Milesian, the new state adopted the 'Chian' weight standard, based on a tetradrachm of about 15.3 g. and so called because it is first attested in slightly heavier (*c*.15.6 g.) form on Chios in the sixth century.[5] Since the rapid spread of this standard throughout western Asia Minor during the fourth century may have been due in part to Rhodian influence, it is often termed Rhodian, but to avoid ambiguity it will here be called Chian. As we shall see, a reduced standard based on a didrachm of *c*.6.8 g. was introduced in the late 340s: I shall call this the Rhodian standard.

Description and Dating of the Coinage

408–*c*.385

The mint probably began operation immediately after the synoecism, striking tetradrachms of Chian weight both with symbols accompanying the rose (eagle, club, pecten, sphinx, shrimp) and without symbol (**1–6**)[6]. Some of the sphinx coins carry to the left of the rose the signature Ξ*ENO* in minute letters, which presumably has the same reference as the

[1] I am grateful to Alain Bresson, Philip Kinns, Koray Konuk, and Andrew Meadows for commenting on drafts of this paper.
[2] For these coinages see *BMC* Caria, c–cii and 223–9; Cahn (1957) 18–26; Cahn (1970) 190; Weiss and Hurter (1998) (an unsatisfactory article); Kraay (1976) 35; Price and Waggoner (1975) 94–6; Fried (1987) 7–8; Kagan (1987) 25–6. Bresson (1981) attributes to Ialysos some staters with palmette of the first quarter of the fifth century (Price and Waggoner (1975) nos. 712–13, 'Caria uncertain'). For Kamiros see also the extensive selection in *SNG* Keckman i, 317–51. Note also Lykian staters with reverse inscribed *POΔION* from the Elmalı hoard, which were presumably struck by or for Rhodians in Lykia: Spier (1987) 36.
[3] The rose is a variety of dog rose, which grows extensively on the island. A characteristic of members of the rose family is that one of their five sepals is 'bearded', i.e. has spine-like growths on either side, two are 'half-bearded' (growths on one side only), and two are 'unbearded' (smooth on both sides). The profile roses on Rhodian coins invariably show the outer sepals with spines, but, because only one side of the outer sepals is shown, it is impossible to judge whether they are intended to be bearded or half-bearded. On early coins the central sepal is invariably bearded, but on later coins it is often unbearded or half-bearded. The tip of the central sepal on coins of the late fifth and early fourth centuries is invariably pointed, as it is in nature. On later coins it is often rounded, a stylization not found in nature. I am grateful to Professor Jakov Lorsche and, in particular, to Professor William Stearn for guidance on the above.

[4] For the identification of Rhodos on the coinage see Robert (1967) 7–14. For the adoption of Helios as patron of the new state see van Gelder (1900) 290–8.
[5] Hardwick (1991) 47 ff., esp. 71; Hardwick (1993) 212.
[6] Numbers in bold type refer to the list of issues in App. 1, most of which are illustrated on Plates 6.1–6.12.

monogram ⌗ on the shrimp issue; like the small letters *TAYPO* above the right of the rose on the issue without symbol, these apparently informal markings are perhaps artists' signatures.

Thirty-two obverse dies can be identified for this first series from just 59 coins; hence, the original number of dies was probably much higher.[7] They were followed by an extensive series of Chian-weight tetradrachms which had control letters as well as symbols on the reverse, and which continued, as we shall see, until the third quarter of the fourth century. Apparently in parallel with the last Chian-weight tetradrachms without control letter, the mint struck coins which were at the same time double *sigloi* on the Persian weight standard and tridrachms on the Chian standard, weighing *c*.11.2 g., of the well-known *ΣΥΝ* type (one obverse die from 24 coins), and accompanying triple *sigloi* (*c*.16.8 g.) of conventional Helios/rose types (7–10); the flans of some of the double *sigloi* look as if they were clipped from larger (tetradrachm or triple *sigloi*) flans. The triple *sigloi* consumed five obverse dies from only six recorded coins; hence, the original number of obverse dies was probably much greater, and these coins were probably driven out of circulation by the lighter contemporary Chian-weight tetradrachms.[8] These larger denominations were accompanied by several issues of Chian-weight hemidrachms and obols, and by some bronzes (11–24, 25–7, 57–66). The early date of all the silver coinages can be demonstrated from the date of the *ΣΥΝ* coinage, from hoards, and by comparisons with coinage of other states.

The most recent interpretation of the *ΣΥΝ* coinages is that they were the product of a pro-Spartan alliance formed in Asia Minor after Lysander's defeat of the Athenians in 405/4.[9] Whether or not this will stand the test of time, the *ΣΥΝ* coinages are most unlikely to postdate the King's Peace. Thus, the Rhodian double *sigloi* and triple *sigloi*, certain issues of hemidrachms which share with the triple *sigloi* a bunch or bunches of grapes as symbol, or share with the double *sigloi* a round incuse (outline of the edge of the punch-die) on the reverse (most unusual in silver coins of Rhodes of this date, whose incuse is normally square), and the Chian-weight tetradrachms without symbol which also have the round incuse belong to this early period. Most of these coinages have on the reverse relatively large rectangular roses with markedly curved petals and sometimes buds, which contrast with the small, square, plain and budless roses of some of the Chian-weight tetradrachms without control letter; it is reasonable to suppose that the latter are slightly earlier in date. If the *ΣΥΝ* coinages date to 404, it is tempting, but far from necessary, to propose that the five symbols on these early Chian-weight tetradrachms represent annual issues starting in 408. If this is so, the symbols on the later Chian-weight tetradrachms with control letters may also represent annual issues. There is nothing to disprove this hypothesis (although it would imply that the system changed with the introduction in the late 340s of the very large grapes issue, which clearly spread over several years: see below), but more evidence is needed before it can be accepted.[10] I should also emphasize that, although I find Karwiese's dating of the *ΣΥΝ* coinage the most satisfactory on offer, there is nothing conclusive in the Rhodian numismatic evidence which would preclude restoration of the alliance to its usual date in the late 390s: it would not be difficult to assign the Chian-weight tetradrachms without control letter and the associated hemidrachms to the period 408/7–late 390s, nor to fit

---

[7] For discussion of the statistical methods whereby the original number of dies employed in a series can be calculated from the recorded numbers of dies and coins see Esty (1986), esp. 211. The higher the ratio (the 'index figure') of known coins to known obverse dies, the closer the number of recorded obverse dies is likely to be to the original number of obverse dies. Very crudely put, if the ratio is about 3:1 or more and consistent throughout the series, and if the recorded coins come from a wide variety of sources, then one can be reasonably confident that the bulk of the original obverse dies is known. Ratios of under 3:1 usually suggest a high probability that newly discovered coins will provide new dies.

[8] Detailed justification for this order of issue is given in Ashton (1993*a*), revising the traditional view, maintained in Bérend (1972), that the triple *sigloi* ('Attic-weight tetradrachms') were the mint's first coinage, and had no connection with the *ΣΥΝ* coinage. Bérend (1995)'s restatement of that view is unconvincing: see Ashton in Ashton *et al.* (forthcoming). Whatever the exact order of the early issues, the abundance of the mint's output during its first twenty years of operation is not in doubt.

[9] Karwiese (1980), with discussion of the later dates (late 390s/early 380s) proposed by earlier scholars. Ashton *et al.* (forthcoming) conclude that the 'Hekatomnos Hoard' supports Karwiese's high dating, and reject the recent proposal of Delrieux (2000) that the Ionian and Karian *ΣΥΝ* mints struck during the period 395–390 and the northern mints (Byzantion, Kyzikos and ?Lampsakos) a little later in 389–387.

[10] For criticism of an attempt to interpret the fourth-century tetradrachms of Amphipolis as annual issues see Wartenberg (1992). Samos is thought to have struck annual issues at the time (Barron (1966) 104–19), but it remains to be seen whether the discovery of new magistrate issues will invalidate the hypothesis: see A. Meadows in Ashton *et al.* (forthcoming).

the first issues of Chian-weight tetradrachms with control letters into the decade around 390.

Secondly, the argument from hoards. In the 1903 Chalki hoard (*IGCH* 1203) 135 early Rhodian hemidrachms from all but one of the 13 varieties known, most of which had seen some circulation, were associated with 82 coins of Chios in worn condition from a series dated by Hardwick to c.435–425,[11] and with 5 Samian tetradrachms, which had seen some circulation, signed by Hegesianax, whom Barron associates with the Samian *ΣΥΝ* coinage.[12] The pre-1820 Chios hoard contained 11 worn Chian staters dated by Hardwick c.480–435 and 435–425, and one fairly fresh Rhodian tetradrachm of the pecten issue.[13] The Marmaris(?) c.1965 hoard (*IGCH* 1202) included early Rhodian hemidrachms together with drachms and fractions of Knidos and Karian Khersonesos and dates to c.400–390.[14] Moreover, two hoards which were probably buried c.390–385 and contain Rhodian tetradrachms of the later series with control letter as well as symbol demonstrate that the preceding coinage must have ended by c.390. Durasalar 1956 (*IGCH* 1201) had two Rhodian tetradrachms with symbol and control letter. The Karia 1977/8 hoard (the 'Hekatomnos' hoard: *CH* 9, 387) included over 100 early Rhodian hemidrachms, all quite worn, *ΣΥΝ* double *sigloi* of Rhodes, Knidos, and Ephesos, all showing some wear, and at least 7 Rhodian tetradrachms with symbol and control letter in quite fresh condition.[15]

Finally, the stylistic argument. The portraits of the nymph Rhodos which occur instead of the usual rose

on the reverse of two die-linked issues of early hemidrachms (**11–12**) are very similar to those of Aphrodite on the reverses of certain Knidian drachms from the first group of Cahn's series VI. Cahn (see above, n. 2, 170) plausibly suggests that in some instances the die-engraver was the same. Since, as we have seen, Cahn VI dates to 411–394 (Cahn) or 411–405 (Karwiese), it may be suggested that the Rhodos hemidrachms were the first of the Rhodian series, struck before the rose became their standard reverse type.

All subsequent Chian-weight tetradrachms (**28–56, 67–89, 93–4, 107**) have both symbol and control letters on the reverse. Forty-one different symbols are known, and until the 340s (see below) there seem to be no accompanying fractions. One control letter at a time accompanies each symbol, but many of the different symbol issues can be divided into sub-issues having different accompanying letters, although the sub-issues often have obverse dies in common. The same letters recur with different symbols. It is difficult to determine what these letters represented: perhaps anvils or workshops. The apparent chronological succession of symbols which the stylistic development of the rose on the Chian-weight tetradrachms without control letters suggested encourages the belief that the symbols on these later tetradrachms also have chronological significance.

Two of the reverse dies of the apparent first issue, with lion-head symbol (**28–30**), have the small letters *Ξ-E* around the rose stalk in addition to the regular control letters *A* and *Δ*: these probably have the same reference as the tiny letters *ΞΕΝΟ* and the monogram 𐅺 on the sphinx and shrimp issues from the previous series. The obverse die used on the corn ear + *Δ* issue (**31**) closely resembles some of those used on the early issues without control letter, and the reverses of some of the issues with control letter have a rosebud or buds similar to those on the triple *sigloi*, and some of their obverse dies are similar to those on the early tetradrachms without control letter. Hence, there was probably little if any gap in production. The Durasalar 1956 and the 'Hekatomnos' hoards, both buried c.390–385, and the Turkey 1993/4 hoard, which may well be contemporary, contained between them at least 16 tetradrachms with symbol and control letter, all in fresh condition: 1 kylix + *Φ* and 1 kithara + *Ι* in Durasalar; 1 corn ear + *Φ*, 2 torch + *Φ*, 1 bucranium + *Φ*, 1 corn grain + *Φ*,

---

[11] Hardwick (1991) 141–2; Hardwick (1993) 215.

[12] Barron (1966) 113, 116 and nos. 117c, 123b, 125d, 126b, 128.

[13] Hardwick (1993) 215 n. 31.

[14] I have not been able to identify any coins from this hoard. *IGCH* dated it c.390–380 on the advice of H. A. Cahn, author of the standard work on the Knidian and Khersonesian coinage (Cahn (1970)). The classification of the Knidian coins is unknown, but they presumably included examples of Cahn's final group VI. If Karwiese (1980, 18) is right in compressing Cahn's group VI from 411–394 to 411–405, Cahn's date for the hoard may be raised a little.

[15] For the date of the Durasalar and 'Hekatomnos' hoards see Ashton *et al.* (forthcoming). The Durasalar hoard contained a Samian tetradrachm in mint condition signed by Aristeides, whom Barron dates 392/1 but who may belong about a decade earlier if Karwiese's dating of the alliance coinage is accepted, and seven Ephesian tetradrachms which comprise three with the early curved-wing bee, three (from the same obverse die) of a transitional type with slightly curved wing, and one with straight-winged bee in mint state. A third hoard, said to have been found in Turkey in 1993/4, included a Hegesianax tetradrachm of Samos (condition not known) and at least seven Rhodian tetradrachms with symbol and control letter; it may well be roughly contemporary with the Durasalar and the 'Hekatomnos' hoards, but it is now dispersed and I have been able to glean few further details.

1 aphlaston + *T* and 1 dolphin + *Φ* in the 'Hekatomnos hoard;[16] 2 ivy leaf and berries + *Φ*, 3 boukranion + *Φ*, 1 corn grain + *Φ*, and 1 patera + *Φ* in the Turkey 1993/4 hoard. Taking into account other issues associated with those in these three hoards by die link or style (for example, the central sepal of the roses on earlier issues is pointed, whereas that on the later is rounded), we may conclude that 20 of the 41 symbols of the symbol/letter tetradrachms had been struck by *c*.385 BC, a total of 81 of the known 129 obverse dies (**28–56**).[17] Only 157 tetradrachms are known from these 81 obverse dies, a ratio of less than 2:1, which suggests that many more dies remain to be discovered (see n. 7). Most of these 20 symbols, and none of the remaining 21, occur in the 1970/1 Marmaris-area hoard (*IGCH* 1209) which, since it is reported to have contained only Rhodian tetradrachms, is of little help for absolute dating, but which does corroborate the precedence of the first 20 symbols.[18]

c.385–late 340s

A tetradrachm in the Durasalar hoard with kithara symbol is the sole representative in these early hoards of the next group of 10 symbol issues represented by 37 coins struck from 21 obverse dies: kithara, trident, Ionic capital, oinochoe, profile eye, trap, askos, uncertain, caduceus, and owl, which are often die-linked together and are stylistically similar (**67–80**). Given the burial of the Durasalar hoard in *c*.390–385, they might reasonably be assigned to the late 380s and 370s.

The next 8 symbols are grouped together because they all occur only with the accompanying letter *A*, and are roughly similar in style: wasp, bearded term, Athena Promachos, unidentified but clear symbol, thymiaterion, head of Helios, horse's head, and satrapal(?) head (**81–8**). Only 8 obverse dies and 11 coins are known. The cutter of the obverse die of the sole surviving satrapal(?)-head tetradrachm appears also to have cut the two obverse dies of two further coins

with uncertain, but perhaps the same, symbol; both have *Φ* (**89**). The same cutter appears responsible for the obverses of the next tetradrachm issue, with symbol club (**93**). He, or a colleague working in the same style, seems to have produced the obverses of the first drachms of the mint, which have no symbol on the reverse, but two drooping buds and the letters *Φ*, *A*, and ⊥ (17 obverse dies from 45 coins: **90–2**).

With the club issue, didrachms occur for the first time. *Φ* is the only control letter used on the tetradrachms, but the didrachms are found with either *Φ* or the new letter *E* (a total of 9 obverse dies from 18 didrachms; **95–6**). There are also hemidrachms with club but no accompanying control letter (**102**; distinguished by style from the much earlier hemidrachms with the same symbol). The club tetradrachms and the next issue of tetradrachms with grapes unattached to the rose, which occur only with *E*, are very similar in obverse and reverse styles, and the accompanying issues of didrachms with club + *E* and unattached grapes + *E* share three obverse dies. The tetradrachms with unattached grapes + *E* (**94**) were struck from two obverse dies (but only 3 specimens are known), while the corresponding didrachms (**98**) were struck from 56 obverse dies (including the 3 obverse dies shared with the club + *E* issue) known from a total of 284 coins. Didrachms with unattached grapes also occur with *Δ* as control letter (5 obverse dies from 30 recorded coins, a significant proportion of which are plated; **97**). Other contemporary issues are drachms with unattached grapes + *Δ* or *E*, and hemidrachms with grapes and no control letter (**100–1**, **103**).[19] A rare issue of diobols (*c*.1.15 g.) also seems to belong to this period. They are the first coins of the mint to show Helios radiate and profile on the obverse; the reverse type is also unprecedented—two buds (for two obols?) in a square incuse with the letter *Φ* or *E* in between (**104–5**). Six of the 12 known obverse dies were used on both issues, which were thus probably struck simultaneously.[20]

The 8 tetradrachm issues mentioned above (**81–8**) which have only the letter *A* and the drachm issues with two drooping buds can be assigned to the 350s

[16] The 'Hekatomnos' hoard was also reported to have contained an early tetradrachm with pecten and no control letter; its state of wear is not known.

[17] This means that, *if* the different symbol issues are interpreted as annual (see above), a date for the *ΣΥΝ* coinages in the late 390s or early 380s is excluded, and only Karwiese's hypothesis of an alliance in 405/404 will hold water.

[18] In Ashton (1988), 81 n. 11, I erroneously suggested that *IGCH* 1209 was concealed *c*.350–340.

[19] Two die-linked issues of hemidrachms with grapes + *E* and ivy leaf + *E* (**171–2**) are placed in the period after 305/4 because they have a shallow round incuse on the reverse. But they may well belong a little earlier, for the style of their obverses recalls that of issues with grapes symbol and square incuse under discussion here. See 86 below.

[20] The same types were used for diobols struck in the mid third century and later: Ashton (1988) 86–87 n. 27; see further below.

and 340s, while the club issue and the beginning of the grapes issue can be dated towards the end of that period. The reasons are as follows:

(1) The reverses of the drachms are similar to those of some pseudo-Rhodian drachms of Karia with on obverse Helios left on a solar disc, and on reverse a rose with two drooping buds and the letters *E—Y*, *M—E* or *N—I* flanking the rose; these can be independently dated to *c*.360–340.[21]

(2) About thirty Rhodian didrachms with symbols club and grapes occurred in the 'Pixodaros' hoard, probably concealed *c*.340, and their fresh condition indicates that they were struck not long before burial. The presence of the rare club didrachms confirms that they are the earliest of this denomination. We may therefore conclude that the didrachms began in the late 340s.[22]

(3) A Rhodian tetradrachm in the Gulbenkian collection (Jenkins and Castro Hipólito (1989), no. 774) with horse's-head symbol, was acquired in 1929 and was said to have come 'from a recent find composed chiefly of tetradrachms of Mausolos'. This may well refer to *IGCH* 1266, a hoard said to have been found in Fethiye in 1929 and probably buried in the mid–late 340s. If the Rhodian tetradrachm formed part of the hoard, its fresh condition suggests that it was struck not long before burial.[23]

(4) *SNG* Delepierre 2748 and 2749 are tetradrachms of, respectively, the thymiaterion and the club issues. According to their tickets in Paris they were acquired by Delepierre in late 1950 from a hoard. This may well have been a hoard of around 200 coins recorded as found at Muğla, Karia, in 1950, and buried in the mid to late 340s.[24] If the Delepierre coins formed part

of it, their good condition suggests that they were struck in the 340s, while the apparent absence of the copious Rhodian didrachm issues suggests that they were not in circulation at the time of burial.

On the above evidence the unique tetradrachm (**88**) with the symbol described tentatively as a satrapal head probably belongs *c*.350–340. The symbol is only two-thirds on the flan, and Kraay questioned Pollard's description of the headdress as a Phrygian hat; he thought that it might be a veil with a modius or polus, suggesting Demeter as a possibility.[25] Nevertheless, close examination of a cast of the coin persuades me that the headdress is indeed a Phrygian cap, and that the head is probably that of a Satrap. Linking symbols on Greek coins to historical events is a hazardous game, but it is tempting to connect this unusual symbol with the Hekatomnid control or influence over the island which persisted from the Social War until, probably, the coming of Alexander.[26] The apparently simultaneous introduction by Rhodes and by Hidrieus of the underweight (see below) didrachm denomination, and the introduction of the new control letter *E* both on the Rhodian series and on the greater part of the tetradrachms of Hidrieus (most if not all of which seem to belong late in his reign) suggest further co-ordination between their respective mints.[27] Nevertheless, whatever the degree of Hekatomnid influence over Rhodes, it clearly neither inhibited the operation of the Rhodian mint nor greatly affected the appearance of Rhodian coinage.[28]

[21] Ashton (1990) 31–2, arguments (a) and (c) ((b) uses the Rhodian drachms to date the 'solar-disc' drachms and would be circular here). For further discussion of the 'solar-disc' drachms see Ashton (1999*a*) 16.

[22] Hurter (1998), 151; *CH* 9, 421. The latest datable coins in the hoard are tetradrachms and didrachms of Pixodaros which are conspicuous for their freshness and large numbers. Hurter suggested burial in the mid-330s, but Konuk (2000) 178 has argued cogently for burial very early in Pixodaros' reign in 341–0. My proposal in Ashton (1988) 85, that the Rhodian grapes + *E* issue began in the 330s should thus be revised.

[23] *IGCH* records its contents as 49 tetradrachms of Ephesos, 12 of Mausolos, 5 of Hidrieus, and 1 of Kos. The absence of any of the copious emissions of Pixodaros points to burial before he succeeded Hidrieus in 341/0. Koray Konuk informs me that a further 2 tetradrachms of Mausolos probably belonged to the hoard, making a total of 14, and that its date of discovery was a little earlier than 1929, for the British Museum acquired in 1928 2 tetradrachms of Hidrieus which came from the hoard.

[24] *IGCH* 1215; *CH* 8, 145. It reportedly contained tetradrachms of Ephesos, Miletos and Rhodes, tetradrachms and drachms of Kos, didrachms and hemidrachms of Knidos, tetradrachms and drachms of Mausolos, drachms of Hidrieus, and a drachm of 'Euthenai' (i.e. a 'solar-disc' drachm with *E—Y*: see above). The absence of coins of Pixodaros again points to burial in the mid to late 340s.

[25] Pollard (1970) no. 101; Kraay (1980) 61.

[26] For Hekatomnid influence over Rhodes see Hornblower (1982) 123–30; Berthold (1984) 31–4. Moysey (1989) 126–30, points out that Hornblower has over-interpreted some of the numismatic evidence for the Hekatomnids' relations with their neighbours. Moysey is also right to distrust the use of solely stylistic criteria to date the satrapal-head tetradrachm to *c*.340 (so Hornblower (1982) 129–30, citing a letter from myself). The above arguments, which do not depend solely on style, may be more convincing.

[27] For the coins of Hidrieus see Konuk (1993) 239; Pixodaros took over the control letter *E* when he came to power in 341/0. See also Konuk (1998) 159, 168, 174–5.

[28] For some apt remarks on the lack of effect which putative Hekatomnid control over Miletos would have had on Milesian coinage see Kinns (1986) 247–50. For the question of sovereignty and the right to coin see also Meadows and Oliver in this volume, respectively 53–62 and 35–51.

The earliest drachms with two drooping buds (**90–2**) were struck to a standard of about 3.6 g. and the very rare earliest didrachms with club + Φ (**95**) to roughly the same standard at about 7.4 g., tolerably close to a drachm and a didrachm on the full Chian-tetradrachm standard of 15.3 g. The club didrachms with the new letter E, and all the didrachms with grapes + E and grapes + $\varDelta$ were struck to a markedly lower standard of about 6.8 g., as were the contemporary fractions. The didrachms of Hidrieus and Pixodaros were struck to a similar low standard. Once introduced on Rhodes, the didrachm became the dominant denomination until the reform of the monetary system in the early second century,[29] and the new 6.8 g. standard, which I shall henceforth call 'Rhodian', remained in force during the same period. However, it is noteworthy that the tetradrachms of Hidrieus, Pixodaros, and Rhoontopates remained on the higher standard of 15.3 g., as did the rare Rhodian tetradrachms with unattached grapes + E, which are contemporary with the new lower-weight didrachms having grapes + E. Some slightly later tetradrachms with attached grapes + E (see below) were likewise still struck on the Chian standard of 15.3 g., while the corresponding didrachms were struck to the new standard of 6.8 g. These tetradrachms were the last to be struck in the fourth century; on the only two occasions when tetradrachms appear again, in the late third and early second centuries (see below), they weigh 13.6 g., i.e. the Rhodian standard on which didrachms and smaller denominations had been struck since the late 340s. It remains unclear why the Rhodian and Hekatomnid mints in the late 340s and a little later struck at the same time Chian-weight tetradrachms at 15.3 g. and Rhodian-weight didrachms at 6.8 g. Perhaps they were short of silver, and, while preserving the full weight of their tetradrachms for international prestige and to remain competitive with such coinages as the copious tetradrachms of Ephesos, saved metal by issuing the lower denominations at a lower weight standard.[30] The frequency of plating noted above in the grapes + $\varDelta$ issue also suggests a shortage of silver. Be that as it may, in about 340 the new lower-weight didrachms may have driven the full-weight tetradrachms out of circulation, and this may account for the absence of Rhodian tetradrachms from the 'Pixodaros' hoard, which had puzzled Hurter (1998, 151). It may also account for the fact that most of the later tetradrachm issues survive today in only one example; many more issues may remain to be discovered.[31]

Late 340s–305/4

It is difficult to judge how long the 56 obverse dies used for the E + unattached grapes didrachms lasted, for there is little variation in style or format, but it would be reasonable to assume a period of at least several years from c.340 onwards.[32] Two of the 56 obverse dies were used to strike a rare variant with

---

of Hidrieus, whose known examples weigh between 0.70 and 0.96 g., were struck in order to make up the difference between the full-weight Chian tetradrachm and two lower-weight didrachms; however, the trihemiobols seem a little too light to perform this function—as do the contemporary diobols of Rhodes (see above).

[29] See further below. The dominance of the didrachm may explain why a public subscription on Rhodes in the late third or early second century took the form of a *didrachmia*: Kontorini and Migeotte (1995) 621–8.

[30] Konuk (1993) 237–9, suggests that foreign tetradrachms of Chian weight were exchanged in the Hekatomnid sphere of influence for two of the lower-weight didrachms, the difference representing a tax to the benefit of the local authorities. He suggests further that the trihemiobols

[31] The same phenomena can be observed at Knidos, which in the 350s introduced didrachms and drachms on the same lower standard of c.6.8 and 3.3–3.4 g., while still preserving the full Chian weight of its rare contemporary tetradrachms. Moreover, many of the drachms were struck from silver of poor quality. See Ashton (1999b) 89–90.

[32] Some bronze coins attributed to an Astyra in Karia at first glance upset this dating. On obverse they have a head of Helios three-quarter facing r. (*BMC* 8–11) or a female head r. (*BMC* 12–19), and on reverse an amphora and $A\Sigma TY$. The head of Helios is modelled on that of the silver tetradrachms, didrachms, and gold staters of Rhodes with grapes + E or $\varDelta$, while the female head resembles that on the early bronze coinage of Rhodes, most of which dates, as we shall see, to the second half of the fourth century. H. P. Borrell, the source of most of the British Museum specimens, claimed that they were discovered at the same time on Rhodes (Borrell (1846–7) 166–8). According to the text of Stephanos of Byzantion on which B. V. Head in *BMC Caria*, xxxviii–xxxix relied, a certain Astyra was a $\pi \acute{o} \lambda \iota \varsigma$ $\Phi o \iota \nu \acute{\iota} \kappa \eta \varsigma$ $\kappa a \tau \grave{a}$ $^{\prime} P \acute{o} \delta o \nu$, $\grave{\epsilon} \nu$ $\mathring{\eta}$ $\grave{\epsilon} \tau \iota \mu \mathring{a} \tau o$ $\mathring{\eta}$ $A \theta \eta \nu \mathring{a}$ $A \sigma \tau \upsilon \rho \acute{\iota} \varsigma$ ('a city in the territory of Phoinix opposite Rhodes, in which Athena Astyris was worshipped'; for the possible translation of $\Phi o \iota \nu \acute{\iota} \kappa \eta$ as 'territory of Phoinix' see Bresson (1991) 166). Phoinix lies near the tip of the Loryma peninsula, and, although absolute proof is lacking, it would almost certainly have been incorporated into the Rhodian state by the fourth century (Fraser and Bean (1954) 94–8). It is most unlikely that an incorporated city in the Peraia would have struck its own coinage, still less one described as being subordinate to another within the Peraia. However, no trace of a Karian Astyra has ever been found, and the standard text of Stephanos (A. Meineke (ed.) (Berlin, 1849)) adopts Holstenius' simple adjustment $\pi \acute{o} \lambda \iota \varsigma$ $\Phi o \iota \nu \acute{\iota} \kappa \eta \varsigma$ $\kappa a \tau^{\prime}$ $^{\prime\prime} A \rho a \delta o \nu$ ('a city of Phoenicia opposite Arados'). Karian Astyra is a ghost: see Bean (1953) 23 n. 61, and Bean and Cook (1957) 95 n. 143. Nonetheless, the Rhodian provenance of the coins which Borrell reported and the Rhodian types which they copied suggest a mint in the vicinity. The best solution seems to be that adopted by H. von Aulock at *SNG von Aulock* 8170, namely to assign the coins to Astypalaia. Although most of the types of its later Hellenistic bronze coinage refer to the myth of Perseus, the head of Dionysos on the issue *BMC* 11–12 offer a connection with the Bacchic types of the coins attributed to Astyra.

grapes attached to the roses by a tendril and the letters E—Π flanking the rose (**99**); the significance of the additional Π is unknown. The symbol attached grapes is also used for some contemporary gold staters, although these have only the letter E (**106**). Four specimens survive, of which at least 3 came from the large gold hoard found at Saida in the last century, which was concealed in the period 323–320.[33] Their mint state and the fact that they were all struck from the same pair of dies suggest emission not long before burial. Rhodian gold issues are extremely rare, and this is the earliest.

These issues seem to have been succeeded by a sub-issue of tetradrachms (10 obverse dies from 24 examples) and didrachms (14 obverse dies from 49 examples) which have attached grapes + E and a square incuse on the reverse, but a completely different obverse style with uniformly heavy and fleshy portraits of Helios occupying more of the flan than the smaller and more refined portraits of the earlier issues with grapes; the roses on the reverse are also larger (**107–8**). Since, however, they still have square incuses, they may be assumed to antedate the succeeding issues of didrachms with round or no incuse. The tetradrachms were struck to the Chian standard of 15.3 g., and give the impression of an exceptional issue isolated amid a long series of didrachms struck to the reduced standard of 6.8 g.

c.305/4–c.250 BC

It is unclear why in the above series the combination grapes + E apparently remained unchanged over several years after the preceding decades during which the symbol changed frequently and was accompanied by different letters. The combination of grapes (both attached and unattached) + E continued into the following series of didrachms, which differ from their predecessors in having a round or no incuse on the reverse, and a markedly different obverse style. The square incuse falls out of use. In the new series grapes, both attached and unattached, also appear in combination with the letters EY; the E + grapes and EY + grapes issues share numerous obverse dies and were clearly struck simultaneously (**157–8**). The EY + grapes issue is die-linked to a smaller issue with EY + thyrsos (**159**). The latter in

turn is closely die-linked to three other small issues having the letters EY and symbols jug, aphlaston, and ivy leaf; they were clearly struck simultaneously (**160–2**).[34] This apparently sudden proliferation of simultaneous issues was accompanied by several symbol–letter combinations which are not die-linked and may thus have been struck sequentially: A + trident, NI + fly, Δ + thunderbolt, and Δ + star (**163–4**, **168–9**). The letters EY, A, and NI also appear on a highly unusual and tightly die-linked series of didrachms (8 obverse dies recorded from 46 coins) with a radiate profile head of Helios on the obverse, and with respective symbols cornucopia, trident, and star (**165–7**). The series was clearly struck at the same time as the conventional series with facing head of Helios and the same letters (there are two 'mules' with a facing-head obverse die from the conventional series and a reverse die from the profile-head series).[35]

Some of the obverse dies of the Δ + star issue are similar to some dies of an issue from the next series of coins which for the first time has an official's name above the rose on the reverse. This issue, with name Aristonomos and symbol prow, was also foreshadowed by some rare hemidrachms of the previous series with symbol prow and monogram ⋈, easily resolved as Ari(stonomos), and obverse style resembling that of the Aristonomos issue (**177**, **180**, **188**, **195**). This is the first occasion when coins bear the names of officials, but thereafter all silver coins of hemidrachm size and above are signed.[36] The Aristonomos issue

[33] IGCH 1508; CH 8, 190; Westermark (1979–80), esp. 29.

[34] Leschhorn (1986) 77–8, suggests that E and EY on the round/no incuse didrachms are the initials of a single official, although perhaps not the same man as the E of the square-incuse didrachms. Since, however, the combination grapes + E was in use from the late 340s until at least the end of the century (see below), the letter is unlikely to represent an individual; nor are E and EY likely to have the same reference, given the introduction of EY with both grapes and several new symbols some four decades after the grapes + E series began and concurrently with its final dies. As noted above, the significance of the letters which began to be added to the coins soon after the opening of the mint is uncertain, but the system under which they were applied seems to have changed with the introduction of the long-lasting grapes + E combination; nor is it clear what, if any, connection existed between the letters and the full names which replaced them (see below). Note that Leschhorn, using the 1966 Uşak hoard (see below) as his base, independently reaches similar conclusions about the dating of the fourth- and early third-century didrachms as Ashton (1988), and as the account given here.

[35] Ashton (1988) 80. I now believe that obverse dies A2 and A3 (ibid., 76) are identical, so that the obverse-die count reduces from 9 to 8. The second hybrid occurred in CH 8, 295: Ashton (1992) 3.

[36] As noted above, the minute letters TAYPO and ΞENO found on some of the earliest tetradrachms may be artists' signatures; they are too inconspicuous and informal to bear comparison with the prominent and regular signatures which appear on almost all Rhodian silver coinage

heads a series of 7 signed issues of didrachms, drachms, and hemidrachms, the other names being Aristolochos, Philonidas, Aristobios, Agesidamos, Antipatros, and Erasikles (181–7, 189–94, 196–8). Agesidamos and Erasikles are die-linked to, respectively, Antipatros + dolphin and Antipatros + corn ear, but not to one another, and recur with the same symbols (respectively, running Artemis and helmet) in the following rayed series, where they are tightly die-linked to one another (see below). Hence, they may well have been striking simultaneously in the present series as well. Only one die link is known among other magistrates in the unrayed series (between Philonidas and Aristobios in the drachm denomination), and it seems more likely than not that they struck consecutively. These issues were accompanied by diobols with rayed profile head of Helios on the obverse and two buds on the reverse (like the first diobols struck in c.340). They are unsigned, but between the buds carry symbols, all but one of which occur on the larger denominations; the exception is the pecten, but this occurs on diobols which are die-linked to an issue with the helmet symbol found on the larger denominations signed by Erasikles (199–203).

Several hoards contain a full or partial range of the didrachm issues discussed above from the square-incuse issues with grapes to the issues signed with a full name, and the gradations of wear on coins in each hoard broadly confirm the order of issues suggested above. Two are of particular importance. The 1966 Uşak hoard contained at least 107 Rhodian didrachms, and 5 Ptolemaic tetradrachms, the latest dating 256/5; its presumed burial date around the middle of the third century provides a useful *terminus ante quem* for its Rhodian didrachms, the freshest of which were representatives of the issue with names in full.[37] The 1991 western Turkey hoard, buried after c.301–297, contained at least 700 Rhodian didrachms and at least 150 Rhodian drachms comprising most of the varieties known up to and including the signed series.[38] Other hoards which confirm by wear the order of the

Rhodian didrachms include Turkey 1988/9 (?), Siphnos 1930, Rhodes 1922, Eretria 1937, Fethiye before 1925, Corinth 1938, and Muğla 1945.[39]

The date when the square-incuse didrachms gave way to round-incuse cannot be determined with precision. The earliest hoards which contain relevant round-incuse issues and which can be dated by non-Rhodian material are the 1960 Pazarlık (Kastabos), 1951/2 Kavalla, and 1953 Phaestos region hoards. The 1960 Pazarlık hoard, buried after 306 and perhaps in 305/4, contained a square-incuse Rhodian drachm with grapes and E (101), a square-incuse hemidrachm with grapes (103), a hemidrachm with ivy leaf and shallow round incuse (172), all in good condition, and a very worn hemidrachm from the late fifth/early fourth centuries. There were no later silver Rhodian coins (for the Rhodian bronzes in the hoard, see below).[40] The obverse style of the die-linked round-incuse hemidrachm issues 171 and 172 (with, respectively, grapes and ivy leaf as symbol) suggests that they belong very early in the round-incuse series or late in the square-incuse period (see n. 19 above). The 1951/2 Kavalla and 1953 Phaestos region hoards,[41] which were concealed in the 270s, are both reported to have contained a single EY + grapes didrachm (158): that in the Kavalla hoard shows little sign of circulation; the condition of the example in the Phaestos hoard is not known. This evidence thus suggests that the round-incuse didrachms may not have been introduced until towards the end of the fourth century, but were in circulation by the 270s.

The round-incuse didrachms with initials and symbols consumed 167 obverse dies, plus 8 for the contemporary exceptional issue with profile rayed head of Helios. The series with officials' names and symbols consumed 69 obverse dies. Between 305/4 and c.250 the mint thus used some 244 recorded

---

from Aristonomos onwards. The function of those who signed these Hellenistic coins is discussed in Appendix 2.

[37] CH 2, 68; CH 8, 287. For details of the hoard see Leschhorn (1986); see also Ashton (1988) 83–4; Ashton (1989) 13, first addendum.

[38] CH 8, 295; Ashton (1992a) 3–4. A posthumous Alexander drachm struck c.301–297 (as Price (1991) no. 1840, not no. L27 of the same mint and date, as erroneously reported in Ashton (1992a)) provides a *terminus*

post quem for its burial, but its remaining non-Rhodian contents, notably an important series of Koan tetradrachms, have not yet been independently dated; similarity of Rhodian content suggests burial around the same time as the 1966 Uşak hoard. For the Koan tetradrachms see Requier (1996).

[39] Respectively CH 8, 294 (Ashton (1992a) 4); IGCH 91 (Nicolet-Pierre and Kroll (1990) 23); IGCH 1284; IGCH 175 (Nicolet-Pierre and Kroll (1990) 27–8); IGCH 1428 (Ashton (1989) 8); IGCH 187 (Nicolet-Pierre and Kroll (1990) 32); and IGCH 1292 (Göktürk (1992)).

[40] IGCH 1288. Price (1966). A regal bronze coin of Demetrios Poliorketes in good condition ensures that burial was no earlier than 306, while the most plausible reason for its concealment is the activity of Poliorketes in the Loryma peninsula during his unsuccessful siege of Rhodes in 305/4.

[41] Respectively IGCH 450 (Thompson (1981)) and IGCH 152.

obverse dies for didrachms, which were by far the dominant denomination. Apart from the rather vague, if consistent, evidence of wear in hoards, it is on present evidence difficult to date individual issues closely within the fifty- to sixty-year span. A working hypothesis is proposed below.

c.250–c.190

The unrayed signed series discussed above seems to have been succeeded around the middle of the third century by an anomalous series of two issues of didrachms, whose obverses have the rayed facing heads of Helios found on all the succeeding issues of tetradrachms and didrachms, but whose reverses revert to a system of control letters (*EY* again, and *ΔI*) rather than names, and introduce a border of dots (**204–5**). They were struck from 39 obverse dies (137 coins). They were absent from the large 1966 Uşak and 1991 western Turkey hoards, and when they do appear in hoards they are mostly in worn condition and associated with the later rayed coins and plinthophoroi; they should be placed after rather than before the unrayed signed series.[42] Two magistrate–symbol combinations from the unrayed signed series, Agesidamos + running warrior and Erasikles + helmet, recur in the next series, which has rayed facing heads on the obverse and a dotted border on the reverse. These two magistrate issues are closely die-linked to one another and to two new magistrate–symbol combinations, Mnasimachos + standing Athena and Timotheos + term (**206–9**). The rayed didrachms signed by these four names consume no fewer than 159 obverse dies (860 coins), and the four magistrates seem to have formed a sort of board which must have overseen the coinage of the state for perhaps a decade or two. The fact that unrayed didrachms of Agesidamos + running warrior and Erasikles + helmet occur in good condition in the 1966 Uşak and 1991 western Turkey hoards, whereas the rayed issues with the same name–symbol combinations are absent, strongly suggests that the latter began shortly after the burial of those hoards around the middle of the third century.[43] The Agesidamos–Erasikles–Mnasimachos–Timotheos board struck no

other silver denomination[44] and no bronze. Agesidamos signed Attic-weight gold staters of autonomous types, and Mnasimachos Attic-weight gold staters with the types of Philip II: only one example of either apparently survives (**210–11**).[45]

This board of four was succeeded by a second board, comprising Ameinias, Aristokritos, Eukrates, and Tharsytas, who struck tetradrachms, didrachms, and (Ameinias and Eukrates only) drachms and hemidrachms (**212–15**, **217–21**, **224–5**, **226–7**). The tetradrachms and didrachms have a rayed head of Helios on obverse and a border of dots on the reverse, like the didrachms of the previous board, but the smaller denominations do not have these features. The tetradrachms, the first of this denomination since the square-incuse tetradrachms of the fourth century, were struck from 25 obverse dies (589 coins), shared by all four magistrates (only Eukrates and Tharsytas have no die in common), and used until they were worn or heavily flawed. The didrachms used 31 dies, and were mostly struck in the names of Ameinias and Eukrates, who also shared numerous drachm and hemidrachm dies. A fifth name, Akesis, occurs on extremely rare (two known) tetradrachms struck from one of the 25 obverse dies mentioned above (**216**). He also struck didrachms and hemidrachms which share obverse dies with the coins of a new magistrate, Anaxandros (**222–3**, **228–31**). Two issues of diobols probably belong to Akesis and Anaxandros, for they are die-linked and have between the two buds on the reverse, respectively, the symbols oval shield and lyre which appear on the didrachms (Apollo with a lyre on the didrachms) (**232–3**). A hoard of some 1,470 Rhodian tetradrachms and didrachms which came on to the market in 1986 (*CH* 8, 347) included tetradrachms and

[42] Ashton (1989).
[43] Their absence from, or slim representation in, other hoards of the second half of the third century confirms this point: Ashton (1988) 83–4.

[44] Four 'drachms' of the Timotheos issue, made from the same pair of dies, are false: Ashton (1999c).
[45] Respectively, BM 1897-3-5-66 (Montagu II, 283), and Sotheby, Wilkinson and Hodge, 6 May 1895 (Ashburnham), 76. The former was struck from dies also used for silver didrachms, an unusual practice which casts doubt on the coin's genuineness; the practice is, however, attested (Kinns (1984) 8 n. 50) and there is no other reason to condemn the piece. The Philip-type stater came from the Northwick collection, dispersed in 1859, and cannot have been part of the 1895 Maeander Valley hoard (*IGCH* 1294), which consisted of at least thirteen posthumous staters of Philip II including some from mints in south-west Asia Minor. In any case, the hoard was probably buried before 275, whereas, as we shall see, the Rhodian Philip was struck several decades later. See further Le Rider (1990) 545; Price (1969) 9–10. Price refers to Rhodian Philips with the names Mnasimachos and Aristoboulos, but the Aristoboulos coin must be the posthumous Lysimachos discussed below in Appendix 3.

didrachms of Ameinias, Aristokritos, Eukrates, Tharsytas, and Akesis, many of which showed a slight amount of wear, and didrachms of Akesis and Anaxandros, all in uncirculated condition. Hence, Akesis may have been a latecomer to the Ameinias/Aristokritos/Eukrates/Tharsytas board or at least inherited one of its tetradrachm dies, and continued to strike with Anaxandros after that board ceased to function. Anaxandros did not strike any tetradrachms, and neither he nor Akesis struck any drachms. The sigma in the name on some of the Anaxandros didrachms is lunate, a form which is unusual on pre-imperial Rhodian coins, but which recurs on the two known reverse dies of the following Stasion + cornucopia didrachms; one of the latter's reverse dies also has a cursive omega (**273**).

The tetradrachms and didrachms of the post c.250 period discussed above were both struck to the Rhodian standard of c.13.6 g. and 6.8 g. respectively. A group of the drachms struck by Ameinias and Eukrates, united by common obverse dies, was also struck to this standard at about 3.2 g., but a second die-linked group in the same names was struck at a significantly lower weight of about 2.8 g.; the latter are now far more common and presumably drove the former out of circulation. All or nearly all of the surviving hemidrachms of the series weigh correspondingly less at c.1.3 g. The lower weights of 2.8 g. and 1.3 g. were used for all the copious subsequent issues of drachms and hemidrachms until the entire system was replaced when the plinthophoroi were introduced in c.190 (see below). The significance of the 2.8 g. weight of the drachms will be discussed below. It should, however, be stressed that the mint continued to strike full Rhodian-weight tetradrachms and didrachms of c.13.6 g. and 6.8 g. alongside the drachms weighing 2.8 g., right up until the plintho-phoric reform.

With the next group of issues we have some firm dating criteria. They were struck in the names of Gorgos and Peisikrates (didrachms, drachms, and hemidrachms), Ainetor (didrachms and drachms), Stasion (tetradrachms, didrachms, and drachms), Theudotos (didrachms only), Aristakos, Teisylos, Damokrines, Diophanes, and Aristoboulos (drachms only), Antigenes, Anaxidikos, Philokrates, Anaxidotos, Athanodoros, and Agesidamos (hemidrachms only) (**259–60**, **268–76**, **282–311**). The tetradrachms and

didrachms are rare (5 and 18 known respectively), but the drachms are common (203 dies from 457 coins, with many more pieces awaiting incorporation into the die-study), particularly those of Gorgos, Ainetor, and Stasion, as are the hemidrachms of Gorgos and Peisikrates. Die-linking is particularly close among the drachm issues of Gorgos, Peisikrates, Ainetor, Aristakos, and Stasion, and among the hemidrachm issues of Gorgos, Peisikrates, Antigenes, Anaxidikos, Philokrates, Anaxidotos, Athanodoros, and Agesida-mos: many were clearly struck simultaneously. The names Ainetor, Stasion, Aristoboulos, Teisylos, Dio-phanes, and Damokrines recur, frequently die-linked, on a series of posthumous Attic-weight Alexander tetradrachms struck by Rhodes, which were clearly issued alongside the autonomous coins of Rhodian weight (**243–58**). Most of these Alexanders, including those with the names mentioned, can be dated on independent grounds to the period 202–190, but some, notably those with monograms resolvable as Ameinias and Eukrates, were struck some years ear-lier. The Alexanders consumed 36 recorded obverse dies, many used very hard, from a total of some 160 recorded coins.[46] The names Gorgos and Ainetor recur among some drachms and didrachms of Rhodian types, but of very low weight and poor silver, which are found in large numbers on Crete and are almost certainly to be associated with the Cretan war of c.205–200. I have suggested elsewhere that these and other issues were struck by Rhodian commanders operating on Crete, and that, although the names Gorgos and Ainetor occur on regular issues of the Rhodian mint, the other names concerned (Straton, Sosikrates, Boulakrates, Kallippos, Herakleitos) do not, and may have been those of the commanders themselves (**333–44**).[47] Aristakos is an extremely rare

[46] Kleiner (1971); Price (1991) nos. 2509–27. The issue of Timaios (Kleiner Series VIII, Price nos. 2526–7) is probably not Rhodian (Ashton (1986) 12 n. 24), and is not included in the Appendix here. For the view that the series began several years earlier than c.202, see Bresson (1993) 154, with refs., to which add Ashton (1993b) 279. For the hard wear on the dies see Kleiner (1971) 114. Three Lysimachos-type gold staters, two signed by an Aristoboulos, are usually attributed to Rhodes in this period; in Appendix 3 I give reasons for doubting the attribution.

[47] Ashton (1987) (issues 1–9: issue 10 is, it was argued, probably an imitation made by a local mint). I take this opportunity to correct a probable error in that account: the only example of the 'hemidrachm' issue 3B looks more like a clipped drachm of issue 3A. For the poor quality of the silver in these issues see Barrandon and Bresson (1997), who also demonstrate the remarkable purity of the silver used for earlier and contemporary regular Rhodian coinage.

name on Rhodes, and is otherwise known only as a hierope from Kamiros, Aristakos the son of Hieron, who appears on an inscription dating to *c*.215; he is probably the same man as the moneyer.[48] Finally, it is worth noting that a member of a board charged with collecting a tax in the late third or early second century was a certain Ainetor, son of Mytion;[49] however, although the context is temptingly financial, Ainetor is a common name on Rhodes, and the absence of patronymics on the coins precludes positive identification.

The final coins of Rhodian weight were a group of tetradrachms and didrachms distinguished by broad flat flans, weakly executed portraits of Helios, and roses with markedly curved central sepals. They were struck in the names of Stasion, Ainetor, Aetion, Agemachos, Damatrios, Onasandros and Xenokrates, and die-linking suggests simultaneous or near-simultaneous emission (**261–7**, **274–81**). Agemachos and Damatrios recur on posthumous Alexanders of Rhodes. As the Alexanders end by *c*.190,[50] the Rhodian-weight tetradrachms and didrachms probably end then too.

This is consistent with the starting date of the next series struck at the mint, the plinthophoroi, which represented a complete reorganization of the monetary system.[51] The Rhodian weight standard was at last abandoned and replaced by a system based on drachms weighing slightly over 3.0 g. accompanied by hemidrachms and diobols but no higher denominations. Because most of the drachms of the preceding series weigh around 2.8 g., the plinthophoric standard is usually regarded as an increase. But, as we shall see, the weight of these earlier drachms was established for a particular purpose, and the Rhodian-weight tetradrachm and didrachm of 13.6 g. and 6.8 g., with a theoretical drachm of *c*.3.4 g., remained the standard. Hence, the plinthophoric drachm represented a reduction. This may well explain why the last tetradrachms and didrachms are now so rare, even though they seem originally to have been an abundant series whose ratios of surviving specimens to obverse dies (respectively 29:12 and 29:18) suggest that significantly

more obverse dies remain to be discovered: the plinthophoroi will have driven the proportionately heavier tetradrachms and didrachms out of circulation. The new plinthophoric system was marked by a change in design: on the drachms and diobols a rayed profile head of Helios replaced the usual facing head, while on the hemidrachms the unrayed facing head became rayed; more startling was the addition to the reverse of a shallow square incuse (*plinthos* = brick or ingot). In a fundamental article in 1951 Louis Robert showed that the series should be removed from its traditional starting date in 166 to at least as early as 173. Subsequent research has shown that the series was in circulation at least as early as the mid-180s.[52] No fewer than 15 or 16 of the names on the immediately pre-plinthophoric coins, including all five of the names on the last Rhodian-weight tetradrachms and didrachms, recur on the earliest plinthophoroi (Jenkins (1989), Group A) with similar patterns of die-linking: Agatharchos, Agemachos, Agesidamos, Aetion, Ainetor, Anaxidikos, Anaxidotos, Antigenes, Aristoboulos, Athanodoros, Damatrios, Onasandros, Philokrates, Stasion, Xenokrates, and perhaps Aristokritos. It seems certain that all, or almost all, these names belong to the same men striking both series.[53] If the Rhodian-weight coinage ended by *c*.190 and the plinthophoroi were in circulation before 184, then, given the large number of overlap magistrates, it would be reasonable to conclude that the plinthophoroi began around 190. The historical implications of this will be discussed below.

The last group of pre-plinthophoric issues can thus be securely dated *c*.205–*c*.190. There is unlikely to have been much of a gap between it and the preceding group, that struck by Ameinias–Aristokritos–Eukrates–Tharsytas–Akesis–Anaxandros, given the

---

[48] *Tituli Camirenses* 40, l. 12. I owe this point to Alain Bresson.

[49] See Kontorini and Migeotte (1995); Bresson (1997), 16–17, n. 19.

[50] Kleiner (1971) 114–16.

[51] Jenkins (1989) gives a conspectus of the series, whose end he places in 84 BC. For the subsequent silver emissions of Rhodes see Ashton with Weiss (1997).

[52] Robert (1951) 166–78; Errington (1989), esp. 286–8 (by 185/4); Ashton (1994) 58, esp. n. 4. Bresson (1998) 84 suggests that the 'old Rhodian drachms' mentioned in I. Milet 148 (redated by Errington to 185/4) may refer to third-century drachms weighing *c*.3.30–3.35 g.; but the light-weight drachms of *c*.2.8 g., introduced in the late third century, will almost certainly have driven these out of circulation by the mid-180s, and it seems preferable to follow the traditional view that 'old drachms' refers to the drachms of *c*.2.8 g., and to allow that the inscription thereby indirectly refers to the plinthophoroi.

[53] The Agesidamos on immediately pre-plinthophoric hemidrachms is almost certainly the same as the man of that name who signed early plinthophoroi; the Agesidamos who struck in the mid third century must be a different man. Aristokritos struck tetradrachms and didrachms in the last quarter of the third century, and may be the plinthophoric magistrate of that name.

apparently short-lived fashion for the lunate sigma shared by certain Anaxandros and Stasion issues, and the uniformity of wear among hemidrachms of the two groups in a hoard which appeared on the London market in 1973.[54] As we shall see, the historical background also suggests continuity. There are no die links or other obvious connections between the Ameinias–Aristokritos–Eukrates–Tharsytas board and the Agesidamos–Erasikles–Mnasimachos–Timotheos board which preceded it, but it is unlikely that there was much gap between them for (i) these two very large groups of coins have to be fitted into the period c.250–c.205; and (ii) the wear of the many specimens of both boards which occur in CH 8, 347 (see 87 above) is roughly similar. It will be argued below that the Ameinias board was in operation by the early 220s.

Bronze Coinage

Kamiros had struck an issue of small (10–11 mm.) bronzes with on obverse a fig-leaf, and on reverse the letters KA within two quarters of a four-spoked wheel. The fabric is chunky and the reverse has a marked round incuse (BMC 15, SNG Keckman 351). The early date of this issue need occasion no surprise, particularly given the links since the archaic period between Rhodes and Sicily where a fiduciary bronze coinage had been introduced before 425 BC, and it is unnecessary to suggest that it was struck by Kamiros for purely local use after the synoecism.[55] The first federal bronze coinage is the abundant series of chalkoi (9–11 mm., c.1.0–1.5 g.) with types head of Rhodos/rose, which is generally assumed to date to the second half of the fourth century.[56] As we shall see, most of these coins were indeed struck in that period, but there are some rare chalkoi with the same types, which seem to be much earlier (57–66). I have firmly identified only 26 from the thousands of

Rhodos/rose chalkoi extant. They differ from most of the later Rhodos/rose chalkoi in their chunky fabric, high proportion of irregular die axes (all silver and almost all other bronze issues of Rhodes were struck with upright axes, with very few individual exceptions), and in certain stylistic features which recall the earliest silver of the mint.[57] The symbols shrimp, grasshopper, ivy leaf, and bucranium on four of the issues may well have the same reference as those symbols on some roughly contemporary hemidrachms and tetradrachms.

Rhodes thus struck federal bronze coinage as soon as the mint opened, although little survives of the earliest emission. By contrast, in the second half of the fourth century the mint struck an abundant series of Rhodos/rose chalkoi in issues distinguished by 26 different symbols and 21 different letters, double letters or monograms on the reverse, together with one issue without any sign (109–56). Twenty-six of these issues can be identified in 3 mixed hoards concealed c.300, and a further 4 in unmixed hoards which also contain representatives of issues found in the mixed hoards.[58] Some of the symbols and letters recur on silver coinage of the fourth and early third centuries, and may have the same reference. It seems likely that the entire series should be dated to the second half of the fourth century, although some of the issues not apparently represented in the hoards may belong a little later. Pace Price (1966) 69–70, the two different positions of the ethnic on these chalkoi (P—O around the rose stalk, or Po in the left

---

[54] CH 1, 85. The mid-second-century date proposed in CH 1 is too late, for all the plinthophoroi belong to Jenkins's (1989) Group A, which is unlikely to have ended much, if at all, after 175, given the large number of magistrates which it shares with the pre-plinthophoric issues.

[55] For the earliest issues of bronze coinage see Price (1968), to which add (for western Asia Minor) Ashton in Ashton et al. (forthcoming).

[56] Head (1911) 639; Price (1968) 101; Price (1966) 70. In the late third century there were probably 8 chalkoi to the Rhodian obol (Ashton (1986) 9 n. 8); there is no reason to suppose that this was not the case from the beginning.

[57] Six of the twenty-six have Rhodos left rather than right, an orientation never found on the other Rhodos/rose issues, and their heads of Rhodos in general resemble those on the reverse of some early hemidrachm issues, particularly in usually having the hair in a sakkos rather than simply rolled, as on the later bronzes. Furthermore, whereas all the later Rhodos/rose coins have upright buds, usually to the right, the squat, square, and budless roses of some of the early chalkoi recall those on the earliest tetradrachms with symbol eagle or club and on two of the three reverse dies of the alliance tridrachms. The position of the ethnic P—O around the body of the rose on most of the early bronzes recalls the hemidrachms of issue 19, while the drooping buds and ethnic POΔION above the rose on early bronze issue 61 recall the hemidrachms of issue 18. (Most later Rhodian coins of small module in either metal use the abbreviated version of the ethnic.) The two drooping buds on some of the bronzes closely resemble those on some early tetradrachms and hemidrachms. The central sepals of the roses, where they can be discerned, have pointed ends: as we have seen, this is characteristic of the earliest silver issues, after which the sepals usually seem to have rounded ends.

[58] Mixed hoards: IGCH 1287 = CH 2, 59; IGCH 1288; IGCH 1289/1290 (see Ashton (1999a) 22 n. 13); (CH 8, 597 is at best badly contaminated, and is of no value for our purposes: see note ad loc.) Unmixed: IGCH 1285 (see Ashton (1999a) 20); IGCH 1286; CH 8, 239.

field) do not seem to have any chronological significance, for the two varieties have several control marks in common, and they do not show any significant difference in pattern of wear in hoards.

The next bronzes seem to have been an extremely rare series of apparent obols and dichalka (3 survive) with profile radiate head of Helios on obverse and a rose on reverse (178–9); their style suggests that they accompanied the special series of didrachms with radiate profile head of Helios struck in the first half of the third century. Thereafter no bronzes are recorded until another apparently special series with unusual types: tetrachalka with head of Zeus right/rose with control letters or monogram; dichalka with veiled female head right on obverse and on reverse either a prow or the more usual rose with control letters also found on the Zeus tetrachalka (234–42).[59]

Next come chalkoi with the rose as a type on both sides (317–31). In most of the major catalogues they are regarded as the earliest Rhodian bronzes and dated to the fourth century. They are, however, conspicuously absent from the hoards of Rhodian bronzes which can be dated to the late fourth century or just after (see above), and the three hoards in which they are firmly attested are much later in date. IGCH 1342 = CH 2, 84 contained 2 Rhodian tetradrachms and 10 didrachms of the second half of the third century, 98 early plinthophoric drachms, 2 rose/rose chalkoi, and 1 chalkous with radiate head of Helios profile right/rose without plinthos (332). The early plinthophoric drachms ensure that the hoard cannot have been buried earlier than the 180s and it is likely that the bronzes were struck not long before the start of the plinthophoric period. The second hoard, CH 7, 106, circulated on the Athens market in the mid-1970s and comprised several hundred Rhodian chalkoi of the rose/rose and plinthophoric varieties. No further information survives (it is legitimate to wonder whether at least some of the plinthophoric bronzes were in fact chalkoi with profile radiate head of Helios and no plinthos), but the association of the two varieties is convincing evidence that the rose/rose chalkoi belong to the late third or early second centuries. The third hoard, found in Rhodes city in 1975/6, contained 239 chalkoi, 2 didrachms, and 1 hemidrachm. The chalkoi included

several dozen worn examples of the Rhodos/rose issues 109–56, while all or most of the rest were rose/rose chalkoi in much better condition. A date of burial in the last quarter of the third century is suggested by the fact that one of the didrachms was of the Aristokritos + aphlaston issue (219; for the date, see above).[60] On the evidence of IGCH 1342 the chalkoi with a radiate profile head of Helios right and a rose without the plinthos belong to about the same period, and as the radiate profile head seems to anticipate the radiate heads which appear on the plinthophoroi, it is reasonable to suppose that this is the last pre-plinthophoric bronze issue.[61]

Thus the mint seems to have struck chalkoi in limited numbers in the late fifth/early fourth centuries and in considerable numbers in the second half of the fourth and early third centuries. Thereafter, apart from some limited and exceptional issues of obols, tetrachalka and dichalka in the early and (as we shall see) the late third century, production of bronze resumed only towards the end of the third century, again in the form of chalkoi. This production continued into the second century and into the plinthophoric period after c.190. Thus in the period under review the mint of Rhodes did not produce a broad multidenominational range of bronze coinage, unlike certain other large mints in western Asia Minor. Nor did it provide small change in the form of extremely small silver denominations such as were issued in large numbers in Karia and elsewhere in the earlier part of the fourth century.[62] The smallest silver coins produced were the obols struck in the two first decades of the mint's existence (see above); thereafter diobols and hemidrachms were the smallest denominations, and it seems that, even allowing for the accidents of survival and collectors' preferences, they were produced in only limited numbers.

[59] Ashton (1986) 1–8.

[60] The hoard was on display in the Palace of the Grand Masters in Rhodes in 1998, when I saw it and recorded the above details; see also AD 31/1976, Chron., 386 (the suggested burial date of the late fourth/early third centuries is too early).

[61] IGCH 1289/1290 contained Rhodos/rose, profile rayed Helios/rose and plinthophoric bronzes, but are of no value for dating purposes because of their apparent contamination (Ashton (1999a) 22 n. 13).

[62] Multidenominational bronzes at, for example, Miletos: Deppert-Lippitz (1984) 152–160, 172–5, 182–3; Erythrai, Teos, Lebedos, Kolophon: Kinns (1980) 420–3, 427–30, 441–64, 469–70, 504–5, 508–13, 516–18, 520–2, 543, 545–8, 559–61, 565–70, 574–9. Fractional silver of the early fourth century from Samos: Barron (1966) 210–13. Fractional silver from mainland Caria: Troxell (1984) 249–57; Troxell and Kagan (1989) 275–81; Konuk (1998) 22–51; see also SNG Keckman i, 837–928.

Volume, Pattern, and Historical Associations of the Coinage

In order to make convenient chronological comparisons of output, I have converted all known obverse dies used for the silver coinage into didrachm equivalents (one tetradrachm obverse = two didrachm obverses; two drachm obverses = one didrachm obverse; four hemidrachm obverses = one didrachm obverse; six diobol obverses = one didrachm obverse), and produced a rounded average figure of annual consumption of such dies for each period adopted. The pitfalls are obvious: for example, I have not taken into account the probably differing rates of die survival over the periods, nor the fact that most Hellenistic fractions were struck at a little less than their theoretical weights, nor the fact that the drachms and hemidrachms of the period c.205–c.190 were significantly reduced in weight (see above), nor the probability that dies of different (and indeed the same) size would produce greatly varying numbers of coins. Hence, the figures produced below are at best extremely rough, but they should give some idea of variation in output between periods.[63]

The extremely low ratio of obverse dies to surviving tetradrachms from c.385 to the late 340s suggests that the survival rate of tetradrachm issues and of dies for that period may be particularly poor

Table 6.1: Variation in output at Rhodes between different periods

Period	Number of didrachm-equivalent dies	Average per year
408–c.385	262	11.4
c.385–c.360	42	1.7
c.360–late 340s	28	1.5
late 340s–305/4	126	3.5
305/4–c.250	294	5.5
c.250–c.230	198	9.9
c.230–c.205	123	4.9
c.205–c.190	241	16.1

(above, p. 84). Nevertheless, the contrast between the first quarter-century of the mint's operation and the next 45 years is stark, as is the absence of small denominations during the latter period, apart from a few drachms. When we consider also the low level of activity at the three old mints on the island immediately before the synoecism, it is difficult to avoid the conclusion that the heavy output of the first two or three decades, a level unsurpassed until the late third century, was prompted by the need to finance construction of the new city of Rhodes on the northern tip of the island. Hemidrachms were issued on a scale unmatched in the later history of the mint, and perhaps represented a day's pay for at least some categories of workmen.[64]

In the last four decades of the fourth century, when didrachms were the dominant denomination, output still seems to have been quite modest, but two phenomena require explanation. First, the production of the small (1 obverse die) issue of gold staters on the Attic standard with the E + grapes control under which most of the contemporary silver coinage was struck. In 1966 Martin Price suggested that the gold staters marked the arrival of Macedonian supremacy in the island in 333/2 and that they initiated the E + grapes issue as a whole. We have seen above that the E + grapes didrachms began in the late 340s, and, as the only recorded find-spot of the gold staters is in the east (the Saida hoard), an alternative explanation might be that they were struck as a contribution to Alexander's war effort, and may have gone with the group of ten ships sent by Rhodes in early 332 to offer the submission of the island to Alexander while he was besieging Tyre.[65]

Secondly, some time after the didrachm was established as the island's principal denomination the mint struck an issue of tetradrachms with E + attached grapes and unusual style together with didrachms of the same style. To judge from the consistency of obverse and reverse style (all the dies look as if they were the work of one engraver), the emission was short-lived, and gives the impression of being struck to meet a sudden need. I have suggested elsewhere

[63] I have not taken account of the minor gold issues struck on rare occasions, nor of the quasi-official issues struck on or for Crete in the late third century (88 and n. 47 above). The didrachms of issues 204–5, dated c.250 BC, have been added to the coins of c.250–c.230 (with which, as we have seen, they are associated in hoards) and not to those of 305/4–c.250.

[64] Construction of the new city: Strabo 14. 2. 5 (653), 14. 2. 9 (654); Dio Chrys. 31. 163; Psd.-Arist. 43 (797–8, 810D); for modern references see Berthold (1984), 56. Compare the rates of pay recorded for construction and other manual workers at Athens in the fifth and fourth centuries (generally higher than a hemidrachm a day): Loomis (1998) 104–20.

[65] Price (1966) 70; Arr. Anab. 2. 20. 2; Curt. 4. 5. 9, 8. 12; Just. 11. 11. 1.

that reconstruction work after the floods of 316 which destroyed Rhodes' fortifications would be a plausible, if unprovable, explanation. Two other serious floods earlier in the fourth century may have prompted the striking of particular issues, but they cannot be dated, and speculation as to what issues might have been involved would be fruitless.[66]

The round-incuse series begins with a sudden proliferation of letter–symbol combinations, tightly die-linked and clearly struck simultaneously, after the long preceding period during which the E + grapes combination had been the only one in use. The dies of the earlier issues often show large flaws—i.e. they were used hard—and the impression is of a rapid initial peak in output followed by a longer period of high but more measured production. I have suggested elsewhere that the high output at the start of the series was prompted by the need to prepare for and resist the great siege of 305/4, and then to repair the damage done by Poliorketes, and to construct the Colossus, which was built from the proceeds (300 talents) of the sale of his siege-train. If this is right, the small and highly unusual series of didrachms with profile radiate head of Helios which was struck simultaneously with the 'regular' issues of the mint and the bronze tetrachalka and dichalka with the same types may have been issued to commemorate the Colossus; the rayed head may in fact portray the Colossus itself.[67]

For several decades thereafter the output of didrachms, by far the dominant denomination, continued at an apparently even pace with no discernible peaks or troughs. The autonomous Attic-weight gold stater signed by Agesidamos may be contemporary with the gold stater in the name of Philip signed by Mnasimachos, which perhaps dates to about the middle of the third century (see above). A connection with the Second Syrian War in the 250s is possible but unprovable.[68] Then, long after the final tetradrachms of the fourth century, tetradrachms are again struck, apparently in some haste and in large numbers, to judge from the hard wear to which the 25 obverse dies involved were subjected. Some of the dies were used until they were badly worn and others until large flaws

developed—treatment which is rarely observed on the dies of other periods. I have argued elsewhere that, as may have been the case with the tetradrachms of the late fourth century, the need to finance urgent construction work lay behind the revival of the tetradrachm denomination in the later part of the third, this time the repair of the damage wrought by the great earthquake of the early 220s. I also argued that the unusual Zeus/rose, veiled female head/rose, and veiled female head/prow bronze issues belong to the same period, and reflect the aid provided by Ptolemy III after the disaster, in particular his gift of large quantities of coined and uncoined bronze (one of the Zeus/rose coins is in fact overstruck on a Ptolemaic bronze coin of much larger module); and that the female head represents Berenice II.[69] It may further be conjectured that the final, much smaller, group of autonomous tetradrachms datable to the late third or early second century was struck to repair damage done by an earthquake attested in 198/7.[70]

As we have seen, the magistrates Ameinias and Eukrates, who struck the bulk of the tetradrachms associated with the earthquake of the early 220s, also reduced their drachms and hemidrachms from the normal Rhodian weights of c.3.3 g. and c.1.6 g. to c.2.8 g. and c.1.3 g., and these weights remained in force until the whole Rhodian system was replaced c.190 by the plinthophoric, although the autonomous tetradrachms and didrachms continued to be struck at the normal Rhodian weights of c.13.6 g. and 6.8 g. This reform is probably to be connected with the minting, almost certainly by Ameinias and Eukrates, of Rhodes' first posthumous Alexander tetradrachms, struck on the Attic standard in parallel with the autonomous Rhodian-weight tetradrachms and didrachms and the reduced drachms. The reduced drachms seem to have passed as tetrobols on the Attic standard, whether or not they were intentionally struck as such, although it is clear from later inscriptions that they continued to be called drachms.[71]

The Alexanders continued to be struck until the end of the Rhodian-weight coins in c.190. This period is characterized by a marked increase in the number

[66] Diod. 19. 45. 1–8; Ashton (1988) 82, 85.
[67] Ashton (1988), esp. 86–8.
[68] For discussion of this ill-documented event see Will (1979) 234–43; CAH vii, 2nd edn., 1, 418–19. For Rhodes's probable involvement see Berthold (1984) 89–92.

[69] Ashton (1986). Other evidence for public expenditure after the earthquake is discussed by Migeotte (1992) 105–8, no. 37, and by Kontorini and Migeotte (1995).
[70] Ashton (1986) 16–17 n. 43.
[71] Bresson (1996) 71 with n. 33; inscriptions: e.g., TN, no. 370.

of magistrates striking coins: after several decades during which at most four or five magistrates were striking at any one time, the die links now show that eight or ten magistrates were probably striking simultaneously. At the same time the die count shows that, rough and ready though the calculation is, the rate of production went up to the equivalent of an average of 16.1 didrachm obverse dies a year for the last years of the third century and first decade of the second, a rate never achieved before or since. These developments (reduced drachms, Alexanders, doubling in number of signing magistrates, increased rate of output) all occurred within a short space of time, and are almost certainly to be connected with the expenses of the wars on Crete and against Philip V and Antiochos III, in which Rhodes was closely involved.[72] It was probably in this period that the Rhodian drachm of reduced weight became established as a standard medium and daily rate of pay for mercenaries, particularly Cretans, and was the model for many imitations struck by a variety of authorities in south-west Asia Minor and mainland Greece. The use of both genuinely Rhodian and pseudo-Rhodian drachms was particularly prevalent during the Third Macedonian War, some twenty years after the Rhodian mint had abandoned the old-style drachms in favour of the plinthophoroi (see n. 112 below).

We have seen that the plinthophoroi probably replaced the Rhodian-weight series in about 190. Louis Robert has made the attractive suggestion that the change reflected a reorganization at the mint to cater for the changes made by the Peace of Apameia in 188, particularly the large amount of mainland territory granted to Rhodes under its terms.[73] Bresson has suggested that the new coinage was introduced because the prestige of the pre-plinthophoric drachms had been diminished by the number of imitations which they had spawned and which would have threatened the closed monetary system which Rhodes enforced over its territories.[74] However, the great bulk of pseudo-Rhodian drachms were struck in the decades

after Apameia, and in 190 the only imitations known to have been in existence were those which had been issued on Crete 205–200—almost all, it seems, struck by Rhodian commanders. They hardly seem sufficient in quantity or close enough in time to have undermined acceptance of genuine products of the Rhodian mint. One further hypothesis may be advanced, although at this stage it is little more than speculative. The early plinthophoric drachm weighed, at just over 3.0 g., the same as the early cistophoric drachm issued by Attalid mints, which in turn weighed slightly less than a quarter of the cistophoric tetradrachm, following the usual Hellenistic practice whereby fractions weighed slightly less than their theoretical weight, presumably to reflect the higher unit cost of minting them. The date when the cistophoroi were introduced is still under debate, but opinion seems to be hardening in favour of an early date, in the 180s or even the late 190s.[75] If this is right, it is legitimate to ask whether it is more than coincidence that two states, which were allies in the wars against Philip V and Antiochos III, both decided to introduce at about the same time coinages which were completely different in design from any previous products of their mints and which apparently adopted the same, otherwise unknown, weight standard. Was the introduction of the cistophoroi and plinthophoroi a co-ordinated response to military events in the late 190s, as the emission of posthumous Alexanders by the two states may have been a decade or more earlier? If so, the co-ordination was short-lived, and the coinages will have gone their separate ways, for the cistophoroi rarely travelled outside the Pergamene economic zone where they enjoyed an overvalued status, whereas Rhodian plinthophoroi are not recorded from Pergamene territory (apart from Telmessos, an isolated enclave granted to the Attalids by the Peace of Apameia and surrounded by Rhodian-controlled lands).[76]

Circulation

The circulation of pre-plinthophoric Rhodian silver has been well discussed by Alain Bresson.[77] He

---

[72] See Berthold (1984) 107–66 for the historical background.

[73] Robert (1951) 172. Robert's further tentative suggestion (174–5; briefly revived by Chankowski-Sablé (1997) 366) that the late pre-plinthophoric and the early plinthophoric coinage may have been struck simultaneously for different purposes is not supported by the evidence of coin circulation and is a priori improbable: see Bresson (1993) 164–6; Apostolou (1995) 18.

[74] Bresson (1993) 165–6; Bresson (1996) 71–2.

[75] Bauslaugh (1990) 61–4 with refs.; Harl (1991); Ashton (1994) 60.

[76] Kleiner and Noe (1977) 18, 124–5; Ashton (1994) 57–8; Ashton *et al.* (1994).

[77] Bresson (1993).

demonstrates that most finds of autonomous-type Rhodian coins are from the island itself and the Peraia, and from nearby areas in Karia and the coast of Lykia under the economic domination of Rhodes; much smaller quantities are found on the neighbouring islands, and Crete, and remarkably few elsewhere in the Greek world. The Attic-weight Alexanders of Rhodes do not conform with this pattern, for, as an internationally accepted currency, they circulated widely, especially in the East. Bresson suggests that the coinage listed as Rhodian in the Delian inventories in 166 BC (in any case only about 10 per cent of the total) may have consisted largely of the imitations struck outside Rhodes, and notes that most of the many Rhodian-type coins circulating in mainland Greece at the time of the Third Macedonian War were imitations struck locally.[78] Thus, pre-plinthophoric Rhodian coinage did not travel to anything like the degree we might expect from the island's commercial prominence, nor does its circulation correspond with what is known of the island's trading relations, as witnessed by, for example, amphora handles: 'le reseau commercial de Rhodes est plus qu'imparfaitement retranscrit par les trouvailles monétaires: en fait il n'y a aucune correspondance réelle entre la distribution des monnaies et ce que l'on sait des relations commerciales de la cité' (Bresson (1993) 161).

The argument is perhaps not as clear cut as Bresson suggests. First, much Rhodian coin may have been melted down by recipient states: Ptolemaic Egypt, Rhodes' principal trading partner, operated a closed currency system where Rhodian coins would not have been allowed to circulate (cf. 97 and n. 91 below); elsewhere in the eastern Mediterranean, the Attic-weight currency of Alexander and his successors was dominant from the late fourth century onwards, and coins of Rhodian weight would have been regarded as anachronistic and difficult to exchange, even in the open currency system of the Seleucid empire. Secondly, the extensive imitation of Rhodian drachms in mainland Greece and south-west Asia Minor in the first half of the second century, often for the payment of mercenaries, shows that genuine Rhodian coins

were widely known and accepted (see n. 112 below). Thirdly, hoards and stray finds in addition to those which Bresson lists indicate that Rhodian coinage was more common in mainland Greece and Crete in the fourth and third centuries than he suggests. Fourthly, the proportion of authentic as against imitation Rhodian drachms in the hoards associated with the Third Macedonian War was higher than he allows, and significant numbers turn up as stray finds from central and northern Greece.[79] Nevertheless, despite these and other adjustments,[80] the overall picture presented by Bresson is broadly convincing. It seems likely that for most foreign commercial transactions Rhodian merchants used foreign currency, particularly Attic-weight or Ptolemaic coinage, and/or instruments of credit, although I know of no direct evidence for the latter. Bresson also demonstrates that

[78] See also Chankowski-Sablé (1997) at 359–66, esp. 364. The idea that the word rhodion refers to a weight standard common to both imitation and genuine non-plinthophoric Rhodian drachms in the Delian inventories (ead., 364) is doubtful, for the former often weighed significantly less than the latter (Ashton (1995) 7 and n. 3).

[79] For example, the 595 Rhodian-type coins examined from the Oreus hoard were not all imitations, as Bresson (1993) 141 asserts. On a conservative estimate (i.e. discounting doubtful coins which may or may not have been authentically Rhodian), at least 152 of the coins were genuine products of the Rhodian mint. Nevertheless, the presence of Rhodian drachms in central and northern Greece during the Third Macedonian War attests only the then popularity of Rhodian and Rhodian-type coinage as payment for mercenaries, and hardly affects Bresson's general thesis; for that reason there is no need to note here the many Rhodian drachms struck c.205–190 which I have recorded as stray finds from mainland Greece (mostly Thessaly and Phokis) and in hoards which came to light after Bresson's study (e.g. CH 8, 419–26, and other material assembled for the forthcoming CH 9). Of more relevance are the following notes, which are not exhaustive, from my file of fourth- and third-century Rhodian coins found as strays in central and northern Greece: 1 each from silver issues 98, 158, 169, 180, 183, 186, 187, 190; 3 bronzes of issues 109–56, 1 bronze of issue 234. Note also the unspecified Rhodian hemidrachm in CH 8, 278 (Thessaly, buried c. 270); the 20 didrachms in CH 8, 517 (north of Larisa, 1985; buried c.75, but the didrachms must antedate c.190, for the denomination was abandoned when the plinthophoroi were introduced); and the fact that the Third Macedonian War hoards CH 8, 419, and 426 included specimens of (CH 8, 419) issues 99 (1) and 157 or 158 (1), and (CH 8, 426) issues 100 (1), 193 (1), 224 (2), and 225 (3). From Crete, in addition to the material assembled by Bresson, I have noted 3 bronzes of issues 109–56 and a didrachm of issue 275. Gabrielsen (1997) 182–3 nn. 73 and 77, following Robert and Hackens, sees evidence for Rhodian trade in coin finds at, respectively, Histiaia and Thebes, but most of these coins are pseudo-Rhodian drachms connected with the Third Macedonian War, not trade.

[80] e.g. 2 chalkoi of issue 332 from excavations at Phanagoria (R. Ashton in a forthcoming volume of Colloquia Pontica); 1 didrachm of issue 158, 5 chalkoi of issues 109–56, and two chalkoi of issue 332 from the Athens Agora excavations (Kroll (1993), nos. 959, 963 and 964; nos. 960–1, 962, and 965–6 are, respectively, pseudo-Rhodian drachms, unidentifiable, and plinthophoric or later); 1 chalkous of issue 119, 2 chalkoi of issues 317–31 from the Corinth excavations (Zervos (1986) 194, no. 122; Williams and Zervos (1985) 88, no. 52; Edwards (1933) 71, no. 456); 1 chalkous of issue 137 from the Kenchreai excavations (Hohlfelder (1978) 15, no. 54). On the other hand, and in support of Bresson's conclusion, the Rhodian coins reported in the fourth-century hoard from Denia in Spain (IGCH 2317) are strikingly anomalous and one wonders if they are in fact coins of nearby Rhoda.

within the island and the Peraia very little non-Rhodian currency circulated and suggests plausibly that Rhodes enforced a closed monetary zone there.[81]

Function of the Coinage

The above discussion has shown that in the period from the foundation of the unified state in 408 to *c*.190 Rhodian coinage was dominated firstly by tetradrachms and then by didrachms. Smaller denominations were struck in significant quantity only during the first two and the last two decades of the period, when they can be explained respectively as pay for workers constructing the new city of Rhodes and as military expenditure in the wars against Cretan pirates, Philip V, and Antiochos III. Bronze chalkoi were struck in significant quantity only in the second half of the fourth century and in the last two or three decades of the period under review; the few larger bronze denominations which survive have the character of exceptional, perhaps quasi-commemorative, emissions of little economic significance. Thus, although the lower survival rate of small change doubtless skews our picture, and although the large denominations may have been used to pay for regular small transactions on a cumulative 'slate' system, the coinage does not seem well adapted for everyday domestic use.[82] Nor, it seems, was it used extensively in foreign transactions (apart from the Attic-weight Alexanders). What then was its purpose? We have seen above that various peaks in production, particularly those involving tetradrachms, can plausibly be associated with construction work or military crises: the construction of the new city from 408; repairs after the floods in 316; the great siege of 305/4 followed by reconstruction work and erection of the Colossus; reconstruction after the earthquakes of 229–226 and 198/7; and intense military expenditure from 205 to 190.[83] But these crises do not account for the apparently regular and increasing emission of coinage, in particular didrachms, from *c*.340 to the end of the period under review.

Although direct evidence is lacking, a significant proportion, perhaps all, of the non-exceptional output of the mint must have been struck to cater for regular state expenditure. The state had many domestic and external commitments, particularly from the time of Alexander onwards, when trade and the need to police trade routes against pirates increased considerably. Such expenditure would have included:

(1)   the maintenance of the standing fleet. By fifth-century Athenian standards, the Rhodian military fleet in the Hellenistic period may have been quite small, perhaps fewer than 40 ships, of which only some would be at sea at any one time in normal circumstances. The largest number of capital ships sent out in a single year seems to have been about 75 in 190. But in the late third century it cost some 10,000 drachms a month to maintain a trireme, and it is difficult to imagine that even in peacetime less than, say, 100 talents a year was spent on the fleet. To this must be added enormous expenditure on the dockyards and other naval infrastructure for which Rhodes was famous, and on the manufacture of armaments;[84]

(2)   the payment of the mercenaries who seem to have made up the rank and file of the Rhodian land army. The land army seems to have been relatively unimportant and used mainly to garrison the Peraia, although detailed evidence is lacking; we hear of a force of 2,600 mercenaries in the Peraia in the early second century, although this was in the exceptional context of the war against Philip V;[85]

(3)   contributions towards the expense of the Nesiotic League revived under Rhodian leadership in or soon after 200;[86]

(4)   payments for jury service, for service on the Council, and for attendance at the Assembly;[87]

(5)   probable payment of numerous military, religious, and civic officials, although direct evidence is lacking;[88]

[81]   Bresson (1993) 132–6, 162–4. I noted a marked paucity of non-Rhodian coinage while working in the Archaeological Museum at Rhodes in the early 1970s.

[82]   This contrasts sharply with the picture of archaic coinage proposed by Kim, 7–20 above.

[83]   For coinage and building programmes at sixth/fifth century Athens see Rutter (1981), esp. 2 and 5.

[84]   *SIG*³581; Strabo 14. 2. 5; Berthold (1984) 42–4; Rice (1991). For the navy see also Gabrielsen (1997) 85 ff., esp. 93–4 (arguing that the fleet may have been larger than earlier commentators have suggested); also 37–42 for dockyards and other naval infrastructure.

[85]   Berthold (1984) 45–6; 138–9 and refs.; Griffith (1935) 90–2; Gabrielsen (1997) 42, 51, 165 n. 30, and 169 nn. 70–2.

[86]   See Gabrielsen (1997) 57–8, with refs.

[87]   Dio Chrys. 31. 102; Psd.-Sall. *ad Caes*. 2. 7. 12; Cic. *Rep*. 3. 35. 48; Fraser (1972) 119–24; Gabrielsen (1997) 27–8.

[88]   Gabrielsen (1997) 28 and 159–60 n. 57, noting that references in several inscriptions to 'unpaid' military officers suggests that such service

(6) an apparently well-organized system of taking care of the needy, although the bulk of this was performed by liturgy.[89]

While allowing that state expenditure was usually the main or only reason for emissions of ancient coinage, C. J. Howgego has recently stressed that it could also be struck for other purposes, such as to allow the State to make a profit from reminting, and to enable individuals to pay taxes, bid for tax-farming rights or fund private activities.[90] On Rhodes one can well imagine, for example, the authorities insisting that customs dues and other goods and services be paid for in Rhodian currency, thus creating a lucrative business in money-changing and reminting, like that attested for third-century Egypt.[91] If Bresson is right in concluding that Rhodes enforced a closed monetary zone in the Peraia, the scope for this sort of activity will have been considerable. The mint may well also have struck coin to enable Rhodian merchants to finance their business on the island (if not abroad: see above), for Rhodes was after all one of the leading second-rank powers in the Hellenistic world, and its prosperity depended on trade. There is, however, as yet no evidence that the mint offered such a service, and, although there is little direct evidence that the non-exceptional output of the mint was struck to fund public expenditure, there is no doubt that such expenditure had to be made, and one can assume that much, if not all, of the mint's output was struck to cater for it.[92]

As at other mints,[93] the amount of silver struck as coin at Rhodes appears small when compared with the occasional figures for expenditure and income which we can glean from literary and other sources. Thus,

very roughly speaking and on the basis of known dies, we can cite an average annual consumption of about 6.2 didrachm-equivalent obverse dies during the 100-year period *c*.305–*c*.205. If we make the usual, though far from reliable, assumption that each die struck on average 30,000 coins, we reach the sum of 1,860,000 didrachms or 64 Rhodian talents a year. The rough and ready nature of this calculation can hardly be over-stressed,[94] but it gives an illuminating order of numbers even if the amounts are multiplied or divided, say, by five, for we learn of figures for revenue and expenditure such as the following:

(1) The sale of Poliorketes' siege-train raised 300 talents: Pliny, *NH* 34. 41.

(2) A loan of 100 talents was made to Argos *c*.300–250 for the improvement of its walls and cavalry: Migeotte (1984) no. 19, with references.

(3) Customs duties were worth 1 million drachms (166 2/3 talents) a year in 167, suggesting that the value of goods in transit alone through Rhodian harbours was at least 25 (possibly 50) million drachms a year: Polyb. 30. 31. 12 with Gabrielsen (1997) 64, 68–9, 178–9 nn. 1, 23–5.

(4) Kaunos was bought for 200 talents during the war against Antiochos III: Polyb. 30. 31. 6, with Walbank (1979) 457; Livy 33. 20. 11–13; App. *Mith.* 4. 23.

(5) Kaunos and Stratonikeia (let alone the rest of the Peraia) produced revenue of 120 talents a year in 167: Polyb. 30. 31. 7.

(6) Gifts to Rhodes after the earthquake of the early 220s included a total of 500 talents of silver, in addition to much else: Polyb. 5. 88–90.

(7) 140,000 drachms' (23 1/3 talents') worth of aid, including 3,000 gold pieces of unspecified type, was

---

was normally paid. For non-military Rhodian officialdom see van Gelder (1900) 256–88; von Gaertringen (1931) col. 767.

[89] Strabo 14. 2. 5; Polyb. 31. 31. 1 (education fund); Gabrielsen (1997) 32–6, 107–8.

[90] Howgego (1990), esp. 15–25; Howgego (1995) 33–8. For tax farming on Rhodes (for which there is no direct evidence) see Gabrielsen (1997) 69.

[91] *P.Cair Zen.* 1. 59021, dated 258/7 BC. See also Bresson (1993) 163–4.

[92] We know surprisingly little about Rhodian banking operations. For the evidence see Bogaert (1968) 213–16 (216: 'Le manque d'information sur les opérations de banque des temples et des banques de Rhodes s'explique en partie par l'excellente situation des finances publique de l'île, tout au moins en ce qui concerne le IIIe siècle avant J.-C.'); Fraser (1972) 116–17; Zoumbaki (1994) 214 n. 7, citing an unpublished dissertation by A. Bresson; Gabrielsen (1997) 80–4; Gabrielsen (1993) 147 (the figures for coin volume attributed to me in his n. 58 are garbled). Note also the parallels and questions posed by Bresson (1993) 138. See also Rostovtzeff (1941) 172–3; Ziebarth (1932), esp. 917–21; *CAH* vii, 2nd. edn., pt. 1, 432–3.

[93] See, for example, Howgego (1995) 35.

[94] For discussion of the number of ancient coins struck per die see de Callataÿ (1995) 296–302, with an overly sceptical response from Buttrey and Buttrey (1997), esp. 129–35. In a recent re-examination of the Delphic treasurers' accounts Marchetti (1999), esp. 109, argues that the average number of Amphiktyonic League staters struck per obverse die in the mid 330s was between 14,350 and 23,333, markedly lower than the range of 23,333 to 47,250 proposed by Kinns (1983), esp. 18–19, which is the basis for the rough figure of 30,000 often applied by numismatists to all Greeek coinage. If right, Marchetti's conclusion confirms the practical work of Sellwood (1963), who reached a result of 10,000–16,000 coins per obverse die when hot striking was used, and accentuates the contrast between the amount of silver coined and the apparently much larger sums which can be inferred for the state's income and expenditure.

sent to Sinope in 220: Polyb. 4. 56. 2–3, with Migeotte, (1984) 83 n. 254, and Gabrielsen (1997) 46 and 167 n. 46.

(8)   A gift of grain from Eumenes II in 161/0 would have yielded a sum of at least 1.2 million drachms (200 talents), the interest from which was to be used for educational purposes on Rhodes: Polyb. 31. 31. 1–2, with Gabrielsen (1997) 80–1.

(9)   A crown of 20,000 gold pieces was voted for Rome in 168/7: Polyb. 30. 5. 4, with Walbank (1979) 421–2; Livy 45. 25. 4–7.

(10)   Cassius stripped 8,500 talents' worth of precious metals from temples, treasuries, and private homes in 42 BC: Plut. Brut. 32; App. BC 4. 73; Cass. Dio 47. 33. 4.

(11)   10,000 drachms (1 2/3 talents) a month was needed to maintain a trireme in the late third century (SIG³ 581). This figure was used above to suggest expenditure of at least 100 talents a year on the fleet alone.

(12)   The sums raised by public subscriptions on Rhodes in the Hellenistic period, as recorded in inscriptions, were considerable. See Migeotte (1992), nos. 37 (2 contributors gave at least 20,000 drachms each); 38 (a total of perhaps about 35,000 drachms, including an individual gift of 10,000 drachms); 42 (a total subscription of 14,000 drachms); 45 (a total of about 26,860 drachms); 46 (a total of perhaps about 37,400 drachms). Note also ibid. no. 10, recording two sums of 18,000 drachms each, perhaps private debts.

These figures are the more impressive for being haphazard, and gleaned from a body of evidence which is at best patchy. Even allowing for the reuse of old coin, it seems likely that the money coined by the mint represented only a fraction of the money paid out and received by the State. One imagines that bullion, foreign coin, and instruments of credit made up the shortfall.

Comparison of Output with Other Mints

We have seen that calculation of output is at best an extremely inexact procedure; the difficulties are compounded when one attempts to compare the output of different mints. Die-studies are often incomplete, survival rates of dies from different mints will differ (and

have not been calculated here), and differing minting practices may have caused production per die at different mints to have varied systematically. Even if one could assume that die survival and mint practices were consistent over all mints, the political or economic circumstances which prompted the production of coinage will have differed from state to state, and can give a misleading picture of relative wealth. A building programme or a war may have provoked an massive short-term output of coinage at a relatively poor state, while a richer neighbour with no need of such military or civic expenditure may have made do with a much lower output of coinage. Nevertheless, a rough comparison of silver output in the fourth century at some major mints in western Asia Minor for which data are available may be worth putting on record as one element in future debates about their relative economic power. As with the statistics for Rhodes (92 above), I have converted all known obverse dies into didrachm equivalents. The results are as follows:

Table 6.2: Comparison of output at Rhodes with that of other mints

Mint and period	Didrachm-equivalent obverse dies	Average per year
Samos, 406/5–365[95]	c.72	c.1.75
Kos, c.390–c.340[96]	142	c.2.8
Ephesos, c.405–c.330[97]	c.350	c.4.7
Miletos, c.350–325[98]	c.88	c.3.5
Chios, c.420–330[99]	90	c.1.5
Hekatomnids 392–336[100]	c.389	c.6.8

[95] Figures from Barron (1996) 96–119. A few new tetradrachm dies have surfaced since that study: A. Meadows in the publications of the 'Hekatomnos' and 'Pixodaros' hoards in CH 9 (forthcoming).
[96] Die count, but not dates, from Ingvaldsen (1994); Ingvaldsen is currently working on a full study of the mint. Meadows and I briefly discuss the chronology of the fourth-century coinage of Kos and provide die-studies of some issues in the publications of the 'Hekatomnos' and 'Pixodaros' hoards in CH 9 (forthcoming).
[97] I have taken the mid point of the rough figure of 150–200 + tetradrachm dies suggested by Kinns (1989) 188; Dr Kinns informs me that, according to a die-study which he has recently conducted, the figure of c.175 seems to be about right. In the same article he provides figures for other smaller mints in Ionia in the fourth century.
[98] Kinns (1989) 191, noting that the number of dies may be inflated by inaccuracies in Deppert-Lippitz's die-study, and that the coinage may have begun as early as 360. In the latter case, the annual average consumption of dies would reduce to c.2.5.
[99] Figures from Hardwick (1991).
[100] Figures from Konuk (1998). I have not taken into account the minor gold issues of Pixodaros.

Rhodes thus seems to have been among the leading producers of city coinage in western Asia Minor in the fourth century, but after c.385 was not pre-eminent. In the third and early second centuries her production increased markedly, whereas that of most other states in western Asia Minor dwindled. Their needs were probably met by the huge quantities of regal silver on the Attic and Ptolemaic weight standards circulating in the area. Rhodes by contrast maintained her own local standard.

APPENDIX I: SUMMARY OF RHODIAN ISSUES 408–c.190

Unless otherwise noted, the obverse and reverse types are, respectively, an unradiate head of Helios three-quarter facing right (left on some dies of issues **8**, **20**, and **21** and on most dies of **334–44**) and a rose. Wherever possible I have given what I judged to be the most accessible published references, but many issues are unpublished or recorded only in obscure publications; note further that I shall publish unillustrated corpora of issues **1–56**, **67–89**, **93–4**, and **107** in Ashton et al. (forthcoming). The figures for obverse dies and specimens are often greater than those published in earlier articles on individual series, and reflect the recording of additional material. The few coins whose obverse dies could not be identified have been excluded. When die-linking within a group of issues is particularly dense, I have simply given totals for the whole group. The statistics do not include some 1,000 recently recorded coins, mostly fourth–third century didrachms and late third-/early second-century drachms, which I have not yet incorporated into my die-study; I have no reason to suppose that they will add significantly to the number of obverse dies recorded below. References for the individual coins illustrated are given in the Key to the Plates.

Table 6.3: Summary of Rhodian issues 408–c.190

Issue	Obverse Dies (figures in brackets refer to dies also used on preceding issues)	Number of Coins Recorded	Reference (numbers refer to coins or issues not pages)
408/7–c.404			
Chian-weight Tetradrachms			
1 Eagle on rock	8	21	Bérend (1972), 7–16
2 Club	4	4	Bérend (1972), 17–19
3 Pecten	9	14	Bérend (1972), 1–6
4 Sphinx	9	16	Bérend (1972), 23–31
5 Shrimp + ⧻	1	1	Bérend (1972), 32
6 Two buds, no symbol	1	3	Bérend (1972), 20–2
Totals of 1–6	32	59	
Triple *Sigloi*			
7 Two buds, no symbol	1	1	Ashton (1993a), 7
8 Grapes on either side	3	4	Ashton (1993a), 8–10
9 Caduceus	1	1	Ashton (1993a), 11
Totals of 7–9	5	6	
Double *Sigloi*/Chian-weight Tridrachms (*ΣΥΝ*) Child Herakles strangling two snakes/Rose.			
10	1	24	Ashton (1993a), 12–14
Hemidrachms (408–c.390)			
11 Rhodos r.	4	38	Ashton (1993a), 18–26
12 Rhodos r., round incuse	1 (+1)	5	Ashton (1993a), 27–9
13 Club	11	25	*SNG* Lockett 2944

Table 6.3: (cont'd)

Issue	Obverse Dies (figures in brackets refer to dies also used on preceding issues)	Number of Coins Recorded	Reference (numbers refer to coins or issues not pages)
14 Two bunches of grapes	3	21	Ashton (1993a), 32–6
15 One bunch of grapes	2	8	Berlin 10516
16 Two thorny branches	2 (+1)	7	SNG Berry 1118
17 One thorny branch	7	27	SNG Keckman i, 365
18 Drooping bud	5	32	SNG Keckman i, 362–4
19 Plain rose, no symbol	28 (+1)	136	SNG Keckman i, 366–8
20 Helmet[101]	12	41	SNG Keckman i, 369–71
21 Astragalos	14	58	SNG Keckman i, 372–4
22 vacat			
23 Pilos	1 (?)[102]	1	Oxford, Robinson 1946
24 Grasshopper	5	17	SNG Keckman i, 375
Totals of 11–24	95	408	
Obols (408–c.390)			
25 Rhodos r.	2	5	Ashton (1993a), 30–1
26 Two thorny branches	1	1	Ashton coll., acq. 1979
27 Plain rose, no symbol	2	6	SNG Keckman i, 376–7
Totals of 25–7	5	11	
404–c.385			
Chian-weight Tetradrachms			
28 Lion's head + A	1	1	Bérend (1972), 33
29 Lion's head + Δ	2 (+1)	4	Bérend (1972), 34–6
30 Lion's head + Φ	1	1	Bérend (1972), 37
31 Corn ear + Δ	4	7	Bérend (1972), 50–5[103]
32 Corn ear + Ι	1	3	Bérend (1972), 56
33 Corn ear + A	1	1	BMC 14
34 Corn ear + Φ	1	5	Bérend (1972), 47–9
35 Wreath + Φ	2	5	Bérend (1972), 38–42
36 Corinthian helmet + A	2	4	Bérend (1972), 43–5 bis
37 Ram's head + A	− (+1)	1	Bérend (1972), 46
38 Torch + Φ	3	7	Bérend (1972), 71
39 Star + Φ	3	6	Bérend (1972), 57–60
40 Grapes and vine leaf + Φ	3 (+2)	7	Bérend (1972), 61–6
41 Ivy leaf and berries + Φ	12 (+1)	16	Bérend (1972), 67–70
42 Boukranion + Φ	2 (+1)	10	Bérend (1972), 72–5
43 Olive sprig + Φ	2 (+1)	8	Bérend (1972), 76–9
44 Kylix + Φ	3	4	McClean 8565
45 Corn grain + Φ	11 (+2)[104]	23	Bérend (1972), 80–4
46 Patera + Φ	5 (+2)	12	Jenkins and Hipólito (1989), 769
47 Aphlaston + T	3	3	BMC 19
48 Aphlaston + Φ	3	3	Boston 2044

[101] The helmet is Corinthian, except on a unique coin from the 'Hekatomnos' hoard, which has a Phrygian helmet.

[102] The unique pilos coin is worn, and its obverse die cannot be identified with certainty.

[103] Obverse and reverse of Bérend 55 (Δ) and 56 (Ι) are transposed on Bérend's plate. Bérend described her nos. 50–1 as having the letter A; they are here regarded as more likely to belong to the sub-issue with Δ (the letter in either case is wholly or partly obscured) because their obverse die is shared with a coin (Bérend 52) which indisputably has corn ear + Δ. The corn ear issue is here placed earlier than in Bérend's catalogue because of the affinity of that obverse die to certain obverse dies used on the eagle and sphinx issues without letters.

[104] The corn grain issue shares one obverse die with the ivy leaf issue and one with the kylix issue.

Table 6.3: *(cont'd)*

Issue	Obverse Dies (figures in brackets refer to dies also used on preceding issues)	Number of Coins Recorded	Reference (numbers refer to coins or issues not pages)
49 Boiotian shield + Φ	1 (+1)	3	Pozzi 2683
50 Boiotian shield + T	1	3	Bérend (1972), 86
51 Boiotian shield + Δ	— (+1)	2	SNG Hart 991
52 Dolphin + Φ	3	3	McClean 8564
53 Dolphin + Δ	3	3	SNG von Aulock 2787
54 Grasshopper + Φ	3	3	Bérend (1972), 85
55 Pecten + Φ	3 (+1)	5	Jenkins and Hipólito (1989), 770
56 Floral motif on pecten + Φ	2	4	BMC 21
Totals of 28–56	81	157	

Bronze (408–c.385)

Head of Rhodos r. or l./rose flanked by P—O. Chalkoi. 26 recorded. No die-study.

57 Rhodos r./no bud	—	—	SNG Keckman i, 380–1
58 Rhodos r./to l., upright bud	—	—	SNG Keckman i, 395
59 Rhodos l./no bud	—	—	Berlin 641/1914
60 Rhodos r./drooping buds to l. and r.	—	—	Berlin, Fox
61 Rhodos r./drooping buds to l. and r., POΔION above	—	—	Ashton coll., acq. 1977
62 Rhodos r./to r., shrimp; P—O around stalk	—	—	Paris 1597
63 Rhodos r./to r., grasshopper, no bud, P to l. (no O)	—	—	Ashton coll., acq. 1972
64 Rhodos l./to l., ivy leaf; to r., bud	—	—	Rhodes Arch. Mus. 2238a
65 Rhodos r./to l., bucranium, no bud; P—O around stalk	—	—	Ashton coll., acq. 1975
66 Rhodos r./to l., olpe; P—O around stalk	—	—	Paris 1596

c.385–c.360

Chian-weight Tetradrachms

67 Kithara + Ⅰ	2	2	BMC 16
68 Trident + Ⅰ	3	4	SNG Copenhagen 726
69 Ionic capital + Ⅰ	— (+1)	1	Superior, 12 June 1978, 3205
70 Oinochoe + A	— (+1)	2	J. Hirsch 21 (1908), 3245
71 Profile eye + A	3 (+2)[105]	7	SNG Fitzwilliam 4779
72 Trap + A	1	2	Jenkins and Hipólito (1989), 771
73 Askos (?) + A	— (+1)	1	Sotheby's, 14 July 1976, 28
74 Uncertain + A	1	1	MMAG 47 (1972), 509
75 Caduceus + Ⅰ	2	4	BMC 17
76 Caduceus + T	5	5	SNG von Aulock 2788
77 Caduceus + Σ	1	1	Jenkins and Hipólito (1989), 772
78 Owl + Σ	1 (+2)[106]	3	Jenkins and Hipólito (1989), 773
79 Owl + Ⅰ	1 (+1)	2	MMAG 76 (1991), 819
80 Owl + Δ	1	2	Sotheby's, 1 December 1924, 180
Totals of 67–80	21	37	

[105] One obverse die unites the trident, Ionic-capital, and eye issues, and another the trident, oinochoe and eye issues.

[106] Of the three obverse dies used in the owl + Σ issue, one was also used with caduceus + T, one with caduceus + Σ, and one with owl + Ⅰ.

Table 6.3: (cont'd)

Issue	Obverse Dies (figures in brackets refer to dies also used on preceding issues)	Number of Coins Recorded	Reference (numbers refer to coins or issues not pages)
*c.*360–late 340s			
Chian-weight Tetradrachms			
81 Wasp + *A*	I	2	Bourgey, 4 November 1975, 45
82 Bearded term + *A*	I	I	J. Hirsch 13 (1905), 4008
83 Athena Promachos + *A*	I	I	Berlin, ex J. Hirsch 25 (1909), 2439
84 Uncertain (but clear) + *A*	I	I	de Hirsch 1557
85 Thymiaterion + *A*	I	I	*SNG* Delepierre 2748
86 Helios head + *A*	I	I	Leu 30 (1982), 185
87 Horse's head + *A*	I	3	Jenkins and Hipólito (1989), 774
88 Satrapal head + *A*	I	I	Pollard (1970), 101
89 Uncertain + *Φ*	2	2	Berlin 1372/1918
Totals of 81–9	10	13	
Drachms (two buds, no symbol; Ashton (1990), p. 32)			
90 *A*	9	18	*SNG* Keckman i, 383
91 *I*	3 (+5)	18	*BMC* 39–40
92 *Φ*	5	9	Boston 2043
Totals of 90–2	17	45	
Late 340s–316			
Tetradrachms			
93 Club + *Φ*	5	5	*SNG* Delepierre 2749
94 Grapes + *E*	2	3	*SNG* Lockett 2945
Totals of 93–4	7	8	
Didrachms			
95 Club + *Φ*	4	9	*SNG* Keckman i, 426
96 Club + *E*	5	9	*SNG* Keckman i, 427–8
97 Grapes + *Δ*	5	30	*SNG* Keckman i, 433
98 Grapes + *E*	53 (+3)	284	*SNG* Keckman i, 436–40
99 Grapes + *E—Π*	3 (+2)	9	*SNG* Keckman i, 435
Totals of 95–99	70	341	
Drachms			
100 Grapes + *Δ*	2	18	*SNG* Keckman i, 434
101 Grapes + *E*	3	8	*SNG* Keckman i, 441
Hemidrachms			
102 Club	5	13	*SNG* Keckman i, 429
103 Grapes	10	19	*SNG* Keckman i, 442–4
Diobols			
Radiate head of Helios profile r./two buds.			
104 *Φ*	9	11	MMAG FPL 538 (1990), 89
105 *E*	3 (+6)	21	*SNG* Keckman i, 430–2
Gold Staters			
106 Grapes + *E*	I	4	Westermark (1979–80), 38–40[107]

---

[107] The fourth specimen is Jenkins and Castro Hipólito (1989) no. 775, of unspecified provenance.

Table 6.3: (*cont'd*)

Issue	Obverse Dies (figures in brackets refer to dies also used on preceding issues)	Number of Coins Recorded	Reference (numbers refer to coins or issues not pages)
316–305			
Tetradrachms			
107 Attached grapes + *E*	10	26	*SNG* Copenhagen 727
Didrachms			
108 Attached grapes + *E*	14	53	*SNG* Keckman 445

Bronze (*c*.350–*c*.300)

Chalkoi. Obv. Head of Rhodos r. in stephane, hair rolled. Rev. Rose; to r., bud; to l., symbol, letter, or monogram; *P—O* around rose stalk, or *Po* to l.; occasionally the bud is to l. and the sign to r. Thousands extant. No die-study.

Issue			Reference
109 Corn ear	—	—	*BMC* 79–81
110 Torch	—	—	*SNG* Keckman i, 391
111 Swastika	—	—	Ashton coll., acq. 1975
112 Horse's head	—	—	*BMC* 99
113 Bee or fly	—	—	*BMC* 105
114 Dolphin	—	—	*BMC* 86–7
115 Caduceus	—	—	Ashton coll., ex MMAG FPL 418 (1980), 204
116 Trident	—	—	*BMC* 88–9
117 Club (to l. or r.)	—	—	McClean 8577 (l.); Müller 18 (1976), 125 (r.)
118 Grapes (to l. or r.)	—	—	*SNG* Keckman i, 386; *BMC* 74–8
119 Ivy leaf (to l. or r.)	—	—	*SNG* Keckman i, 388, 393–4, 397
120 Pentangle	—	—	*SNG* Keckman i, 384
121 Palm branch	—	—	Ashton coll., acq. 1972 (*CH* 2, 59)
122 Star	—	—	*SNG* Keckman i, 390
123 Star above M	—	—	American Num. Soc.
124 Harpa	—	—	Ashton coll., acq. 1972 (*CH* 2, 59)
125 Hook	—	—	Oxford
126 Spearhead	—	—	Ashton coll., acq. 1972 (*CH* 2, 59)
127 Bow in case (to l. or r.)	—	—	Berlin, Löbbecke (l.); *BMC* 102–3 (r.)
128 Thyrsos	—	—	Ashton coll., acq. 1972 (*CH* 2, 59)
129 Helmet	—	—	Ashton coll., acq. 1972 (*CH* 2, 59)
130 Wreath	—	—	Turin DC 24392
131 Pecten (to l. or r.)	—	—	*BMC* 93–6
132 Thunderbolt	—	—	*BMC* 83–4
133 Arrow or spear	—	—	Dresden 1499
134 Cornucopia	—	—	*BMC* 90
135 *A*	—	—	CNA 20 (1992), 361
136 *Γ*	—	—	Price (1966), 64
137 *Δ*	—	—	Price (1966), 69–70
138 *E*	—	—	*BMC* 109
139 *H*	—	—	Jacquier FPL 17 (1995), 126
140 *I*	—	—	*BMC* 110–11
141 *K*	—	—	Ashton coll., acq. 1972 (*CH* 2, 59)
142 *M*	—	—	*BMC* 112–13
143 *N*	—	—	Ashton coll., acq. 1972 (*CH* 2, 59)
144 *Π*	—	—	*SNG* Keckman i, 398–9

Table 6.3: (cont'd)

Issue		Obverse Dies (figures in brackets refer to dies also used on preceding issues)	Number of Coins Recorded	Reference (numbers refer to coins or issues not pages)
145	Σ	—	—	Oxford, Milne gift 1924
146	T	—	—	Ashton coll., acq. 1972 (CH 2, 59)
147	Φ	—	—	Ashton coll., acq. 1972 (CH 2, 59)
148	X	—	—	BMC 116–17
149	Aꟼ	—	—	BMC 108
150	ℍ	—	—	Kroll (1993), 963a ('H')
151	IA	—	—	Ashton coll., acq. 1972 (CH 2, 59); G. Hirsch 185 (1995), 336
152	ΛI	—	—	Ashton coll., acq. 1998
153	ℳ	—	—	Ashton coll., acq. 1972 (CH 2, 59)
154	EP above rose	—	—	Pushkin Museum of Art, Moscow
155	ΔA above rose or to l.	—	—	G. Hirsch 194 (1997), 251
156	No sign	—	—	BMC 106–7

305–c.275 BC

Didrachms

157	E + grapes	—	—	SNG Keckman i, 449–53
158	EY + grapes	—	—	SNG Keckman i, 454–60
159	EY + thyrsos	—	—	Leschhorn (1986), 69–71
160	EY + jug	—	—	SNG Keckman i, 461
161	EY + aphlaston	—	—	SNG Keckman i, 462
162	EY + ivy leaf	—	—	Leu 33 (1983), 393
Totals of 157–62		137	648	
163	A + trident[108]	16	74	SNG Keckman i, 475
164	NI + fly	4	23	Leschhorn (1986), 78–9
165	EY + cornucopia	4	26	Ashton (1988), 1–10, and n. 35 above
166	A + caduceus	2 (+1)	7	Ashton (1988), 11–15
167	NI + star	2	13	Ashton (1988), 16–19

(Nos 165–7 have on obverse rayed head of Helios profile r.)

168	Δ + thunderbolt	6	73	SNG Keckman i, 477
169	Δ + star	4	42	Leschhorn (1986), 77
Totals of 163–9		38	258	

Drachms

170	Δ + star	5	34	SNG Keckman i, 478–82

Hemidrachms

171	E + grapes[109]	12	19	SNG von Aulock 2795; SNG Keckman i, 468–9
172	E + ivy leaf	10 (+2)	35	SNG Keckman i, 446–8, 464–6
173	No symbol or letter	— (+2)	5	SNG Keckman i, 473
Either 171 or 172		2	3	
174	Λ + grapes	7	14	SNG Keckman i, 470–1
175	A + trident	4	4	SNG Keckman i, 476

[108] A rare variant has A—M below the rose stalk instead of A to left of the rose: Leschhorn (1986) no. 86.

[109] The control letter is off-flan, obscured by wear or corrosion, or perhaps absent altogether, from many hemidrachms of this issue. Such coins are grouped with the E + grapes issue rather than the Λ + grapes issue solely on the grounds of their obverse style.

Table 6.3: (*cont'd*)

Issue	Obverse Dies (figures in brackets refer to dies also used on preceding issues)	Number of Coins Recorded	Reference (numbers refer to coins or issues not pages)
176 *Δ*	7	19	*SNG* Keckman i, 483–5
177 *Ꞧ* + prow	2	3	*SNG* Keckman i, 486
Totals of 171–7	44	102	
Bronze (contemporary with nos. 165–7)			
178 Profile rayed Helios/rose; obol	1	1	Ashton (1988), 68
179 As last; dichalkon	2	2	Ashton (1988), 69
***c*.275–*c*.250 BC**			
Didrachms			
180 *ΑΡΙΣΤΟΝΟΜΟΣ* + prow	16	82	*SNG* Keckman i, 487
181 *ΑΡΙΣΤΟΛΟΧΟΣ* + torch	9	22	*SNG* Keckman i, 490
182 *ΦΙΛΩΝΙΔΑΣ* + lamp	3	13	*SNG* Keckman i, 491
183 *ΑΡΙΣΤΟΒΙΟΣ* + wreath	13	43	*SNG* Keckman i, 493
184 *ΑΓΗΣΙΔΑΜΟΣ* + running Artemis	2	3	Ashton (1992*b*), 6–7
185 *ΑΝΤΙΠΑΤΡΟΣ* + dolphin	3 (+1)	8	*N. Circ.* Sep. 1994, 5433
186 *ΑΝΤΙΠΑΤΡΟΣ* + corn ear	20	103	*SNG* Keckman i, 503–4
187 *ΕΡΑΣΙΚΛΗΣ* + helmet	3 (+7)	41	*BMC* 47
Totals of 180–7	69	315	
Drachms			
188 *ΑΡΙΣΤΟΝΟΜΟΣ* + prow	5	8	*SNG* Keckman i, 488
189 *ΑΡΙΣΤΟΛΟΧΟΣ* + torch	1	1	Ashton coll., acq. 1992
190 *ΦΙΛΩΝΙΔΑΣ* + lamp	6	10	*SNG* Keckman i, 492
191 *ΑΡΙΣΤΟΒΙΟΣ* + wreath	7 (+1)	12	*SNG* Keckman i, 494
192 *ΑΓΗΣΙΔΑΜΟΣ* + running Artemis	5	15	*SNG* Keckman i, 495–6
193 *ΑΝΤΙΠΑΤΡΟΣ* + corn ear	5	11	*SNG* Keckman i, 505
194 *ΕΡΑΣΙΚΛΗΣ* + helmet	10	30	*SNG* Keckman i, 506
Totals of 188–94	39	87	
Hemidrachms			
195 *ΑΡΙΣΤΟΝΟΜΟΣ* + prow	6	8	*SNG* Keckman i, 489
196 *ΑΓΗΣΙΔΑΜΟΣ* + running Artemis	6	10	*SNG* Keckman i, 497–502
197 *ΑΝΤΙΠΑΤΡΟΣ* + corn ear	3	9	*SNG* Manchester 1276
198 *ΕΡΑΣΙΚΛΗΣ* + helmet	19	30	*SNG* Keckman i, 507–10
Totals of 195–8	34	57	
Diobols			
Radiate Helios profile r./two buds			
199 Lamp	5	13	*SNG* Keckman i, 511
200 Wreath	6	15	*SNG* Keckman i, 512–13
201 Running Artemis	13	17	*SNG* Keckman i, 515
202 Helmet	18 (+2)	33	*SNG* Keckman i, 517–23
203 Pecten	6 (+3)	12	*SNG* Keckman i, 524–7
Totals of 199–203	48	90	

Table 6.3: (cont'd)

Issue	Obverse Dies (figures in brackets refer to dies also used on preceding issues)	Number of Coins Recorded	Reference (numbers refer to coins or issues not pages)
c.250			
Didrachms (Helios radiate)			
204 *ΔI* + star or star on pileus	11	63	Ashton (1989)
205 *EY* + harpa	28	74	Ashton (1989)
c.250–c.230			
Didrachms (Helios radiate)[110]			
206 *ΑΓΗΣΙΔΑΜΟΣ* + running Artemis	—	—	*SNG Keckman* i, 534–5
207 *ΕΡΑΣΙΚΛΗΣ* + helmet	—	—	*SNG Keckman* i, 536
208 *ΜΝΑΣΙΜΑΧΟΣ* + Athena[111]	—	—	*SNG Keckman* i, 537–9
209 *ΤΙΜΟΘΕΟΣ* + term	—	—	*SNG Keckman* i, 540–1
Totals of 206–9	159	860	
Gold Stater, Autonomous Types (Helios radiate)			
210 *ΑΓΗΣΙΔΑΜΟΣ* + running Artemis	– (+1)	1	See n. 45 above
Gold Stater, Types of Philip II			
211 *ΜΝΑΣΙΜΑΧΟΣ* + rose, *Po*	1	1	See n. 45 above
c.230–205			
Tetradrachms (Helios radiate)			
212 *ΑΜΕΙΝΙΑΣ* + prow	—	—	*SNG Keckman* i, 542
213 *ΑΡΙΣΤΟΚΡΙΤΟΣ* + aphlaston	—	—	*SNG Keckman* i, 544–5
214 *ΕΥΚΡΑΤΗΣ* + thunderbolt	—	—	*SNG Keckman* i, 547–8
215 *ΘΑΡΣΥΤΑΣ* + eagle	—	—	*SNG Keckman* i, 550
Totals of 212–15	25	589	
216 *ΑΚΕΣΙΣ* + dolphin	– (+1)	2	*BMC* 119
Didrachms (Helios radiate)			
217 *ΑΜΕΙΝΙΑΣ* + stern	—	—	*SNG Keckman* i, 543
218 *Vacat*			
219 *ΑΡΙΣΤΟΚΡΙΤΟΣ* + aphlaston	—	—	*SNG Keckman* i, 546
220 *ΕΥΚΡΑΤΗΣ* + anchor	—	—	*SNG Keckman* i, 549
221 *ΘΑΡΣΥΤΑΣ* + eagle	—	—	*SNG Keckman* i, 551
Totals of 217–21	31	200	
222 *ΑΚΕΣΙΣ* + Apollo with lyre	5	33	*SNG Keckman* i, 567
223 *ΑΝΑΞΑΝΔΡΟΣ* + oval shield	4 (+4)	39	*SNG von Aulock* 2805
Drachms			
224 *ΑΜΕΙΝΙΑΣ* + trident	—	—	*SNG Keckman* i, 552–4
225 *ΕΥΚΡΑΤΗΣ* + tripod	—	—	*SNG Keckman* i, 559–60
Totals of 224–5	46	105	

[110] On some of these didrachms, usually coins of rather crude style, the name on the reverse is in the genitive, and the ethnic is sometimes rendered *M—O*, presumably a die-cutter's error for the usual *P—O*.

[111] Two anomalous didrachms are on record with the name Mnasimachos in combination with the symbol running Artemis which is on all other coins associated with the moneyer Agesidamos: Emporium 8 (1987) 85, and Kurpfälzische Münzhandlung 26 (1984) 84 = Athena 12 (1982/3) 30 = Brandt and Sonntag 4 (undated) 78. The two coins are struck from the same obverse and reverse dies, which do not recur on any other coin recorded from the series. The style of the obverse is very crude, and the only known weight, that of the second coin, is, at 6.15 g., very light. It seems likely that these coins were ancient imitations of some sort.

Table 6.3: (cont'd)

Issue	Obverse Dies (figures in brackets refer to dies also used on preceding issues)	Number of Coins Recorded	Reference (numbers refer to coins or issues not pages)
Hemidrachms			
226 ΕΥΚΡΑΤΗΣ + anchor	15	29	SNG Keckman i, 561
227 ΑΜΕΙΝΙΑΣ + term	13 (+8)	41	SNG Keckman i, 555–8
228 ΑΚΕΣΙΣ + dolphin	4 (+2)	10	SNG Keckman i, 578
229 ΑΚΕΣΙΣ + lyre	2	2	SNG Keckman i, 577
230 ΑΚΕΣΙΣ + lamp	1	6	Ashton coll. (2, acq. 1973, 1977)
231 ΑΝΑΞΑΝΔΡΟΣ + trident	2 (+1)	9	SNG Keckman i, 569–73
Totals of 226–31	37	97	
Diobols			
Radiate Helios profile r./two buds.			
232 Lyre	6	13	SNG Keckman i, 617
233 Shield	— (3)	11	Paris 1470 = Babelon (1898), 2795
Bronze			
Head of Zeus r./rose; to l., letters, monogram, or monogram + letter. Tetrachalka.			
234 ΤΕ	7	27	Ashton (1986), 19–41
235 ΦΙ	4 (+1)	23	Ashton (1986), 42–62
236 ⚕ and variants	—	—	Ashton (1986), 63–84
237 ⚕ and variants + E	—	—	Ashton (1986), 63–84
238 ⚕ and variants +	—	—	Ashton (1986), 63–84
Totals of 236–8	11	28	
Veiled head of Berenike II (?) r./rose; to l., EP, TE, or ΦI. Dichalka.			
239 EP	3	5	Ashton (1986), 7–10
240 ΤΕ	3	4	Ashton (1986), 11–14
241 ΦΙ	1 (+1)	5	Ashton (1986), 15–18
Veiled head of Berenike II (?) r./prow; above, lotus. Dichalka.			
242.	5	8	Ashton (1986), 1–6
c.205–190			
Alexander-type Tetradrachms			
243 ⚕ (ΑΜΕΙΝΙΑΣ?)	—	—	Price (1991), 2509
244 ⚕ (ΕΥΚΡΑΤΗΣ?)	—	—	Price (1991), 2510
245 ⚕ (ΤΕΙΣΥΛΟΣ?)	—	—	Price (1991), 2511
246 ⚕ (ΣΤΑΣΙΩΝ?)	—	—	Price (1991), 2512
247 ⚕ (ΑΙΝΗΤΩΡ?)	—	—	Price (1991), 2513–14
248 ⚕ (ΑΡΙΣΤΟΒΟΥΛΟΣ?)	—	—	Price (1991), 2515
249 ΑΡΙΣΤΟΒΟΥΛΟΣ	—	—	Price (1991), 2516–16A
250 ΣΤΑΣΙΩΝ	—	—	Price (1991), 2517
251 ΑΙΝΗΤΩΠ	—	—	Price (1991), 2518–19
252 ΤΕΙΣΥΛΟΣ	—	—	Price (1991), 2520
253 ΔΑΜΑΤΡΙΟΣ	—	—	Price (1991), 2521
254 ΗΦΑΙΣΤΙΩΝ	—	—	Price (1991), 2522
255 ΔΑΜΟΚΡΙΝΗΣ	—	—	Price (1991), 2523
256 ΔΙΟΦΑΝΗΣ	—	—	Price (1991), 2524
257 ΑΓΑΘΑΡΧΟΣ	—	—	Price (1991), 2525
258 ΑΓΕΜΑΧΟΣ	—	—	Price (1991), 2525A
Totals of 243–58	36	160	

Table 6.3: (cont'd)

Issue	Obverse Dies (figures in brackets refer to dies also used on preceding issues)	Number of Coins Recorded	Reference (numbers refer to coins or issues not pages)
Chian-weight Tetradrachms (Helios radiate)			
259 ΤΕΙΣΥΛΟΣ + female cult figure	3	3	BMC 128
260 ΣΤΑΣΙΩΝ + Asklepios	1	2	Ashton coll., ex Lanz 44 (1988), 226
261 ΣΤΑΣΙΩΝ + snake on omphalos	—	—	BM 1929-11-5-3
262 ΑΙΝΗΤΩΡ + butterfly	—	—	Berry (1971), 524
263 ΑΡΙΣΤΟΒΟΥΛΟΣ + thunderbolt	—	—	SNG Copenhagen 755
264 ΟΝΑΣΑΝΔΡΟΣ + star on pilos	—	—	SNG von Aulock 2803
265 ΑΕΤΙΩΝ + cup	—	—	BMC 118
266 ΔΑΜΑΤΡΙΟΣ + hook	—	—	SNG Berry 1124
267 ΑΓΕΜΑΧΟΣ + star	—	—	Ashton coll., ex Buckland, Dix, and Wood (London) 28 June 1995, 22
Totals of 261–7	12	29	
Didrachms (Helios radiate)			
268 ΓΟΡΓΟΣ + hippocamp	1	6	Ashton coll., ex Lanz 20 (1981), 250
269 ΠΕΙΣΙΚΡΑΤΗΣ + petasos (?)	2 (+1)	7	SNG Keckman i, 568
270 ΘΕΥΔΟΤΟΣ + cornucopia	— (+1)	1	Paris 1447
271 ΤΕΙΣΥΛΟΣ + palm branch	1	1	American Numismatic Society
272 ΑΡΙΣΤΑΚΟΣ + cult statue	1	1	BMC 136
273 CΤΑCΙωΝ + cornucopia	2	2	Ashton coll., ex NFA 29 (1992), 149
274 ΣΤΑΣΙΩΝ + bow in case and club	—	—	BMC 149
275 ΑΙΝΗΤΩΡ + bee	—	—	Coin Galleries 19 November 1973, 235
276 ΑΡΙΣΤΟΒΟΥΛΟΣ + corn ear	—	—	BMC 137
277 ΑΓΕΜΑΧΟΥ + wreath	—	—	BMC 129
278 ΑΕΤΙΩΝ + filleted thyrsos	—	—	BMC 133
279 ΔΑΜΑΤΡΙΟΣ + arrowhead	—	—	BM 1948-11-3-26
280 ΟΝΑΣΑΝΔΡΟΣ + eagle	—	—	BMC 148
281 ΞΕΝΟΚΡΑΤΗΣ + snake	—	—	BMC 147
Totals of 274–81	18	29	
Drachms[112]			
282 ΑΙΝΗΤΩΡ + butterfly	—	—	SNG Keckman i, 586–7
283 ΑΙΝΗΤΩΡ + aphlaston	—	—	Ashton coll., ex Kricheldorf 38 (1984), 239

[112] Many similar issues often listed as Rhodian drachms of the period are in fact imitations struck in Crete around 205–200 (see above), and south-west Asia Minor and central/northern Greece in following decades: see my articles in NC 147 (1987) 8–25; NC 148 (1988) 21–32, 129–34; NC 152 (1992) 1–39; NC 155 (1995) 1–20; NC 157 (1997) 188–91; NC 158 (1998) 223–8; NC 160 (2000) 93–116; RN 6th. ser., 31 (1989) 41–8; SM 146 (1987) 34–5 (issue 10); SM 151 (1989) 67–70; and (with J. Warren) RBN 143 (1997) 5–16. Several other issues with the Rhodian ethnic can probably be regarded as imitations on the grounds of weight, die-axis, find-spot, and style, but have not yet been discussed in detail, e.g. ΓΟΡΓΟΣ + torch or club or caduceus; ΚΑΛΛΙΣΘΕΝΗΣ + thunderbolt or club; ΣΩΠΟΛΙΣ + thunderbolt or club; ΑΡΙΣΤΟΚΡΑΤΗΣ + club; ΚΑΛΛΙΣΤΡΑΤΟΣ + club; ΠΑΥΣΑΝΙΑΣ + thunderbolt. I am also doubtful about ΤΕΙΣΥΛΟΣ + club or trident (301–2), known only from single examples in the 1902 Oreus hoard (IGCH 232), both of suspiciously low weight and odd style, and about ΔΙΟΦΑΝΗΣ + star (295), known only from low-weight examples found in mainland Greece. J. Svoronos, JIAN 5 (1902) 325–8, several times used as a reference in the following catalogue, lists the many varieties of Rhodian and pseudo-Rhodian drachms found in the 1902 Oreus hoard; the bulk are pseudo-Rhodian struck at the time of the Third Macedonian War. Note also that I have excluded from the totals of dies and specimens recorded for the ΣΤΑΣΙΩΝ + crossed bow and club issue (297) eighteen dies and forty-two coins which I am certain (on the grounds of their find-spots, irregular die-axes, crude style, and often low weights) were imitations struck in northern or central Greece during the Third Macedonian War. I am suspicious of a dozen or so other dies among the total of 203 listed for the series as a whole, but at present have insufficient hard evidence to exclude them.

Table 6.3: (*cont'd*)

Issue		Obverse Dies (figures in brackets refer to dies also used on preceding issues)	Number of Coins Recorded	Reference (numbers refer to coins or issues not pages)
284	*AINHTΩP* + bow in case	—	—	*JIAN* 5 (1902), 326, no. 160
285	*APIΣTAKOΣ* + caduceus	—	—	*SNG* Keckman i, 588–90
286	*APIΣTOBOYΛOΣ* + ivy leaf	—	—	Berlin, Löbbecke
287	*APIΣTOBOYΛOΣ* + corn ear	—	—	CNG 34 (1995), 161
288	*ΓOPΓOΣ* + bow in case	—	—	*SNG* Keckman i, 582–4
289	*ΓOPΓOΣ* + bow in case and tripod	—	—	*JIAN* 5 (1902), 326, no. 373
290	*ΓOPΓOΣ* + bow in case and club	—	—	*JIAN* 5 (1902), 326, nos. 374–6
291	*ΓOPΓOΣ*, no symbol	—	—	*JIAN* 5 (1902), 327, nos. 399–406
292	*ΓOPΓOΣ* + griffin forepart	—	—	*JIAN* 5 (1902), 327, no. 398
293	*ΔAMOKPINHΣ* + pentangle	—	—	*SNG* Copenhagen 784
294	*ΔAMOKPINHΣ* + helmet	—	—	*JIAN* 5 (1902), 327, nos. 431–3
295	*ΔIOΦANHΣ* + star	—	—	*BCH* 1969, 716, no. 12 (misread)
296	*ΠEIΣIKPATHΣ* + Athena Promachos	—	—	*SNG* Keckman i, 579
297	*ΣTAΣIΩN* + crossed bow and club	—	—	*BMC* 182–3
298	*ΣTAΣIΩN* + winged thunderbolt	—	—	*SNG* Manchester 1281
299	*TEIΣYΛOΣ* + snake	—	—	*SNG* Keckman i, 591
300	*TEIΣYΛOΣ* + palm branch	—	—	Ashton coll., acq. 1977
301	*TEIΣYΛOΣ* + club	—	—	*JIAN* 5 (1902), 328, no. 554
302	*TEIΣYΛOΣ* + trident	—	—	*JIAN* 5 (1902), 328, no. 558
Totals of 282–302		203	457	
Hemidrachms				
303	*ΓOPΓOΣ* (?) + spearhead	1	1	Private coll., Finland
304	*ΓOPΓOΣ* + hook	15	36	*SNG* Keckman i, 585
305	*ΠEIΣIKPATHΣ* + spearhead	9 (+4)	24	*SNG* Keckman i, 580–1
306	*ANTIΓENHΣ* + aphlaston	3	4	Ashton coll., ex G. Hirsch 178 (1993), 372
307	*ANAΞIΔIKOΣ* + amphora	2 (+1)	4	Artemis Antiquities 6 (1972), 69
308	*ΦIΛOKPATHΣ* + tripod	—	—	Ashton coll., ex Lennox Gall. FPL 3 (1996), G160
309	*ANAΞIΔOTOΣ* + trident	—	—	BM 1973-12-6-45
310	*AΘANOΔΩPOΣ* + Isis crown	—	—	*SNG* Fitzwilliam 4787 (symbol misidentified)
311	*AΓHΣIΔAMOΣ* + star	—	—	Münz Zentrum Köln 97 (1999), 305
Totals of 308–11		7	17	
Diobols				
Helios radiate r./two buds.				
312	Snake	2	4	*SNG* Keckman i, 620
313	Star	1 (+1)	3	H. Weber 6722 (now BM)
314	Grapes	2	4	*SNG* Keckman i, 619
315	Torch	1 (+1)	2	*SNG* von Aulock 2819
316	Double axe	1	1	SKAB FPL 52 (1988), 323
Totals of 312–16		7	14	

Table 6.3: (cont'd)

Issue	Obverse Dies (figures in brackets refer to dies also used on preceding issues)	Number of Coins Recorded	Reference (numbers refer to coins or issues not pages)
Chalkoi			
Late Third Century BC(?)			
Rose with or without bud(s)and control letter/rose, *P—O* around stalk or body of rose, bud, or buds; usually a control letter. Hundreds extant. No die-study.			
317 No control letter/no control letter	—	—	*SNG* Copenhagen 747
318 No control letter/*H* to l.	—	—	Oxford, Milne gift 1924
319 No control letter?/*Δ* to l.	—	—	Lisbon, Gulbenkian reserve coll.
320 No control letter/*Δ* to l., no ethnic	—	—	BM 1939-12-10-6
321 No control letter/*I* to l., no ethnic	—	—	Paris, Delepierre coll. (not *SNG*)
322 Uncertain/Λ to l.	—	—	Athens 1911/12 ΞΘ'.106
323 No control letter/*T* to l.	—	—	G. Hirsch 185 (1995), 335
324 No control letter/*Σ* to l.	—	—	*BMC* 73 (obv. and rev. inverted)
325 No control letter/*E* to l., no ethnic	—	—	*SNG* Copenhagen 749 (K, in error)
326 *E* to l./*Σ* to l.	—	—	*SNG* Fitzwilliam 4827
327 *Π* to l./*Σ* to l.	—	—	*SNG* Keckman i, 599
328 *T* to l./*Σ*? to l.	—	—	Rhodes Arch. Mus. 538κβ
329 *T—I*/*Σ* to l.	—	—	American Numismatic Society
330 Uncertain/*Σ* to l., no ethnic	—	—	Turin, Fabretti 4275
331 Uncertain/above rose, [...]*N*	—	—	London market 1973
Early-Second Century BC			
Radiate head of Helios r./rose, *P—O* around stalk or body, bud on either side; no control letter.			
332 Hundreds extant; die-study not yet attempted	—	—	*SNG* Keckman i, 607–16.
Quasi-official Reduced Didrachms and Drachms Struck on Crete c.205–200			
Didrachms			
On obverse, head of gorgon.			
333 *ΓΟΡΓΟΣ* + star	1	50	Ashton (1987), 1
Drachms			
On obverse, Helios usually three-quarter facing left.			
334 *ΓΟΡΓΟΣ* + butterfly	5	10	Ashton (1987), 2
335 *ΣΤΡΑΤΩΝ* + dolphin or dolphins	1	23	Ashton (1987), 3 (and n. 47 above)
336 *ΣΤΡΑΤΩΝ* + caduceus	—	5	Ashton (1987), 4A
337 *ΣΤΡΑΤΩΝ* + caduceus and bucranium	—	1	Ashton (1987), 4B
338 *ΣΩΣΙΚΡΑΤΗΣ* + caduceus and bucranium	—	1	Ashton (1987), 5
339 *ΑΙΝΗΤΩΡ* + caduceus (and variants)	79	139	Ashton (1987), 6A
340 *ΑΙΝΗΤΩΡ* + caduceus and bucranium	—	4	Ashton (1987), 6B

Table 6.3: (cont'd)

Issue		Obverse Dies (figures in brackets refer to dies also used on preceding issues)	Number of Coins Recorded	Reference (numbers refer to coins or issues not pages)
341	*ΑΙΝΗΤΩΡ* + deer (?)	4	II	Ashton (1987), 6C
342	*ΗΡΑΚΛΕΙΤΟΣ* + palm tree	2	5	Ashton (1987), 7
343	*ΚΑΛΛΙΠΠΟΣ* + prow	2	2	Ashton (1987), 8
344	*ΒΟΥΛΑΚΡΑΤΗΣ* + prow or no symbol	3	3	Ashton (1987), 9
Totals of 334–44		96	204	

APPENDIX 2: THE MONEYERS ON RHODIAN COINS

We have seen that all Hellenistic Rhodian silver coins above diobol size from the second quarter of the third century onwards bear signatures, but in no case is the office of the moneyer identified. In the early imperial period, the moneyers who signed certain large bronze drachms identified themselves explicitly as *tamiai* (RPC I, 2748 ff.). Between five and seven of these officials (the number seems to have varied) held office at the same time and were appointed for terms of six months.[113] It is possible that three or four *tamiai* at a time signed the individually small issues of Attic-weight silver drachms which preceded the bronze drachms in the first century BC, but this is far from certain (Ashton with Weiss (1997), 21–2). Jenkins (1989), 104, thought that *tamiai* may have signed the plinthophoroi, but admitted that this was pure speculation. The fact that no fewer than fifteen or sixteen 'overlap' moneyers signed both late pre-plinthophoric and early plinthophoric coins suggests that they were not *tamiai* or other semi-annual or annual officials, for this would involve an improbable number of re-elections. Moreover, we have seen above that the moneyers who signed coins in the period c.250–c.205 must have been functioning for several years at a time, and this also seems to have been the case with at least one of the moneyers in the period c.205–c.190, Ainetor, who occurs on coins struck for use on Crete in the late third century and on early plinthophoroi from c.190 onwards. The fact that two of the four moneyers who signed in the

period c.250–c.230, Agesidamos and Erasikles, had also signed preceding issues suggests that the moneyers of this first phase of signed coinage were likewise not annual or semi-annual officials.

In the absence of other evidence it is not possible to determine what function the Hellenistic moneyers had. However, as Jenkins (1989, 104) explains, at no time were they the eponymous magistrates of Rhodes, the annual priests of Helios.

APPENDIX 3: THE 'RHODIAN' LYSIMACHI

Two rare issues of gold staters of Lysimachean types, one unsigned, one with the name Aristoboulos, have been plausibly attributed to Rhodes because of the rose symbol which they have on the reverse and because the name Aristoboulos occurs on some Rhodian Alexanders and autonomous coinage dating to c.200–c.190 (issues **249, 263, 276, 286–7**). Only three specimens are recorded, struck from one obverse and three reverse dies:

Obv. Head of Alexander the Great r. with horn of Ammon.

Rev. Athena Nikephoros enthroned l.; below throne, trident decorated with dolphins; in l. field, rose.

Rev. To r., *ΒΑΣΙΛΕΩΣ*; to l., *ΛΥΣΙΜΑΧΟΥ*.

1. 8.27 g. 10h British Museum; R. Payne Knight, *Nummi Veteres* (London, 1830), 86, no. 12. Pierced twice. (**Pl. 6.12. A**).

Rev. To r., *ΛΥΣΙΜΑΧΟΥ*; to l., *ΑΡΙΣΤΟΒΟΥ-ΛΟΣ*.

2. 8.56 g. 12h British Museum 1896-6-1-78 (Montagu I, 619). (**Pl. 6.12. B**).

3. 8.64 g. Paris, de Luynes 1812.

---

[113] van Gelder (1900) 256–7.

If these staters are Rhodian, they were undoubtedly inspired by the mint of Byzantion which reverted to the use of Lysimachos-type coinage around 220, added a trident below the throne on the reverse of its gold staters in c.215, and an abbreviated ethnic to the throne on its gold staters and silver tetradrachms in c.205; between c.220 and c.205 the Byzantine Lysimachi carried no ethnic.[114] Since an Aristoboulos was signing silver coins on Rhodes in the years around 200, it would be natural to associate these Lysimachi with the wars fought by Rhodes on Crete and against Philip V and Antiochos III.

However, there is no obvious reason why Rhodes should have struck gold in the form of Lysimachi at that time, and, given that no other mint south of the Dardanelles was striking them, our three staters look remarkably isolated. Moreover, all other Rhodian coinage, including the posthumous Philip (**211**) and Alexanders, carried the ethnic *POΔION*, *POΔI*, or *PO*, and, despite the lack of an ethnic on the presumed Byzantine model, its absence from the three staters is worrying, for the rose was not an exclusively Rhodian symbol.[115] The name Aristoboulos is not uncommon (114 examples in *LGPN* 1, of which at most 26 from Rhodes; 88 in *LGPN* 2; 25 in *LGPN* 3A) and, although it is not attested numismatically at Byzantion, at least two men with that name are known from the city.[116]

Although no other contemporary Lysimachi of Byzantion are known to carry the names of moneyers in full, there thus seems to be a reasonable case for transferring the three staters to Byzantion or to one of the Black Sea states which imitated its Lysimachi, and for dating them c.215–c.205. Nevertheless, in the absence of a die-study of the northern staters, the question remains unresolved.

POSTSCRIPT

After this article went to press, details came to light of the important 'Magnesia 1995' hoard (*CH* 9, 463), which was dispersed before it could be fully recorded but apparently contained at least 83 Rhodian didrachms, whose obverses, but not reverses, are recorded on some rather indistinct photocopies recently unearthed in the British Museum. To judge from the obverse dies, 75 of these didrachms belong to the varieties with square incuse on the reverse, and 8 to varieties with round incuse. About 57 of the square-incuse coins appear to belong to the unattached grapes + Δ and E issues (**97–8**), and about 18 to the attached grapes + E issue (**108**). The obverse dies of 7 of the 8 coins from the round-incuse series are found only on the Δ + thunderbolt and Δ + star issues (**168–9**). (I cannot determine the die of the eighth.) The remainder of the hoard seems to have comprised coins of Magnesia, Miletos, Ephesos, the Hekatomnids, and Rhoontopates, and suggests formation in the 320s. If this is right, it suggests that (i) the Rhodian square-incuse series may well have ended by that time, rather than possibly continuing down towards the end of the century; (ii) the attached grapes + E tetradrachms and didrachms should be uncoupled from the earthquake of 316; (iii) the Δ + thunderbolt and Δ + star issue will be the first of the round-incuse issues, and will be datable to the 320s. The calculations of output in the periods late 340s–305/4 and 305/4–c.250 made above (92) would have to be modified slightly, but the new hoard does not upset the connection made above between the siege of 305/4 and the closely die-linked proliferation of other round-incuse issues, nor the possible association of issues **165–7** and **178–9** with the erection of the Colossus.

However, the evidence in favour of dating the introduction of the round-incuse didrachms a couple of decades later, while far from conclusive, retains some weight (see 85–7 above), and it remains possible that the 8 round-incuse Rhodian didrachms in the 'Magnesia 1995' hoard were added later to the main body of the deposit in ancient or modern times.

[114] Seyrig (1968), esp. 199; see also Mørkholm (1991) 147, 157.
[115] Compare, for example, the use of the rose as a symbol on lifetime and posthumous coins of Alexander struck at places as diverse as Macedonia, Miletos, Sardes, Cilicia, Paphos, Babylon and Memphis: Price, (1991) 564 (index).
[116] Information kindly provided by Elaine Matthews from material assembled for future *LGPN* volumes.

REFERENCES

APOSTOLOU, E. (1955). 'Les Drachmes rhodiennes et pseudo-rhodiennes de la fin du IIIe et du début du IIe siècle av. J.-C.', *RN* 150: 7–19.

ASHTON, R. H. J. (1986). 'Rhodian Bronze Coinage and the Earthquake of 229–226 BC', NC 146: 1–18.

——(1987). 'Rhodian-type Silver Coinages from Crete', SM 146: 29–39.

——(1988). 'Rhodian Coinage and the Colossus', RN⁶ 30: 75–90.

——(1989). 'A Series of Rhodian Didrachms from the Mid-Third Century', NC 149: 1–13.

——(1990). 'The Solar Disk Drachms of Caria', NC 150: 27–38.

——(1992a). 'A Third Century BC Hoard of Coins of Western Asia Minor', CNR 17/3: 3–4.

——(1992b). 'Some Forgeries of Rhodian Didrachms of the Mid Third Century BC', in H. Nilsson (ed.), Florilegium Numismaticum: Studia in Honorem Ulla Westermark Edita (Stockholm), 29–32.

——(1993a). 'A Revised Arrangement for the Earliest Coinage of Rhodes', in M. Price et al. (eds.), Essays in Honour of Robert Carson and Kenneth Jenkins (London), 9–15.

——(1993b). NC 153: 276–80 (review of Price (1991)).

——(1994). 'The Attalid Poll-tax', ZPE 104: 57–60.

——(1995). 'Pseudo-Rhodian Drachms from Central Greece', NC 155: 1–20.

——(1999a). 'The Coinage of Nisyros', in M. Amandry et al. (eds.), Travaux de numismatique grecque offerts à Georges Le Rider (Paris), 15–24.

——(1999b). 'The Late Classical/Early Hellenistic Drachms of Knidos', RN 154: 63–95.

——(1999c). 'Some Early Forgeries of Rhodian Coins', NC 159: 293–4.

—— et al. (1994). R. H. J. Ashton, M. Arslan, and A. Dervişağaoğlu, 'The Köyceğiz Hoard of Late Rhodian Plinthophoric Drachms', CH 8: 84–7.

—— et al. (forthcoming). R. H. J. Ashton, P. Kinns, K. Konuk, and A. R. Meadows, 'The Hecatomnos Hoard', CH 9.

ASHTON, R. with A.-P. WEISS (1997). 'The Post-Plinthophoric Drachms of Rhodes', NC 157: 1–40.

BABELON, E. (1898). Inventaire sommaire de la collection Waddington (Paris).

BARRANDON, J.-N. and A. BRESSON (1997). 'Imitations crétoises et monnaies rhodiennes: analyse physique', RN 152: 137–55.

BARRON, J. P. (1966). The Silver Coins of Samos (London).

BAUSLAUGH, R. (1990). 'Cistophoric Countermarks and the Monetary System of Eumenes II', NC 150: 39–65.

BEAN, G. E. (1953). 'Notes and Inscriptions from Caunus', JHS 73: 10–35.

—— and J. M. COOK (1957). 'The Carian Coast III', ABSA 52: 58–146.

BÉREND, D. (1972). 'Les Tétradrachmes de Rhodes de la première période', SNR 51: 5–39.

——(1995). 'Rhodes, encore', RN 150: 251–5.

BERRY, B. Y. (1971). A Numismatic Biography (Lucerne).

BERTHOLD, R. M. (1984). Rhodes in the Hellenistic Age (Ithaca and London).

BOGAERT, R. (1968). Banques et banquiers dans les cités grecques (Leiden).

BORRELL, H. P. (1846–7). 'Unedited Autonomous and Imperial Greek Coins', NC 9: 143–72.

BRESSON, A. (1981). 'Notes rhodiennes', RÉA 83: 211–12.

——(1991). Recueil des inscriptions de la pérée rhodienne (pérée intégrée) (Paris).

——(1993). 'La Circulation monétaire rhodienne jusqu'en 166', DHA 19/1: 119–69.

——(1996). 'Drachmes rhodiennes et imitations: une politique économique de Rhodes?', RÉA 98/1–2: 65–77.

——(1997). 'La Monnaie rhodienne au Ier s. a. C.: nouveautés et interrogations', Topoi 7/1: 11–32.

——(1998). 'Rhodes, Cnide et les Lyciens au début du IIe siècle av. J.-C.', RÉA 100: 65–88.

BUTTREY, S. E., and T. V. BUTTREY (1997). 'Calculating Ancient Coin Production, Again', AJN 9: 113–35.

CAHN, H. A. (1957). 'Die archaischen Silberstatere von Lindos', in K. Schauenberg (ed.), Charites, Studien zur Altertumswissenschaft (Festschrift E. Langlotz; Bonn).

——(1970). Knidos. Die Münzen des sechsten und fünften Jahrhunderts v. Chr. (AMUGS 4; Berlin).

CHANKOWSKI-SABLÉ, V. (1997). 'Les Espèces monétaires dans la comptabilité des hiéropes à la fin de l'indépendance délienne', RÉA 99: 357–69.

DE CALLATAŸ, F. (1995). 'Calculating Ancient Coin Production: Seeking a Balance', NC 155: 289–311.

DELRIEUX, F. (2000). 'Les Ententes monétaires au type et à la légende ΣΥΝ au début du IVe siècle', in O. Casabonne (ed.), Mécanismes et innovations monétaires dans l'Anatolie achéménide (Varia Anatolica XII; Istanbul), 185–211.

DEPPERT-LIPPITZ, B. (1984). Die Münzprägung Milets vom vierten bis ersten Jahrhundert v. Chr. (TYPOS 4, Aarau, Frankfurt am Main, Salzburg).

EDWARDS, K. (1933). Corinth vol. VI, Coins 1896–1929 (Cambridge, Mass.).

ERRINGTON, M. (1989). 'The Peace Treaty between Miletus and Magnesia (I. Milet 148)', Chiron 19: 279–88.

ESTY, W. (1986). 'Estimation of the Size of a Coinage', NC 146: 185–215.

FRASER, P. M. (1972). 'Notes on Two Rhodian Institutions', ABSA 67: 113–24.

—— and G. E. BEAN, (1954). The Rhodian Peraea and Islands (Oxford).

FRIED, S. (1987). 'The Decadrachm Hoard: An Introduction', in I. A. Carradice (ed.), Coinage and Administration in the Athenian and Persian Empires (BAR Int. Series 343, Oxford), 1–10.

GABRIELSEN, V. (1993), 'Rhodes and Rome after the Third Macedonian War', in P. Bilde et al. (eds.), Centre and Periphery in the Hellenistic World (Aarhus), 132–61.

——(1997). *The Naval Aristocracy of Hellenistic Rhodes* (Aarhus).

GÖKTÜRK, M. T. (1992). *Annual of the Anatolian Civilisations Museum, Ankara*, 172–81.

GRIFFITH, G. T. (1935). *The Mercenaries of the Hellenistic World* (Cambridge).

HARDWICK, N. N. M (1991). 'The Coinage of Chios from the Sixth to the Fourth Century B.C.' (Univ. of Oxford D.Phil. thesis).

——(1993). 'The Coinage of Chios from the VIth to the IVth century B.C.', *ProcINC* XI (Louvain), 211–22.

HARL, K. (1991). 'Livy and the Date of the Introduction of the Cistophoric Tetradrachma', *Classical Antiquity*, 10: 268–97.

HEAD (1911). *Historia Numorum*, 2nd edn. (Oxford).

HOHLFELDER, R. (1978). *Kenchreai, iii. The Coins* (Leiden).

HORNBLOWER, S. (1982). *Mausolus* (Oxford).

HOWGEGO, C. J. (1990). 'Why Did Ancient States Strike Coins?', *NC* 150: 1–25.

——(1995). *Ancient History from Coins* (London and New York).

HURTER, S. (1998). 'The "Pixodaros" Hoard', in R. Ashton and S. Hurter (eds.), *Studies in Greek Numismatics in Memory of Martin Jessop Price* (London, 1998), 147–53.

INGVALDSEN, H. (1994). 'Utmyntningen på Kos 366–190 f.Kr.' (Univ. of Oslo MA thesis).

JENKINS, G. K. (1989). 'The Rhodian Plinthophoroi—A Sketch', in G. Le Rider *et al.* (eds.), *Kraay–Mørkholm Essays: Numismatic Studies in Memory of C. M. Kraay and O. Mørkholm* (Numismatica Lovaniensia 10; Louvain, 1989), 101–19.

—— and M. CASTRO HIPÓLITO (1989). *A Catalogue of the Calouste Gulbenkian Collection of Greek Coins*, pt. 2 (Lisbon, 1989).

KAGAN, J. (1987). 'The Decadrachm Hoard: Chronology and Consequences', in I. A. Carradice (ed.), *Coinage and Administration in the Athenian and Persian Empires* (BAR Int. Series 343, Oxford), 21–8.

KARWIESE, S. (1980). 'Lysander as Herakliskos Drakonopnigon', *NC* 140: 1–27.

KINNS, P. (1980). 'Studies in the Coinage of Ionia: Erythrae, Teos, Lebedus, Colophon, *c.*400–30 B.C.' (Univ. of Cambridge Ph.D. thesis).

——(1983). 'The Amphictionic Coinage Reconsidered', *NC* 143: 1–22.

——(1986). 'The Coinage of Miletos', *NC* 146: 231–60.

——(1989). 'Ionia: The Pattern of Coinage during the Last Century of the Persian Empire', *RÉA* 91/1–2: 183–93.

KLEINER, F. S. (1971). *The Alexander Tetradrachms of Pergamum and Rhodes*, ANSMN 17: 95–125.

—— and NOE (1977). *The Early Cistophoric Coinage* (ANSNS 14; New York).

KONTORINI, V. and L. MIGEOTTE (1995). *ΛΟΓΕΙΑ ΤΑΣ ΔΙΔΡΑΧΜΙΑΣ à Rhodes*, *BCH* 119: 621–8.

KONUK, K. (1993), 'Quelques Réflexions sur le monnayage des satrapes hécatomnides de Carie', *ProcINC XI* (Louvain), 237–42.

——(1998). 'The Coinage of the Hekatomnids of Caria' (Univ. of Oxford D.Phil. thesis).

——(2000). 'Influences et éléments achéménides dans le monnayage de la Carie', in O. Casabonne (ed.), *Mécanismes et innovations monétaires dans l'Anatolie achéménide* (Varia Anatolica XII; Istanbul), 171–83.

KRAAY, C. M. (1976), *Archaic and Classical Greek Coins* (London).

——(1980). 'Notes on the Courtauld Collection of Greek Coins at the University of Zimbabwe', *Proceedings of the African Classical Associations*, 15: 59–61.

KROLL, J. H. (1993). *The Athenian Agora. xxvi. The Greek Coins* (Princeton, NJ).

LE RIDER, G. (1990). 'Antiochos II à Mylasa', *BCH* 114: 543–51.

LESCHHORN, W. (1986). 'Zu den rhodischen Didrachmen des 4. und 3. Jh. v. Chr.', *JNG* 36 (1986, pub. 1989): 67–94.

LOOMIS, W. T. (1998). *Wages, Welfare Costs and Inflation in Classical Athens* (Ann Arbor, Mich.).

MARCHETTI, P. (1999). 'Autour de la Frappe du nouvel amphictionique', *RBN* 145: 99–113.

MIGEOTTE, L. (1984). *L'Emprunt public dans les cités grecques* (Quebec/Paris).

——(1992). *Les Souscriptions publiques dans les cités grecques* (Geneva/Quebec).

MØRKHOLM, O. (1991). *Early Hellenistic Coinage* (Cambridge).

MOYSEY, R. A. (1989). 'Observations on the Numismatic Evidence Relating to the Great Satrapal Revolt of 362/1 B.C.', *RÉA* 91, nos. 1–2: 107–139.

NICOLET-PIERRE, H., and J. KROLL (1990). 'Athenian Tetradrachm Coinage of the Third Century B.C.', *AJN*, 2nd ser., 2: 1–35.

POLLARD, G. (1970). *A Catalogue of the Greek Coins in the Collection of Sir Stephen Courtauld at the University College of Rhodesia* (Salisbury = Harare, Zimbabwe).

PRICE, M. J. (1966). 'The Coins', in J. Cook and W. Plommer, *The Sanctuary of Hemithea at Kastabos* (Cambridge), 66–71.

——(1968). 'Early Greek Bronze Coinage', in C. M. Kraay and G. K. Jenkins (eds.), *Essays in Greek Coinage Presented to Stanley Robinson*, 90–104.

——(1969). 'Greek Coin Hoards in the British Museum', *NC*, 7th ser., 9: 1–14.

——(1991). *The Coinage in the Name of Alexander the Great and Philip Arrhidaeus* (Zurich/London).

—— and N. WAGGONER (1975). *Archaic Greek Coinage: The 'Asyut' Hoard* (London).

REQUIER, P. (1996). 'Les Premiers Tétradrachmes hellénistiques de Cos', *SNR* 75: 53–64.

RICE, E. E. (1991). 'The Rhodian Navy in the Hellenistic Age', in W. Roberts and J. Sweetman (eds.), *New*

Interpretations in Naval History (Annapolis, Md., 1991), 29–50.

ROBERT, L. (1951). *Études de numismatique grecque* (Paris).

——(1967). *Monnaies grecques: types, légendes, magistrats monétaires et géographie* (Hautes Études Numismatiques, ii, Geneva/Paris).

ROSTOVTZEFF, M. (1941). *The Social and Economic History of the Hellenistic World* (Oxford).

RUTTER, K. (1981). 'Early Greek Coinage and the Influence of the Athenian State', in B. Cunliffe (ed.), *Coinage and Society in Britain and Gaul: Some Current Problems* (London), 1–9.

SELLWOOD, D. G. (1963). 'Some Experiments in Greek Minting Technique', NC^7 3: 217–31.

SEYRIG, H. (1968). 'Monnaies hellénistiques de Byzance et de Calcédoine', in C. M. Kraay and G. K. Jenkins (eds.), *Essays in Greek Coinage Presented to Stanley Robinson*, 183–200.

SPIER, J. (1987). 'Lycian Coins in the "Decadrachm Hoard"', in I. A. Carradice (ed.), *Coinage and Administration in the Athenian and Persian Empires* (BAR Int. Series 343, Oxford), 29–37.

THOMPSON, M. (1981). 'The Cavalla Hoard (*IGCH* 450)', *ANSMN* 26: 33–49.

TROXELL, H. (1984). 'Carians in Miniature', in A. Houghton et al. (eds.), *Festschrift für/Studies in honor of Leo Mildenberg* (Wetteren), 249–57.

—— and J. KAGAN (1989). 'Cilicians and Neighbors in Miniature', in G. Le Rider et al. (eds.), *Kraay–Mørkholm Essays: Numismatic Studies in Memory of C. M. Kraay and O. Mørkholm* (Numismatica Lovaniensia 10; Louvain, 1989), 275–81.

VAN GELDER, H. (1900). *Geschichte der alten Rhodier* (The Hague).

VON GAERTRINGEN, F. H. (1931). 'Rhodos', *RE supp.* 5, cols. 731–840.

WALBANK, F. W. (1957, 1967, 1979). *An Historical Commentary on Polybius*, vols. 1–3 (Oxford).

WARTENBURG, U. (1992). *NC* 152, 193–5 (review of C. Lorber, *Amphipolis. The Civic Coinage in Silver and Gold* (1990, Los Angeles, Calif.)).

WESTERMARK, U. (1979–80). 'Notes on the Saida Hoard (*IGCH* 1508)', *NNÅ* 1979–80: 22–35.

WILL, E. (1979). *Histoire politique du monde hellénistique*, i, 2nd edn. (Nancy).

WILLIAMS, C. and O. ZERVOS (1985). 'Corinth, 1984: East of the Theater', *Hesperia*, 54: 55–96.

ZERVOS, O. (1986). 'Coins Excavated at Corinth, 1978–1980', *Hesperia*, 55: 183–205.

ZIEBARTH, E. (1932). 'Zur Handelsgeschichte der Insel Rhodos', *Mélanges Gustave Glotz* ii (Paris), 909–24.

ZOUMBAKI, S. (1994). 'Ρωμαῖοι ἐγγαιοῦντες in Elis', *Tyche*, 9: 213–18.

7

TEMPLES, CREDIT, AND THE CIRCULATION OF MONEY

John K. Davies

THIS CHAPTER[1] ATTEMPTS TO MAP THE WAYS in which the adoption of coined money by most Greek microstates by or soon after 500 BC affected the economic activity and attitudes of collectives. Building on Henry Kim's chapter, it focuses on mainland and Aegean Greece, leaving the material from Magna Graecia aside for separate treatment. It concentrates on the behaviour of those bodies—demes, phratries, *gene*, as well as whole *poleis*—which used or were responsible for communal resources, whether beneficially owned by the collective or owned by a deity, temple, or sanctuary, whose assets the collective managed for the purposes of divine service. The topic has become a prime focus of study in recent years, and has stimulated much useful recent work,[2] which has shown the value and complexity of exploring the interface between (a) cult, ritual, and theology, (b) economic (especially agrarian) history, and (c) administrative practices and their underlying value structures. Since the question 'What difference did the adoption of coined money make?' risks further complicating the scholarly quest, clarity is best served by concentrating on the long-term

logic of such divine service and by illustrating the various alternative behaviours via (mostly epigraphic) quotation, while acknowledging that wider issues—of public finance, of cultic propriety, of attitudes towards asset accumulation and 'increase',[3] or of the scale of monetary activity by collectives—cannot be ignored.

Rhamnous: The Evidence and the Problem

Discussion can usefully start from a well-known example. For five (probably sequential) years in the 440s BC, the Athenian deme of Rhamnous inscribed on a stone *stele* the summary accounts of the monies of their goddess Nemesis. The flavour of the document[4] emerges readily from a translation: section numbers and words in round brackets are insertions to assist understanding.

Text A

I Autokleides being demarch, sum of the money of Nemesis which (was) with those owing the 200 drachmae was 37,000 (drachmae). Sum of the other money of Nemesis 2,728 (drachmae) 3 (obols).

II Mnesiptolemos being archon, sum of all the sacred money 51,397 (drachmae) 5 (obols).

[1] This paper has undergone drastic, and I hope productive, revision since its first outing, not least before and after delivery to a postgraduate seminar at Berkeley. My warmest thanks for helpful comments to the editors, to the Press readers, to Ron Stroud, and especially to colleagues and postgraduates at Berkeley; in particular, Bridget Buxton, Michael Clark, Leslie Kurke, Donald Mastronarde, and Leslie Threatte. Yet again I thank the Leverhulme Trust for its unobtrusive support since 1995. Translations are my own unless otherwise stated.

[2] Cf. Bogaert (1968) 279–304; Jameson (1982); Migeotte (1984); Linders and Nordquist (1987); Knoepfler (1988); Osborne (1988); Ampolo (1989/90); Walbank (1991) 145–207; Linders and Alroth (1992); Hellström and Alroth (1996).

[3] For this rendering of *tokos* cf. Cohen (1992) 45.

[4] ML 53 = IG I[3] 248, with Finley (1952) 284 f.; Pouilloux (1954) 147–50; Whitehead (1986) 160 and 167; Millett (1991) 175–6.

III   Nausimenes being archon, sum of the sacred money which (was) with those owing the 200, 37,000. Of the other, 11,723 (drachmae) 2 (obols).

IV   Euainetos being archon, sum of the 300-drachmae (lots) 13,500. Of the whole, 55,712 (drachmae) 1 (obol).

V   Demophanes being demarch, sum with the *hieropoioi* 5,206 (drachmae) 4 (obols). Of the 300-drachmae (lots) 14,400. Of the 200-drachmae (lots), 37,000. Of the whole, 56,606 (drachmae) 4 (obols).

Complete though it is, with arithmetic which adds up (as it does not always in fifth-century accounts), this much-discussed document is telegraphic enough to need some explanation. Five aspects are of importance.

(1) The word *argyrion*, here translated as 'money', is clearly money in coined form, for otherwise it could hardly comprise packets of 200 or 300 drachmae.

(2) That money, owned by the goddess, was evidently seen by the demesmen of Rhamnous as being under their full control and as properly subject to being administered not by priests or priestesses but by the *hieropoioi* cited in year-entry V, whose vague title ('sacred-doers') makes them, like their counterparts elsewhere in Attika, secular officials concerned with cult affairs but leaves their precise roles opaque and variable.[5]

(3) The money was being lent out, presumably to individuals, in packets initially of 200 drachmae, later (from Year IV) in 300-drachmae packets as well. Individuals may have borrowed more than one packet apiece,[6] while commentators have noted the parallel pattern of lending adopted by Demosthenes père, whose estate, according to his son, included 'about a talent deployed in 200s and 300s' (Dem. 27. 11). The oscillations in, and the rate of growth of, the 'sum' need explanation. A 'windfall gain' in Year II is one possibility, but parallel practice elsewhere (see below) suggests that interest was being charged. In fact, if there was no windfall gain, to move from 39,528 to 56,606 drachmae represents a compound interest rate of over 7 per cent over the quinquennium[7] (even

higher if we assume that 'the other money' (Year II) was idle), but we need not assume that the men of Rhamnous thought in such terms. They did think, though, that their stewardship of the goddess's money was worth recording, and may perhaps have copied the format of the First Stele of the Tribute Lists, with its notion of a sequence of annual entries on a single stone.

(4) As with the First Stele, we are clearly well beyond the start of the system. The idea of the '200-drachmae lot' is in place, and the distinction between 'working monies' and cash in hand is already established: developments such as the introduction of '300-drachmae lots' or the greater precision in presentation visible in Year V are refinements to a going concern.

(5) However, since presumably little or nothing of Nemesis's movable assets survived 480, the origin of the funds we here see being deployed is a matter of some consequence, to be explored further below.

Prima facie, then, the goddess and her temple, with its stewards, are using the flexibility of coin in order to employ money as a commodity for their own advantage. They have been exploiting her possession of resources which either were or could be transformed into coin, by lending out her monies at interest, thereby increasing her wealth and resources, and are advertising the achievement with some pride. Even if with Millett we incline to locate such activity within *philia* relationships rather than within market-based relationships, monetization has clearly affected behaviour. This collective at least, the deme of Rhamnous, has come to see what would otherwise be 'dead' resources locked up (probably literally) in the premises of a deme, or shrine, or temple, or phratry, or tribe, as resources which could be put to work: *energa*, in Demosthenes' terminology (Dem. 27. 10).

Their activity poses the question whether such a use of sacred monies, or a comparable use of resources owned by civic or private collectives, was exceptional or normal. Since Paul Millett has already reviewed the limited Athenian evidence for such money-lending,[8] it may illuminate the theme of this book most helpfully to locate it spatially and chronologically

---

[5] For *hieropoioi* at deme level see Whitehead (1986) 142–6; at national level, *Ath. Pol.* 54. 6–7, with Rhodes ad loc., and Rhodes (1972) 127–30.

[6] Thus rightly Pouilloux (1954) 149.

[7] For the various attested rates see Millett (1991) 104. The rate of one drachma per day per talent, well attested for the loans from Athene to the

Athenian state before 426/5 (ML 72, p. 215), will not be enough to generate the growth.

[8] Millett (1991) 171–8.

within a wider framework of needs, opportunities, hindrances, and scruples concerning the manipulation of resources. The default assumption will be that we are reconstructing the behaviour of men who are acting above all as pious stewards of the assets of their gods, as fearful of divine or human retribution for acts done without divine approval, and yet as deeming human and divine interests to be coterminous rather than in conflict.

Coin and the Zero Base

Conceptually, if not historically, the new start of post-Mycenaean Greece can be seen as a build-up from a zero base. Historically, indeed, continuity of cult from LM IIIB is now becoming a reality,[9] so that the assignation of landed resource to deities as *temene* may have had a long past before its first attestation at *Odyssey* 8. 363. Conceptually, though, our baseline of divine service should comprise those shrines—surely the vast majority at all times—which had no 'capital resources' (of land, bullion, or dedications) out of which to draw material with which to carry out their rituals and ceremonies. Such shrines had to rely entirely on offerings made by worshippers, on fees for consultations, and on unpaid devotion by priests, sacristans, etc. Offerings will primarily have been animals, or foodstuffs, or other specific *things*, via a custom accessible to us only through the literary or documentary record.

Typical as illustration are the two texts which follow. Part of a *lex sacra* of *c*.510–480 from the Eleusinion in Athens[10] records:

Text B

    [——of barley?, hal]f-sixths s[e]ven, of w[ine ch-]
    [oes s]ix and a [h]alf-chous, [——]   60
    [——a six]th, of ho[n]ey cu[ps]
    [ei]ght, of olive oil half-chou[s——]
    [——a hal]f-fourth, of cheese [thr-]
    [ee] fourths, [of b]ean[s——, of sesa-]
    [me white th]ree cho[inikes], of bl[a-]   65
    [ck three choi]nike[s, ————]
    [————t]wo [————].

Similar in its specification of the composition of sacrifices, though less detailed, is part of a treaty of *c*.450 between Argos, Tylissos, and Knossos,[11] fragmentarily preserved in both Argos and Tylissos:

Text C

When we sacrifice to Machaneus the sixty full-grown rams, to Hera as well shall be given the leg of each victim. If several cities take property from the enemy, as the Knossians and Argives jointly decide, so shall it be. To Ares and Aphrodite shall the Knossian priest make sacrifice, and he shall keep the leg of each victim. The Archos shall keep the precinct at Acharna. For those who sacrifice, the Knossians shall provide gifts, while the Argives (shall provide them) for the chorus.

Such texts reflect and regulate a cultic regime functioning entirely *en nature*. Their preoccupation is above all with specifying in greater or less detail which offerings in kind for which ritual are to be offered to which deity on which day, who is to provide what, or who keeps which bit of the sacrificial victim. They reflect practices whose principle will have been long-standing by the time they begin to be codified in publicly accessible written form.

Nonetheless, however stable that regime *en nature*, it was invaded by coin with some rapidity. One illustration is provided by the shift in the meaning of *pelanos*. Originally denoting a cake of flour and honey to be burned on an altar, it seems to retain that tangible sense *c*.425 in the regulations for the Andrian *theoroi* at Delphi.[12] Yet an only slighter later document from Delphi (*CID* I 9) specifies that:

Text D

It seemed good to Delphians that Phaselitai are to give the *pelanos*: the public one, 7 Delphian drachmae 2 obols, the private one, 4 obols. When Timodikos and Histiaios were *thearoi*, Herylos was archon.

Here, *pelanos* has become the word for a consultation fee levied in coin. Indeed, another Delphian inscription of *c*.500, though brief and fragmentary, so links '*pelanos*' and '15 drachmae' as to imply that the

---

[9] Cf. Morgan (1997).   [10] *IG* I[3] 232, ll. 59–68.

[11] *IC* I viii 4* and xxx, 1 = *Staatsverträge* II no. 148 = Piccirilli (1973) nos. 18–19 = ML 42. Translation of ML 42B, ll. 29–38, from Fornara (1977) no. 89.
[12] *CID* I 8, ll. 24–8, with Amandry (1950) 86–103, and Rougemont (1977) 9 with n. 4.

pelanos-fee was monetized[13] remarkably soon after Delphi began to coin, a decade or so before 500.[14]

Other indications of the tendency to monetize are the insertions, into calendars of sacrifices, of monetary fees to priests and of the prices of offerings and victims. A classic early example is provided by the regulations, set out *c*.460,[15] for the Mysteries in the City Eleusinion at Athens:

Text E

```
[———]obol [———]                                    5
[———]: festiv[al-organizers]
[are to take ha]lf-obol [per]
[d]ay [from t]he initiate e[a-]
[ch one]. The priest[es]s of Demeter
is to take at My[st]eries t[h]e L-                 10
[e]sser from [the in]itiate each
one an obol and at [the G]rea[ter]
[M]ysteries an o[bol from the in-]
[iti]ate each one. A[ll the obo-]
ls are [to be] of the goddesses [except] for si-   15
x hundred an[d thousand dr]achm-
ae. From the si[x hundre]d an-
d thousand drachm[ae the pr]iestes-
s is [to give] the expenditures [just]
as was previously spent. E[u]m[olpid]ai an-        20
d Her[a]lds are to tak[e from] the in-
itiat[e e]ach fiv[e obols from t-]
he [ma]les, but from female[s three].
[Scotfree an in]itiate it is not per[mitted to ini-]
[tiate nobo]dy except for the [initian]d from [hearth.]
```

Few documents reveal so clearly the irresistible convenience of coin, not least by providing the facility to top-slice revenue and to earmark it for the traditional expenditures (whatever they were). A century later, the sacrificial calendar of the Greater Demarchy of Erchia *c*.375–350[16] was to take the process even further by specifying the price of each offering and dividing the aggregate cost of all the deme's offerings into five equal shares: considerations of cost expressed in coin, and of dividing its burden evenly, had determined the deme's decisions and thereby the very form of the document.

Below the Line, I: Temple Building

Monetized or not, the acts and rituals envisaged in the texts cited so far do not involve investment in premises, and require no more than space round an altar which might itself be nothing but a heap of ashes. In accountancy terms they are clearly 'above the line', involving no more than current income and expenditure within a given period. However, since many cults and collectives came to own land and other assets, the roles which coin could play in their management need consideration. No single answer will suffice, for at any one historical juncture managers might need simply (i) to accommodate and guard a growing congeries of dedications of uncontrollably various shapes, sizes, values, fragility, and convertibility, or more actively (ii) to accumulate resources in order to lay out a site and build on it, or more proactively still (iii) to procure resources from which a reliable income of indefinite duration could be derived, in the forms of produce or rent or interest. The difference between these tasks is profound. The first is essentially a caretaker role, the second envisages getting resources in order to spend them, while the third envisages getting resources in order to husband them and to draw income therefrom on a regular basis for (say) the maintenance of premises, for procuring the goods (spices, animals for sacrifice) needed for honouring the god appropriately, for feasting, or for providing perquisites for deme or phratry officials, priests, or priestesses.

The first two tasks need brief notice, since they overlap and since two distinctions need to be made. The first is between resources for temple construction made available by polities or *koina* out of accumulated funds, and resources made available by individuals or families. Obvious examples of the former are the temples financed by the Athenian state after 450 from the monies deposited with Athene (Thuc. 2. 13. 3, etc.), of the latter the shrine of Artemis Aristoboule founded in Melite by Themistokles (Plut. *Them*. 22. 2–3). The second distinction is between resources provided by singleton donations and those provided through recurrent revenues or ongoing liens on activities. Examples of the former are the two huge known donations to Delian Apollo, the first when Polykrates of Samos gifted the island of Rheneia to him by

---

[13] *CID* I 1. *CID* I 13, ll. 8 ff. (mid-fourth century) shows comparable provisions and language, but *CID* I 11–12 do not, maybe because the Asklepiadai were exempt (thus Rougemont (1977) 123–4). Lines 36 ff. of the Eleusis First-Fruits decree (ML 73: see below, TEXT I) may also use *pelanos* to denote a cash sum to finance the three-animal sacrifice. For further discussion see Dow and Healey (1965) 40–1.

[14] Kraay (1976) 121.   [15] *IG* i³ 6 C, ll. 5–50.

[16] *SEG* xxi 541, with update in xxxiv 111; Whitehead (1986) 199 ff.

chaining it to Delos, the second when Nikias of Athens bought the hippodrome area on Delos for 10,000 drachmae, probably in 417, and gifted it with equal éclat to the god.[17] An example of the second is the credit of the order of 150–200,000 Aiginetan drachmae made available by the City of Delphi to the *naopoioi* to help finance the reconstruction of the Apollo temple after the 373 earthquake, a credit which was drawn on over a number of years and could therefore be met from the city's normal annual income.[18]

These two distinctions could cross-cut each other, and were clearly blurred in practice. We cannot tell, for example, whether the temples in Corinth, at Perachora, and at Isthmos attributed to the 'families' of the Bacchiadai or the Kypselidai[19] were financed by one-off donations or by recurrent liens, even if 'public' and 'private' revenues can be effectively distinguished. However, to be aware of the distinctions helps to locate the conceptual space within which the utility of coin came into play. Three sixth-century temple-building projects illustrate the timescale of change. The first is Herodotos' well-known tale of the rebuilding of the Apollo temple at Delphi after the fire of 548.[20] The cost was estimated at 300 talents, one-fourth to be provided by the Delphians, who famously took their begging bowl as far as Egypt, while the 'family' which gained the contract, the Athenian Alkmaionidai, are portrayed as behaving both as contractors and as *euergetai*. Procedures, though monetary, were essentially pre-coinage, for the fund-raising profile which emerges emphasizes gifts, in kind or as bullion, and ostentatious euergetism on the part of *privati*.

The second and third projects, both from Asia Minor, show both similarity with, and difference from, the Delphian procedure. One of them is known from a temple dedication of *c.* 525–500 from Sidene on Propontis,[21] which records that:

Text F

[—son of–]enos and his companions made the roof from the sacred precincts and the skins. [—]os son of Leukippos finished off the temple with his own hand.

Again, a part is played by ostentatious euergetism, this time via one craftsman's own personal service, but more than that is involved, for the first sentence contains a procedural ellipse. The 'sacred precincts and the skins' must have been converted into man hours somehow, and the use of coin, though not essential, is quite likely. That inference is inescapable with the third project, the so-called 'Kroisos-temple' of Artemis at Ephesos. While the 'many columns' which Kroisos gave (Hdt. 1. 92. 1) attest lavish and ostentatious euergetism, a double-sided silver plaque from the foundation deposit[22] records that :

Text G

(Side A) [——] forty *mnai* were first weighed from the gi[fts(?)] of gold: they were brought from the *polis*. Five and twenty silver *mnai* were brought in the first gold. From the wood six *mnai* were weighed. Ten *mnai* of gold were weighed from here. Three and thirty *mnai* of silver were weighed from here. Silver fr[om the] flee[t——] seventy *mnai*. [——] ten from the salt.
(Side B) [——] in addition to(?) the half-mna [from the w]ood [of silv(e?)]r twenty *mnai* lacking a [half]-mna. [Th]irty *mnai* w[ere weighed(?) — to a (?)s]tater and a sixth from the salt. [——]fourteen *mnai*. There resulted from this [–] a half-mna of the cup and five half-sixths. (two vacant lines) [Of (or 'From')] what we worked forty *mnai* [–] and eight stat[ers were weighed(?). From the gar]den thirty-five *mnai* of silver were brought.

Much here is unintelligible, but the most straight-forward assumption is that the plaque records the origin of at least some of the resources used for the construction of the Chersiphron–Metagenes temple. Some looks like bullion, from the (akro?)*polis* or 'from here' (whatever that means), but the mentions of 'fleet', 'salt', 'wood', and 'garden', though problematic,[23] strongly suggest that some kind of turnover tax was being levied. Moreover, though in themselves *mnai* are simply units of weight and do not imply coined currency, the references to staters, and even more to fractions, point firmly towards coin as the medium in question. It is hard to avoid the inference that the Ephesians wished to exploit the practical advantages of the easy convertibility of resources offered by the adoption of money in coined form.

[17] Respectively Thuc. 1. 13. 6 and 3. 104. 2, with Kent (1948) 245 f., and Shipley (1987), 74–80; Plut. *Nikias* 3. 5–8.
[18] *CID* II **31–32**, with Bousquet's commentary.
[19] Sources and discussion in Salmon (1984) 59 ff.
[20] Hdt. 2. 180 and 5. 62. 2–3.
[21] Robert (1950) 78ff. pl. 10 = Jeffery (1961), 372 no. 50.
[22] Jeffery (1961) 339 and 344 no. 53, pl. 66 = *IK Ephesos* Ia 4, with *SEG* XXXIV 1079.
[23] For a documented sketch of alternative interpretations see Talamo (1984).

Below the Line, II: Using Assets Productively

We may now turn to task (iii), that of acquiring resources from which an income could be drawn for cultic purposes. This was far from being a straightforward matter, for varied reasons which take us into a confused morass of conflicting ideas and priorities. Though simplistic and probably over-linear, it will be helpful to distinguish five stages in this process. First and basic is that resources should accrue, via donation and dedication. That could pose problems. All fundraisers know that it is much easier to attract resources for new building than for maintenance, for new buildings can carry the donor's name—the treasury of Kypselos, the stoa Peisianakteios, the Philippeion—and enhance his prestige, while maintenance is unglamorous and often invisible: few benefactors were as willing to repair and maintain as Eumenes II of Pergamon was, by sending a squad of workmen under his Master of Works to Delphi in 197/6.[24] Unhelpful too might be the consecration of property to a deity, if accompanied by the stipulation or expectation that from its revenue there should be some commemoration of the donor,[25] or behaviour such as that of Telemachos of Acharnai, importing the cult of Asklepios to Athens and treating it as his own property.[26]

If they were not to remain as passive caretakers and inventory-compilers, swamped by a clutter of useless dedications, like the fourth-century curators of the goods of Artemis Brauronia,[27] cult managers had to move to a second stage, that of getting a grip on their possessions and of seeing them as potentially productive assets. The mental jump required lay in the unrecorded past, but challenges to the propriety of so doing are visible. One well-known such case is the Pelargikon area below the Athenian Akropolis, kept unused in accordance with a (misinterpreted?) oracle until the accommodation crisis of spring 431 forced a reconsideration.[28] Equally well known is the Sacred Land of Apollo by Delphi, to be left fallow in terms of a decision enforced periodically by the

Amphiktyones, enshrined in the Amphiktyonic Law of 380 but certainly of long standing by then, and chartered by the story of the First Sacred War irrespective of its historicity.[29] Nor was that Sacred Land unique, for quarrels over the use to be made of the tract of land on the border between Attika and Megara called the Sacred Orgas nearly triggered a war in 353/2 and were only resolved by referring the decision to Apollo at Delphi. It was more than a squabble over Jenkins's Ear, for the issue at stake was whether the 'King Archon should lease out the parts now under cultivation [of the Sacred Orgas, those wi]thin the markers, towards the building of the po[rch and the repair of th]e sanctuary of the Two Goddesses' or 'to leave them holy-idle for the Two Goddesses'. The criterion was 'that matters regarding the Two Goddesses should be as pious as possible', and the decision, as with the Sacred Land of Delphi, was to leave it uncultivated.[30] The issue of the ritual propriety of using a god's property for raising an income was therefore a real one, even when the intended use of the income was as ostensibly pious and as proper as the Athenians proposed. It comes as no surprise to find confirmation of such values in another oracular consultation,[31] this time at Dodona by a small community from somewhere in northwest Thessaly:

Text H

The community of the Mondaiatai consults Zeus Naios and Dione concerning the money of Themis, whether it is permissible and better to put it out on loan for Themis.

The unknown answer matters less than the enquiry: already at stage two if not well beyond, but caught between piety and practicality, the Mondaiatai sought guidance from an authority which could not itself be accused of impiety.

---

[24] SIG³ 671 B, ll. 12–3.
[25] Isaios iv. 9 for an allegation, with Wyse's edition ad loc. for other examples.
[26] IG II² 4960, with SEG xxxix 240.
[27] Cf. IG II² 1514–31, with Linders (1972).

[28] See Thuc. 2. 17. 1, with Hornblower ad loc., ML 73, ll. 54 ff., and Hurwit (1999) 78, with 69 fig. 48 for its conjectured location.
[29] CID I 10, ll. 15–21. For other sources and discussion see Kahrstedt (1954).
[30] IG II² 204 (quotations from ll. 25–30 and 51–2), with Androtion, FGrH 324 F 30, and Philochoros, FGrH 328 F 155. Translations are based on those in Harding (1985), no. 78. The word translated as 'repair', episkeuen, is wholly restored but must reflect the general sense. For the rare word anetos, here translated as 'holy-idle', see Ael. NA 11. 2 (used of a sanctuary of Apollo in Epeiros) and Pollux 1. 10.
[31] Dodona, lead roll, no date ascribed: SGDI 1557, ed. and tr. Parke (1967), 260, with further refs.

Income in Kind versus Income Monetized

Nonetheless, some communities clearly overcame such scruples and were able to move to the third stage, that of actually making their assets productive. The sanctuary of the Two Goddesses at Eleusis provides two complementary examples. The first is its holding of land in the Rarian Plain, known from the record of its leasing out to the politician Hypereides for the quadrennium 332/1 to 329/8 for an annual rent of 619 *medimnoi*, a literal tithe of which (61 *medimnoi*) went 'to the priests and priestesses according to custom'.[32] More complex were the arrangements in the First Fruits decree of *c*.420:[33]

Text I

They shall perform sacrifice with the *pelanos* in accordance with what the Eumolpidai [enjo]in, and the triple sacrifice led by the bull with gilded horns to each of the Two Goddesses from the barley and the wheat, and to Triptolemos and to the [go]d and to the goddess and to Euboulos a full-grown victim to each, and to Athene a bull with gilded horns. The *hieropoioi* together with the Council are to sell the other barley and wheat and are to dedicate dedications to the Two Goddesses, having done whatever seems fit to the people of the Athenians, and are to inscribe on the dedications that they were dedicated from the first fruits of the harvest, and of Greeks the offerer of first fruits. [To tho]se who do these things there are to be many good things and good harvest and abundant harvest, [who]soever do not injure Athenians or the city of Athenians or the Two Goddesses.

This excerpt is fundamental, for it shows how stage three, the direct deployment for ritual purposes of resources accruing in kind as tithes, can generate (and coexist with) stage four, the monetization of those resources via market-based exchange. Here, some of the barley and wheat is to be used directly, to buy the animals for sacrifice to the Eleusinian deities, while the rest is to be sold off, the proceeds (in silver coin, undoubtedly, by this date) being then stored in a convenient format by being converted into dedications.

This was the mechanism which generated at least some of the monetary assets attested as being in the beneficial ownership of shrines and collectives. It offered opportunities, but also posed dilemmas, for cultic communities and polities alike. Once monetized, the resource could either (as at Eleusis) be stored, or (as at Rhamnous) be put to work as *energa*. If the latter procedure is regarded as stage five, it becomes clear that the practices attested at Rhamnous in the mid-fifth century represent a comparatively 'advanced' stage in the use of cult-owned assets. Consequential questions of the scale and frequency of such practices are best put within the context of Greek practice as a whole.[34] Three fifth-century examples suffice. The first is Delos. By the start of extant documentation, in the 430s,[35] a system of leasing out the lands and properties of the Apollo temple was already in full swing, fully monetized and extending, as at Rhamnous, to the loan of money at interest to individuals. (Whether the Amphiktyones were already also lending money to cities and communities in the Aegean, as they were doing by the 370s and almost certainly by 393/2, cannot be ascertained.[36]) When the system began, or when it was monetized, is indeterminable. We do not have to postulate Athenian influence,[37] and, while Apollo's acquisition of Rheneia is plausibly assumed by Kent to have been rapidly followed by the conversion of that part of the island which Apollo retained into the ten estates which are identifiable from the fourth century till 166 BC,[38] it is unlikely to have been Apollo's first property holding. In any case, rents were not necessarily levied in coin right from the start, for the shift from tithes to coin could have occurred after any of several *caesurae* in the history of Delos.

However, a *terminus ante quem non* can be applied to the second example, a possibly comparable system at fifth-century Hyampolis in Phokis. A lead tablet

---

[32] *IG* II² 1672, ll. 252–8.

[33] ML 73 = *IG* I³ 78. Translation of ll. 36–47 based on that of Fornara (1977), no. 140. I am most grateful to Ron Stroud for emphasizing to me the value of this text.

[34] Cf. Bogaert (1968) for an assemblage of evidence, which, however, blurs essential distinctions of period and function.

[35] ML 62 = *ID* 89 = *IG* I³ 402.

[36] Cf. *ID* 98 for the 370s, and for 393/2 *ID* 97, ll. 9 ('increase from Delians') and 13–4 ('sum total from the cities'). The note 'Individuals owe' at *ID* 91, l. 9, implies its contrast, communal borrowing, but *ID* 91 is not closely dated within the late fifth century.

[37] Peisistratos' intervention on Delos (Thuc. 3. 104. 1) need not have affected Rheneia. Neither the year-long residence of two Kerykes as *parasitoi* on Delos (Athen. 6. 234e–f) nor Philochoros, *FGrH* 328 F 75, reliably attest Athenian interest in Delos before Peisistratos' *démarche*.

[38] Kent (1948) 244–52, esp. 245.

found in the sanctuary of Apollo and Artemis at Kalapodhi, published in 1987, reads: 'When Ennaios was secretary, first month: [Go]rgos has paid (back?) 20 *mnai*. These Menondas borrowed. Hyanpolioi guarantors of interest of 10 st(aters).'[39] The words 'possibly comparable' are meant to acknowledge the absence of any explicit indication that the monies involved are the gods'. However, against the hypotheses that the monies were the property of the polity (whether Hyampolis or Phokis), on the pattern of Plotheia in Attika (see below), or alternatively that the transaction was wholly private, stands the role of the Hyanpolioi as guarantors, for on the first hypothesis the community would then be offering its members *carte blanche* to default on interest payments, and on the second would be giving itself an extraordinary role in private transactions. If instead the monies were the gods', the polity would be acting in a recognizable but limited way by guaranteeing that the gods' interests (and interest) suffered no harm. It therefore seems safe to assume that the sanctuary did, indeed, function as a resource-lending entity. Since the temple was sacked in 480 by the Persians,[40] the resources available for such purposes will have accumulated subsequently.

A third well-known text, from a tiny deme of fifth-century Attika,[41] encapsulates the interaction of competing ideals:

Text J

(1–10) Totals: to demarch 1,000. To two treasurers for the sacred things through the year 5,000. For the Herakleion 7,000. For the Aphrodisia 1,200. For the Anakia 1,200. For the tax exemption 5,000. For Apollo 1,100. For Pandia 600. From rents 144 (dr.) 2 1/2 (ob.).
(11–22) Resolved by Plotheieis, Aristotimos moved: the archons responsible for the money are to allot of which each office controls, and these (officers) are to keep the money safe for Plotheieis. In the case of any (money) about which there is a decree of lending or a fixed interest, they are to lend in accordance with the decree or are to exact (the interest), but lending such money as is lent annually (to) whoever may give the greatest interest, he who may persuade the lending officials by valuation or guarantor.

(22–28) From the interest and the rents, in place of whatever of the totals there may be purchases bearing rent, to make the holy acts, both those which are common to Plotheieis and those (made) to Athenians on behalf of the commonwealth of Plotheieis and those to the quadrennial festivals: (28–33) and also for the other holy acts, whenever it is necessary for all Plotheieis to contribute money for holy acts, whether to Plotheieis or to Epakreis or to Athenians, from the common fund the officials who may be in charge of the money for the tax exemption are to pay on behalf of the demesmen.
(33–40) And for the common holy acts in which Plotheies feast, they are to provide sweet wine from the commonwealth, for the other holy acts up to a half-*chous* to each Plotheus present, [and—] to the producer a jar [—] to the burner-off [—] public official? [——]

Such a document is a warning to minimalists. For all its small size and unremarkable profile in the local life of Attika, the deme of Plotheia could make a surprisingly high level of resource available to its officials (lines 1–10): the money was to be kept safe 'for Plotheieis' rather than for any particular deity: the income was seen as being largely bespoken for 'holy acts' but was also seen as usable to pay the taxes due on behalf of the demesmen and to pay for feasting (hence the demesmen had a double direct personal interest in the maximization of the surplus): and deme officials therefore had *carte blanche* to lend out the remaining monies '(to) whoever may give the greatest interest'. The text suggests a society not perhaps driven by 'economic rationality' in the sense of maximizing profit come what may, but one in which that idea was a significant component, albeit embedded within a structure of codified practice which had other values and other objectives and which showed the conflicting interests of private debtors and of a creditor collective in some sort of (precarious?) balance. Above all, it reflects a society in which money in the form of coin was being taken for granted, as a prime enabling feature of its institutions.

Large-scale Lending: The Pros and Cons

On this evidence some cult communities and polities clearly felt themselves able to advance to stage five without impropriety. It therefore becomes a real question why the practice was not more widespread. Lack of resources, an attachment to *philia* relationships,

[39] *SEG* xxxvii 422, with *BE* (1988) 670.
[40] Hdt. 8. 33, with further refs. in Morgan (1997) 184.
[41] Deme decree of Plotheia, c.420; *IG* I³ 258.

or preferences for feasting or for priestly prebends may all have helped to inhibit cultic money-lending, but wider issues were at stake. They emerge most visibly if the lending patterns attested on Delos, at Kalapodhi, and within the microcosms of Attika's regional cults and groups are juxtaposed with the large-scale role assigned to Athene as the national deity of Attika and with those envisaged for the resources held in the sanctuaries of other major deities.

The latter are suggestive. So early as the planning stage of the Ionian Revolt Hekataios is said to have suggested to Aristagoras that he should finance a navy by 'removing' the dedications made by Kroisos to Apollo at Branchidai.[42] Likewise, some seventy years later the Korinthians broached the idea of 'borrowing' monies from the treasures at Delphi and Olympia for a similar purpose (Thuc. 1. 121. 3), and this time there is a clear hint in the truce document of Spring 423 that some of those at Delphi were used, incurring Sparta's ostensible disapproval.[43] Since, after initial opportunism, the Arkadians in 364/3 showed an equal reluctance to use the Olympia treasures in such a way (Xen. *Hell.* 7. 4. 33–5), while the peal rung over the Phokians for their comparable use of the Delphian treasures in 356–346 is notorious, we are left with a very odd bifurcation of attitude. Some actual or proposed uses of temple resources for non-sacral purposes, whether military or money-lending, whether as 'borrowing' or as 'removing', pass without the least adverse comment: others, though functionally indistinguishable, incur doubt, disapproval, and even ferocious (though sanctimonious) condemnation. It cannot be the nature of the deity which made the difference, for Apollo was Apollo, whether at Branchidai, Delos, or Delphi; nor the distinction between military and non-military use, for Athene helped to finance both; nor the distinction between a more casuistical Ionian world and a more puritanical mainland, for Korinthians and Hyampolitans adopted or at least contemplated the practice; nor even the distinction between 'national' and 'international' gods or shrines,[44] for Delos and Branchidai were no less international than Delphi or Olympia. The only distinction which may hold is that between naval and land warfare, for it cannot be

chance that the aim of using temple monies to finance ships and crews was common to Aristagoras, to the Athenians, and to the Korinthians, and that disapproval or self-denial emanated from powers which thought primarily in landward terms or thought it wholly improper to use temple monies for land warfare (Sparta in 423, Arkadia in 364/3, Boiotia in 356). If that distinction is tenable, it suggests that it was the horrendous costs of naval warfare in the new, trireme-based era which led the Greek powers which were most aware of them to view temple resources in a more detached and manipulative way. That suggestion in turn focuses attention on coin, the medium whose use was virtually essential in order to transmit resources to rowers whether indigenous or mercenary, as a cultural innovation and on a hypothesis that it may have generated radical ideological change in a fundamental aspect of communal life.

That is rather more than a hypothesis. The very next lines of the Eleusinion decree quoted above[45] (Text E) run:

> Of the sacred money [——]
> [it is perm]itted? to Athen[ians — to]
> [us]e? as far as they may wis[h, just]
> as of the [money] of Athene,   35
> that on Akropolis. The mo[ney th-]
> e festival organizers [—— o-]
> [n] Akropolis is to be stewarded [–]

Given its battered state, this text cannot be proof, but it is at least consistent with the view taken by the Athenian state, in the fourth century as in the fifth, of the full availability for public purposes of the monies owned by, or deposited with, both Athene and some (but not all) of the Other Gods. It does not greatly matter whether with Linders we think in terms of the 'secularization' of cultic resources,[46] nor which approach we adopt to the old (but still real) argument between Gomme and the editors of *ATL* about whether the monies kept on the Akropolis by 431 were comparable in status to those attested in the

---

[42] Hdt. 5. 36. 3, with no suggestion of 'borrowing' or of sacrilege.

[43] Thuc. 4. 118. 3, with Hornblower ad loc. and Parker (1983) 173–4.

[44] *Pace* Parker (1983) 173.

[45] Anne Jeffery's conservative text at *IG* i³ 6 C, ll. 32–8, runs: τõ δὲ hιερõ ἀργυρί[ο ... 7 ...] / [.]Εs[... .]ναι Ἀθεν[αίοισι..] / [.]σθαι hέος ἂν βόλο[νται καθά]- / περ τõ τε͂ς Ἀθεναια[s ἀργυρίο] / τõ ἐμ πόλει τὸ δὲ ἀρ[γύριον τὸ]- / s hιεροποιὸs [...]το[...7...ἐ] / [μ] πόλει ταμιεύεσθ[αι .. 6 ...] / [.]δ[....] χεν ἐν τõι/[....8...]. The translation offered in the text above reflects the gist of restorations made by Clinton, Meritt, and others, as reported in the app. crit. There is fortunately little doubt about the *Wortlaut* of the crucial lines 34–6.

[46] Linders (1975) 7 ff.

demes, i.e. that the goddess was the 'beneficial owner' (the *ATL* view), or whether they were deposited with her as with a bank but were owned by the Athenian state or the 'Athenians and their allies' (Gomme's view).[47] The aspects which matter are that monies—however acquired, and whosesoever 'possessions' they were—were being stockpiled, mostly in coined form, rather than being loaned out Plotheia-style for the sake of 'increase' (still less investment); that in the effort to maximize such resources the assets of many gods were added to the pile by being amalgamated managerially if not physically[48] under Athene's protection, only those monies being exempt for which (as with those of Eleusis) a strong case based on tradition had been recognized; that any use of them comprised a loan from Athene, to be repaid with interest; and, above all, that they could be used only for below-the-line divine service (i.e. temple construction) or for military and naval purposes.

These ideas did not vanish with the 1,000-talent reserve: expedients derived from this 'Periklean' tradition continued to mould Athenian financial management throughout the fourth century. A complete list is impractical, and in any case Ferguson documented the main known instances long ago,[49] but it is pertinent to call attention in particular to the decisions to turn the proceeds from the confiscation of the properties of the Thirty into *pompeia* of, it seems, roughly standard weight,[50] to a detectable fourth-century decision to require uniform weights for honorific crowns voted by the Demos and then dedicated on the Akropolis by the honorand,[51] to Androtion's activity, probably in the 360s, in melting down the temple treasures,[52] and even to the uniform weights (respectively 100 and 500 dr.) of the manumission *phialai* dedicated in the 330s and 320s and of the liturgists' *phialai* of 331/0.[53] Not, of course, that all dedications could be made as, or transformed into, easily countable units of uniform weight in such a way, but Lewis was right to comment that:

'the practical Androtion always saw the temple-treasures as an iron-reserve, something which could be turned into money, if it should be necessary. He was, if only in theory, the predecessor of Lachares, and of course the same idea was always inherent in the policy of Pericles, though Demosthenes prefers to ignore this. An essential preparation for such coining was the melting of unwieldy crowns of varying weights into objects of stock size, which could easily be checked and coined.'[54]

Furthermore, the fourth-century material, even in Demosthenes' two speeches, betrays no notion (or polite fiction) that the monetization and use of such resources would count as a loan by the goddess to the State, or was in any sense impious.[55] In the fourth century as in the fifth, a city could not run a serious navy without taking a coldly instrumental attitude towards the assets of its gods.[56]

Conclusion

The set of practices which I have tried to map has emerged as a more complex one than is often acknowledged. On the one hand there came to be a reservoir of resources in the system, accruing to cults, shrines, sanctuaries, and other cultic or secular collectives from a variety of sources. These included rents in kind or in coin from productive land owned by the cult or collective, rents in coin from houses similarly owned, tithes of produce, booty dedicated or deposited, other dedications from a variety of sources, fees from participants in rituals, fines, or rents from hosting markets or panegyrics.[57] Some of

---

[47] For basic orientation see Wade-Gery and Meritt (1957). Also Kallet-Marx (1989*a*) and (1989*b*); Giovannini (1990); Samons (1993).

[48] ML 58, of immaterial date for present purposes.

[49] Ferguson (1932) 85–95 and 111–27.

[50] Philochoros, *FGrH* 328 F 181, with Ferguson (1932) 113 n. 2.

[51] *IG* II[2] 1496, ll. 52 ff., with Kirchner ad loc. and Ferguson (1932) 113 f.

[52] Dem. 22. 69 ff. and 24. 176 ff., with Lewis (1954) 39–49.

[53] *IG* II[2] 1553–78+, with *SEG* XXXIX 168; Lewis (1968); Linders (1989/90) 281–5.

[54] Lewis (1954) 49.

[55] The nearest approach is a Council decree of 353/2 that a list of what was in the Chalkotheke should be made and read out to the Council, which 'was to consider beforehand if there was need of anything and bring (the matter) to the Demos, so that the Demos, having heard, should consider how what was lacking shall be replenished, so that matters pertaining to the Goddess are best and most pious' (*IG* II[2] 120, ll. 28–32, with Rhodes (1972) 92 f.: restorations are heavy, but the general sense is clear): but here, to judge from the three-line whip sent to all the elected military officials and to all the *tamiai* in post since 362/1, it was a matter of doing an emergency audit in the presence of responsible parties, not of challenging the practices of storing surplus resources with the Goddess and of lending them for profit or spending it for survival. The defalcation by the *tamiai* reported by Schol. Dem. 24. 136 was probably a separate occasion.

[56] For other comparable non-Athenian examples of the thesaurization and public deployment of sanctuary-owned resources see Ampolo (1989/90).

[57] The extensive relevant material cannot be assembled here. Note also Smith (1996) 147, for hypotheses about the economic role of temples in archaic Central Italy.

such resources or revenue had to be regarded as bespoken, whether for the maintenance of sacred or secular premises, for new buildings, for purchasing spices and sacrificial animals, for maintaining cult personnel, for feasting, or for priestly perquisites. However, in fortunate circumstances some resources might be left over, on a windfall or recurrent basis. The problem of how to use them will therefore have presented itself across the Greek world (and, indeed, not only the Greek world), no doubt spasmodically and irregularly, but on a large enough scale to prompt the evolution of widespread institutionalized common practices. As the above review of possible courses of action has shown, solutions had to be seen to be pious, and might therefore be subject to a divine veto via oracular consultation. They had to ensure that in practical terms the interests of the god or of the collective suffered no harm, and therefore generated documents of public accountability, some few examples of which have survived for us. They might even have to ensure that those interests were maximized, which could lead to close specification of how leased-out land was to be worked,[58] or to pressure to seek the best income or the highest interest. At such junctures, however, awkward choices had to be made, the alternative resolutions of which generate our disarticulated picture. Those taking the decisions in any one case might themselves become borrowers or lessees, and would therefore have an interest in securing low rates of rent or 'increase', but might equally—and simultaneously—benefit from high rates *qua* participants in the cult and its privileges. They might also have to decide whether the interests—especially the military and naval interests—of the polity of which they were citizens took priority over ancestral custom, the perquisites of priests, or the attractions of 'increase'.

In all these ways the adoption of coin had deep long-term effects. By transforming the ways in which the assets of collectives, cults, and sanctuaries were held, regarded, and used, and especially by forcing the pace of change within those states which went over to trireme fleets by or soon after 500, above all in Athens, it brought the worlds of cult practice, administration, and warfare together. The scholarly consequence for us is that the worlds of the numismatist and of the historian must coalesce if the processes involved are to be mapped satisfactorily.

REFERENCES

AMANDRY, P. (1950). *La Mantique apollinienne à Delphes* (Paris).

AMPOLO, C. (1989/90 [1991]). 'Fra economia, religione e politica: tesori e offerte nei santuari greci', in *Anathema. Regime delle offerte e vita dei santuari nel Mediterraneo antico* (= *Scienze dell' Antichita. Storia, archeologia, antropologia*, 3/4 (Roma), 271–9.

BOGAERT, R. (1968). *Banques et banquiers dans les cités grecques* (Leiden).

COHEN, E. (1992). *Athenian Economy and Society: A Banking Perspective* (Princeton, NJ).

DOW, S. and R. F. HEALEY, SJ (1965). *A Sacred Calendar of Eleusis* (Harvard Theological Studies, xxi, Cambridge, Mass.).

FERGUSON, W. S. (1932). *The Treasurers of Athene* (Cambridge, Mass.).

FINLEY, M. I. (1952). *Studies in Land and Credit in Ancient Athens* (New Brunswick, NJ; repr. 1973; new edn. with additional material by P. Millett, New Brunswick, 1985).

FORNARA, C. W. (1977). *Translated Documents of Greece and Rome*, i (Baltimore, Md. and London).

GIOVANNINI, A. (1990). 'Le Parthénon, le Trésor d'Athéna et le Tribut des Alliés', *Historia*, 39: 129–48.

HARDING, P. (1985). *Translated Documents of Greece and Rome*, ii (Cambridge).

HELLSTRÖM, P. and B. ALROTH (1996) (eds.), *Religion and Power in the Ancient Greek World* (Boreas, 24, Uppsala).

HURWIT, J. M. (1999). *The Athenian Acropolis* (Cambridge).

JAMESON, M. H. (1982). 'The Leasing of Land in Rhamnous', in *Studies in Attic Epigraphy, History and Topography Presented to Engene Vanderpool* (Hesperia, suppl. 19, Princeton, NJ), 66–74.

JEFFERY, L. H. (1961). *The Local Scripts of Archaic Greece* (Oxford; new edn. with additional material by A. W. Johnston, Oxford, 1990).

KAHRSTEDT, U. (1954). 'Delphoi und das Heilige Land des Apollon', in G. E. Mylonas (ed.), *Studies Presented to David Moore Robinson on his Seventieth Birthday* (St. Louis, Mo.) ii, 749–57.

KALLET-MARX, L. (1989a). 'Did Tribute Fund the Parthenon?', *CSCA* 29: 252–66.

—— (1989b). 'The Kallias Decrees, Thucydides, and the Outbreak of the Peloponnesian War', CQ^2 39: 94–113.

KENT, R. G. (1948). 'The Temple-estates of Delos, Rheneia, and Mykonos', *Hesperia*, 17: 243–338.

KNOEPFLER, D. (1988) (ed.), *Comptes et inventaires dans la cité grecque* (Neuchâtel–Genève).

---

[58] Jameson (1982) 71.

KRAAY, C. (1976). *Archaic and Classical Greek Coins* (London).

LEWIS, D. M. (1954). 'Notes on Attic Inscriptions', *BSA* 49: 17–50.

—— (1968). 'Dedications of Phialai at Athens', *Hesperia*, 37: 274–80.

LINDERS, T. (1972). *Studies in the Treasure Records of Artemis Brauronia Found in Athens* (Stockholm).

—— (1975). *The Treasurers of the Other Gods in Athens and their Functions* (Meisenheim am Glan).

—— (1989/90 [1991]). 'The Melting Down of Discarded Metal Offerings in Greek Sanctuaries', in *Anathema. Regime delle offerte e vita dei santuari nel Mediterraneo antico* (= *Scienze dell'Antichita. Storia, archeologia, antropologia* 3/4 (Roma), 281–5.

—— and B. ALROTH (1992) (eds.), *Economics of Cult in the Ancient Greek World* (*Boreas*, 21, Uppsala).

—— and G. NORDQUIST (1987) (eds.), *Gifts to the Gods* (*Boreas*, 15, Uppsala).

MIGEOTTE, L. (1984). *L'Emprunt public dans les cités grecques. Recueil des documents et analyse critique* (Quebec and Paris).

MILLETT, P. (1991). *Lending and Borrowing in Ancient Athens* (Cambridge).

MORGAN, C. (1997). 'The Archaeology of Sanctuaries in Early Iron Age and Archaic *Ethne*: A Preliminary View', in L. Mitchell and P. J. Rhodes (eds.), *The Development of the polis in Archaic Greece* (London and New York), 168–98.

OSBORNE, R. (1988). 'Social and Economic Implications of the Leasing of Land and Property in Classical and Hellenistic Greece', *Chiron*, 18: 279–323.

PARKE, H. W. (1967). *The Oracles of Zeus* (Oxford).

PARKER, R. (1983). *Miasma* (Oxford).

PICCIRILLI, L. (1973). *Gli arbitrati interstatali greci*, i (Pisa).

POUILLOUX, J. (1954). *La Forteresse de Rhamnonte* (Paris).

RHODES, P. J. (1972). *The Athenian Boule* (Oxford).

ROBERT, L. (1950). *Hellenica*, ix (Paris).

ROUGEMONT, G. (1977). *Corpus des Inscriptions de Delphes*, i: *Lois sacrées et règlements religieux* (Paris).

SALMON, J. (1984). *Wealthy Corinth* (Oxford).

SAMONS II, L. J. (1993). 'Athenian Finance and the Treasury of Athena', *Historia*, 42: 129–38.

SHIPLEY, G. (1987). *A History of Samos 800–188 BC* (Oxford).

SMITH, C. J. (1996). *Early Rome and Latium: Economy and Society c.1000 to 500 BC* (Oxford).

TALAMO, C. (1984). 'Sull' Artemision di Efeso', *PdelP* 39: 197–216, at 216.

WADE-GERY, H. T. and B. D. MERITT (1957). 'Athenian Resources in 449 and 431 B.C.', *Hesperia*, 26: 183–97.

WALBANK, M. B. (1991). 'Leases of Public Lands', in *The Athenian Agora*, xix. (Princeton, NJ), 145–207.

WHITEHEAD, D. (1986). *The Demes of Attica* (Cambridge).

8

MONEY AND THE ÉLITE IN CLASSICAL ATHENS

Kirsty Shipton

There are ten *poletai*, one appointed by lot from each tribe. They lease out all the leasings and sell the mines and the taxes . . . in the presence of the *boule*. And they ratify the granting of the mines to whoever the *boule* selects, both those ready to be worked [*ergasima*] which have been sold for three years, and those which have been given up which have been sold for ten years.[1]

[Ar.] *Ath. Pol.* 47.2

The *archon basileus* introduces the leases of the sacred territories, writing them up on whitened tablets. These too are leased out for ten years[2] and the payment is made in the ninth prytany.

[Ar.] *Ath. Pol.* 47.4

Introduction

LEASING OF THE SILVER MINES AND PUBLIC land were two important money-using institutions in the public economy of classical Athens.[3] Not

only did the silver mines of Athens produce her owl coinage. The leasing of the silver mines, together with the proceeds from the leasing of public land, produced cash which the State could widely redistribute. Democratic payments, other benefits to citizens in cash and in kind, money spent on the navy or on public building projects, were all important ways in which the money from these different areas of activity—the non-landed and the landed—were recirculated in the economy.[4]

99–108; and a very general account in Shepherd (1993). A valuable study of some aspects of mine leasing appears in Osborne (1985a). Most recent are G. G. Aperghis (1997–8); J. E. Jones and S. D. Lambert (1999). Literary sources are Dem. 37; 40. 52; 42. 3; Hyper. 4, together with allusions in Aristoph. *Knights* 362; *Birds* 593, 1105; *Frogs* 1422; and schol. on *Peace* 451. Literary sources are discussed most recently by Faraguna (1992) 289–322. Archaeological evidence now provides detailed evidence of washeries in Laureotike: J. E. Jones (1982, 1984/5, 1988, and 1990). On other recent archaeology see Osborne (1985a) 242 nn. 4 and 5. For bibliography on BSA research in Laurion see *AR* 43 (1996/7), 10–11. For an account of a metal-working complex at Thorikos, from the second half of the fifth century to the fourth century, see *AR* (1996/7) 16. The most recent edition of the public-land leases is by Walbank in *Agora*, xix, whose text I follow. The leases discussed below are Walbank's L6, L9–12. For a history of the leasing of public land see Walbank (1991) 152–62. On other sources on land leasing apart from the *poletai* records see Osborne (1985a) 226 n. 3. Major discussions of the public-land leases are: Kent (1948) and Hennig (1983) on Delos; Behrend (1970); Lewis (1973); Andreyev (1974); Jameson (1982); Walbank (1983, 1984, 1991); Osborne (1985a, 1985b, 1988); Whitehead (1986); Lambert (1993) on phratry and *genos* leasing; Parker (1996) on phratry and *orgeones* leasing. Osborne (1988) 287 estimates that between 300 and 400 properties were leased out by the state in the fifth and fourth centuries BC. For the increase in public- and private-land leasing in the classical period see Osborne (1987) 42–3. For a detailed study of the mine and land leases see Shipton (2000).

Acknowledgement: I am grateful to the Institute of Classical Studies, School of Advanced Study, University of London, for permission to reproduce below some of the charts and tables which appear in Shipton (2000).

[1] I follow the *OCT* in reading 'ten' and not 'seven'. For the meanings of the mine classifications see Crosby (1950); Hopper (1953); Langdon (1991); and Shipton (1998).

[2] It may be, however, that leases changed hands more frequently, as can be seen to happen in the Delos records (cf Osborne (1985b) 125–6: eleven lessees take over the same estate between 313 and 246 BC). Records L6 and L9 appear to be renewals of leases ten years apart (Walbank (1991)). The leases made by demes and other bodies include a variety of other lengths of leases: 5 years (*SEG* xxviii, 103), 25 years (*IG* II² 411), 30 years (*SEG* xxiv, 203), 40 years (*IG* II² 2492), and even 'for all time' (*SEG* xxiv, 151, *IG* II² 2497, *IG* II² 2497, *SEG* xix, 181, *SEG* xix, 182, *IG* II² 2501, *SEG* xxi, 644). In the fifth century the state itself leases the sanctuary of Neleus and Kodros for 20 years.

[3] The most recent editor of the mine leases is Langdon in *Agora* xix (1991), whose text I follow. This now supersedes Crosby (1950, 1957). For studies of the silver mines see: Ardaillon (1897); Hopper (1953, 1961, 1968); Lauffer (1979), 2nd edn.; Conophagos (1980); Kalcyk (1982); Lohmann (1993) 77–9,

[4] For a discussion of another important circulator of cash—the private banks—see Shipton (1997).

In the context of this collection the mine and land leases have a particular significance. By looking at these two institutions we may hope to explore further some of the changes which the monetization of the economy produced.[5] John Davies draws attention to the ideological change in attitudes towards the use of temple monies.[6] What I explore here is the effect of monetization on another ideology about the use of wealth, viz. the high status of investing in land and the disdain of the wealthy élite for cash-based activities which aimed at profit.[7] Does this ideology prevail when the wealthy élite have the choice of spending money on leasing land from the State and spending on the non-landed activity of exploiting the state-owned silver mines which, if successful, could lead to large profits in cash?[8]

A study of the mine and land leases may also reveal another aspect of the use of money to which Jane Rowlandson draws attention below, viz. the role of money as an aspect of social relationships.[9] While she focuses, in the records of Roman Egypt, on the relationship between peasant tenant farmers and their wealthy landlords in the private economy, I focus on the relationship between the State and the men who leased state-owned property.[10]

We may surmise at the outset that wealthy lessees will have experienced a different relationship with the State from that of the many (as we shall see) prosopographic nonentities—once we have made due allowance for the possibility that some of the latter were in reality men of wealth and social standing. But the precise nature of these relationships will depend on the roles which the wealthy élite, and other social groupings, actually play in the silver-mine and public-land leases.

I therefore focus in my discussion on two main issues: What role do the wealthy élite play in the cash-based public economy of classical Athens? And, given the choice of using their money in both non-landed (the mines) and landed (public-land leasing) activity, how does this wealthy élite behave?

Methodology: An Index of Prominence

To date, much discussion about the social configuration of economic activity has been conducted in terms of the distinction between élite and non-élite, with attention tending to focus on the economic behaviour of the élite.[11]

In an attempt to nuance the role of the élite and the nature of their involvement in the cash economy of fourth-century Athens, I have devised an 'index of prominence' based on the evidence which has survived about the other activities of the men involved in our two cash-based institutions. The index distinguishes six levels of prominence ranging from the performance of expensive liturgies to a single appearance in the records of one of the institutions which I examine. This index of prominence is shown on all the Tables and Charts under the column headed 'Index'. It uses the letters A to F. These ratings fall into two parts which have different implications. 'A' and 'B' refer to specific levels of wealth. 'C'–'F' merely refer to frequency of attestation.[12]

The six categories of prominence naturally fall into three groupings. 'A' and 'B' are wealthy élite. They are applied to the men who appear in Davies's *Athenian Propertied Families* and thus include men who performed major state liturgies—both trierarchic and agonistic—or who show other evidence of

---

[5] On the role of early money see Kim above chapter 1. On the monetization in general of the Athenian economy see Shipton (1997) 403–9. On the existence of money before coinage see C. Howgego (1995) 13–15. On pre-coinage Athens see also T. Martin (1996) and J. Kroll (1998). For evidence on the fluctuations of money flow in the fifth and fourth centuries BC see Burke (1992) n. 62. On the spread of early owl coinage see C. Kraay (1976) on the wide distribution of Athenian tetradrachms. Athenian coinage formed 19 per cent of the Egyptian Asyut hoard of 475 BC (Howgego (1995) 97). On the growth of the Athenian economy between the sixth and fourth centuries see I. Morris (1994) 351–66; E. M. Burke (1992). On the increasing monetization of the fourth century see Osborne (in Rich and Wallace-Hadrill (1991) 119–45). On the links between monetization and democracy see Osborne (1991).

[6] See above chapter 7.

[7] See Dem. 37 (attack on the money-lender Nikoboulos); Dem. 36. 30 (justification for former metics failing to conform to citizen ideology, which prized citizenship above wealth in cash).

[8] See Xen. *Poroi* 4 on mine exploitation as an effective way of raising cash.

[9] See below chapter 9.

[10] The Athenian public-land leases do, of course, put lessees and their guarantors into an important relationship with each other. But this topic, while important, is outside the scope of the present investigation.

[11] For the élite and their spending power see Davies (1971) and (1981). For non-citizens and their economic role see Whitehead (1977). For an analysis of Athenian social groups based on economic/military criteria see Hansen (1991) 109–16. For glimpses of the economic behaviour of poorer citizens and 'social outcasts' such as money-lenders and traders see Millett (1991) 179–217.

[12] This task has been greatly facilitated by the recent appearance of *LGPN* II (= M. J. Osborne and S. G. Byrne (eds.) (1994)).

a wealthy background.[13] They both use as a major criterion the performance of the most expensive state liturgy—the trierarchy. 'A' refers to those mine operators and public-land lessees who themselves performed this liturgy.[14] 'B' refers to men who are not themselves seen to perform this liturgy but who have a direct ascendant or descendant who did.[15]

'C' and 'D' can also be taken together. They are men who are active in public life, while not seen to belong to the trierarchical top echelon. Both groups are involved in such activities as holding various magistracies, belonging to local delegations, acting as *bouleutai*, being honoured by decrees, proposing decrees, acting as arbitrators in local disputes, or contributing to public dedications. My criterion of 'prominence' here is the range of activities an individual was involved in rather than the importance of any one activity itself. 'C' thus refers to men who appear in at least two areas of activity outside the silver-mine and public-land leases, while 'D' refers to men who appear in only one 'outside' activity. 'C' and 'D' thus distinguish different degrees of attestation.

The men categorized by 'C' and 'D' *need* not be very wealthy, and, on the evidence of what has survived, they are not in a top liturgical band. But some of them—particularly those of political prominence—are likely to have been wealthy to some extent.[16]

'E' and 'F' may similarly be taken as a group. While 'A'–'D' ratings apply to all the men who are 'otherwise known', 'E' and 'F' refer to men found only in one particular set of records. Following the same methodology as with 'C' and 'D', 'E' and 'F' distinguish different levels of attestation within the same body of records, viz. the silver-mine and public-land leases. Both indices thus indicate men who are not 'otherwise known'. 'E' refers to men who appear to be involved in two or more mining or land-leasing activities. The 'E' index also has the additional significance that it enables us to see whether one economic activity rather than another attracted repeated investment. 'F' refers to men whose names appear only once in any of the records we examine. The 'F' rating is the least informative of the indices. It essentially marks a lack of information about the individual so categorized. It does not, of course, necessarily imply that the 'F'-rated man lacked wealth or social distinction or that he was politically inactive.

It will be apparent from my use of this index of prominence that its primary function is to allow comparisons to be drawn between the socio-economic profile of the two cash-using institutions which we examine here. Using the index we may hope to see, for example, whether men from a trierarchical background play a more or less significant part in the silver-mine or public-land leases. It is important to recognize that the index in itself cannot provide an adequate way of distinguishing precisely a series of different socio-economic groups and is not intended to do so.[17]

Evidence

Most of our detailed evidence about the administration of the silver mines comes from the

---

[13] See Davies (1971), pp. xx–xxvii (criteria for inclusion in *Athenian Propertied Families*). For the uselessness of Solon's property classes (cf. Pollux 8. 130) as effective criteria of wealth see Davies (1981) 36. Dem. 20.21 puts the number of agonistic liturgies in 355/4 at 60 per annum—a figure which Davies (1981) 27 raises to 97 (and to 118 in a *Panathenaia* year). Davies (1981) 27 suggests an agonistic class of 200–300, but regards this as the 'same class under another aspect' as the trierarchical class.

[14] In practice virtually all the As in the databases were trierarchs, but occasionally an A may not be seen to be of trierarchical status but shows other evidence (on the criteria in *Athenian Propertied Families*) of a wealthy background. I have also consulted Spence's list of *Hippeis* (Spence (1993) 294–31) as a likely indication of considerable wealth, but the few individuals in the mine and land leases who appear there also feature in *Athenian Propertied Families* (103 *hippeis* are listed in the fourth century who do not appear in *Athenian Propertied Families*). For an Athenian (possibly tendentious) view on the disparity of wealth within the trierarchic class see Dem. 18. 102–8. Undoubtedly, by no means all performers of the trierarchy were extremely rich. However prejudiced Demosthenes may have been, we have to take into account the fact that the syntrierarchy appears in the last decade of the fifth century and continues to 323/2 BC with three or even more men sharing in the last half of the fourth century. And in 406/5 BC the *choregia* can also be shared (see Gabrielsen (1994) 173–5).

[15] While As and Bs are defined in terms of the trierarchy, these index ratings do not, of course, indicate the whole range of economic and other activities which are often attested for the men put into these categories. Thus As and Bs are also seen to perform the same kind of economic or other activities as Cs and Ds. And they may also at times be involved in repeated activity, like the men in category E.

[16] That men who were *bouleutai* or proposers of decrees tended to come from wealthy backgrounds is argued by Osborne (1985a) 66–9. See too Whitehead (1986) 236–41, esp. 240 n. 74.

[17] No individual appears in more than one category, so the indices are mutually exclusive. Thus, given the possibility of categorizing a man as either an A, because he was a trierarch, or (for example) a C because he is 'otherwise known' on more than two occasions, my practice has been to select only the highest index to which he is entitled. I have adopted this procedure so as to gain the fullest picture our ancient sources allow of the wealthy élite. Thus A and B indicate those silver-mine and public-land lessees who are known to come from wealthy families. But the C–D groupings enable us to put the role of these wealthy individuals into perspective by pointing up the comparative importance of men who, while not known to belong to the wealthy élite, also appear to be relatively prominent through the number of their attestations in our sources.

fourth-century inscribed records of the *poletai* to which [Aristotle] refers.[18] They contain a wide range of factual information.[19] The typical lease[20] gives the location, and (often) the name of the mine, its classification, the names and demotics of the registrants and lessees, and the sums paid. Some also give a date, either in the heading (where this has survived) or in the course of the text.

The land-lease documents which I examine here are the bulk records produced by the State and recorded, like those of the mines, on stelae set up in the Agora.[21] Like the mine records the land leases largely belong to the middle and later decades of the fourth century.[22] And they contain very similar information: dates, the property leased out, the names and demotics of the lessees, and the sums paid.

Their main difference from the mine leases is the presence of guarantors who guaranteed the payment due to the State by the lessee. The guarantors are not directly involved in land leasing, unlike the registrants in the mine records who operate, or have at some time operated, mines themselves. A guarantor would not be called upon to make a payment to the State unless the lessee defaulted. I have, however, included the guarantors in my investigation since, as potential contributors of cash for public land, they may reasonably help to provide a fuller picture of the types of men involved in the public-land-based cash economy.

Both sets of records, inscribed on stelae set up in the Agora, present a number of difficulties for the historian.[23] They contain many gaps and it is frequently impossible to date the records precisely. Nor can we have any means of knowing how many records were originally produced. In the case of both the mine and public-land leases we know that detailed records were kept on wooden tablets, which have not survived.[24]

Given all these limitations in the evidence any conclusions have to be regarded as suggestive ways of approach and not as definitive explanations of how money was used in the cash-based economy of classical Athens.

Tests of Dominance

In order to evaluate the role of the élite in the silver-mine and public-land leases I apply a number of tests of 'dominance'. The first asks whether the élite dominate by the size of their presence in our two sets of records. I then ask three questions which form tests 2, 3, and 4. Do the élite dominate in the mines by the amounts which they pay to the State? Secondly, do the élite dominate by the frequency of their investment? Finally, do they dominate by family links—that is, does investment in the mines tend to involve different generations of élite families?

If we find clear evidence that, for example, the wealthy élite made large cash investments in the silver mines then we may draw one conclusion about their role in this particular area of the cash-based economy. But if, on the other hand, men from a liturgical background do not spend more than we might expect from the level of their representation in our sample of sums paid, then our conclusion will be different. Again, if repeated leasing of silver mines turns out to be more common among the wealthy élite than among the other index groups, this would suggest that men from a liturgical background played a more significant role in this area of the public economy.

A pattern of family investment would also lead to interesting conclusions both about the dominance, or otherwise, of the wealthy élite and about the way in which they invested in the cash-based economy. The family was a vital unit in the land-based economy,

---

[18] The mines were almost certainly leased by the *poletai* in the fifth century as well, though no explicit record so far survives (see Langdon (1991) 61 and nn. 25 and 26).

[19] Strictly speaking there were two sets of mine records—those on the stelae set up in the Agora and those on whitened tablets kept (probably in the *Metroon*) by a public slave who deleted the sums due when they were paid up ([Ar.] *Ath. Pol.* 47. 5). The apparent popularity of inscribing public records in the middle decades of the fourth century has its counterpart in the private sphere, where grave inscriptions (including demotics) also proliferate during this period, apparently reflecting Athenian democratic emphasis on the importance of citizenship (see Meyer (1993)). Both public and private records may be part of the same phenomenon of democratic consciousness.

[20] I argue elsewhere that the *poletai* records are not strictly leases but record sums due, to meet a mining tax whose amount depended on the length of exploitation (Shipton (1998)). A number of the *poletai* mine inscriptions include records of property confiscated by the State—this may have been a common procedure, but the fragmentary condition of many of the records makes it impossible to be certain.

[21] Walbank (1991), 158 suggests that the *poletai* who were responsible for the mine records and sales of confiscated property were also responsible for the bulk land leases.

[22] The longest land and mine records are closely contemporary: land 343/2 (L6); mine 342/1–339/8 (P26).

[23] On the role of stelae—which preserve both the silver-mine and public-land leases—as records see Thomas (1989) 46 and 64–8.

[24] Cf. *Ath. Pol.* 47. 5.

with estates passing on through marriage or inheritance to different family members. Landed wealth thus tended to have the conservative effect of keeping land in the control of the family who had originally come to own it. But the silver mines and public land were state assets and as such could not pass on by marriage or inheritance.[25] A pattern of family investment, in whatever index group it occurred, would have the interest of showing that economic behaviour traditionally displayed by landowners continued to be displayed in money-based activities where ownership by inheritance played no part.

I begin with the first test of dominance:

Test 1: What is the socio-economic profile of the silver-mine lessees? Does it suggest dominance by a wealthy élite?

The results of this test of dominance are summarized in Table 8.1 and the accompanying chart.[26] The thirty men in categories 'A' and 'B' form 19 per cent of the total number of identifiable investors—159 names in all.[27] Within this group it is apparent that those who have paid for the expensive triremes in the Athenian navy are almost twice as prominent as the men who merely belong to a trierarchical family. This is perhaps an indication that the very rich were at least of some relative prominence among the élite buyers of mines.

In the case of men who are otherwise known, but not seen to come from a liturgical background (Cs and Ds) both the subgroups are almost equally important: the relevant figures are 5 and 4, accounting for 3 per cent each of the overall total. To judge from the figures, men who on existing evidence are

Table 8.1: Mine buying/registering by index

Index	Count of Index	% of Total
A	19	11.95
B	11	6.92
C	5	3.14
D	4	2.52
E	38	23.90
F	82	51.57
Total	159	100.00

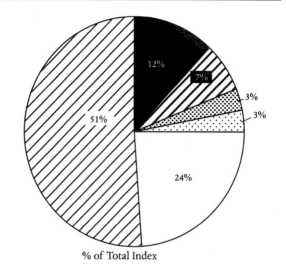

% of Total Index

■ (A) liturgist
▨ (B) immediate ascendant/descendant a liturgist
▦ (C) involved in several areas of activity apart from mining
▫ (D) involved in one area of activity apart from mining
□ (E) involved in several activities in mining only
▧ (F) involved in one activity in mining only

more active in a range of social, political, and economic activities (= C) are not more involved in mining than the men who appear to be less active in public life (the Ds). Looking at the comparative ratios of A, B, C, and D, I would therefore tentatively conclude that mining may be more closely associated with the possession of considerable wealth (category A) than with other types of prominence where the individual is not seen to be very wealthy.[28]

---

[25] When Mantitheos claims ([Dem.] 40. 52) to have 'shared out' his mining property with his half-brother, such 'sharing', even if true, was not a permanent gift. The State leased out different types of mining property for set periods of three or ten years, after which the mines would have to be re-registered and either given up or re-leased for a period of three years. For a detailed discussion of the administration of the mine leases see Shipton (1998). There is the occasional explicit recognition of family 'inheritance' in the land leases: in the case of a cleruchy c.510–500 BC the lease may be transferred, but only to another family member.

[26] The data used in all the silver-mine tables and charts have been collected from the new edition of the mine leases by Langdon in Agora, xix (1991), 76–137. Data used in the public-land-lease tables and charts come from the new edition by Walbank in Agora, xix (1991), numbers L6, L9, L10, L11, and L12.

[27] Throughout the ensuing analyses 'men' is a convenient shorthand for registrations and buyings (in the mine leases) or buyings and guaranteeings (in the public-land leases) by men who can be identified.

[28] The men categorized as 'C' or 'D' are 'prominent' in the sense that, typically, they appear on lists of bouleutai, or as the subjects of honorific decrees, or as the dedicators of various gifts. Men categorized as A or B may also be prominent in any or all of these ways but are distinguished from Cs and Ds by their known wealthy backgrounds.

If we now set these results against the comparable figures from the land leases, we can nuance this conclusion in an interesting way. The chart in 8.2 shows the relative proportions of the different index bands, using the classification of A–F, as was used with the mine records. The accompanying Table gives the actual figures on which the various percentages are based. The most striking figures here in comparison with those in the mine records are the very large preponderance of men who are not attested outside the land-lease records, and the very small numbers who are seen to belong to the liturgical élite. Thus the 'not otherwise knowns' (Es and Fs) account for more than 87 per cent of the 87 lessors

Table 8.2: Land leasing/guaranteeing by index

Index	Count of Index	% of Total
A	3	3.45
B	1	1.15
C	0	0.00
D	7	8.05
E	2	2.30
F	74	85.06
Total	87	100.00

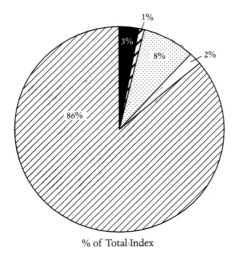

% of Total Index

■ (A) liturgist

▨ (B) immediate ascendant/descendant a liturgist

▦ (C) involved in several areas of activity apart from public-land leasing

▫ (D) involved in one area of activity apart from public-land leasing

□ (E) involved in several activities in public-land leasing only

▨ (F) involved in one activity in public-land leasing only

and guarantors named in the bulk records of the State; the corresponding figure for the Es and Fs in the mine leases is just over 75 per cent. And while men from a liturgical background account for about 19 per cent of the mine lessees who can be identified, this wealthy élite forms less than 5 per cent of the public-land lessees and guarantors. The comparison thus serves to point up the importance of very wealthy men in silver-mine leasing.

As a result of applying Test 1, and of comparing the mine leases with the public-land leases, we may now suggest two conclusions. First, the mine leases were particularly attractive to men from a liturgical background. Secondly, while a significant proportion of the men who operate the mines are not seen, on existing evidence, to be socially prominent (the 75 per cent made up of Es and Fs), the higher proportion of these groups in the land-lease records (88 per cent), and in particular the much greater proportion of Fs in the land-lease records, may suggest that men not seen to be prominent were more attracted to land-based activities.

But there is an important qualification to be made. To put these comparisons into proper perspective, ideally we need to know the total number of As–Ds attested for the period of our mine records (367/6–307/6 BC). In the case of the Cs and Ds this is not at present a practicable exercise.[29] But we can make a more or less reasonable estimate of the (minimum) numbers of As and Bs over this period thanks to our knowledge of how many liturgies had to be performed.[30] We also have numbers (again minima) of liturgical men currently attested for the relevant

[29] LGPN II contains all attested individuals in Attica, but a manual search for all those attested two or more times would be impossibly time-consuming. We may, however, note Davies (1971), pp. xxxii–xxxiii, who demonstrates that over the period 366–300 BC covered by the mine records only 38.6 per cent of the liturgical class (my As and Bs) are attested (38.6 is an average of Davies's figures of 43 per cent for the generation of 366–333 BC and 34.3 per cent for that of 333–300 BC).

[30] The actual numbers of men whose wealth was of liturgical status is likely to be larger—possibly very much larger. Demosthenes clearly envisaged the possibility of 2,000 men, rather than the 1,200 in the reform of Periandros, being available for the performance of liturgies (Dem. 14. 16–17). Whatever the precise function of this group (cf. Gabrielsen (1994), 182–93 on Periandros' reform), and however much it may have suited Demosthenes' rhetorical purpose to exaggerate the number of wealthy men, the figure of 2,000 must have been likely to sound plausible to his audience. But 2,000 is, of course, no more an accurate estimate of the actual numbers of the very rich than the 1,200 of Periandros. Both Periandros and Demosthenes are concerned to ensure that enough men can be found to perform the liturgies—especially the trierarchy. Neither has the interests of a demographer.

period.[31] On the basis that each generation in the fourth century had a minimum of 600 men in the liturgical class, then, over the two generations covered by our records the 30 As and Bs attested in the silver mines represent only 2.5 per cent of the 1,200 needed to perform the liturgies between 366 and 300 BC. They do, however, form a larger 5.5 per cent of the 540 attested members of the liturgical class during these years. Seen against these figures the role of the very rich in the silver mines must not be exaggerated. Moreover, these conclusions about the role of the wealthy in the mine and land leases may need to be altered, or at least nuanced further, in the light of the remaining tests. In the rest of this Chapter I look at three patterns of investment which may serve as further tests of the dominance or otherwise of the élite. Once more I attempt to clarify the significance of the results by comparing them with results obtained from asking the same questions about land leasing.

Test 2: Do the élite dominate by size of investment?

The evidence here is based on 45 prices from mines bought or registered by men whose names have survived in the records. Table 8.3 and the accompanying chart present an analysis of all 45 prices by the index rating of the men who paid them. Again we must recollect that the 220 leases we can still trace will all originally have mentioned a price.[32]

We have to acknowledge that the sample of sums paid by men who are otherwise known (As–Ds) is small. We know the amounts paid by 12 As and Bs, and only 5 Cs and Ds (the remaining 28 sums are paid by Es and Fs). So conclusions about the dominance or otherwise of the wealthy élite have to be suggestive. The most striking feature in the sums paid for mine leasing is the very different pattern in the sums paid by the liturgical élite and those paid by the remaining 'otherwise knowns' who are not seen to come from very wealthy backgrounds. As the figures in Table 8.3 reveal, As and Bs together spent 2,240 dr. The overall total is 6,330 dr. So the contribution of As and Bs—the wealthy élite—is 35.38 per cent. If we compare this with their presence in the sample—which is 27 per cent (12 of the 45 sums)—we see that these men from a liturgical background are spending more than we might expect. But the sums paid by the Cs and Ds present a different picture: these men spend much less than we might expect. They form 11 per cent of the sample (5 out of 45) but their contributions account for only 4 per cent of the sums paid.

On the basis of the sums which happen to have survived, these different patterns suggest the conclusion that men from a liturgical background play a particularly significant part in the sums paid for leasing the mines, and that their contribution to this sector of the public economy is much more important than that of the men who are otherwise known but not seen to belong to the wealthy élite.[33]

Once more I turn to the public-land leases in order to put this conclusion into perspective. As in the mine records, we have to take account of the gaps in our evidence. The public-land leases which we are using contain traces of some 86 leases, but only 21 complete lease prices now survive.[34] Of these, 19, analysed in Table 8.4 and the accompanying chart, were paid by identifiable individuals to whom the index can be applied.[35]

[31] The figures used here are those produced by Davies (1971), pp. xxxii–xxxiii (minima, as *Athenian Propertied Families* is currently being revised). For a more recent estimate of the number of liturgists needed over a three- or five-year period see Gabrielsen (1994) 178–80. The basis of the figures in Gabrielsen (1994) and Davies (1971) is different, since Gabrielsen challenges Davies's view that Demosthenes' law on the trierarchy reduced the numbers liable from 1,200 to 300 (Gabrielsen (1994) 210–12).

[32] As will be apparent the prices reveal some regular patterns, with 20 dr. and 150 dr. by far the most common. I have recently made a detailed study of the patterns discernible in the mine-sale prices, in Shipton (1998), where I argue for a new interpretation of the periodicity which the prices reveal. I suggest that sums above 500 dr. involve payment by a single individual for a number of different exploitations in the same, large, mine. I accept the standard interpretation of the frequent 20 dr. and 150 dr. prices as being payments for new/reopened mines and renewals of mining concessions respectively. The patterns of the prices are discussed in detail by Conophagos (1980), Hopper (1953) 224–239, and Crosby (1950) 196–204. See too Osborne (1985a) 116–18 (includes suggestion that the lessees paid rent to the landowners in the mining areas).

[33] It is possible, however, that the unusually large sum of 1,550 dr. may be a skewing factor. If we remove this figure from both the A and F columns where it occurs we find that A and B together now invest 690 dr., which is 21.36 per cent of the new total of 3,230 dr. But the wealthy élite are still investing slightly more than we might expect from their level of representation in the sample.

[34] Walbank (1991) argues that the sums represent some 8 per cent of the value of the property.

[35] Traces of a further 25 prices also appear, but these cannot give an accurate picture of the original sum.

Table 8.3: Mine prices by index

Index	Price (in drachmas)								Total	% of Total
	20	50	130	150	160	200	500	1,550		
A	60	50	0	300	0	200	0	1,550	2,160	34.12
B	80	0	0	0	0	0	0	0	80	1.26
C	20	0	0	0	0	0	0	0	20	0.32
D	60	0	0	150	0	0	0	0	210	3.32
E	80	0	130	900	0	0	500	0	1,610	25.43
F	240	0	0	300	160	0	0	1,550	2,250	35.55
Total	540	50	130	1,650	160	200	500	3,100	6,330	100.00
No. of prices	27	1	1	11	1	1	1	2	45	

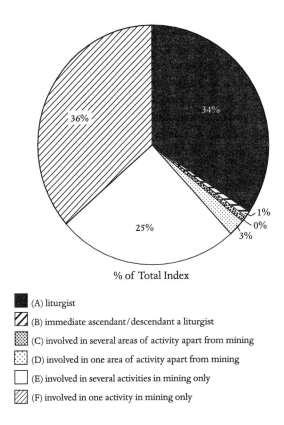

% of Total Index

- ■ (A) liturgist
- ▨ (B) immediate ascendant/descendant a liturgist
- ▦ (C) involved in several areas of activity apart from mining
- ▨ (D) involved in one area of activity apart from mining
- ☐ (E) involved in several activities in mining only
- ▨ (F) involved in one activity in mining only

The chart accompanying Table 8.4 shows the contributions of the different index groups within the overall sum of the complete prices which have survived. The hazards of survival restrict our information to only three of the index groups—A, D, and F. Of these, the Fs are clearly dominant, accounting for 79.5 per cent, while the liturgical As make up 11.9 per cent of the whole as against the 8.6 per cent of Ds. A breakdown of the individual prices appears in Table 8.4. The prices range from 60 dr. to 681 dr., with 5 prices, around a quarter of the sample, being in the higher range of 600 dr. or above.[36] To throw further light on the possible significance of these figures we

[36] Sums of 600 and above would require two guarantors—but both names have not always been preserved. Given the confines of this paper my current analysis of the sums in the land leases does not distinguish those involving land from those which refer to buildings. But it is interesting to note in passing that if we look at the size of rent paid in each of these categories we find a very similar pattern to that in the Delian land-lease records. In both sets of records the rent for land is considerably higher than the rent for buildings. Thus in the Athenian leases the average rent for houses is 155 dr., but for land it is 271 dr. The corresponding figures in the Delian records (at the beginning of the third century) are 50 dr. for buildings but 300 dr. for land. (Delian figures are from Osborne, 1988.)

Table 8.4: Land prices (in drachmas) by index

	A	D	F	Total	% of Total
	0	0	60	60	1.12
	0	0	90	90	1.69
	0	122	0	122	2.29
	0	0	126	126	2.36
	0	157	0	157	2.94
	0	0	164	164	3.07
	0	0	175	175	3.28
	0	0	176	176	3.30
	0	180	0	180	3.37
	0	0	195	195	3.66
	0	0	200	200	3.75
	0	0	212	212	3.97
	0	0	350	350	6.56
	0	0	351	351	6.58
	0	0	410	410	7.69
	0	0	450	450	8.43
	0	0	600	600	11.25
	636	0	0	636	11.92
	0	0	681	681	12.76
Total	636	459	4,240	5,335	100.00
% of Total	11.92	8.60	79.48	100.00	

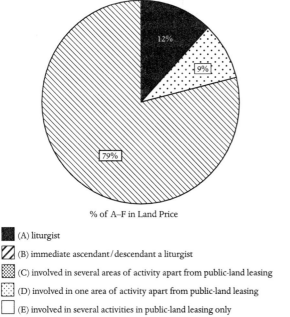

% of A–F in Land Price

■ (A) liturgist

▨ (B) immediate ascendant / descendant a liturgist

▨ (C) involved in several areas of activity apart from public-land leasing

▨ (D) involved in one area of activity apart from public-land leasing

□ (E) involved in several activities in public-land leasing only

▨ (F) involved in one activity in public-land leasing only

may adopt the same procedure as we did earlier, in the case of the mine leases, and compare the relative size of contributions made by different index bands with their various levels of representation within our sample of sums paid by the lessees of public land.[37]

The liturgical élite form 5 per cent of the sample of lease prices, while the remaining 'otherwise knowns' (the Cs and Ds) form 16 per cent. One feature is immediately striking: the liturgical élite spend more than we would expect (almost 12 per cent of the total prices) from their level of representation in the sample; and the remaining 'otherwise knowns' spend less—under 9 per cent compared with their 16 per cent representation in the sample of land-lease prices. We have to recognize, however, that our information about the sums paid both by the wealthy élite and by the remaining 'otherwise knowns' is very restricted—only 1 sum and 4 sums, respectively, are certain. Results based on such figures cannot be seen as conclusive.

On the basis of the comparatively few prices which happen to have survived intact we may therefore suggest, very tentatively, that the wealthy men from a liturgical background do dominate by the amount of cash which they paid to lease both the silver mines and public land. But there is one difference between the role of the liturgical élite in the prices of the mine and land leases which suggests that they play an even more significant role in the mines than in the land leases.

If we now compare the actual sums paid by the wealthy élite in the two sets of records, the role of the wealthy élite in the mines seems to gain even more significance. Table 8.4 above shows that the total spent by As to Fs was 5,335 dr., of which 636 dr., i.e. a little above one seventh of the total, comes from the wealthy élite—the As and Bs. In the mines, Table 8.3 above showed that the total sum spent by As to Fs was 6,330 dr., of which 2,240 dr., i.e. more than a third of the total, was contributed by the As and Bs together.[38] In other words, the contribution of the wealthy élite to the total sums paid in the mine records is more than double the contribution made by the same socio-economic groups to the total sums paid in the land leases. Correspondingly, the role of the wealthy élite in the mine records takes on an even greater significance.

I move on to the second question about pattern of investment.

[37] As and Bs form 5 per cent of this sample; Cs and Ds 16 per cent; and Es and Fs 79 per cent (viz. 1; 3; 15 respectively out of 19 prices).
[38] As contributed 2,160 dr., Bs 80 dr.

Test 3: Do the élite dominate by the frequency of their investments?

The evidence appears in Table 8.5, which shows the total number of mining activities by the men who bought and registered the mines which the records reveal. It includes not just buying and registering but also the ownership of workshops, or of 'neighbouring properties', or involvement in other, indeterminate, mining activities.

Table 8.5 and the accompanying pie chart analyse these various activities by the different index ratings

of A–F, with the numbers 1, 2, 3, 4, and 12 referring to the numbers of individual activities by individual men who appear in our records. Thus, for example, only 1 man in the Table was involved in 12 activities in the mines and he has an index rating of A. But 22 men were involved in 2 mining activities, of whom only 4 have an index rating of A or B. And so on. For the purposes of this test I am not primarily concerned with the one-off activities but for comparative purposes I include them as well, and note the proportions of As to Fs both in single activities

Table 8.5: Mining activities by index

Index	Mining activities					Total	% of Total
	1	2	3	4	12		
A	4	3	1	2	1	11	9.65
B	6	1	1	0	0	8	7.02
C	4	0	0	0	0	4	3.51
D	2	1	0	0	0	3	2.63
E	1	16	2	1	0	20	17.54
F	67	1	0	0	0	68	59.65
Total	84	22	4	3	1	114	100.00

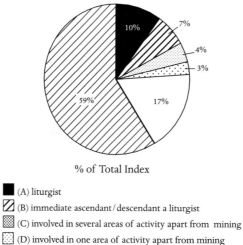

% of Total Index

■ (A) liturgist

▨ (B) immediate ascendant/descendant a liturgist

▦ (C) involved in several areas of activity apart from mining

⠿ (D) involved in one area of activity apart from mining

□ (E) involved in several activities in mining only

▨ (F) involved in one activity in mining only

and in the repeated activities (2 up to 12). This comparison immediately points up the importance of repeated activity in the silver mines: the total number of repeated activities is 80, almost as many as the 84 one-off activities.[39] Do the wealthy men from a liturgical background play a dominant role in this common practice of repeated investment in the mines?[40]

The actual numbers of men involved in the various repeated activities are small, so any conclusions can only be suggestive. But, despite the limitations of our evidence about repeated involvement, two features do seem to stand out. The most common pattern of repetition—being involved in two mining activities—does not appear to be typical of the élite As and Bs. A clear majority—34 of the 44 instances—involve men who are not otherwise known (the Es). On the other hand, being active in the mines 3 or more times appears to be more typical of the men who are seen to be prominent (A–D). The 'A'-rated Pheidippos of Pithos (record 1. 3) is outstanding for his 12 mining activities.

In any conclusion we have to remember, as we noted at the outset of this test, that the sample numbers are small, especially for any repetition above the level of 2 activities. If more evidence had survived, the picture suggested by these smaller samples might well be altered. Nevertheless, on the evidence which has survived there are reasonable grounds for claiming that repeated investment at the higher levels of 3 or more times is associated with men from a liturgical background.

The evidence about repeated leasing in the land records is too slight to point up the significance of the liturgical élite in the mine records. As Table 8.6 reveals, of the 84 occasions where men act as lessees or guarantors, 82 are one-off activities. We have, of course, to bear in mind that the bulk state records which we are examining belong to one of only two years—343/2 or 333/2. If we had records of land leased by the State for a larger number of years,

Table 8.6: Land activities by index

Index	Land activities			Total	% of Total
	1	2	3		
A	3	0	0	3	3.57
B	1	0	0	1	1.19
C	0	0	0	0	0.00
D	4	0	1	5	5.95
E	0	1	0	1	1.19
F	74	0	0	74	88.10
Total	82	1	1	84	100.00

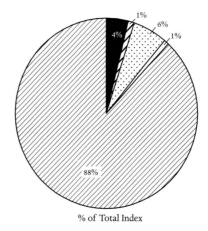

% of Total Index

■ (A) liturgist

▨ (B) immediate ascendant/descendant a liturgist

▨ (C) involved in several areas of activity apart from public-land leasing

▨ (D) involved in one area of activity apart from public-land leasing

□ (E) involved in several activities in public-land leasing only

▨ (F) involved in one activity in public-land leasing only

repeated leasing/guaranteeing might feature more prominently.[41] But on the existing evidence the most significant conclusion to be drawn as a result of applying this test of dominance is that there appears to be very little repeated leasing of public land from the State.[42]

---

[39] The total of 80 repeated activities is made up of: 22 men with 2 activities each (= total of 44); 4 men with 3 activities each (= total of 12); 3 men with 4 activities each (= total of 12); 1 man with 12 activities (= total of 12).

[40] These results suggest a different picture of mining investment from that suggested by Osborne's claim that there was a 'minimal number... of multiple lessees' (in Osborne (1985a) 115).

[41] On the other hand, since leases were normally for ten years, we might expect, if repeated leasing were common, to find evidence of this repetition in records L6 (342/1) and L9 (333/2)—but this does not happen.

[42] The significance of this result is put into sharper focus once again by the records from Delos (cf. Osborne (1985b) and (1988)). The *hiera syngraphe* which lays down the conditions for the leases of the temple estates imposes a 10 per cent increase in rent if a lessee renews his lease at the end of its ten-year term (ID 503). Such a stipulation itself suggests that re-leasing was a not unexpected pattern of behaviour. The records themselves bear out the habit of repeated leasing, both of the same estate and of other estates by the same person. We are particularly well

We may, however, give our results about the role of the wealthy élite in the silver mines additional perspective if we view them in the context of the repeated investments as a whole. If we now take into account the lowest, and commonest, level, viz. repetition on 2 occasions only, we find that men from a liturgical background still play a larger role than we would expect, even though the huge majority of men who invest on only 2 occasions are not known outside the mine records.[43] Of the 30 men involved at the level of 2 or more activities, 9, or 30 per cent belong to the wealthy élite.[44] But in the mining activities as a whole these men from a liturgical background form less than 17 per cent.[45]

This result, together with the dominance of the wealthy élite in the higher levels, of repeated activity, strongly supports the conclusion that the wealthy élite play a particularly important role in the mine leases from the point of view of repeated investment.

Test 4: Do the élite dominate by family invesment?

We hear in the literary sources of wealthy families where mining assets appear in several generations, or are distributed across collateral lines.[46] And in the mine records themselves we find, for example, that the man whom we see investing most frequently in the mines—Pheidippos of Pithos (A)—also has a son who follows his mining interests (and, incidentally, becomes a trierarch himself). Is dominance by family investment typical of the wealthy élite, or is it an equally popular strategy throughout the various groups we have identified?

We have to note at the outset that, given the lacunose state of the mine records, where names are often missing, we cannot see the full extent of family involvement even in those records which happen to have survived. The final results are therefore likely to be an underestimate of the true levels of family links.[47]

Table 8.7 shows the relative involvement of the different index ratings in family investment. An

Table 8.7: Family investment by index (mines)

Index	Sons	% of Total
A	3	25.00
B	1	8.33
C	0	0.00
D	4	33.33
E	0	0.00
F	4	33.33
Total	12	100.00

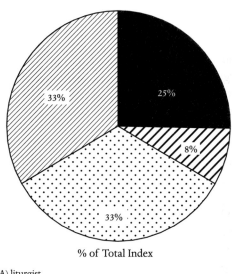

% of Total Index

■ (A) liturgist
▨ (B) immediate ascendant/descendant a liturgist
▦ (C) involved in several areas of activity apart from mining
▫ (D) involved in one area of activity apart from mining
□ (E) involved in several activities in mining only
▨ (F) involved in one activity in mining only

informed about the leasing habits of the descendants of Pherekleides: 8 are involved in leasing various estates over the period 258–169 BC and only 2 lease on a single occasion. They may not, of course, have been typical of leasing patterns in general but there are at least 19 instances of men successively leasing 2, and even 3, different estates. Osborne also refers to another 16 men who repeatedly lease buildings. Repetition does seem to be a marked feature of the Delian leases.

[43] Viz. the 1 F (a man who appears only once as registrant or buyer—hence his F classification despite his reappearance as the owner of a workshop) and 16 Es who account for 17 of the 22 men involved in only 2 mining activities.

[44] Viz. 7 As and 2 Bs.

[45] 19 of the 114 men are As and Bs. For percentages see the final column of Table 8.5.

[46] Cf. [Dem.] 40. 52 (father and son share mining; sharing of mines by half-brothers); Aeschin. 1. 105 (Timarchos ought to have invested in the silver mines like his father).

[47] The problem here is similar to that faced by Hansen (1985) in estimating the numbers of bouleutai serving twice (cf. Osborne's review of Hansen in JHS 107: 233).

interesting feature is that family investment in the mines occurs in equal proportions among the wealthy As and Bs, the active—but not seen to be very rich—Cs and Ds, and the men who are not otherwise attested, the Es and Fs. The actual numbers involved are very small, with only 4 men appearing in each of these three groups. So conclusions have to be cautious.

But if we consider only two broader groupings, the men seen to have some degree of prominence (Ds and above) and those who appear only in the silver-mine records (Es and Fs), it is at once observable that the more prominent groups A–D heavily dominate family investment. In Table 8.7 they form 66.7 per cent, and this degree of dominance far outweighs their overall representation in our total sample in Table 8.1. There, the As–Ds together make up only 24.4 per cent of the men who can be identified in the mine-sale records. *Pari passu*, the least prominent groupings E–F form 75.5 per cent in the total sample shown in Table 8.1, but they represent only 33.3 per cent of family investment in Table 8.7.

Table 8.7 shows up the smallness of our family investment sample—only 12 cases clearly appear in our records of which 8 belong to index ratings A–D. Results based on this numerical evidence must be suggestive rather than conclusive. But there does seem to be some indication that family involvement in mine leasing, where it occurs, is to be associated with men who are otherwise known, including the liturgical élite, rather than with those who are prosopographic nonentities. On the other hand, there is no evidence to suggest that wealthy men from a liturgical background play a more important role in family investment in the silver mines compared with the other lessees who are otherwise known.

As we noted earlier the mine records as they happen to have survived cannot be expected to point up the full extent of family involvement. So any evidence of such links between mine lessees is likely to underestimate the true extent of this phenomenon. If we attempt to give these results more significance by looking at family investment in the public-land leases the most striking observation is the very small numbers involved—too small to form an adequate basis for analysis.

The actual figures appear in Table 8.8. These very small numbers suggest that kinship links may not

Table 8.8: Family investment by index (land)

Index	Sons	% of Total
A	0	0.00
B	0	0.00
C	0	0.00
D	2	66.67
E	0	0.00
F	1	33.33
Total	3	100.00

have been significant among the public-land lessees. We do find at least one example of a father acting as guarantor for his son, while on another occasion a father is a guarantor in one lease and his son is the lessee in another.[48] Again, as with repeated leasing, more examples might well have appeared had the records been less fragmentary.[49] But if we look at the Delian records, where problems of identification are much less severe, it appears that family links did not play a strong role.[50] It may then be that, as in Delos, land leases at Athens tended to change hands across different families.

The very small evidence from both sets of records, and particularly from the land leases, must make conclusions on this last test extremely tentative. What the two sets of records put together do suggest is, first: there do not appear to be particularly strong family links in these cash-circulating activities; secondly: this pattern of investment is commoner in the mines, and does appear to show some skewing towards the men who are otherwise known. But there is no evidence to suggest that the wealthy élite were likely to dominate mine leasing through family involvement.

Results

In the context of this book on the uses of money our study of the silver-mine and public-land leases has

---

[48] Father guarantor for son in L9. 75–6. This may also happen in the incomplete L6. 116–18. Father guarantor: L6. 18–19; son lessee: L6. 33–4.

[49] There must originally have been at least 177 men named in our 86 records (given the rents which appear to have required 2 guarantors) but only 87 have survived.

[50] Osborne (1988) 301. But there are examples of a single family, like that of Pherekleides, leasing a variety of estates over several generations.

produced interesting results both about the use of
money by the wealthy élite and others and also about
the different economic patterns in these two areas of
the public economy. It makes sense to claim that the
wealthy élite played a dominant role in the silver
mines. They spend more than we would expect from
their level of representation in the sample of sums
paid for leases. And the sheer number of the wealthy
élite in the mine leases, particularly when compared
with their numbers in the public-land leases, does
seem significant.

The public-land leases, on the other hand, appear
dominated by large numbers of prosopographic
nonentities. Even allowing for the likelihood that
some of these will in fact have been socially prominent, and wealthy, we still have a very different social
profile from that in the Delian land leases, where
wealthy individuals are clearly important.

We have also found different patterns of investment in the silver mines and land leases. Both repeated investment and, where they can be detected,
family links between investors are much more
common in the silver mines than in the land leases.

In evaluating our results we have, of course, to
take into account that mine exploitation and land
leasing do not work on a level playing field. Each of
these economic activities has its individual bias
which is likely to have skewed the results of our
various tests. The silver mines were locationally
limited and will therefore have attracted men who
had the resources to travel—sometimes considerable
distances.[51] Lessees also need to have slaves who can
be dedicated to mine exploitation. But land leasing
tended to attract men from the same locality as
the leasehold, and in any one locality there is likely to
be a limited number of very wealthy individuals.[52]
Nor did land leasing necessarily demand the same
level of resources as the mines in terms of slaves
and equipment.

It would also be rash to make any inferences about
the landed and non-landed economies in general on
the basis of these results. They must be tested in a

wider study of uses of money in classical Athens. But
on the evidence which happens to have survived we
may at least make some tentanive suggestions. We
have found some indications that the wealthy élite
dominate in the mine leases and that they prefer
investing their money in the silver mines to investing it
in public land. We may reasonably assume that this
wealthy élite will also be wealthy landowners. But it
must be significant that they are not seen to take the
opportunity offered by the State to invest in public land
for profit, whereas in the mines they invest heavily—in
the amounts they spend, in the degree of family
involvement, and in high levels of repeated activity.

Pari passu, leasing of public land is heavily dominated by men who are not otherwise known, and
who appear to invest on single rather than multiple
occasions. We may put this apparent importance of
the prosopographic nonentities into perspective by
comparing the evidence of other, contemporary,
Athenian land leases in the *Hekatostai* inscriptions.[53]
In these records the 'otherwise knowns' account for
30 per cent of the lessees, a much higher proportion
than the comparable figure in the public-land leases,
where the 'otherwise knowns' account for just over
11 per cent. Against the background of the *Hekatostai*
the role of the prosopographic nonentities in the
public-land leases seems all the more striking.

Conclusion

These results suggest that the use of money in the
public economy of classical Athens will have produced different types of relationships between
individuals and the State in different areas of cash-
based activity. Mine leasing seems likely to have
reinforced the ties between the wealthy élite and the
State whereby each profits from the other. The lessees gain a profitable asset while the State in its turn
may expect to receive liturgical service.[54]

[51] Osborne (1985a), Table 9: of 161 lessees with demotics no fewer than 116 come from outside the mining demes.

[52] There will, of course, have been regional differences in the levels of wealthy élite. Osborne (1985a) Table 2(a) shows an average 'wealth index' for 127 demes of 1.39, but 14 demes are more than double this figure (Leukonoion has an index of 6).

[53] The *Hekatostai* contain documents relating to landed property belonging to demes and cult bodies which attracted a 1 per cent tax. For a persuasive argument that these documents are not sales but leases (with the tax being 1 per cent of the property value) see Osborne (1988). Unlike the public-land leases, the *Hekatostai* relate to a single occasion in the late fourth century. For the date (c.335 BC) see Lewis (1973) and Osborne (1988). Data on the *Hekatostai* has been taken from Osborne (1988).

[54] At some point in the fourth century mine workings were exempt from liturgical asssessment ([Dem.] 13. 17–9). Hopper (1953) 251 n. 376 suggests the period of Euboulos. But in 345 BC (Aesch. 1. [*Against*

But the ties between individual and State may well have been different for at least some, perhaps even many, of the numerous prosopographic nonentities who appear only once in the public-land leases. For these men the State may have been providing land for subsistence living rather than as an agricultural asset to be exploited for profit. If that is indeed the case then many of the lessees of public land may have felt dependent on Athens for providing a vital resource—a situation very different from that in Delos with its many wealthy land lessees.

Ties within the family can also be seen to be affected by the uses of money which we have been exploring. The family is likely to have been an important economic unit long before the spread of monetization. And its significance is likely to have been greatest in agricultural activity. But, on the evidence we have been investigating, the family—in so far as it actually appears in our records—appears to have economic importance not in agricultural leasing but in the exploitation of the silver mines by men of some standing.[55] So in this case at least it is non-landed, profit-seeking activity which is seen to involve and thus help to strengthen the bonds of kinship.

From the point of view of the traditional land-based ideology of wealth from which we began, our results now suggest that the wealthy élite of classical Athens, when faced with a choice of using their money to acquire either landed or non-landed assets from the State, do not in fact choose to invest in land. Instead they are seen to play a dominant role in non-landed activity which had the potential to produce considerable cash profits.

REFERENCES

ANDREYEV, V. N. (1974). 'Some Aspects of Agrarian Conditions in Attica in the Fifth to Third Centuries BC', *Eirene*, 12: 5–46.

APERGHIS, G. G. (1997–8). 'A Reassessment of the Mining Lease Records', *BICS* 42: 1–20.

ARDAILLON, E. (1897). *Les Mines du Laurium dans l'antiquité* (Paris).

BEHREND, D. (1970). *Attische Pachturkunden* (Munich).

BURKE, E. M. (1992). 'The Economy of Athens in the Classical Era: Some Adjustments to the Primitivist Model', *TAPA* 122: 199–226.

CONOPHAGOS, C. (1980). *Le Laurium antique* (Athens).

CROSBY, M. (1950). 'The Leases of the Laureion Mines', *Hesperia*, 19: 189–312.

—— (1957). 'More Fragments of Mining Leases from the Athenian Agora', *Hesperia*, 26: 1–23.

DAVIES, J. K. (1971). *Athenian Propertied Families, 600–300 B.C.* (Oxford).

—— (1981). *Wealth and the Power of Wealth in Classical Athens* (New York).

FARAGUNA, M. (1992). 'Atene nell' età di Alessandro: problemi politici, economici, finanziani', *MAI* ser. 9, 22: 165–447.

GABRIELSEN, V. (1994). *Financing the Athenian Fleet: Public Taxation and Social Relations* (Baltimore, Md.).

HANSEN, M. (1985). *Demography and Democracy: The Number of Athenian Citizens in the Fourth Century B.C.* (Herning).

—— (1991). *The Athenian Democracy in the Age of Demosthenes* (Oxford).

HENNIG, D. (1983). 'Die "heiliger Hausen" von Delos', *Chiron*, 13: 411–95.

HOPPER, R. J. (1953). 'The Attic Silver Mines in the Fourth Century BC', *ABSA* 48: 200–54.

—— (1961). 'The Mines and Miners of Ancient Athens', *GR* 8: 138–51.

—— (1968). 'The Laurion Mines: A Reconsideration', *ABSA* 63: 293–326.

HOWGEGO, C. (1995). *Ancient History from Coins* (London).

JAMESON, M. H. (1982). 'The Leasing of Land at Rhamnous', *Hesperia*, suppl. 19, 60–74.

JONES, J. E. (1982). 'The Laurion Silver Mines: A Review of Recent Researches and Results', *GR* 29: 169–83.

—— (1984–5). 'Laurion, Agrileza 1977–83', *Archaeological Reports for 1984–85*, 106–23.

—— (1988). 'An Athenian Silver-mine Ergasterion at Agrileza in the Laureotike', in Πρακτικα του ΞΠ Διεθνους Συνεδριου Κλασικης Αρχαιολογιας. (Acts of the Twelfth International Congress of Classical Archaeology, Athens, 4–10 September, 1983) 3 vols. (Athens).

—— (1990). 'The Planning and Construction of Attic Ergasteria', *Bautechnik der Antike* (Internationales Kolloquium in Berlin, 15–17 February).

—— and S. D. LAMBERT (1999). 'Two Security Horoi from an Ore Washery at Agrileza', *ZPE* 89: 131–6.

KALCYK, H. (1982). *Untersuchungen zum attischen Silberbergbau. Gebietstruktur, Geschichte und Technik* (Frankfurt).

Timarchos] 101), the father of Timarchos gets rid of his mining property so as to avoid liturgies.

[55] Although outside the scope of this enquiry it is striking that there are apparently very few family links between the many partnerships of lessee and guarantor(s) which we find in the public-land leases.

Kent, J. H. (1948). 'The Temple Estates of Delos, Rheneia and Mykonos', *Hesperia*, 17: 243–338.

Kraay, C. (1976). *Archaic and Classical Greek Coins* (London).

Kroll, J. (1998). 'Silver in Solon's Laws', in R. Ashton and S. Hurter (eds.), *Studies in Greek Numismatics in Memory of Martin Jessop Price* (London), 225–32.

Lambert, S. D. (1993). *The Phratries of Attica* (Ann Arbor, MI).

Langdon, M. K. (1991). 'Poletai Records', in *The Athenian Agora*, xix (1991).

Lauffer, S. (1979). *Die Bergwerksklaven von Laureion*, 2nd edn. (Wiesbaden).

Lewis, D. M. (1973). 'The Athenian Rationes Centisimarum', in M. I. Finley, *Problèmes de la Terre en Grèce Ancienne* (Paris), 181–212.

Lohmann, H. (1993). *Atene 1* (Cologne).

Martin, T. (1996). 'Why Did the Greek Polis Originally Need Coins?', *Historia*, 45: 257–83.

Meyer, E. A. (1993). 'Epitaphs and Citizenship in Classical Athens', *JHS* 113: 99–121.

Millett, P. (1991). *Lending and Borrowing in Ancient Athens* (Cambridge).

Morris, I. (1994). 'The Athenian Economy Twenty Years after *The Ancient Economy*', *CP* 89: 351–66.

Osborne, M. J., and S. G. Byrne (1994). *A Lexicon of Greek Personal Names*, ii. *Attica* (Oxford).

Osborne, R. (1988). 'Social and Economic Implications of the Leasing of Land and Property in Classical and Hellenistic Greece', *Chiron* 18: 225–70.

—— (1991). 'Pride and Prejudice, Sense and Subsistence: Exchange and Society in the Greek City', in J. Rich and A. Wallace-Hadrill (eds.), *City and Country in the Ancient World* (London), 119–45.

—— (1985b). 'Buildings and Residence on the Land in Classical and Hellenistic Greece: The Contribution of Epigraphy', *ABSA* 80: 119–28.

—— (1987). *Classical Landscape with Figures* (London).

—— (1985a). *Demos: The Discovery of Classical Attika* (Cambridge).

Parker, R. (1996). *Athenian Religion: A History* (Oxford).

Rich, J. and A. Wallace-Hadrill (1991). (eds.), *City and Country in the Ancient World* (London and New York).

Shepherd, R. (1993). *Ancient Mining* (London and New York).

Shipton, K. M. W. (1997). 'The Private Banks in Classical Athens', *CQ* 47: 396–422.

—— (1998). 'The Prices of the Athenian Silver Mines', *ZPE* 88: 57–63.

—— (2000). *Leasing and Lending in Fourth-Century Athens*, *BICS* Supplement 74 (London).

Spence, I. G. (1993). *The Cavalry of Classical Greece* (Oxford).

Thomas, R. (1989). *Oral Tradition and Written Record in Classical Athens* (Cambridge).

Walbank, M. B. (1983). 'Leases of Sacred Properties in Attica, Parts I–IV', *Hesperia*, 52: 100–35 and 177–231.

—— (1984). 'Leases of Sacred Properties in Attica, Part V', *Hesperia*, 53: 361–8.

—— (1991). 'Leases of Public Lands', in *The Athenian Agora*, xix.

Whitehead, D. (1977). *The Ideology of the Athenian Metic*, *PCPS* suppl. 4 (Cambridge).

—— (1986). *The Demes of Attica* (Princeton, NJ).

9
MONEY USE AMONG THE PEASANTRY OF PTOLEMAIC AND ROMAN EGYPT

Jane Rowlandson

Introduction

MY CONTRIBUTION MAY SEEM AT FIRST sight something of an interloper in this volume, since I am no numismatist, nor even strictly an economic historian; moreover, the primary focus of this paper, Roman Egypt, is not normally regarded as part of the Ancient Greek world. But, as a social historian who has become interested in exploring what impact money actually had on the lives of the people I study, I hope to justify the relevance of taking Ptolemaic and Roman Egypt over *la longue durée* as a case-study of the gradual penetration of money use into the rural society and culture of the Greek world more generally. Interaction with indigenous and other peoples is a consistent backdrop to Greek expansion, in the archaic and classical no less than the Hellenistic periods, while the impact of Rome was again an experience shared by the entire Greek world.

Moreover, Hellenistic Egypt, as well as being an important part of the Greek east in its own right, is particularly advantageous as a case-study because of the abundance of papyrological evidence, an advantage which is significantly increased if the study is prolonged into the even better-documented Roman period. Although in many respects the Roman conquest certainly marked a sharp change from the Hellenistic past (cf. Meadows, Ch. 4 above), it happens that in the two main areas of concern here, rural society and monetary history, change was relatively slow and progressive rather than an immediate result

of Roman rule.[1] One consequence of the major administrative reorganization set in train by Augustus and continued by his successors, enhancing the *metropoleis*[2] as centres of wealth and Hellenic culture, may indeed have been to make the villages actually regress economically as they lost social amenities, including, it seems, banks, the institution most relevant to the present study.[3]

Recent work has done much both to clarify the monetary history of Ptolemaic and Roman Egypt and to establish widespread monetization as a basic fact of the whole period.[4] This relative consensus leaves me free to adopt a somewhat different focus, which looks at money as an aspect of social relationships. For, although money is often considered to 'depersonalize'

---

[1] See Lewis (1984), esp. 1079–80 on rural life; Rathbone (1997), esp. 215, and see further below, on money; Bowman and Rathbone (1992) on administrative changes. For abbreviations of Greek papyri and related works see J. F. Oates *et al.*, *Checklist of Editions of Greek and Latin Papyri, Ostraca and Tablets*, fourth edn. (*BASP* supp. 7, 1992); http:// scriptorium.lib.duke.edu/papyrus/texts/clist.html.

[2] The chief town of each administrative region, or nome, given full civic status only by Septimius Severus; but at least the larger and best known *metropoleis* (such as Oxyrhynchus, Herakleopolis, or Arsinoe) were in all practical ways cities long before that.

[3] Contrast the full evidence for village banking institutions in the Ptolemaic period (Bogaert (1994) ch. 17) with the more equivocal testimony of the Roman period (ibid., ch. 18; I am also unconvinced that all the cases listed by Bogaert on p. 386 do refer to a local village bank, particularly *P.Oxy.* XII 1435). On the operation of banks in the Ptolemaic period see also Bogaert (1998–9).

[4] On monetary history, Maresch (1996), summarized, elucidated, and amended by Cadell and Le Rider (1997) (Ptolemaic period) and Rathbone (1997) 187–90 (Roman period); see also Hazzard (1995). On monetization, von Reden, ch. 5 above, Howgego (1992).

exchange, replacing the socially determined barter transactions of 'primitive' societies with transactions articulated only within a clearly differentiated economic sphere, this is far from the case. The substantive change in the nature of the transaction is magnified by a shift of our own perspective, from a focus primarily on the social aspect of barter to an exclusively economic view of monetary exchange. In recent decades, anthropologists and sociologists have helped to break down this distinction (e.g. Crump (1981)). From this perspective, money becomes the mediator of particular types of social relationship. Mary Douglas, in a fertile and much quoted passage in *Purity and Danger* has written that: 'Money is only an extreme and specialized form of ritual'.[5] Certainly we might usefully view money use as constituting a distinctive set of rituals; the use of money puts individuals into particular types of relationship with each other, which may on occasion be ephemeral, but can also be of long duration. Moreover, these monetary transactions interlock into the more general pattern of interpersonal exchanges, each gaining significance from its relationship to the others. Even in our highly complex and mobile economy, each person's behaviour tends to fall into patterns, so that, for instance, we tend to shop regularly in the same shops and supermarkets, and become familiar with the individuals who take our payment at the tills (who in some cases may even be our own students!), and perhaps exchange words with them. If modern monetary transactions are not wholly 'disembedded' from other social relationships, how much less so were those of a relatively unsophisticated and isolated ancient peasantry.

A preliminary word must also be said about the nature of the papyrological evidence. It is essential to bear in mind how selective this source of information is if we are to gain a proper understanding of the significance of this study. The papyri offer an illusion of detail, but the picture they present, of an essentially static world of agrarian communities (mainly in the Lower Nile valley and the Fayum) almost untouched by the international trade that was passing along the Nile, should not be taken as representative of the Egyptian economy as a whole. In particular, the papyri reveal almost nothing of the economic sophistication of Alexandria, which after its foundation in 331 BC

rapidly became the wealthiest city of the Greek world, and even after losing its political independence to Rome continued to expand as a centre of manufacture and international trade. Papyri of the third century BC amply document the close connection which the first generations of Greek immigrant entrepreneurs maintained with Alexandria, while parts of the Delta (again largely undocumented by papyri) and a few other places (Koptos, for instance) developed and maintained through the Roman period close economic ties with Alexandria and the wider Mediterranean.

But the relative isolation of many villages in the Nile valley and the Fayum may be more than a construct of our evidence, as the development of the *metropoleis*, particularly during the Roman period, increasingly gave them the role of economic mediators between the villages and the wider world. The evidence for some *metropoleis*, most notably Oxyrhynchus, is, of course, excellent, and recent work has explored their economic role within the Roman province, demonstrating that they were far from being 'agro-towns' whose populations depended almost wholly upon agriculture. Although the urban élite was primarily a class of landowners, a significant proportion of the wider population of the *metropoleis* was engaged in manufacture, trade, services, and other non-agrarian occupations.[6] The economy of the *metropoleis* was undoubtedly thoroughly monetized, although the degree of sophistication of their financial institutions and transactions is a subject that might benefit from further study.

But here my focus is, rather, primarily on the agrarian villages, which form a 'limiting case' of monetization; it is here, among the population of peasant farmers, that we should expect to find the least frequent and sophisticated uses of money, the most obvious limitations on the monetization of the Egyptian economy.

Money Within the Agricultural Economy

We need to start by picturing a countryside with a lot of nucleated villages (with populations varying from under a hundred to several thousand), surrounded by land worked under a mixture of agricultural regimes. Although, particularly during the Roman period, the

---

[5] Douglas (1970) 85–6.

[6] Alston and Alston (1997); Alston (1998).

number of large estates, like the one discussed by Dominic Rathbone (1991), gradually increased, most land remained in small parcels, worked by villagers either as peasant proprietors (*autourgoi*), or as tenants of landowners from the *metropolis*, or as tenants of royal (later public) land. The first Ptolemies claimed ultimate control over all agricultural land, assigning it variously to holders of different status in return either for appropriate duties or for revenues: the temples and their personnel, high officials and smaller scale military settlers (*klerouchoi*), royal farmers; a relatively small amount was classed as 'privately owned' (*ge idioktetos*). The Romans, although modifying this system to create a substantial proportion of private land (perhaps 50 per cent in the Fayum; up to around 75 per cent in the Nile valley), continued to assess the main land revenues in taxes in kind from all arable land, whether private or public.

As Sitta von Reden shows above (Ch. 5), monetization of the Egyptian countryside developed rapidly after coined currency was first introduced by Ptolemy I, even if coin itself was not always in plentiful supply. This was ensured not least by the royal decision to set the key capitation taxes, as well as taxes on some processed and other agricultural produce, in money, although tax on the main cereal crops remained in kind.[7] The division thus created, between crops (primarily cereals) habitually subject to dues in kind and those (such as fodder crops and fruit trees) whose revenues were normally assessed in money, spread from the sphere of royal taxation to that of leasing arrangements between private individuals, and remained fundamental to the agricultural economy right through to the late Roman period. Crops subject to money taxes needed marketing, which in some cases was strictly regulated by the early Ptolemaic government;[8] but by the Roman period we see clearest evidence of lively markets in precisely those products traditionally subject to money tax.[9]

The persistence of taxes and private rents in kind constitutes the most obvious limitation on the monetization of the agrarian economy, and as I shall argue, did have important consequences for the role that money played among the peasantry; but we also have to remember certain qualifications to the practice of taxation in kind. For instance, there were subsidiary money taxes even on arable land, such as the *naubion*, a tax associated with the upkeep of the canal system, although the rural population was also obliged to contribute to work on the dykes through personal, corvée, labour. There is also some evidence, for the Roman period, of commutation of taxes in kind into cash payments, although the scale of this is very uncertain.[10] In so far as commutation into cash payments did occur, it is most likely to have mainly involved owners of large estates, who we certainly know sometimes exacted cash rents for arable land from their own tenants.[11]

We are, on the other hand, well informed about the elaborate administrative mechanism (again inherited by the Romans from the Ptolemaic period) for collecting the taxes in wheat from small and medium landholders. After the grain was harvested and threshed, farmers would hand over what was due in taxes to the collector of grain taxes, and, where appropriate, their rent to private landlords. The grain might be handed over actually on the village threshing floor, or paid by the farmer directly into the local granary. All villages of any size had a public granary, overseen by *sitologoi*, granary officials, whose activities have left copious documentation. As well as receiving tax payments in grain, the granaries held deposit accounts for individual landowners, who through the *sitologoi* could make payments by giro transfer, either for tax in their own name due at another village, or to the accounts of other individuals held at the same or a different granary.[12] Thus we can see that in Roman Egypt wheat itself served some of the functions of a currency.

---

[7] On capitation taxes see D. J. Thompson and W. Clarysse, *Counting the People* (forthcoming).

[8] See *P.Rev.Laws* on wine and orchard crops and on oil; the tax on vineyards was collected in wine and then sold.

[9] Rathbone (1997) contrasts wine (and donkeys) with wheat; the market in the latter was also affected by government purchases at fixed price. The market in fodder seems to have been particularly volatile (Rowlandson (1996) 21–2), but fodder prices are unfortunately not amenable to a systematic analysis such as Rathbone conducted for wheat, wine, and donkeys because of uncertainty over the size of measures.

[10] Rathbone (1997) 198; earlier (Rathbone (1989)) he hypothesized a very large scale of commutation, approaching half the total assessment, on the ground that it is difficult to envisage how the government disposed of the enormous quantity of wheat due to it. Surely much of the surplus may be accounted for by sale within Egypt, particularly to supply Alexandria.

[11] e.g. *P.Oxy.* XIV 1630, relating to Claudia Isidora's estate at the Small Oasis.

[12] e.g. *P.Oxy.* XXXI 2588–91, XXXVIII 2863–72.

As Howgego (1992) has pointed out, the system of taxing arable land in kind was perpetuated by the Romans not because Egypt was inadequately monetized to support money taxes, but because it suited the Roman government to receive some of its taxes in kind, and made sense within the overall economy. But it did have wider consequences for the agrarian economy. For, the large number of small-scale farmers did not need to sell part of their crop in order to obtain cash for the land tax, although they did need to acquire some money to meet their personal taxes and to buy goods like salt for their personal needs. The poll tax paid by the lower classes in the Roman period varied from nome to nome (12–40 dr.), but on average one villager's poll tax and other personal taxes could have been met by selling two or three *artabae* of wheat (at 8–12 dr. in the first to second century AD). This was by no means a negligible sum, particularly since many households must have had more than one member liable to the poll tax (which was paid by males only, aged fourteen to sixty-two), but it is very much less than a tenant of, say, ten *arourae* of public land would have needed to sell in order to meet a basic land tax in money rather than in kind.

Thus it could be argued that the Ptolemaic and Roman policy of collecting a substantial portion of the revenues on land in kind contributed very significantly to preserving the existence of large numbers of small-scale peasants in Egypt. In practice, it would have been very difficult for them to have marketed a substantial amount of their produce, whether in wheat or if they changed to other cash crops, since estate owners would always be able to use their greater power and influence to compete more effectively in marketing their crops. The villages provided limited scope for selling agricultural produce, to resident craftsmen and scribes, but most villagers grew the same basic range of crops, restricting the scope for selling any surplus to other villagers. Fodder, for which there was considerable demand because of the lack of rough grazing in Egypt, seems to have been the main exception; numerous references attest a lively and volatile market in fodder, and it seems that even estates might prefer to buy fodder rather than producing it themselves.

By the Roman period, the *metropoleis* certainly provided a much bigger potential market for agricultural produce. The population of Oxyrhynchus has been estimated at around 25,000; that of Hermopolis and Arsinoe perhaps nearer 40,000, the bulk of the population probably not themselves agricultural producers. But it is doubtful how far even the *metropoleis* served, or could potentially have served, as a market for the surplus produce of the rural peasantry. As a class of *rentiers*, the urban élite, who themselves received the bulk of their rents in kind (largely wheat), must surely, together with the estates, have been the main suppliers of staple foods to the *metropoleis*. This is corroborated by the survival of orders of the Prefect to precisely these classes in time of food crisis to declare the stocks of corn they were holding.[13] (The Roman government's attitude to taxation in kind was not, of course, determined by any concern to preserve peasant vitality; rather they were content to continue a system which produced a large quantity of wheat, which they had a use for. In practice, during the course of the Principate, the system was progressively modified to the detriment of small-scale farmers, particularly the tenants of public land.)

The fact that the urban landowners received much of their rent in kind also, of course, had an impact on the livelihoods of the villagers who were their tenants, again absolving them of the need to sell part of the crop in order to acquire cash. The private lease contracts form a very large, detailed, and homogeneous body of documentation; over one thousand survive from different parts of Egypt throughout the Ptolemaic and Roman periods. The contracts were normally made for short periods, of one to four years, although we know of cases of contracts being renewed on expiry, for as long as a total of forty years.[14] This large body of documentation makes quite clear that whether to set the rent in kind or in money was rarely a matter of choice by the parties to the contract based on economic considerations, but instead followed from the convention dating back to the early Ptolemaic period that cereal crops paid in kind, while 'processed' and fodder crops usually yielded money. In the the early Roman period there was some tendency for cash rents on fodder to expand at the expense of wheat, but interestingly the

---

[13] *P.Oxy.* XLII 3048, XLVII 3339.
[14] Rowlandson (1996) 252–4; the longest known case is that of Kronion's family from Tebtunis: *P.Kron.*, p. xxvii.

basic pattern was maintained right through the currency problems of the third and fourth centuries AD, with little sign of an increasing use of rents in kind.

Thus, as in the case of the government land tax, we can see wheat operating in the leases as a medium of payment, and significantly wheat rents were charged not only on wheat or other cereal crops, but sometimes on a range of other arable crops too, whereas it was extremely rare for any other crop to serve as a medium of rent payment unless it were actually to be sown.

To sum up the argument so far, the government's collection of the main land tax in kind (mainly wheat) from the primary producers does in one sense constitute a significant limitation on the monetization of the agricultural economy, protecting these small producers from the need to sell much of their crops; and this limitation was further buttressed by the convention of also collecting private rents in kind on certain crops. In these contexts, wheat can in fact be seen serving two distinct functions of a currency: as a medium of payment (of tax and rent), and as a store of value (in the granaries). Other transactions in kind, such as the occasional rent payments in lentils or radish-seed, played a very small role. This currency-like role for wheat, however, was restricted to the unmonetized areas of the agricultural economy just described; and it deserves emphasis that there is virtually no evidence of wheat being used as a medium of exchange within the wider economy.

Moreover, a closer examination of some aspects of the agricultural economy suggests that, despite the prominence of wheat in the roles just outlined, the use of coined money may have been more pervasive than appears at first sight. The land leases again supply our best evidence, although we should not assume that they always represent 'typical' agricultural practice, despite their survival in large numbers. Nor were tenants necessarily peasants, particularly in the Ptolemaic period, when cleruchs often leased their plots to colleagues or to civilian entrepreneurs who possessed the resources to exploit them effectively (Bingen (1978)). But in the Roman period leases made between urban *rentiers* and village tenants commonly specify a system of crop rotation, annually alternating wheat with a fodder crop. This often therefore meant that tenants were paying wheat rent in one year and money rent the next,

although some leases did split the land equally between the two crops in each year. We also find leases in which the tenant was allowed to choose what crops to grow, but which seem to presuppose the practice of crop rotation by setting a rent divided between wheat and money.[15] In all these cases, as well as the leases of vineyards or orchards for a money rent, tenants presumably needed to sell part of their crop in order to pay the money rents. As we saw earlier, fodder and wine are precisely those which have produced most plentiful evidence of marketing, on both a large and small scale.

From vineyard leases, we can see the full complexity of the processes involved in cultivation, which often required the participation, alongside the tenant, of other workers who received money payments.[16] Irrigators (*hydroparochoi*) were needed to ensure a constant water supply (vineyards needed watering once every five days); an irrigation machine (*sakia*) might involve the employment of *mechanarioi*, carpenters, and guards; donkeys and their drivers were hired to bring manure. Even if responsibility for the harvest was contracted out to *karponai*, their labourers probably received their wages primarily in money.

On arable land, too, it looks as if in some cases the process of cultivation involved the employment of extra workers for money. Some leases provide the tenant with a loan of cash until the harvest to cover his expenses,[17] but the arable leases themselves are largely silent on day-to-day procedures, from sowing, weeding, and guarding the crops (often the task of young boys), to harvesting, threshing, and winnowing.[18] While these processes must often have involved the use of extra labour, we remain uncertain how far this was normally supplied by the unpaid work of family members, or by arrangements of mutual benefit, and how far they involved money payments.

This is one point at which we are straining at the very limits of the evidence. Surviving estate accounts

---

[15] Rowlandson (1996) 236–47.

[16] Rowlandson (1996) 228–36. Cf. the contract for carrying manure in a vineyard, *SB* XVIII 13311 (= *BASP* 23 (1986), 61–4, corr. in *ZPE* 86 (1991), 243 f.), of AD 131, at 8 obols per donkey per 6 trips for dung, and likewise for the conveyance of *sebakh*, 8 obols per donkey per 8 trips.

[17] e.g. *SB* X 10274, a loan of 28 dr. on a very small area of land (AD 99).

[18] These are costed only in exceptional circumstances, such as the case of a widow's brother-in-law, obliged to farm his deceased brother's plot of land in order to meet the tax arrears on it, who itemizes all the expenses of the cultivation (which include 4 dr. paid to a man for scaring ibises); *P.Coll.Youtie* I 24, from Tebtunis, AD 121/2.

frequently list money payments to men or boys (and occasionally women and girls) for these types of casual agricultural labour,[19] but it is difficult to prove that similar monetary payments for agricultural work were customarily made outside the context of large estates, precisely because outside this context such arrangements would rarely produce any kind of written record. Various contracts for agricultural work do survive among the papyri (although the 'work contract' is not a single homogeneous type of document, but could be articulated through various legal forms; Hengstl (1972)), but these are relatively rare in comparison, say, with the leases, and unsurprisingly tend to refer to large-scale activities, such as the harvesting of fifty-two and a half *arourae*, rather than to casual labour on a small scale.[20]

But, on the whole, I think it is likely that the employment of casual labour was far from confined to the larger estates which kept written accounts. In fact, I would guess that it was at least as much through engaging in this kind of work on both estates and the medium-sized landholdings (or by getting their children to do so), as through the sale of their own crops, that the smallest-scale peasant proprietors and farmers of public land got hold of the money they needed to pay their personal taxes. It would admittedly be very difficult to prove this assertion, but it does seem to accord best with what we do know (often in detail) of the way the agricultural regimes of Egyptian villages operated.

If this is the case, it would have important implications for both the significance of money use and for social relationships generally within the village communities. We are well informed about the social ties between villagers and wealthy landlords through tenancy and loan arrangements (both in kind and in money); but if payment for peripheral agricultural work was as pervasive as I am suggesting, wage payments would form yet another strand in the nexus of social ties. It was suggested earlier that taxation in kind maintained the peasantry in a position of relative independence; this independence was, of course, limited to the extent that the farmers became obligated

to any particular landlord. Surviving archives of the papers of tenant farmers show how some independence was maintained, despite persistent indebtedness, through the spread of obligations between several different local magnates,[21] and, up to a point, casual work remunerated in money would seem unlikely to involve the creation of more permanent ties. That is, of course, if the payments were actually made in cash. But Rathbone's study (1991) of the third-century AD estate of Appianus has revealed the extent to which not only the permanent workers on the estate but even their relatives employed on a more casual basis actually received the payments into their accounts with the estate. While this system from one perspective demonstrates an impressive extension of the sphere of monetization while requiring no increase in the actual amount of coin, it obviously means that the estate workers, for good or ill, were locked into a permanent economic relationship with the estate, and thus drawn into social dependence on it.

It therefore makes a considerable difference to the significance of money payments for agricultural work whether they involved actual transfers of coin or were payments on account. The Appianus estate was certainly not unique in keeping detailed accounts; a few well-documented parallels, and many more fragments, stretch back at least to the early Roman period.[22] However, such a complex system of written accounting seems too sophisticated for the needs of the average metropolitan landowner, let alone a primary tenant, who might be the person actually responsible for employing supplementary workers. In these cases, it seems likely that the payments were normally made in coin, unless they could be credited against some specific debt.

A further role which coin played in agricultural tenancies provides a link with the final section of this paper, on the social significance of money payments. Leases, of both arable land and vineyards, not uncommonly refer to extra payments, termed *sponde* or *thallos*, which the tenant must provide annually. Sometimes these involved a small gift in kind, often a

---

[19] e.g. *P.Fay.* 102, on the estate of the veteran L. Bellienus Gemellus.

[20] *P.Mich.* 123 recto XIII 26; cost 210 dr. One letter draws an interesting distinction between harvesting 'for a [daily (?)] wage (*pros misthon*)' and harvesting 'by the *aroura* measurement (*pros arourismon*)', though the latter also involved a money payment, of 2 dr. 3 ob. per *aroura* (Gonis (1997)).

[21] See esp. Bagnall (1980), on *P.Soter.*; also *P.Kron.*

[22] For a range of parallels see Rathbone (1991) 401–2; for the second-century AD 'Laches archive' see esp. *P.Mil.Vogl.* VII. *SB* XX 14409 (= *P.Oxy.* VI 985) is a fragmentary but substantial account from *c.* AD 100 (long enough for Euripides' *Hypsipyle* to be copied on the verso).

loaf of bread, a fowl, or even a piglet; but the *sponde* could also be in money, invariably one or more tetradrachms. There was in fact also a tax on vine land, the *sponde Dionysiou*, assessed at the fixed sum of 8 drachmae plus supplement irrespective of area, unusual for land taxes, which were mostly assessed on the area. The name evokes an origin in connection with the libation that would be traditionally poured to the wine god (with whom the Ptolemaic dynasty claimed an association) at the vintage.[23]

In the leases, the *sponde* is sometimes described as 'for the *paidaria*', for the boys; presumably those helping with the harvest. These instances serve to remind us not only of the shadowy figures who lurk behind our evidence assisting with the agricultural work, and possibly, as I have suggested, receiving formal payment for it, but also of the strong ritual element involved in both the leasing of land and the employment of labour, in which the handing over of a coin is not merely an economically convenient means of payment, but loaded with symbolic significance. It is naturally tempting to interpret the use of coin in this context, as Eitrem (1937) does, as a development from earlier payments in kind, which somehow 'devalues' the ritual significance into a mere token exchange; but if we think for a moment of the later history of 'earnest money' and the 'King's shilling', this does not work; there is no linear development from symbolically significant offerings in kind to less significant money payments. The *sponde Dionysiou* tax may indeed have lost any connection with ritual, and have become merely a convenient source of government revenue, but this is different from the arrangements made between individual landowners and their tenants who were at liberty to dispense with, or change the nature of, the gift if they wished. Gifts of money and of other objects persisted in conjunction over a period of time, just as the conjunction of payments in kind along with money has remained a feature of wage payments right through from antiquity even to the present day.

The use of coins in these extra payments does, of course, presuppose a certain level of monetization, and indeed the availability of suitable coins, and it is interesting that the fowl and piglets were also commonly valued in money (loaves normally by weight). But far from representing a devaluation of some earlier highly symbolic payment in kind, the appearance of coin in this context must, I think, reflect the importance of coinage itself as a bearer of meaning, as it was incorporated into the wider pattern of symbolism that marked rural social relationships.

Money and its Meanings

This leads to a consideration of other contexts in which to explore the social meanings of coined money. The inclusion of coin in dowries, alongside the monetary valuation of other (but not all) dowry items, offers an interesting case, amply documented through from the pre-Ptolemaic to the late Roman period, also allowing us to see the integration of Greek with Egyptian preconceptions and practices.

Although Egypt did not have a coinage for internal use until the Ptolemaic period, it possessed monetary units expressing value, which von Reden (1997) has suggested were, by their abstract nature, in some ways more sophisticated in their use than a simple coinage. In the Ptolemaic period, these traditional units of value, the silver *deben* and *kite*, were used in demotic Egyptian documents with reference to the Ptolemaic silver currency, so that 1 *deben* (= 10 *kite*) was equivalent to 20 drachmae. The stater (= 4 drachmae) also appears as a monetary unit in some marriage documents. There were three patterns of Egyptian marriage payment, one given by the husband to his wife, the others by the wife to the husband; these payments were normally expressed in monetary terms, though they could also be expressed in kind.[24] In addition, the documents specify obligations on the husband to provide annually for his wife's maintenance, again differing in detail according to the pattern of document; this would typically include grain and oil for food, plus sums of silver for clothing and expenses. It will be observed that, although the Egyptian marriage documents are conspicuously more generous than Greek ones in thus providing for the wife's support (as well as in other respects), they share the fundamental use of

---

[23] Wallace (1938) 62–3; cf. de Cazanove (1995) on vintage rituals.

[24] See Pestman (1961), Smith (1995); two examples are translated in Rowlandson (1998) nos. 118 and 119.

monetary evaluation for the main components of the dowry.

The earlier known Greek marriage agreements from Egypt often refer to the dowry as a single monetary sum, although this in fact may include the value of non-cash items, like the dowry returned on dissolution of a marriage in 154 or 143 BC, of total value 46 talents 4,100 drachmae bronze, consisting of 30 talents coin in addition to a slave girl (valued at 15 talents) and clothing.[25] By the Roman period greater complexity is introduced, not only by the tendency to list dowry items in more detail, but also by the fact that what are in effect Egyptian marriage documents are also found written in Greek.[26]

Of particular interest here is the innovative use of a loan received through a bank to formalize the receipt of the dowry.[27] For instance:

Tryphon, son of Dionysios, Persian of the epigone, to Saraeus, daughter of Apion, with as guardian Onnophris son of Antipatros, greeting. I acknowledge that I have received from you at the Serapeum in Oxyrhynchos city through the bank of Sarapion son of Kleandros, forty silver drachmae of imperial and Ptolemaic coinage, and for the value of one pair of gold earrings, twenty silver drachmae, and for a milk-white *chiton*, twelve silver drachmae, making in total a principal of seventy-two drachmae of silver, to which nothing at all has been added, concerning which I am satisfied. And I will repay to you the seventy-two drachmae of silver on the 30th of Phaophi in the coming second year of Gaius Caesar Germanicus New Augustus Imperator without any delay. If I do not repay in accordance with the above terms I will pay to you the said principal with the addition of half its amount, for which you are to have the right of execution upon me and upon all my property, as in accordance with a legal decision.

This way of facilitating a traditional Egyptian procedure through a distinctively Greek financial institution is most clearly in evidence among the more Egyptianized families of the *metropolis* of Oxyrhynchus; in a village, a similar loan format might be employed without recourse to a bank (e.g. *P.Tebt.* II 386).

The relationship between the monetary and other content of dowries deserves further investigation. By the Roman period, the 'core' of the dowry, the *pherne*, was often supplemented by a *parapherna* consisting of jewellery and clothing, which also formed an increasingly significant part of the *pherne*. However, the *parapherna* never included cash, nor was it given a monetary valuation; the standard formula in fact ran 'and as *parapherna*, without valuation . . .'. This would seem a very significant distinction, since in the case of death or more particularly of a contentious divorce it was important to establish the exact value of the *pherne* that had to be returned. However, although it continued to be normal throughout the Roman period to give a total monetary value to the *pherne*, this was not invariable, the weight of gold items of jewellery being regarded in itself as an adequate valuation (a monetary valuation for any clothing in the *pherne* was more essential).[28] If the practice of not valuing gold objects in the *pherne* gradually spread, this does not seem to be a consequence of any distrust of the value of the monetary currency, since it predates the significant debasement of the Egyptian coinage, and the earliest examples seem to come from Alexandria in Augustus' reign.[29] Rather it appears to result from a shift of focus from viewing the dowry primarily as a global sum, providing security for the wife in the event of the failure of her marriage, to a greater preoccupation with the detail of its individual components, which the wife might use for conspicuous display in addition to the latent function of insurance. It is perhaps significant that the mummy portraits which appear from the early first century AD onwards show women wearing clothes and jewellery of precisely the sort that would compose their dowries. And even humble village women did wear their jewellery in public, sometimes in surprisingly risky situations.[30]

This shift of focus seems to be borne out by the increased complexity of the dowry's composition. This, then, raises the question of how the remaining cash component of the *pherne* was seen; was it sharply

---

[25] *P.Mert.* II 59; *P.Giss.* 2 also includes a slave (and her offspring). The famous *P.Eleph.* I (= *Select Papyri* I 1) of 311 BC reads 'bringing clothing and ornaments [worth] 1000 drachmae', while (e.g.) *P.Tebt.* III 815 frag. 4 recto col. i 2–11 and *P.Tebt.* I 104 give a total monetary value only; cf. the acknowledgements of receipt for dowries from the 230s BC, *CPR* XVIII 6, 8, 9, 12, 13, 17, 20, 28.

[26] These are so-called alimentary contracts, *syngraphai trophitides*. In the Roman period, demotic Egyptian rapidly ceased to be used for writing legal contracts.

[27] See Gagos *et al.* (1992). The text quoted is *P.Oxy.* II 267, as translated in Rowlandson (1998), no. 132.

[28] See Whitehorne (1986).

[29] For examples see Reekmans (1975), 752–3.

[30] A tenant of public land from Euhemeria in the Fayum complained that his wife and mother-in-law had lost jewellery and a bowl when attacked at the village bathhouse; *P.Ryl.* II 124.

differentiated from the items of adornment or personal use? The dowry of one wealthy family from Oxyrhynchus included a sum of cash specifically intended for the purchase of further dowry goods,[31] but otherwise there is little indication of the uses to which the cash was put. A dissolute husband was perfectly capable of squandering the non-cash items in the dowry by pawning or selling them, as did Kronion the younger of Tebtunis, as his divorce contract testifies:

The jewellery that all the aforementioned affirm Kronion received from his sister Taorsenouphis—gold, weighing one mina and ten quarters, and uncoined silver, weighing twenty-eight staters—and which he converted into cash for his own use, the declarant Kronion must repay to his sister Taorsenouphis in equivalent jewellery within sixty days from the present day.[32]

On the other hand, both coins and jewellery might be hidden away in a box in a wall cupboard for decades, if another petitioner from Euhemeria is to be believed; Orsenouphis, a 'notable' of the village, complained that, in his absence making a living, a builder employed on alterations to his house discovered the box, hidden some thirty years earlier, containing gold and silver jewellery and 60 drachmae in coin, which he gave to his maiden daughter, claiming to Orsenouphis on his return that he had found the box empty.[33] Again, whether Orsenouphis' allegations were true or not, the story presupposes a close equivalence between the coins and the jewellery, both serving as a reserve of wealth that could be drawn on in time of need. Given the ease with which jewellery, and indeed other household items, could be pawned for cash, their potential exchange value was almost as useful to a peasant family as their other more obvious functions.[34]

Gold jewellery held a particularly close relationship with the gold currency, in that the weight of items of jewellery often seems to have reflected the weight standard of the aureus, although the jewellery was often less pure. This may have been encouraged by the practice of using coins as the raw material for jewellery.[35] A gold coin could also be set into a necklace, as we see depicted on mummy portraits, making the coin itself into an item for display and distancing it from more obviously economic functions.[36] A peasant family would be most unlikely to meet gold coins in circulation;[37] but instead their wealth could be stored in the jewellery handed down or acquired as dowries for their womenfolk.

On the other hand, it is clear that even villagers made regular, if hardly copious, use of the standard copper and 'silver' coinages of the Ptolemaic and Roman periods. It is striking that, despite the appearance of extensive money use in early Roman Euhemeria already noted by Howgego, fewer than one hundred Ptolemaic and Roman specimens were recovered when the site was excavated for papyri.[38] And the total of over 30,000 coins found at Karanis appears less impressive if we consider that fewer than 1,000 date from before the third century AD, and that Karanis was an unusually large settlement (in fact a town, although technically a *kome*), with a large proportion of veterans and other Roman citizens among the population.[39] It appears that coins were not so plentiful that their loss could be readily tolerated.

This is confirmed by numerous references in papyrus letters which suggest that the difficulty of laying hands on ready cash, which Sitta von Reden identifies (Ch. 5 above) in the third century BC, remained a persistent problem right through the Roman period. Often a crop would need to be sold to raise the cash for a tax or other payment. Correspondents directing the recipient to make a payment

---

[31]   P.Coll.Youtie II 67; for the family, see Rowlandson (1996), 111–12.

[32]   P.Kron. 52, trans. Rowlandson (1998) no. 102; cf. BGU IV 1105 (ibid. no. 257), from Alexandria.

[33]   P.Ryl. II 125 (= Select Papyri II 278); see the discussion by Reekmans (1975).

[34]   For evidence of pawnbroking see Reekmans (1975), 759, and more recently Sijpesteijn (1993).

[35]   Ogden (1996); cf. the instruction in a letter from Paniskos to his wife: 'make the three gold solidi into anklets for my daughter', P.Mich. III 218 (c. AD 297).

[36]   See Parlasca (1964), pl. 31 for two examples.

[37]   The hoard of gold coins found in the second-century house BII at Karanis is assumed to have been brought home by a Roman officer serving abroad (Haatvedt and Peterson (1964), 14–15).

[38]   Howgego (1992), 21, referring to the series of petitions to the chief of police that has preserved the two cases quoted earlier. Other interesting cases are P.Ryl. II 127, concerning the theft of items from a house, including 120 dr. kept in a casket which the petitioner had received in payment from an imperial freedman, another 4 dr. in a wooden box, and 4 copper dr. in a belt; and P.Ryl. II 128, another theft of a cloak and of 40 dr. which the petitioner was keeping to pay the rent. Coin finds from Euhemeria are listed in P.Fay., intro., p. 69; even fewer were found at Theadelphia and Philoteris.

[39]   Haatvedt and Peterson (1964), table 1 (pp. 4–5); the bulk date from the late third century (from Probus to the Tetrarchs). See also Alston (1998), 176, for a brief survey of the coin evidence surviving from Fayum villages.

would include the necessary coins with the letter, just as they also might send small gifts of foodstuffs. With one letter, Dionysios sent his mother 112 drachmae, with which to redeem his clothes from pawn for 100 drachmae plus 8 drachmae interest; the remaining 4 drachmae were for her to spend on a festival. He assured her that he would have sent her more if he could; he had borrowed even to find that sum.[40]

Conclusion

Since one of the main needs of villagers for cash was to pay their taxes, it would be tempting to see the currency as a symbol of oppression by a foreign and alien rule, parallel perhaps to the imposition of Greek as the language of administration.[41] Certainly the motifs on the Ptolemaic currency were wholly Hellenistic, in contrast to the representation of the dynasty in other contexts through both Greek and Egyptian iconographic traditions. And when Egyptian motifs do appear, starting with the bronze coins of Augustus, these surely reflect Roman 'Egyptomania' more than a genuine attempt to make the currency more familiar to the population of the province.[42] But, as with the use of the Greek language, the evidence in fact provides little justification for thinking that coinage was viewed as alien by the rural population of Egypt; who rather seem to have given both innovations a remarkably positive reception, eager to appropriate their advantages in whatever directions they could be readily assimilated into aspects of the existing culture.

We are thus left with the apparently paradoxical impression of a rural society at once thoroughly penetrated by monetization, and used to thinking in monetary terms, while often finding the actual use of money, and particularly coin, problematic, and certainly less flexible than economic theory might lead us to expect. To elucidate this paradox, the linguistic parallel may again prove helpful. Whereas it used to be fashionable to view literacy as a unitary phenomenon which in its impact transformed the mentality of an entire society, a more nuanced view has now developed which emphasizes its complex, often

partial, nature and uneven development, with orality and literacy coexisting in close proximity. Similarly, a rural society could be thoroughly monetized in the sense of having assimilated both the concept and, to a lesser extent perhaps, the actual use of money into its pre-existing culture and traditional practices, without being significantly transformed by them.

The reason why money could be assimilated in this way is that, in the context of rural Egypt, money use does not seem to have produced any clearly differentiated category of social relationships or activities, but instead became incorporated within the wider existing patterns of interaction. This is not because Ptolemaic and Roman Egypt was economically 'primitive'; it would be true of any agrarian society, at least until the last hundred years. However, it may help to explain why sociological writers seem to have so much difficulty identifying the distinctive characteristics of money; it is not as distinctive as it appears.[43] Coin does indeed have particular messages to convey within the overall conceptual webs of significance which constitute our experience, but in this it is more closely related to other potential bearers of meaning, from piglets to gold bracelets, than it is differentiated from them.

REFERENCES

ALSTON, R. (1998). 'Trade and the City in Roman Egypt', in H. Parkins and C. Smith (eds.), *Trade, Traders and the Ancient City* (London and New York), 168–202.
——and R. D. ALSTON (1997). 'Urbanism and the Urban Community in Roman Egypt', *JEA* 83: 199–216.
BAGNALL, R. S. (1980). 'Theadelphian Archives: A Review Article', *BASP* 17: 97–104.
BINGEN, J. (1978). 'The Third-century BC Land-leases from Tholthis', *Illinois Classical Studies*, 3: 74–80.
BLAND, R. (1996). 'The Roman Coinage of Alexandria, 30 BC–AD 296: Interplay Between Roman and Local Designs', in D. M. Bailey (ed.), *Archaeological Research in Roman Egypt: Proceedings of the XVII British Museum Classical Colloquium* (London), 113–27.

---

[40] *P.Oxy.* III 530.   [41] Cf. Hopkins (1991).
[42] On the iconography of the Roman coins, see Bland (1996).

[43] Cf. Dodd (1994). Dodd's own suggestion that the distinctiveness of money depends on the 'ideal of unfettered empowerment, of complete freedom to act and assimilate at will' (p. 154), assumes a total transformation of the mentality of its users; precisely what I have argued does not seem to have happened in rural ancient Egypt.

BOGAERT, R. (1994). *Trapezitica Aegyptiaca: recueil de recherches sur la banque en Egypte gréco-romaine* (Pap. Flor. 25; Florence).

—— (1998–9). 'Les Opérations des banques de l'Égypte ptólémaïque, *Ancient Society*, 29: 49–145.

BOWMAN, A. K. and D. W. RATHBONE (1992). 'Cities and Administration in Roman Egypt', *JRS* 82: 107–27.

CADELL, H. and G. LE RIDER (1997). *Prix du blé et numéraire dans l'Egypte Lagide de 305 à 173* (Pap. Brux. 30; Brussels).

CRUMP, T. (1981). *The Phenomenon of Money* (London).

—— (1990). 'Money', in *The Anthropology of Numbers* (Cambridge), ch. 8.

DE CAZANOVE, O. (1995). 'Rituels romains dans les vignobles', in O. Murray and M.-M. Tecusan, *In Vino Veritas* (London), 214–23.

DE LIGT, R. (1990). 'Demand, Supply, Distribution: The Roman Peasantry Between Town and Countryside: Rural Monetization and Peasant Demand', *MBAH* 9: 24–56.

DODD, N. (1994). *The Sociology of Money* (New York).

DOUGLAS, M. (1970). *Purity and Danger* (Harmondsworth; paperback edn.; first published (in hardback) 1966).

EITREM, S. (1937). 'A Few Remarks on *Sponde*, *Thallos* and other Extra Payments in Papyri', *Symbolae Osloenses*, 17: 26–48.

GAGOS, T., L. KOENEN, and B. E. McNELLEN, (1992). 'A First Century Archive from Oxyrhynchos: Oxyrhynchite Loan Contracts and Egyptian Marriage', in J. H. Johnson (ed.), *Life in a Multi-cultural Society: Egypt from Cambyses to Constantine and Beyond* (Chicago, Ill.), 181–205.

GARA, A. (1988). 'Aspetti di economia monetaria dell'Egitto romano', *ANRW* II.10.1, 912–51.

GONIS, N. (1997). 'Troubled Fields: CPR VII 52 Revised', *Tyche*, 12: 47–50.

HAATVEDT, R. E. and E. E. PETERSON (1964). *Coins from Karanis* (Ann Arbor, Mich.).

HAZZARD, R. A. (1995). *Ptolemaic Coins: An Introduction for Collectors* (Toronto).

HENGSTL, J. (1972). *Private Arbeitsverhältnisse freier Personen in den hellenistischen Papyri bis Diokletian* (Bonn).

HOPKINS, M. K. (1991). 'Conquest by Book', in *Literacy in the Roman World* = *JRA* supp. 3: (Ann Arbor, Mich.), 133–58.

HOWGEGO, C. (1992). 'The Supply and Use of Money in the Roman World, 200 BC–AD 300', *JRS* 82: 1–31.

HUNT, A. S. and EDGAR, C. C. (1932/1937). *Select Papyri*, vols. I and II (Cambridge, Mass.).

LEWIS, N. (1984). 'The Romanity of Roman Egypt: A Growing Consensus', *Atti del Congresso Internazionale di Papirologia XVII* iii. (Naples), 1077–84.

MARESCH, K. (1996). *Bronze und Silber. Papyrologische Beiträge zur Geschichte der Währung im ptolemaischen und römischen Ägypten zum 2 Jahrhundert n. Chr.* (Opladen).

OGDEN, J. (1996). 'Weight Units of Romano-Egyptian Gold Jewellery', in D. M. Bailey (ed.), *Archaeological Research in Roman Egypt: Proceedings of the XVII British Museum Classical Colloquium* (London), 191–6.

PARLASCA, K. (1964). *Mumienporträts und verwandte Denkmäler* (Wiesbaden).

PESTMAN, P. W. (1961). *Marriage and Matrimonial Property in Ancient Egypt: A Contribution to Establishing the Legal Position of the Woman* (Pap. Lugd. Bat. 9; Leiden).

RATHBONE, D. W. (1989). 'The Ancient Economy and Graeco-Roman Egypt', in L. Criscuolo and G. Geraci (eds.), *Egitto e storia antica dell'ellenismo all'età Araba: bilancio di un confronto* (Bologna), 159–76.

—— (1991). *Economic Rationalism and Rural Society in Third-century AD Egypt: The Heroninos Archive and the Appianus Estate* (Cambridge).

—— (1996). 'Monetisation, not Price-inflation, in Third-century A.D. Egypt?', in C. E. King and D. G. Wigg (eds.), *Coin Finds and Coin Use in the Roman World: The Thirteenth Oxford Symposium on Coinage and Monetary History* (Berlin), 321–39.

—— (1997). 'Prices and Price Formation in Roman Egypt', in J. Andreau, P. Briant, and R. Descat (eds.), *Économie antique: Prix et formation des prix dans les économies antiques* (Entretiens d'archéologie et d'histoire; Saint-Bertrand-de-Comminges), 183–244.

REEKMANS, T. (1975). 'Treasure Trove and *Parapherna*', in J. Bingen *et al.* (eds.), *Le Monde grec: Hommages à Claire Préaux* (Brussels), 748–59.

ROWLANDSON, J. L. (1996). *Landowners and Tenants in Roman Egypt: The Social Relations of Agriculture in the Oxyrhynchite Nome* (Oxford).

—— (1998) (ed.). *Women and Society in Greek and Roman Egypt* (Cambridge).

SIJPESTEIJN, P. (1993). 'A Pawnbroker's Account', *Ancient Society*, 24: 51–9.

SMITH, H. S. (1995). 'Marriage and Family Law', in M. J. Geller and H. Maehler (eds.), *Legal Documents of the Hellenistic World* (London), 46–57.

VON REDEN, S. (1997). 'Money and Coinage in Ptolemaic Egypt: Some Preliminary Remarks', in *Akten des 21. Internationalen Papyrologenkongresses, Berlin 1995* (Archiv für Papyrusforschung, Beiheft 3; Berlin), 1003–8.

WALLACE, S. L. (1938). *Taxation in Egypt from Augustus to Diocletian* (Princeton, NJ).

WHITEHORNE, J. E. G. (1986). 'The Valuation of Gold Dowry Objects in Papyri of the Roman Period', *Archiv*, 32: 49–53.

Index

Inevitably inconsistencies appear in the spelling of ancient names. In general, the spelling in the index reflects that used in the body of the text.

Telemachos of Acharnai 122
Telmessos 94
Temnos 56
tenancy, agricultural 147, 149
Tenedos 56
Teos 10, 56, 91 n. 62
Termessus 55–6
thallos 150
Tharsytas 87–90, 106
Thasos 13, 16
Thebes 35, 95 n. 79
Themis 122
Themistokles 120
Theocritus 67–8
Thessaly 38, 53, 95 n. 79
Theudotos 88, 108
Thorikos 44, 47, 129 n. 3
Thrace 11, 58
Thraso 42
Thrason 72
Tigranes II 57 n. 22
Timaios 88 n. 46
Timarchos 140 n. 46, 143 n. 54
Timodikos 119
Timokles 70–1
Timotheos (Rhodes) 87, 90, 106
Timotheus (general) 29 n. 67
Tisamenos 29
Tomi 56
trade 11, 12, 17, 68, 96, 146
Traducta 54
Tralles 58
trierarchy/trireme/navy *see* navy
Tripolis 57, 60
Triptolemos 123
Tylissos 119
Tyre 57, 60–1, 92

Vespasian 54
village 145, 146, 147, 148

wages 24, 70, 71, 72, 73, (for agricultural work) 149,
    150, 151
weighing systems/weight standards 17–9, 29 n. 72, 31,
    ch. 6 *passim*
work contracts 150

Xenokrates 89, 108

Zenon of Caunus 70–3
Zenon of Citium 32, 37–8, 42
Zeus 60, 67, 69, 91, 122

Hoards:
Almyros (*CH* 8. 424) 95 n. 79
Artemisium (*IGCH* 1154) 10
Asia Minor (*CH* 1. 3) 15–6, 18
Asyut (*CH* 2. 17) 15

Campana (*IGCH* 2029) 70 n. 41
Caria 1965 (*IGCH* 1287) 90 n. 58
Caria 1968/9 (*IGCH* 1289/1290) 90 n. 58 , 91 n. 61
Caria 1977 (*CH* 9. 387) 81–2
Caria 1979 (*CH* 9. 421) 83–4
Caria 1988 (*CH* 8. 294) 86
Carystus (*IGCH* 117) 47 n. 87, 51
Chalki (*IGCH* 1203) 81

Chios, before 1820 81
Corinth (*IGCH* 187) 50–1, 86

Denia (*IGCH* 2317) 95 n. 80
Durasalar (*IGCH* 1201) 81–2

Eretria (*IGCH* 175) 47 n. 87, 51, 86
Eretria (*CH* 8. 282) 50

Fethiye (*IGCH* 1266) 83
Fethiye (*IGCH* 1428) 86

Cent./N. Greece (*CH* 8. 423) 95 n. 79

Hija e Korbit (*CH* 8. 299) 47 n. 87, 50–1

Jabucovac (*IGCH* 447+458) 50

Kakovatos (*IGCH* 190) 70 n. 41
Karanis, 1926 153 n. 37
Karditsa (*IGCH* 162) 47 n. 87 , 51
Kato Kleitoria (*IGCH* 184) 70 n. 41
Kavalla (*IGCH* 450) 86
Kozani (*IGCH* 457) 50–1
Krcedin 1953 48, 50

Larisa (*CH* 8.517) 95 n. 79
Leros (*CH* 1. 54) 90

Macedonia (*CH* 8. 419) 95 n. 79
Maeander Valley (*IGCH* 1294) 87
Marmaris (*IGCH* 1202) 81
Marmaris (*IGCH* 1209) 82
Meydancikkale (*CH* 8. 308) 66 n. 12
Montagna di Marzo (*IGCH* 2242) 70 n. 41
Muğla (*IGCH* 1215) 83
Muğla (*IGCH* 1292) 86

Olympia (*IGCH* 176) 50–1
Oreus (*IGCH* 232) 95 n. 79, 108 n. 112

Pazarlk (*IGCH* 1288) 86, 90 n. 58
Pella (*CH* 8. 420) 95 n. 79
Phaestos (*IGCH* 152) 86
Phayttos (*IGCH* 159) 48, 50
Pherai (*IGCH* 168) 47 n. 87, 50
Pontolevadi Kilkis (*IGCH* 445) 50

Ras Shamra (*IGCH* 1478) 15
Rhodes (*IGCH* 1284) 86
Rhodes (*IGCH* 1285) 90 n. 58
Rhodes (*IGCH* 1286) 90 n. 58
Rhodes (*CH* 8. 239) 90 n. 58
Rhodes? (*CH* 8.347) 87–8, 90
Rhodes (*IGCH* 1342) 91
Rhodes (*CH* 7. 106) 91
Rhodes city 1975/6 91
Rougha (*CH* 8. 425) 95 n. 79

Saida (*IGCH* 1508) 85, 92
Sambiase (*IGCH* 1872) 15
Selinus (*CH* 8, 35) 15–6
Sicyon (*IGCH* 183) 70 n. 41
Siphnos (*IGCH* 91) 47 n. 88, 86
Sophikon (*IGCH* 179) 48 n. 92, 50–1
Sparta (*IGCH* 181) 47 n. 87, 50–1

Taranto (*IGCH* 1874) 15
Thebes (*IGCH* 193) 46 n. 80, 51
Thessalonike? (*CH* 8. 426) 95 n. 79

Key: Plates to Chapter 1

A selection of coins and uncoined silver from CH I 3 (coins are enlarged 2: 1)
Coins: (1) 0.17 g., (2) 0.22 g., (3) 0.44 g., (4) 0.49 g
Silver disks: (5) 0.24 g., (6) 0.92 g., (7) 4.01 g
Silver scraps: (8) 0.47 g., (9) 0.84 g., (10) 2.89 g

All objects are in the Ashmolean Museum, Oxford.

Key: Plates to Chapter 3

1. AR tetradrachm of Athens (Pi style) BM 1977-2-4-29
2. AR tetradrachm of Athens (Quadrigidité) BMC Athens 141
3. AR tetradrachm of Athens (Heterogeneous F) BM 1920-8-5-368
4. AR tetradrachm of Athens (Early 2nd cent. BC) BM 1968-12-7-2
5. AR pentobol of Athens BM 1908-4-8-10
6. AR tetrobol of Athens BM 1949-4-11-497
7. AE dichalkon of Athens (Eleusinian types) BMC 252

All coins are in the British Museum and are illustrated by courtesy of the trustees.

Key: Plates to Chapter 4

1. AE coin of Ancyra, reign of Nero. 1922-6-21-1
2. AE coin of Corinth, reign of Domitian. 1920-8-5-892 Earle Fox bequest
3. AR tetradrachm of Phaselis. BMC Alexander 2849a
4. AR tetradrachm of Aspendos. BMC Alexander 2891c
5. AR stater of Phaselis. 1979-1-1-823, SNG von Aulock 4419
6. AR tetradrachm of Perge. BMC 1
7. AR stater of Aspendos. 1979-1-1-870, SNG von Aulock 4547
8. AR tetradrachm of Athens. BMC 286
9. AR tetradrachm of Chalcis. BMC 85
10. AR tetradrachm of Cyzicus 146. BMC 146
11. AR tetradrachm of Heracleia Latmos. 1979-1-1418, SNG von Aulock 1976
12. AR drachm of Tlos. 1979-1-1-833, SNG von Aulock 4462
13. AR drachm of Rhodes. 1973-12-6-34
14. AR tetradrachm of Ptolemy VIII of Egypt, mint of Alexandria. BMC 60
15. AR tetradrachm of Aradus. BMC 18
16. AR tetradrachm of Alexander I of Syria, mint of Berytus. BMC 5
17. AR tetradrachm of Antiochus IX of Syria, mint of Ake-Ptolemais. BMC 2
18. AR tetradrachm of Antiochus VIII of Syria, mint of Ascalon. 1947-4-6-518
19. AR tetradrachm of Ascalon. 1935-11-17-924
20. AR tetradrachm of Seleuceia Pieria. 1924-5-6-11
21. AR tetradrachm of Tripolis. BMC 3
22. AR cistophorus of Ephesus. 1979-1-1-231, SNG von Aulock 7844
23. AR drachm of Ephesus. 1979-1-1-404, SNG von Aulock 1850
24. AE coin of Amaseia. SNG Black Sea 1049
25. AE coin of Pimolisa. SNG Black Sea 1351
26. AE coin of Comana. SNG Black Sea 1260
27. AE coin of Sinope. SNG Black Sea 1534
28. AR didrachm of Panticapaeum. SNG Black Sea 934
29. AR didrachm of Phanagoria. SNG Black Sea 997
30. AE coin of Sestos. BMC 12
31. AE coin of Ake-Ptolemais, reign of Antiochus IV of Syria. BMC 72
32. AE coin of Hierapolis Castabala, reign of Antiochus IV of Syria. 1991-1-30-51
33. AE coin of Sidon, reign of Antiochus IV of Syria. BMC 50
34. AE coin of Sidon, reign of Antiochus IV of Syria. 1931-4-6-165
35. AE coin of Berytus, reign of Antiochus IV of Syria. 1931-4-6-162
36. AE coin of Tyre, reign of Antiochus IV of Syria. 1979-8-15-11
37. AE coin of Alexandria ad Issum, reign of Antiochus IV of Syria. BMC 1
38. AE coin of Ascalon, reign of Antiochus IV of Syria. 1931-4-6-126

All coins are in the British Museum and are illustrated by courtesy of the trustees.

Key: Plates to Chapter 6

1. Munich
2. BM 1914-1-16-1 (Lawson)
3. Bérend (1972), 2
4. *BMC* 11
5. Bérend (1972), 32
6. Bérend (1972), 21
7. Berlin 66/1875
8. Berlin, Imhoof-Blumer
9. Boston 2037
10. Paris, de Luynes 2720
11. MMAG Deutschland 1 (1997), 235
12. Berlin 48/1978
13. Ashton coll., acq. 1976
14. Istanbul 7423
16. *SNG* Berry 1118
17. Peus 332 (1991), 212
18. Aufhäuser 13 (1997), 189
19. Lanz 44 (1988), 223
20. Müller (Solingen) 56 (1987), 127
21. Peus 351 (1997), 228
25. Private coll., Switzerland
26. Ashton coll., acq. 1979
27. Stockholm
28. Bérend (1972), 33
30. Bérend (1972), 37
31. Bérend (1972), 52
34. Bérend (1972), 48
35. Bérend (1972), 42
36. Bérend (1972), 45
37. Bérend (1972), 46
38. Jenkins and Hipólito (1989), 767
39. Bérend (1972), 58
40. Bérend (1972), 62
41. Bérend (1972), 70
42. Bérend (1972), 73
43. Bérend (1972), 77
44. Sternberg 19 (1987), 202
45. Lanz 36 (1986), 410
46. Leu 59 (1994), 137
48. Boston 2044
50. NAC 1 (1989), 214
53. *SNG* von Aulock 2787
54. *SNG* Berry 1120
55. Jenkins and Hipólito (1989), 770
56. Brussels, du Chastel 268
57. Princeton, Art Museum 55-365
59. Ashton coll., acq. 1993
61. Ashton coll., acq. 1977
63. Ashton coll., acq. 1972

65. Ashton coll., acq. 1975
67. Istanbul (*IGCH* 1201)
68. *SNG* Copenhagen 726
69. Superior, 12 June 1978, 3205
70. J. Hirsch 21 (1908, Consul Weber), 3245
71. Leu-MMAG 3 December 1965 (Niggeler), 414
72. Jenkins and Hipólito (1989), 771
73. Sotheby's, 14 July 1976, 28
74. MMAG 47 (1972), 509
75. London market 1999
79. MMAG 76 (1991), 819
81. Bourgey, 4 November 1975, 45
82. J. Hirsch 13 (1905, Rhousopoulos), 4008
83. Berlin 568/1909, ex J. Hirsch 25 (1909, Philipsen), 2439
84. Brussels, de Hirsch 1557
85. *SNG* Delepierre 2748
86. Leu 30 (1982), 185
87. Jenkins and Hipólito (1989), 774
88. Pollard (1970), 101
90. Lanz 78 (1996), 295
91. Lanz 44 (1988), 225
92. Stockholm
93. Auctiones Basel 20 (1990), 1369
94. The Israel Museum, Jerusalem, inv. 1423
95. NAC E (1995), 2378
96. *SNG* Keckman i, 427
97. Giessener MH 73 (1995), 180
98. Jenkins and Hipólito (1989), 776
99. Ashton coll., ex G. Hirsch 205 (1999), 351
100. Ashton coll., acq. 1992
101. Lanz 64 (1993), 254
102. G. Hirsch 184 (1994), 297
103. NFA, 20 March 1975, 178
104. G. Hirsch 187 (1995), 534
105. Lanz 74 (1995), 227
106. *BMC* 10
107. Giessener MH 78 (1996), 222
108. CNG 31 (1994), 344
109. Kress 152 (1971), 206
111. Ashton coll., acq. 1975
113. Stockholm

115. US market 1986
119. Cast in Winterthur, Stadtbibliothek
129. Ashton coll., acq. 1996
132. Stockholm
134. Stockholm
135. Ashton coll., acq. 1983
151. Ashton coll., acq. 1972; *CH* 2, 59
152. Ashton coll., ex Peus 355 (1998), 136 part
153. Ashton coll., acq. 1972; *CH* 2, 59
155. Ashton coll., acq. 1983
157. G. Hirsch 191 (1996), 500
158. G. Hirsch 185 (1995), 324
159. G. Hirsch 199 (1998), 202
160. G. Hirsch 184 (1994), 290
161. CNG 29 (1994), 208
162. Leu 33 (1983), 393
163. CNG 32 (1994), 1328
164. G. Hirsch 184 (1994), 281
165. Ashton (1988), 76, no. 4b
166. Ashton (1988), 77, no. 11a
167. Berk 89 (1996), 165
168. *CNR* 17/3 (1992), 731
169. G. Hirsch 199 (1998), 194
170. Ashton coll., acq. 1986
171. *SNG* von Aulock 2795
172. Ashton coll., acq. 1993
173. Ashton coll., acq. 1980
174. MMAG 66 (1984), 271
175. Ashton coll., acq. 1977
176. Ashton coll., acq. 1992
177. Ashton (1988), 89, no. 70
178. Ashton (1988), 89, no. 68
179. Ashton (1988), 89, no. 69
180. MMAG 41 (1970), 235
181. H. Schulman 26 April 1951, 3031
182. London market 1994
183. MMAG FPL 144 (1955), 16
184. Ashton (1992b), 30, no. 6
185. *CNR* 17/3 (1992), 740
186. G. Hirsch 185 (1995), 329
187. Giessener MH 62 (1993), 291
188. Lanz 66 (1993), 280
189. Ashton coll., acq. 1992
190. MMAG FPL 243 (1964), 24
191. Lanz 66 (1993), 279
192. Giessener MH 79 (1996), 235

193. L. Cancio coll.; G. Hirsch 175 (1992), 393
194. G. Hirsch 175 (1992), 392
195. Stockholm
196. BM 1925-9-3-4
197. Princeton, Art Museum 55-361
198. Triton 1 (1997), 545
199. Frankfurter MH (SBV) 135 (1990), 1479
200. G. Hirsch 178 (1993), 348
201. CNG 37 (1996), 553
202. G. Hirsch 202 (1998), 207
203. London market 1983
204. MMAG FPL 257 (1965), 15
205. G. Hirsch 195 (1997), 349
206. Toronto, Royal Ontario Museum 949.15.385
207. Brussels; *SNG* Lockett 2955
208. MMAG 41 (1970), 236
209. Stockholm
210. See n. 45 above.
211. See n. 45 above.
212. Lisbon, Gulbenkian coll.
213. Peus 340 (1994), 392
214. Toronto, Royal Ontario Museum 924.6.4
215. Stockholm
216. Ashton coll., ex Christie's 28 April 1993, 13
217. Stockholm
219. Olympia, *IGCH* 270
220. Stockholm
221. G. Hirsch 178 (1993), 349
222. Sternberg 14 (1984), 134
223. Tkalec and Rauch 25 April 1989, 138
224. BM 1954-10-13-1
225. BM 1979-1-1-616 = *SNG* von Aulock 2814

226. Bucharest, Institute of Archaeology 1261/A.4825
227. Ashton coll., acq. 1983
228. Giessener MH 87 (1998), 238
230. Ashton coll., acq. 1973
232. Ashton (1988), 90, no. 84
233. Ashton (1988), 90, no. 83
234. G. Hirsch 172 (1991), 274
235. Sternberg 34 (1998), 45
238. Ashton coll., acq. 1977; Ashton (1986), 7, no. 75
239. Ashton coll., ex Lennox Gallery FPL 3 (1996), G161
242. Ashton coll., acq. 1975; Ashton (1986), 2, no. 6a
246. NAC H (1998), 1275
250. Lanz 54 (1990), 226
251. Lanz 48 (1989), 345
253. Peus 343 (1995), 156
254. Peus 330 (1991), 140
259. *BMC* 128
260. Ashton coll.; ex Lanz 44 (1988), 226
261. BM 1929-11-5-3
263. BM 1929-11-5-1
264. Leu 50 (1990), 174 = *SNG* von Aulock 2803
265. Vinchon 26 April 1999, 204
266. *SNG* Berry 1124
267. Ashton coll., ex Buckler, Dix and Wood 28 June 1995, 22
268. Stockholm
269. BM 1948-11-3-12
272. *BMC* 136
273. Ashton coll., ex NFA 29 (1992), 149
274. *BMC* 149
275. Ashton coll., acq. 1993
276. BM 1948-11-3-25
277. *BMC* 129
278. BM 1948-11-3-21

279. BM 1948-11-3-26
280. Spink 25 (1982), 108
281. BM 1927-1-5-2
282. Toronto, Royal Ontario Museum 925.9.1
283. Private coll., Athens (1979)
285. Berk 91 (1996), 195
286. Gotha coll.
288. NAC D (1994), 1503
291. Brussels
293. Ashton coll., ex Hornung 19 (1981), 384
294. Ashton coll., acq. 1973
296. Nummorum Auctiones (Vecchi, London) 10 (1998), 390
297. NAC D (1994), 1506
298. Turin DC 24373
299. G. Hirsch 25 (1960), 1772
300. Ashton coll., acq. 1977
304. Ashton coll., acq. 1977
305. Stockholm
306. Ashton coll., ex G. Hirsch 178 (1993), 372
308. Ashton coll., acq. 1984
309. BM 1979-1-1-623
312. Hesperia Art 34, 108
313. Ashton (1988), 90, no. 86
314. G. Hirsch 189 (1996), 274
315. Ashton (1988), 90, no. 88
323. G. Hirsch 185 (1995), 335
332. Ashton coll., acq. 1979
333. CNG 45 (1998), 457
335. G. Hirsch 174 (1992), 316
337. Ashton coll., acq. 1984
338. *BMC* 185
339. Stockholm
341. Ashton coll., acq. 1998
342. CNG 35 (1995), 242
A See Appendix 3
B See Appendix 3

PLATE I.I

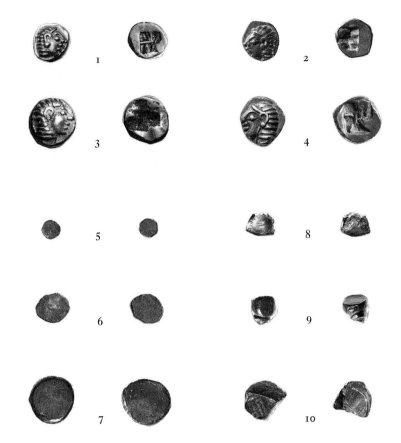

A selection of coins and uncoined silver from *CH* I, 3 (coins are enlarged 2:1)

Coins: (1) 0.17 g, (2) 0.22 g. (3) 0.44 g. (4) 0.49 g.
Silver disks: (5) 0.24 g. (6) 0.92 g. (7) 4.01 g.
Silver scraps: (8) 0.47 g. (9) 0.84 g. (10) 2.89 g.

PLATE 3.1

1. AR tetradrachm of Athens (Pi style) BM 1977-2-2-4-29.
2. AR tetradrachm of Athens (Quadrigidité) BMC Athens 141.
3. AR tetradrachm of Athens (Heterogeneous F) BM 1920-8-5-368.
4. AR tetradrachm of Athens (Early 2nd cent. BC) BM 1968-12-7-2.
5. AR pentobol of Athens BM 1908-4-8-10.
6. AR tetrobol of Athens BM 1949-4-11-497.
7. AE dichalkon of Athens (Eleusinian types) BMC 252.

PLATE 4.1

1. AE coin of Ancyra, reign of Nero. 1922-6-21-1.
2. AE coin of Corinth, reign of Domitian. 1920-8-5-892, Earle Fox bequest.
3. AR tetradrachm of Phaselis. BMC Alexander 2849a.
4. AR tetradrachm of Aspendos. BMC Alexander 2891c.
5. AR stater of Phaselis. 1979-1-1-823, SNG von Aulock 4419.
6. AR tetradrachm of Perge. BMC 1.
7. AR stater of Aspendos. 1979-1-1-870, SNG von Aulock 4547.

PLATE 4.2

8

9

10

11

12

13

8. AR tetradrachm of Athens. BMC 286.

9. AR tetradrachm of Chalcis. BMC 85.

10. AR tetradrachm of Heracleia Latmos. 1979-1-1418, SNG von Aulock 1976.

11. AR tetradrachm of Cyzius. BMC 146.

12. AR drachm of Tlos. 1979-1-1-833, SNG von Aulock 4462.

13. AR drachm of Rhodes. 1973-12-6-34.

PLATE 4.3

14. AR tetradrachm of Ptolemy VIII of Egypt, mint of Alexandria. BMC 60.
15. AR tetradrachm of Aradus. BMC 18.
16. AR tetradrachm of Alexander I of Syria, mint of Berytus. BMC 5.
17. AR tetradrachm of Antiochus IX of Syria, mint of Ake-Ptolemais.
18. AR tetradrachm of Antiochus VIII os Syria, mint of Ascalon. 1947-4-6-518.
19. AR tetradrachm of Ascalon. 1935-11-17-924.
20. AR tetradrachm of Seleuceia Pieria. 1924-5-6-11.
21. AR tetradrachm of Tripolis. BMC 3.

PLATE 4.4

22. AR cistophorus of Ephesus. 1979-1-1-404, SNG von Aulock 7844.
23. AR drachm of Ephesus. 1979-1-1-404, SNG von Aulock 4419.
24. AE coin of Amaseia. SNG Black Sea 1049.
25. AE coin of Pimolisa. SNG Black Sea 1351.
26. AE coin of Comana. SNG Black Sea 1260.
27. AE coin of Sinope. SNG Black Sea 1534.
28. AR didrachm of Panticapaeum. SNG Black Sea 934.
29. AR didrachm of Phanagoria. SNG Black Sea 997.

PLATE 4.5

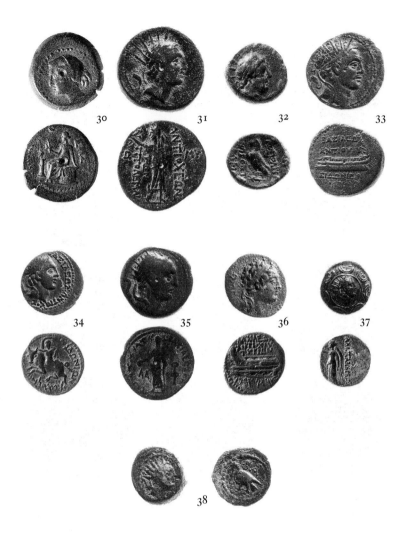

30. Coin of Sestos. BMC 12.
31. AE coin of Ake-Ptolemais, reign of Antiochus IV of Syria. BMC 72.
32. AE coin of Hierapolis Castabala, reign of Antiochus IV of Syria. 1991-1-30-51.
33. AE coin of Sidon, reign of Antiochus IV of Syria. BMC 50.
34. AE coin of Sidon, reign of Antiochus IV of Syria. 1931-4-6-165.

35. AE coin of Berytus, reign of Antiochus IV of Syria. 1931-4-6-162.
36. AE coin of Tyre, reign of Antiochus IV of Syria. 1979-8-15-11.
37. AE coin of Alexandria ad Issum, reign of Antiochus IV of Syria. BMC 1.
38. AE coin of Ascalon, reign of Antiochus IV of Syria. 1931-4-6-126.

PLATE 6.1

1. Munich
2. BM 1914-1-16-1 (Lawson)
3. Bérend (1972), 2
4. *BMC* 11
5. Bérend (1972), 32
6. Bérend (1972), 21
7. Berlin 66/1875
8. Berlin, Imhoof-Blumer

9. Boston 2037
10. Paris, de Luynes 2720
11. MMAG Deutschland 1 (1997), 235
12. Berlin 48/1978
13. Ashton coll., acq. 1976
14. Istanbul 7423
16. *SNG* Berry 1118
17. Peus 332 (1991), 212

18. Aufhäuser 13 (1997), 189
19. Lanz 44 (1988), 223
20. Müller (Solingen) 56 (1987), 127
21. Peus 351 (1997), 228
25. Private coll., Switzerland
26. Ashton coll., acq. 1979
27. Stockholm
28. Bérend (1972), 33

PLATE 6.2

30. Bérend (1972), 37
31. Bérend (1972), 52
34. Bérend (1972), 48
35. Bérend (1972), 42
36. Bérend (1972), 45
37. Bérend (1972), 46

38. Jenkins and Hipólito (1989), 767
39. Bérend (1972), 58
40. Bérend (1972), 62
41. Bérend (1972), 70
42. Bérend (1972), 73

43. Bérend (1972), 77
44. Sternberg 19 (1987), 202
45. Lanz 36 (1986), 410
46. Leu 59 (1994), 137

PLATE 6.3

48. Boston 2044
50. NAC 1 (1989), 214
53. *SNG von Aulock* 2787
54. *SNG Berry* 1120
55. Jenkins and Hipólito (1989), 770
56. Brussels, du Chastel 268
57. Princeton, Art Museum 55-365

59. Ashton coll., acq. 1993
61. Ashton coll., acq. 1977
63. Ashton coll., acq. 1972
65. Ashton coll., acq. 1975
67. Istanbul (*IGCH* 1201)
68. *SNG Copenhagen* 726
69. Superior, 12 June 1978, 3205

70. J. Hirsch 21 (1908, Consul Weber), 3245
71. Leu-MMAG 3 December 1965 (Niggeler), 414
72. Jenkins and Hipólito (1989), 771

PLATE 6.4

73. Sotheby's, 14 July 1976, 28
74. MMAG 45 (1972), 509
75. London market 1999
79. MMAG 76 (1991), 819
81. Bourgey, 4 November 1975, 45

82. J. Hirsch 13 (1905, Rhousopoulos), 4008
83. Berlin 568/1909, ex J. Hirsch 25 (1909, Philipsen), 2439
84. Brussels, de Hirsch 1557
85. *SNG* Delepierre 2748

86. Leu 30 (1982), 185
87. Jenkins and Hipólito (1989), 774
88. Pollard (1970), 101
90. Lanz 78 (1996), 295
91. Lanz 44 (1988), 225
92. Stockholm

PLATE 6.5

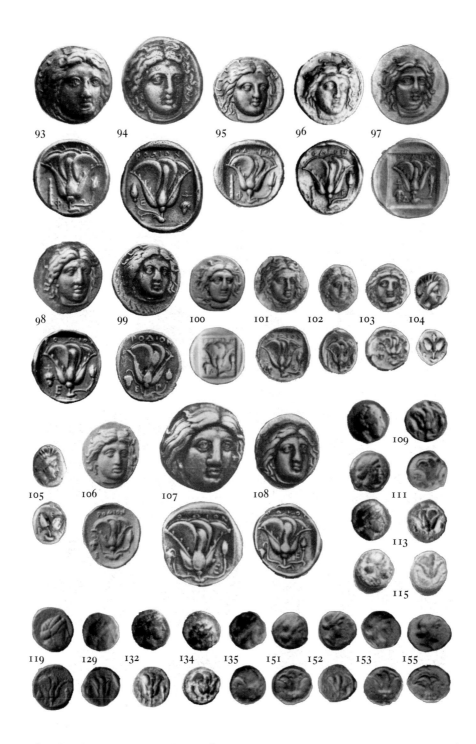

93. Auctiones Basel 20 (1990), 1369
94. The Israel Museum, Jerusalem, inv. 1423
95. NAC E (1995), 2378
96. *SNG* Keckman i, 427
97. Giessener MH 73 (1995), 180
98. Jenkins and Hipólito (1989), 776
99. Ashton coll., ex G. Hirsch 205 (1999), 351
100. Ashton coll., acq. 1992
101. Lanz 64 (1993), 254

102. G. Hirsch 184 (1994), 297
103. NFA, 20 March 1975, 178
104. G. Hirsch 187 (1995), 534
105. Lanz 74 (1995), 227
106. *BMC* 10
107. Giessener MH 78 (1996), 222
108. CNG 31 (1994), 344
109. Kress 152 (1971), 206
111. Ashton coll., acq. 1975
113. Stockholm
115. US market 1986

119. Cast in Winterthur, Stadtbibliothek
129. Ashton coll., acq. 1996
132. Stockholm
134. Stockholm
135. Ashton coll., acq. 1983
151. Ashton coll., acq. 1972; *CH* 2, 59
152. Ashton coll., ex Peus 355 (1998), 136 part
153. Ashton coll., acq. 1972; *CH* 2, 59
155. Ashton coll., acq. 1983

PLATE 6.6

157. G. Hirsch 191 (1996), 500
158. G. Hirsch 185 (1995), 324
159. G. Hirsch 199 (1998), 202
160. G. Hirsch 184 (1994), 290
161. CNG 29 (1994), 208
162. Leu 33 (1983), 393
163. CNG 32 (1994), 1328
164. G. Hirsch 184 (1994), 281
165. Ashton (1988), 76, no. 4b
166. Ashton (1988), 77, no. 11a
167. Berk 89 (1996), 165
168. *CNR* 17/3 (1992), 731
169. G. Hirsch 199 (1998), 194
170. Ashton coll., acq. 1986
171. *SNG* von Aulock 2795
172. Ashton coll., acq. 1993
173. Ashton coll., acq. 1980
174. MMAG 66 (1984), 271
175. Ashton coll., acq. 1977
176. Ashton coll., acq. 1992
177. Ashton (1988), 89, no. 70
178. Ashton (1988), 89, no. 68
179. Ashton (1988), 89, no. 69

PLATE 6.7

180. MMAG 41 (1970), 235
181. H. Schulman 26 April 1951, 3031
182. London market 1994
183. MMAG FPL 144 (1955), 16
184. Ashton (1992b), 30, no. 6
185. *CNR* 17/3 (1992), 740
186. G. Hirsch 185 (1995), 329
187. Giessener MH 62 (1993), 291
188. Lanz 66 (1993), 280

189. Ashton coll., acq. 1992
190. MMAG FPL 243 (1964), 24
191. Lanz 66 (1993), 279
192. Giessener MH 79 (1996), 235
193. L. Cancio coll.; G. Hirsch 175 (1992), 393
194. G. Hirsch 175 (1992), 392
195. Stockholm
196. BM 1925-9-3-4

197. Princeton, Art Museum 55-361
198. Triton 1 (1997), 545
199. Frankfurter MH (SBV) 135 (1990), 1479
200. G. Hirsch 178 (1993), 348
201. CNG 37 (1996), 553
202. G. Hirsch 202 (1998), 207
203. London market 1983

PLATE 6.8

204. MMAGFPL 257 (1965), 15
205. G. Hirsch 195 (1997), 349
206. Toronto, Royal Ontario Museum
    949.15.385
207. Brussels; *SNG* Lockett 2955
208. MMAG 41 (1970), 236

209. Stockholm
210. See n. 45 above.
211. See n. 45 above.
212. Lisbon, Gulbenkian coll.
213. Peus 340 (1994), 392

214. Toronto, Royal Ontario Museum
    924.6.4
215. Stockholm
216. Ashton coll., ex Christie's 28
    April 1993, 13
217. Stockholm

PLATE 6.9

219. Olympia, *IGCH* 270
220. Stockholm
221. G. Hirsch 178 (1993), 349
222. Sternberg 14 (1984), 134
223. Tkalec and Rauch 25 April 1989, 138
224. BM 1954-10-13-1
225. BM 1979-1-1-16 = *SNG von Aulock* 2814

226. Bucharest, Institute of Archaeology 1261 / A.4825
227. Ashton coll., acq. 1983
228. Giessener MH 87 (1998), 238
230. Ashton coll., acq. 1973
232. Ashton (1988), 90, no. 84
233. Ashton (1988), 90, no. 83
234. G. Hirsch 172 (1991), 274
235. Sternberg 34 (1998), 45

238. Ashton coll., acq. 1977; Ashton (1986), 7, no. 75
239. Ashton coll., ex Lennox Gallery FPL 3 (1996), G161
242. Ashton coll., acq. 1975; Ashton (1986), 2, no. 6a
246. NAC H (1998), 1275

PLATE 6.10

250
251
253

254
259
260
261

263
264
265
266

250. Lanz 54 (1990), 226
251. Lanz 48 (1989), 345
253. Peus 343 (1995), 156
254. Peus 340 (1991), 140
259. *BMC* 128

260. Ashton coll.; ex Lanz 44 (1988), 226
261. BM 1929-11-5-3
263. BM 1929-11-5-1

264. Leu 50 (1990), 174 = SNG von Aulock 2803
265. Vinchon 26 April 1999, 204
266. *SNG Berry* 1124

PLATE 6.11

267. Ashton coll.; ex Buckland, Dix &
    Wood 28 June 1995, 22
268. Stockholm
269. BM 1948-11-3-12
272. *BMC* 136
273. Ashton coll.; ex NFA 29
    (1992), 149
274. *BMC* 149

275. Ashton coll., acq. 1993
276. BM 1948-11-3-25
277. *BMC* 129
278. BM 1948-11-3-21
279. BM 1948-11-3-26
280. Spink 25 (1982), 108
281. BM 1927-1-5-2
282. Toronto, Royal Ontario Museum
    925.9.1

283. Private coll., Athens (1979)
285. Berk 91 (1996), 195
286. Gotha coll.
288. NAC D (1994), 1503
291. Brussels
293. Ashton coll.; ex Hornung 19
    (1981), 384
294. Ashton coll., acq. 1973

PLATE 6.12

296. Nummorum Auctiones (Vecchi,
       London) 10 (1998), 390
297. NAC D (1994), 1506
298. Turin DC 24373
299. G. Hirsch 25 (1960), 1772
300. Ashton coll., acq. 1977
304. Ashton coll., acq. 1977
305. Stockholm
306. Ashton coll., ex G. Hirsch 178
       (1993), 372

308. Ashton coll., acq. 1984
309. BM 1979-1-1-623
312. Hesperia Art 34, 108
313. Ashton (1988), 90, no. 86
314. G. Hirsch 189 (1996), 274
315. Ashton (1988), 90, no. 88
323. G. Hirsch 185 (1995), 335
332. Ashton coll., acq. 1979
333. CNG 45 (1998), 457
335. G. Hirsch 174 (1992), 316

337. Ashton coll., acq. 1984
338. *BMC* 185
339. Stockholm
341. Ashton coll., acq. 1998
342. CNG 35 (1995), 242
A See Appendix 3
B See Appendix 3